REWRITING PAUL

REWRITING PAUL

Original Translations of the Letters of Paul

(1 Thessalonians, Galatians, Philippians, Philemon, and Romans)

Timothy W. Seid

Copyright © 2019 Timothy W. Seid

APeX Life Media

All rights reserved.

ISBN-13: 978-0-578-53701-6

DEDICATION

*To the scholar and teacher
who impacted my thinking the most,
with gratitude:*

*Stanley K. Stowers,
Professor Emeritus of Religious Studies,
Brown University*

TABLE OF CONTENTS

Preface i

Chapter 1: Introduction 1

Basis for a Rewriting of Paul 9

    Chapter 2: Primary Principles 11

    Chapter 3: Placing Paul in the First Century 23

    Chapter 4: Paul as Philosophical Guide Within Households of Patrons 37

    Chapter 5: Philosophy as the Art of Living 55

    Chapter 6: The Hellenistic Context of Paul 77

Overview of Paul's Letters 95

    Chapter 7: First Thessalonians 97

    Chapter 8: Galatians 111

    Chapter 9: Philippians Correspondence 135

    Chapter 10: Philemon 175

    Chapter 11: Romans 179

Appendix One: Letters of Paul 239

Appendix Two: Chart of Terms 283

Bibliography 291

Preface

I am grateful to have had online access to the Thesaurus Linguae Graecae (*TLG*) (stephanus.tlg.uci.edu). When I started my Ph.D. program in Religious Studies at Brown University, the *TLG* was in beta, and I got to be an early user. In the same way, a big part of my life was going to the basement of "the Rock" at Brown to find the shelves of the little green and red books that made up the Loeb Classical Library (*LCL*). The online Loeb (loebclassics.com) has been of great help. I have also made use of computer programs like EndNote Web, ProWritingAid, Microsoft Word, and Accordance.

I have followed as closely as I can the style of *The SBL Handbook of Style*, Second Edition. Where I have diverged is in providing a full citation to the *LCL* volumes within footnotes. Quotations from ancient works have an in-text citation to the standard reference and a footnote to the modern translation. When quoting the Biblical text, I have used and noted the New Revised Standard Version (NRSV).

In appendix one of this book I provide my translations of 1 Thessalonians, Galatians, Philippians, Philemon, and Romans. I intend to publish a second volume on the Corinthian correspondence. I do not mean the overview section to be a commentary but an explanation of the context of my translation. My approach is to expand on a literal translation with more of a paraphrase. While going through graduate school, I happened to work as a custodian at Tyndale House and had an occasion to chat with Ken Taylor (creator of The Living Bible) while I was emptying his trash. Now I want to present my paraphrase. I have put into italics any words I've added for interpretation and clarity. I have detected in Philippians and Romans some editorial combining of two or more related documents. Scribes in the early phase of the copying have added glosses that reflect a later period than Paul. What's most noticeable is that those texts often contain harsh apocalyptic language. I have tried to show references to biblical quotations with a note if Paul's Greek is very similar to what we have in the Septuagint (LXX) tradition of a Greek Bible. My purpose is to help non-academic readers see the degree to which Paul depended on a Greek text of the Bible.

I am thankful to have received a grant in 2008 from the National Endowment for the Humanities (NEH) to attend a classical studies seminar at the American Academy in Rome, "Identity and Self-Representation Among the Sub-cultures of Ancient Rome," led by Eve D'Ambra and Eleanor Leach. My research interest was the depiction and function of philosophical advisors in households.

I am indebted to Jay Marshall, who hired me to join the faculty where he was the dean, as an administrator of a distance learning program and to give me an appointment as Assistant Professor of New Testament Studies. Over the seventeen years I had many students who were gracious and encouraging of my research and teaching.

The women in my life, my spouse and our five daughters, have listened to me over the past thirty to forty years talk about the research of this book and have been supportive of my career, even when it meant moving so many times.

I have learned much from the teachers I have had at Grace College (Winona Lake, IN), Wheaton College Graduate School, and Brown University. I owe much to them and to those scholars whose books I've read. I cannot cite every monograph and commentary that has been valuable to me in my research, but I cite every work I quote or depend on.

Because I am an independent scholar and not in need of publication credits, I am self-publishing this book as a member of the Alliance of Independent Authors. I have formatted the book and designed the cover myself. I hope it cannot be said of me that people who have themselves as an editor have a fool for a client.

Chapter 1:
Introduction

This book is the culmination of a life's journey trying to understand the origins of Christianity for myself. The first part of this book explains how I approach the interpretation of the earliest New Testament texts. The latter part of the book contains explanations and translations I have made of the principal letters of Paul.[1] I had not planned on my work to be a translation project. It has seemed necessary to compose my own translations because I found that I cannot convince anyone of the validity of my approach when they are reading the texts through the lens of translations that are intended to support and perpetuate traditional Christian theology and practice.

I do not mean for my work to be an attack on Christianity. I do not even mean to suggest that my interpretation is the right one. My work has led me to experiment whether I can explain my approach in a coherent and consistent way. I am persuaded that I have been able to do that to my satisfaction. Smarter people than I will beg to differ. No doubt some will want to argue with me, take me to task, and show how deficient I am in my knowledge and expertise. I don't need anyone to tell me that. I quite know of my deficiencies, but I have done the best I can with the knowledge I've gained (what I can remember) and the skills I've developed. I hope that some people, who may agree with my guiding principles, will find benefit in my attempt to explain the approach and to translate/paraphrase these early Christian texts in keeping with that interpretation. I hope that the reader will take the time to give me a fair reading before criticizing my work. Most of the criticism I have received is that I must be wrong because it is not the traditional view or the scholarly consensus. I fully know of that. It was not my purpose to be iconoclastic or damage anyone's faith. The reason for that

---

[1] I hope to publish a second book with translations and discussions of the Corinthian correspondence.

is that I cannot prove my theories or my interpretation of New Testament texts. I believe them to be viable alternatives and ones based on honest and careful research meant to satisfy my curiosity.

Some might accuse me of being a Marcionite. However, I do not think the letters of Paul are the only foundation for Christianity. But we should interpret the Gospels as the portrayal of Jesus composed by the Gospel writers. To me the "quest for the historical Jesus" is at an impasse. Archaeologists reject any interpretation of the text that can't be proven by the "bones and stones" they find. Scholars continue to argue over the "synoptic problem" and the existence of Q. The Gospels reflect their own period of writing, but I haven't deleted all of the non-Pauline texts from electronic versions. While I think that Hellenistic Jews, whether followers of Jesus or not, thought about God in ways Stoics thought about God, I say that gentile followers of Jesus were taught to worship the one God of Israel. My focus on Paul may just be a product of my educational focus on Paul.

There are a few key principles that have guided my thinking about Christian origins and earliest Christianity. I will try to explain them concisely and carefully. One need not agree with every one of my principles to find benefit in my approach. I will try to summarize what my approach is.

Radical New Perspective

As a student of the "Radical New Perspective on Paul,"[2] "Paul within Judaism,"[3] or more recently the "*Sonderweg* reading," I attempt to read consistently the letters of Paul as written to the gentile peoples[4] in the Roman Empire. For Paul there are a sequence of events that led him to the mission of telling the gentile peoples what God—the one, true, and living God who formed a covenant with the Israelite tribes and continues that relationship with Jewish people in the Judean country then and Jews today—has done regarding the gentile peoples because of the "faithful"

---

[2] Magnus Zetterholm, *Approaches to Paul: A Student's Guide to Recent Scholarship* (Minneapolis: Fortress Press, 2009).

[3] Mark D. Nanos and Magnus Zetterholm, eds., *Paul within Judaism: Restoring the First-Century Context to the Apostle* (Minneapolis: Fortress Press, 2015).

[4] I am using "gentile peoples" as way of referring to non-Jewish ethnic groups without implying anything about their political structure as in the word "nation."

and noble death of Jesus as understood within the Greek martyrologic tradition as best characterized in the description at the end of 4 Maccabees of what the death of Eleazar and the others accomplished. The Judeans hoped Jesus's death would bring about God's action of removing the Roman occupation from the ancestral land and once again blessing God's covenant people. Paul travels and writes letters to household communities in various cities in the Roman Empire in his capacity as a herald or envoy to deliver the good news that God no longer holds the guilt of their sinfulness against them and will not only be the God of the Judeans but the God who will bring blessing to people of all nations. Paul believes this because he witnessed the movement of God's presence as evidenced by the experience of God's Spirit not only in Jerusalem but in far-flung places and not only in Jews but also in gentiles. For Paul gentile people should learn what God has done and not insult God's gift by trying to become Judean citizens through circumcision and adherence to the Torah. Cultural appropriation was unnecessary and even something negative in Paul's view. The first crucial factor is that gentiles would worship the one God and no longer revere Roman deities and images. Second, they would seek to be moral people. Apparently, Paul had an upbringing in a form of Hellenistic Judaism that relied on a Greek translation of the Bible (referred to as the Septuagint or LXX) and interpreted the moral life in terms of the Greek ideals of moral philosophy, particularly that of Stoicism. Those members of households following Jesus were to practice the philosophical life by learning to form proper judgments about virtue and vice to progress toward a mature and flourishing life that transformed their thinking and character as a fully human and thoroughly divine being. If they achieved this, then these people would accomplish the imitation of Jesus both in the qualities of their lives but also in apotheosis at their deaths to be like God and to be immortal. Paul functioned in these households as a philosophical advisor or spiritual guide to help members of his "school," who form themselves within the social construct of friendship, achieve the goal of becoming people who could be self-controlled, self-sufficient, unperturbed by negative emotions, and living in a tranquil state of empowered living.

Paul's Adaptation to his Gentile Audience

In Paul's letters to gentile people, he seems to use "we" language as well as "you." Traditionally, people implicitly understand the "we" language to mean "we Christians" as opposed to other Jews and gentiles who have not become Christians. I have tried to see if I can consistently translate Paul's use of "we" as "we gentiles." At first, I took this to be a rhetorical use of the author identifying with the audience. During my translation work I came across texts I think might explain his usage of "we" as he writes to gentiles. Paul refers to an experience of visiting the Galatians in which he had some problem that was both a reason for his "gospel" mission and a source of embarrassment and shame for him (Gal 4:13). It is in this context that Paul tells the gentiles in Galatia, "I also have become as you are" (Gal 4:12 NRSV). I am not convinced by the traditional view that Paul had some eye problem. What came to my mind was something Paul mentions elsewhere as a practice not advisable (1 Cor 7:18). I began thinking, what if Paul, at some early point in life during which he was interested in Hellenistic culture, underwent a circumcision reversal procedure which left him disfigured and prone to infection or bleeding?[5] What if this is the reason that Paul can both identify with gentile people but also still consider himself an observant Jew? When living among gentiles and frequenting the public bath, the gymnasium, and the latrines, he would insert the pin or needle that held the skin over the tip of his penis, despite whatever pain it might cause him. His friends cared for him to the degree that they did not want to cause him shame and would avert their gaze as if they were blind to his condition (Gal 4:15). Paul could refer to this obliquely when he says he has a "pin" in his flesh (2 Cor 12:7) and when he describes the *stigmata* (Gal 6:17), which is the term used for pin pricks used in tattooing. The reader will have to judge how well this editorial license in translation helps us understand the context of Paul. I have taken the "you (plural)" of Paul to refer to the gentile audience in the particular city. Paul also makes use of the singular pronoun when addressing an "imaginary

---

[5] For a more detailed discussion, see page 37.

interlocuter" in diatribe sections.⁶ I have especially tried to clarify these sections in my translations.

Paul as Founder of Jesus Movement among Gentiles

A major diversion from traditional approaches is the placement of the letters of Paul as the witness not only to the earliest Christian movement but also the foundational one for those people who are not Jewish and locate themselves in the Christian tradition. The basic issue for me is that Paul does not seem to have knowledge of the Gospel tradition of the life of Jesus. The way I put it is that I find it hard to believe that, if the so-called "oral tradition" existed at the time of Paul, he wouldn't have known of it. If he had known of it, surely, he would have referred to it. Therefore, I suggest that there did not exist at the time of Paul a collection of sayings in Aramaic that were part of an eyewitness recollection shared among the followers of Jesus. What we have in the Gospels is a later practice of authors making use of the literature known as the "Life," which progressed to a next stage in the composition of narrative stories of persons from birth to death.⁷

I contend that we have in Christian origins an early understanding of Jesus within a Hellenistic Jewish environment that later in the century becomes "Judaized" as Jewish followers of Jesus encounter a struggle with other Jews within Roman cities over who is the rightful heir of the ancient scriptures and religion and the claim to follow a legal religion in the eyes of the Roman authorities. We have the attempt of the Gospel of Matthew to strain "prophetic" texts as foretelling the Messiah, Jesus. In

---

⁶ Stanley K. Stowers, *The Diatribe and Paul's Letter to the Romans*, SBLDS, (Chico, CA: Scholar's Press, 1981).

⁷ My study has made use of the following: Tomas Hägg, *The Art of Biography in Antiquity* (New York: Cambridge University Press, 2012); Bryan P. Reardon, *Form of Greek Romance* (Princeton, NJ: Princeton University Press, 2016); Bryan P. Reardon, *Collected Ancient Greek Novels* (Berkeley: University of California Press, 1989); Marília P. Futre Pinheiro, Richard Pervo, and Judith Perkins, eds., *The Ancient Novel and Early Christian and Jewish Narrative: Fictional Intersections*, Ancient Narrative Supplementum (Havertown: Barkhuis, 2013); Ross Shepard Kraemer, *When Aseneth Met Joseph: A Late Antique Tale of the Biblical Patriarch and His Egyptian Wife, Reconsidered* (New York: Oxford University Press, 1998); Richard A. Burridge, *What are the Gospels?: A Comparison with Graeco-Roman Biography*, 2nd ed. (Grand Rapids: William B. Eerdmans Pub. Co., 2004).

the Gospel of John, those Jews who have been "put out of the synagogue (*aposynagōgos*)" (John 9:22; 12:42; 16:2) place in the mouth of Jesus their own animosity and vitriol (John 3:19–21; 8:44) about their fellow Jews as a secondary editor expands the first part of the Fourth Gospel with extended speeches appended to pericopes and adds a second half composed primarily of long speeches.

Minimal Expression of Apocalypticism and Messianism

I have also undertaken an exercise which I have referred to as "de-eschatologizing." I take apocalypticism as being a trait of minor groups pessimistic about any hope for national restoration and removal of the Roman occupation. To me this is a fringe element in early Christianity and one that became more popular in the late first century. I am inclined to think—though I cannot prove it—that the primary identity of Jesus was not as the Jewish Messiah. I tend not to think Paul's motivation grew out of an apocalyptic sense of urgency to bring in the end of the age. In my close reading of his letters while translating them, I discovered that the few sections that had apocalyptic language seemed to interrupt the flow of the text, have unusual Greek grammar and vocabulary, and be more expansive and florid in its style. Therefore, I have speculated that these sections were the work of editors and scribes during the collection and copying process. I have bracketed those sections in my translations and give my reasons in the overview sections.

It has been challenging to translate the Greek word we know of as "Christ" (*Christos*). It has been popular to think wherever "Christ" appears in the biblical text, the author has in mind the Jewish concept of messiah, the "anointed," who would become the king to restore Israel and bring about God's kingdom on earth. Paul primarily uses "Christ" as a name rather than a title. I'm content to go along with Novenson and call it an "honorific,"[8] but I wonder if it grew out of some confusion about what word was being said. We commonly know that Suetonius refers to a Chrestus who was responsible for the expulsion of Jews from Rome (*Lives of the Caesars V* [Claudius] 25.4). There is evidence people

---

[8] Matthew V. Novenson, *Christ Among the Messiahs: Christ Language in Paul and Messiah Language in Ancient Judaism* (Oxford: Oxford University Press, 2016).

took the names *Chrīstos* and *Chrēstos* to be a pun on the meaning of *Chrēstos* as "the beneficent one."[9]

My speculation is that, initially, people confused the language in Greek of "anointed one" with the Greek epithet of "beneficent one." In Greek the pronunciation would not have been distinguishable. It was an easy step from the Greek idea of a "son of God" to the Hebrew concept of the Messiah being the king whom the Israelites thought God adopted as a "son of God" upon his inauguration. Throughout the early Christian texts Greek terms known from the Greek translation of the Bible took on their meaning within Greek culture and particularly within Greek philosophy. I take Rom 2:4 as an instance of Paul making a pun with this terminology.

Another thorny issue is how to understand Paul's use of *kyrios*. Is he using the term generically as a ruler or master, or does Paul have in mind the way *kyrios* was used to translate the divine name in the Bible? I'm not of a mind to think Paul was equating Jesus with the divine name of the God of Israel. But I also don't think Paul is referring to Jesus every time he uses *kyrios* by itself. I'm persuaded that the God Paul wants gentiles to commit to is the God of Israel, though I think Paul has probably conflated some notions of the God of the Bible with attributes of the Greek conception of deity.

Paul as a Philosophical Guide

Over the years I've become more and more convinced that the most coherent way to understand Paul is within the Hellenistic context. It is ironic to me that an interpretation that is thoroughly Hellenistic results in viewing Paul as thoroughly Jewish, at least in the way he seems to have understood what that means. This eclectic Paul adapts not only philosophical language but also philosophical practices. I contend that Paul even goes so far as making the goal of life to be quite the same as the Roman philosophers like Epictetus, Seneca, or Musonius Rufus. By imitating Jesus and progressing in the development of the soul, the followers of Jesus could achieve "perfection," in the sense of maturity and completeness and experience a divine quality of life, a "flourishing

---

[9] Thomas Scott Caulley, "The Chrestos/Christos Pun (1 Pet 2:3) in P72 and P125," *Novum Testamentum* 53, no. 4 (2011).

life" (*eudaimonia*). I go a step further by attempting to place Paul within the context of functioning like a household advisor in those households where Paul formed "assemblies." These groups are not just meeting for an hour on the weekend but are part of the daily life within households either as members of the family or friends and clients of the householder.

These are some important ways in which I understand Paul. Because I decided I needed to compose fresh translations of Paul's letters, I have followed the pattern of Gager's *Reinventing* and Stowers's *Rereading* by titling my book *Rewriting Paul*.

BASIS FOR A REWRITING OF PAUL

Chapter 2:
Primary Principles

What Kind of Book is the Bible?

For many years I held to the evangelical view that God inspired the Bible down to the exact words of the original text and to the Bible in its entirety. To me, however, nothing I learned about the composition and copying of the biblical texts supported such a view. I learned that one reason for the popularity of the King James Version was that the translation was based on a series of manuscripts, copies of copies, that agreed in the wording of the text. This was proof that the Spirit of God was preserving the Word of God. But modern textual criticism developed the principle that it's not the number of copies that agree but the quality and diversity of the readings: we don't count manuscripts but "weigh" them, my professor taught me. Although the textual variants in the New Testament manuscripts aren't glaring attempts to deceive the reader and are mainly slight differences in word choice or word order, that copyists treated the early manuscripts of the Bible as a liquid text speaks against the view that scribes considered them to contain the exact words of God. It is also not well-known that the 1611 King James Bible first included the so-called deuterocanonical or apocryphal texts. From the very beginning church leaders in different regions did not agree on the list of books and their order until church councils established the canon of the Bible—and there is still no universal agreement.

This whole process of collating manuscripts, establishing a text, organizing a structure to the whole, producing copies, and creating versions in different languages is mainly the work of the Church. Publishers of modern English translations produce Bibles for Christian worship, and we expect translation committees to produce a volume that has every appearance that one person wrote it.

It's easy to forget that our Protestant Bible contains an Old Testament written in Hebrew—although the evidence of the New Testament is that

Christians were working with a Greek text of the Bible—and a New Testament written in Greek with very few transliterated words from Aramaic. I need to repeat this: THE ENTIRE NEW TESTAMENT WAS WRITTEN IN GREEK. Christians keep pretending they can read the Bible as if it's all the same thing. Even the Greek of the Gospels, when the Synoptics (Matthew, Mark, and Luke) agree, show that the authors felt free to use synonymous terms and put sentences in different syntactical constructions. Sometimes they move whole sections (pericopes) to appear in a different order.

Not only are the documents of the New Testament written in Greek, there is no evidence that NT authors originally wrote in Hebrew or Aramaic. The Hellenistic dialect of the New Testament often shows an influence of words and expressions readers of the Greek of the Bible had learned. Yet the Greek texts show that the authors composed the documents in the Greek language with Greek idioms, puns, and literary devices. Paul chose the form of the Greek letter to communicate with his groups in Roman cities and used a variety of literary devices and the hortatory language and form found in Greek philosophers like Musonius Rufus, Epictetus, and Seneca.

Here's an example of how an early Christian author tells a story and adds a "Hebrew" flavor to it. It's a story found in Acts and told three different times (Acts 9:1–20; 22:1–21; 26:1–23). In the third narration of the story of Paul's "conversion," Paul delivers a defense speech to Agrippa against the charges that his detractors made against him. Luke apparently adds some elaboration and verisimilitude to the story by saying that Jesus in the vision spoke to Paul in Hebrew (*tē Hebraidi*). The irony here is that the phrase put into the mouth of Jesus is a rather typical Greek expression, "to kick against the goads (*pros kentra laktizein*)" (Acts 26:14). This is not a new discovery, just one that scholars seem to ignore. Aeschylus's play, *Agamemnon*, first performed in 458 BCE, contains the line, "Do you have eyes and lack understanding? Do not kick against the goads (*pros kentra mē laktize*) lest you strike to your own hurt" (*Ag.* 1624).[10] Again, Euripides using the same expression in the *Bacchae*, produced in

---

[10] Aeschylus, *Oresteia: Agamemnon. Libation-Bearers. Eumenides.* trans. Alan H. Sommerstein, Loeb Classical Library 146 (Cambridge, MA: Harvard University Press, 2009), 197.

405 BCE, "I would sacrifice to the god rather than kick against his spurs (*pros kentra laktizoimi*) in anger, a mortal against a god" (*Bacch.* 795).[11] These are but two of the instances in Greek literature centuries before the rise of early Christianity. The author of Acts, composing the second volume as Greek literature, as he had the first, made use of a Greek idiom. But for the sake of the story he amplified it with a Hebrew characterization.

What is less well-known is the form of the Gospels. For many years classicists have ignored the literature called Greek novel or romance. Scholars like to study classical poetry (Homer's Iliad & Odyssey), plays (Euripides, Aeschylus, Sophocles, etc.), praise speeches (Gorgias), philosophical texts (Aristotle and Plato), and prose narratives of the histories (Thucydides and Herodotus). What is of less interest has been the development of the composition of fiction. Some writers borrowed from the structure of praise speeches devoted to the life and character of someone to expand to a fuller birth-to-death composition. Then some writers went a step further and imagined an entertaining and exciting adventure of the hero or heroes. These stories often involved young love in which the protagonists get separated, travel around the Mediterranean world, nearly reunite, but ultimately come back together to live happily ever after with their families. The Gospels have many things in common with these Greek novels. Rather than thinking about the Gospels as written by barely literate people just trying to put down exactly what Jesus did and said, we have texts from nearly fifty years after Jesus's death composed in a form of the novel which was just coming into its own as a genre.

Scholars have struggled with how to understand the writing of the Gospels. The prevailing consensus is that the followers of Jesus became eyewitnesses and passed along various sayings of Jesus in oral form in Aramaic. Eventually literate people began writing the sayings down and collecting them. All or part of this collection, known in scholarly circles as Q (for the German Quelle, "source"), we know as the material common to Matthew and Luke but not present in Mark. The theory is that the evangelist Mark, because of the brevity and lack of an infancy and death narrative in the Gospel of Mark, wrote first. Then Luke and

---

[11] Euripides, *Bacchae. Iphigenia at Aulis. Rhesus.* trans. David Kovacs, Loeb Classical Library 495 (Cambridge, MA: Harvard University Press, 2003), 85.

Matthew both use Mark, the Q collection of sayings, and their own independent sources.

Although Bibles place the Gospels first in the New Testament, they were not the first to be written. The dating of the Gospels is typically in the second half of the first century and even as late as the last quarter and beyond. The contention is that the core of the Gospels comes from that early oral transmission of the sayings of Jesus. Yet scholars seem to overlook the fact that we only know of Q in its Greek form. I have some problems with the theory.

For one, if the followers of Jesus knew the actual words of Jesus spoken in Aramaic, then why wouldn't they have continued to pass those along? What we know is that people from this period considered words in Aramaic to be powerful and even magical. Yet not only do we only have Q in Greek, but the Gospel authors don't seem concerned to preserve the Greek of the sayings either.

Most significant to me, the earliest texts of early Christianity, the letters of Paul, dating in the fifties and sixties, contain very little evidence of an existing sayings source. If there had been a collection of the actual sayings of Jesus in Aramaic, I find it hard to believe that Paul wouldn't have known about it. If Paul had known about it, I find it even harder to believe that Paul wouldn't have written about it. The basic principle in historiography is that events are substantiated by texts written at that same time. The only conclusion is that people did not remember much about what Jesus said and did. Christians composed "lives" of Jesus for the purpose of describing the person they believed Jesus to have been and the teaching that represents the way of life of the communities. To give the texts the sense that they come from that time and place, the authors did what authors usually did and added features to provide verisimilitude.

The consensus is that the origins and development of early Christianity follow a pattern. The theory is that Christianity formed within an Aramaic-speaking, messianic, apocalyptic Jewish group. Whatever the historian discovers to be closest to Jewish tradition is the most authentic and whatever shows Greek influence is a later adulteration. I use strong language because I keep hearing people talking as though people like Paul perverted the original, pristine Jewish Christianity by the later adoption of Greek culture for to evangelize the heathens. I don't think the evidence of the New Testament texts supports this view.

I'm convinced that earliest Christianity was a phenomenon growing out of the synthesis of Jewish and Greek culture. Centuries before Jesus and Paul there were Jews who not only were literate in the Greek language and culture but read their Bible in Greek and interpreted it through the lens of the Greek language and culture. Greek was not just a way of representing the meaning of Hebrew, but Jews interpreted the Bible through the lens of Greek history and philosophy. Paul represents a form of Hellenistic Judaism like that found in texts like 4 Maccabees and Wisdom of Solomon. Just as Jews in the Diaspora were gathering in households as an association, so Paul had his groups meet within the household as associations as others might meet as a guild, club, or philosophical school. Paul functioned as a philosophical or household guide with the householder functioning as a patron or sometimes a partner.

Radical New Perspective on Paul

There have been important advances in the study of earliest Christianity and the "Judaisms" of the Second Temple period. One of the most prominent books has been the work of E. P. Sanders in his book *Paul and Palestinian Judaism*.[12] Sanders's comparison of patterns of religion among Jews during the second temple period has been a watershed of renewed interest in Pauline research.

During the past century, scholars have become more and more aware that texts on Judaism (or late Judaism) described Judaism from the viewpoint of Christian theology.[13] Rabbinic Judaism—the surviving form of Judaism following the destruction of the temple in Jerusalem in

---

[12] E. P. Sanders, *Paul and Palestinian Judaism: A Comparison of Patterns of Religion* (Minneapolis: Fortress Press, 1977).

[13] G. F. Moore, "Christian Writers on Judaism," *Harvard Theological Review* 14 (1921): 197-254; G. F. Moore, *Judaism in the First Centuries of the Christian Era, the Age of the Tannaim*, 3 vols. (Cambridge: Harvard University Press, 1927-30); S. Schechter, *Some Aspects of Rabbinic Theology* (New York: Macmillan, 1923); A. Marmorstein, *The Doctrine of Merits in Old Rabbinical Literature* (New York: KTAV, 1968); C. G. Montefiore, "On Some Misconceptions of Judaism and Christianity By Each Other," *Jewish Quarterly Review* 8 (1896): 193-216.

70 CE and the Bar Kochba Revolt in 135 CE—was the type of Judaism made into a caricature. It was the perfect foil for Christian views about law and grace. Besides the Tannaitic literature (Mishnah, Talmud, Targums), there was also a large body of material that came to be associated with Second Temple Judaism. This was literature written in Greek by Jews after the Hellenization program of Alexander the Great in the early fourth century BCE. It included such works as the philosophical writings of Philo of Alexandria, the collections we refer to as the Apocrypha and the Pseudepigrapha, and the historical works of Josephus from the late first century. To this literature in Greek was added the new Aramaic and Hebrew Dead Sea Scrolls material after its discovery and gradual publication over the past fifty years.

Sanders's main conclusion after comparing this body of literature comes to us in the expression "covenantal nomism." He defines it as "the view that one's place in God's plan is established on the basis of the covenant and that the covenant requires as the proper response of man his obedience to its commandments, while providing means of atonement for transgression."[14] In other words, Judaism was not a religion based on legalistic works. The Hebrew people were transferred into this relationship with God by means of the covenant. Torah observance was the means to stay in right relationship with God as a people. This part of Sander's contribution has received wide acceptance, although some other things he had to say have not been as enduring.[15]

Another important figure has been Krister Standahl. In several articles he crystallized an emerging paradigm shift from an Augustinian-Lutheran view of the Christian Paul to the Jewish Paul.[16] Stendahl shifted the focus from the Paul of Rom 7, who can't be right with God through

---

[14] Sanders, *Paul and Palestinian Judaism: A Comparison of Patterns of Religion*, 75.

[15] An alternate view is available from Baker Academic: D. A. Carson, Peter Thomas O'Brien, and Mark A. Seifrid, *The Complexities of Second Temple Judaism*, vol. 1, Justification and Variegated Nomism, (Grand Rapids, MI: Baker Academic, 2001); D. A. Carson, Peter Thomas O'Brien, and Mark A. Seifrid, *The Paradoxes of Paul*, vol. 2, Justification and Variegated Nomism, (Grand Rapids, MI: Baker Academic, 2004).

[16] Krister Stendahl, *Paul among Jews and Gentiles: and other essays* (Philadelphia: Fortress Press, 1996). The section on "Call Rather Than Conversion" (pp. 7–22) and the essay "The Apostle Paul and the Introspective Conscience of the West" (pp. 78–96) have been particularly influential.

the law, to the Paul of the robust conscience: "as to righteousness under the law blameless" (Phil 3:6 NRSV). Instead of the Paul who converted to Christianity, Stendahl described a Jew who became a follower of Jesus and received a prophetic call to be the apostle to the gentiles.

From this type of research going on in the early to mid-twentieth century has arisen what has been called the New Perspective on Paul. The term New Perspective is attributed to James D. G. Dunn from the University of Durham, England.[17] Along with him is a fellow Anglican, N. T. Wright, chair of New Testament and Early Christianity at the School of Divinity at the University of St. Andrews.[18] Both are well-regarded New Testament scholars as well as being popular authors. Both build on the work of Sanders and continue the thesis that Paul did not depict Judaism as a legalistic religion based on fulfilling works of the law.

Following the New Perspective on Paul have been scholars who have written books with Re- in the title. The small paperback published in 2000, written for a non-specialist audience, is titled, *Reinventing Paul*, by John Gager of Princeton.[19] His most recent work is *Who Made Early Christianity?: The Jewish Lives of the Apostle Paul*.[20] The primary work for me is by Stanley Stowers, Professor Emeritus of Religious Studies at Brown University, in his 1994 book, *A Rereading of Romans: Justice, Jews, and Gentiles*.[21] These scholars have developed their ideas in dialogue with Lloyd Gaston, who was a Professor Emeritus of the Vancouver School of Theology, having taught New Testament there from 1973 to 1995.[22] This approach is distinguished within the "Paul within Judaism" movement

---

[17] James D. G. Dunn, *Jesus, Paul, and the Law: Studies in Mark and Galatians* (Louisville: Westminster/John Knox Press, 1990).

[18] N. T. Wright, *What Saint Paul Really Said: Was Paul of Tarsus the Real Founder of Christianity?* (Grand Rapids: Wm. B. Eerdmans Publishing Company, 1997).

[19] John G. Gager, *Reinventing Paul* (Oxford: New York, 2000).

[20] John G. Gager, *Who Made Early Christianity?: The Jewish Lives of the Apostle Paul* (New York: Columbia Press Press, 2015).

[21] Stanley K. Stowers, *A Rereading of Romans: Justice, Jews, and Gentiles* (New Haven: Yale University Press, 1994).

[22] Lloyd Gaston, *Paul and the Torah* (Vancouver: University of British Columbia Press, 1987).

by some with the designation *"Sonderweg."*[23] In a published dissertation I only noticed after finishing my research and writing, Jacob Mortenson credits Franz Mussner[24] with coining the term.[25] Some refer to it as a two covenant view.

For the Radical New Perspective group, the New Perspective group doesn't go far enough. Sanders for instance draws the conclusion, "In short, this is what Paul finds wrong in Judaism: it is not Christianity."[26] The Radical New View argues that Paul says nothing negative about the Law except as it pertains to gentiles. Paul writes letters to gentiles to further establish his objective to announce to gentile peoples across the empire that, though they had been excluded from God's covenant with Israel and, therefore, had no means for being right with God or dealing with sins apart from becoming a Jew through circumcision and law-keeping, Jesus by his obedience and faithfulness to God in death had provided the means for gentiles to be right with God as they participate in the new life in Christ.

With the method and approach I describe in these chapters, I think I have support for the so-called *Sonderweg* or two-covenant view. I translate Gal 4:4–5 in this way. (Italics is used to indicate paraphrase to aid in interpretation but also for foreign words like the Greek and Hebrew in this passage.)

> 4:4 However, when the chronological moment had come, God commissioned his son, birthed by a Jewish mother and therefore a Jew by law, 4:5 for the *dual* purpose of restoring those under Torah, *the Jewish people,* and for the reception of us, *the gentile peoples,* as adopted children. 4:6 Because you are full-fledged sons, God commissioned the Pneuma of God's son to infuse your being resulting in crying out: *Jews cry "Abba"* and *gentiles cry "Patēr."*

---

[23] Terence L. Donaldson, "Jewish Christianity, Israel's Stumbling and the *Sonderweg* Reading of Paul," *Journal for the Study of the New Testament* 29, no. 1 (2006).

[24] Franz Mussner, *Traktat über die Juden* (München: Kösel, 1979).

[25] Jacob P. B. Mortensen, *Paul Among the Gentiles: A "Radical" Reading of Romans,* Neutestamentliche Entwürfe zur Theologie, (Tubingen: Narr Francke Attempto, 2018), 308. (Note 77)

[26] Sanders, *Paul and Palestinian Judaism: A Comparison of Patterns of Religion,* 552.

Two ways are also distinguished in Rom 3:30.

> So then, God is One. God will rectify the circumcised based on faithfulness *to the covenant* and the foreskinned by means of the faithfulness *of Jesus*.

When I came to Rom 8:28–30, I consistently applied my method, and this text came out this way.

> We know that everything that happens results for good for those who love God, to those *gentile peoples* being invited *to be part of God's people* according to God's overall plan. It stands to reason that, those *gentile peoples* whom God knew in antiquity, he also determined in antiquity for them one day to share in the form of the likeness of God's son for the purpose of him being a firstborn among many siblings. It also stands to reason that those *gentile peoples*, whom God made a determination in antiquity, God also invited *to join God's people*. Those invited God also made upright; those made upright God also immortalized.

I did not feel like I had to force the text, but I needed to keep an open mind about the possibilities of the Greek text. Rather than let a Greek New Testament lexicon dictate how to interpret words based on the way others have understood them, I would consult the *Liddell-Scott-Jones Greek-English Lexicon* and also use the online Greek texts in *TLG* and the *LCL* to find similar contexts, most often searching for multiple terms where they occur in the same context.

Recent Scholarship on Greco-Roman Moral Philosophy and Early Christianity

The current movement interested in locating early Christianity within a Greco-Roman context is not the same as that of past generations, such as the History of Religions school. This one focuses on Greco-Roman literature, rhetoric, and philosophy within its social context. This is not to be confused with the earlier movement interested in Greco-Roman mystery religions or the anti-Semitic attempt to portray Nazi Germany as the embodiment of Greek ideals and the successor to the Roman Empire.[27]

In recent years several major collections of articles have been published that focus on the Greco-Roman context and early Christianity. In 1990, on the occasion of Abraham Malherbe's sixtieth birthday, a festschrift was published under the title *Greeks, Romans, and Christians*. Former students and colleagues of Malherbe contributed articles related to Christianity within the Greco-Roman context.[28] A collection of articles called *Paul in His Hellenistic Context* was published in 1995 based on a conference convened by Troels Engberg-Pedersen and held in June 1991 in Copenhagen.[29] In the following year a collection of articles, written by members of the Hellenistic Moral Philosophy and Early Christianity Group of the Society of Biblical Literature (*SBL*), was published with the title *Friendship, Flattery and Frankness of Speech: Studies on Friendship in the New Testament World*.[30] Another book based on a conference held in Denmark and convened by Engberg-Pedersen in 1997 was published in 2001 as *Paul Beyond the Judaism-Hellenism Divide*.

Another contribution was made by J. Paul Sampley in 2003. He edited a project called *Paul in the Greco-Roman World: A Handbook*.[31] In the introduction he notes, "… it is only in the last few decades that renewed interest has been paid to setting Paul's letters in the Greco-Roman world, and this enterprise is clearly on the cutting edge of Pauline scholarship

---

[27] For a survey of historical developments related to interpreting early Christianity within a Greco-Roman context, see Dale B. Martin, "Paul and the Judaism/Hellenism Dichotomy: Toward a Social History of the Question," in *Paul Beyond the Judaism/Hellenism Divide*, ed. Troels Engberg-Pedersen (Louisville: Westminster John Knox, 2001).

[28] David L. Balch, Everett Ferguson, and Wayne A. Meeks, eds., *Greeks, Romans, and Christians: Essays in Honor of Abraham J. Malherbe* (Minneapolis: Fortress Press, 1990).

[29] Troels Engberg-Pedersen, ed., *Paul in His Hellenistic Context* (Minneapolis: Fortress Press, 1995).

[30] John T. Fitzgerald, ed., *Friendship, Flattery, and Frankness of Speech: Studies on Friendship in the New Testament World*, vol. 82, Supplements to Novum Testamentum (Leiden: E.J. Brill, 1996).

[31] J. Paul Sampley, ed., *Paul in the Greco-Roman World: A Handbook* (Harrisburg, PA: Trinity Press International, 2003).

today."[32] He goes on to refer to the tendency of some Pauline scholars to prejudice Paul's Jewishness as theologically "safe and pure" over against Paul's "somehow tainted and dangerous" displays of being knowledgeable of Greek rhetoric and philosophy as a Roman citizen.[33] He makes the point that both are essential to an understanding of Paul.

> The decision to affirm both Paul's Jewish ethos as well as his Greco-Roman ethos is not a theological choice offered over against what I have labeled a theological prejudice in favor of Judaism. On the contrary, the judgment that both must ultimately be considered is not an option but rather a necessity, given that all the Judaisms at the time of Christian beginnings are already Hellenized.[34]

Terms referring to Paul's use of Greco-Roman traditions such as "borrowed" or "adopted" are misleading and ignore the fact that "Paul was a Roman Jew, both together."[35] Sampley adds one further, related consideration. Traditionally, the metaphor of the kernel and the husk has been used to play down or even disparage the historical context as though the skilled interpreter can just peel off the husk and throw it away to get to the real message of the gospel. Sampley counters, "The gospel, however, has never been presented without some incarnation in socially viable conventions and assumptions. There is no such thing as a version of the gospel without culturally situated suppositions and conventions."[36]

Once again in 2003, a festschrift for Abraham Malherbe was published, this time with the title *Early Christianity and Classical Culture*.[37]

---

[32] Sampley, ed., *Paul in the Greco-Roman World*, 1.

[33] Sampley, ed., *Paul in the Greco-Roman World*, 4.

[34] Sampley, ed., *Paul in the Greco-Roman World*, 4-5.

[35] Sampley, ed., *Paul in the Greco-Roman World*, 5.

[36] Sampley, ed., *Paul in the Greco-Roman World*, 5-6. This applies equally to Israelite religion and the emerging Judaism of the late prophetic period. There is no pure Judaism for Jesus and Paul to inherit that is without influence by local cultures and religions.

[37] John T. Fitzgerald, Thomas H. Olbricht, and L. Michael White, eds., *Early Christianity and Classical Culture: Comparative Studies in Honor of Abraham J. Malherbe*, Supplements to Novum Testamentum (Leiden: Brill, 2003).

In the same year John T. Fitzgerald, who can be found as a contributor and editor to preceding volumes, along with several others, collected contributions as an outcome of work by the Hellenistic Moral Philosophy and Early Christianity Section of SBL for a book on the first century BCE Epicurean philosopher from Gadara, Syria, titled *Philodemus and the New Testament World*.[38] Then in 2008 Fitzgerald edited another collection of articles from the same group, this one with the title *Passions and Moral Progress in Greco-Roman Thought*.[39]

In more recent developments, a new commentary series is underway called *Brill's Ancient Philosophical Commentary on the Pauline Writings*. The description of the project takes this position:

> Among modern scholars there is an increasing awareness of the way that Paul's ideas about ethics, anthropology, cosmology and social issues match those expressed by the philosophers of his day.[40]

The first volume on Romans is expected to be available in 2020/21.

---

[38] John T. Fitzgerald, Dirk Obbink, and Glenn Holland, eds., *Philodemus and the New Testament World*, vol. 111, Supplements to Novum Testamentum (Leiden; Boston: Brill, 2004).

[39] John T. Fitzgerald, ed., *Passions and Moral Progress in Greco-Roman Thought*, Routledge Monographs in Classical Studies (London; New York: Routledge, 2008).

[40] https://www.rug.nl/research/centre-for-religious-studies/philosophical-commentary-pauline-writings/philosopher-paul

Chapter 3:
Placing Paul in the First Century

Earliest Christian Texts: Letters of Paul

Although the events of the Gospels are chronologically the earliest, the Gospels are thought to have been written later in the first century, most likely in the last quarter of that century. Paul's letters, therefore, are the earliest written witness of the rise of early Christianity. They are, moreover, the best source for understanding this phenomenon of a Greek-speaking Jew, a Roman citizen, becoming a follower of Jesus and bringing a message of good news to the gentile peoples who are part of the Roman Empire.

Since literary narratives around this period were composed to tell a story from a certain perspective and not strictly as an unbiased report of events and actual dialogue, the content of the Gospels and Acts have to be interpreted within their own context in the latter half of the century. Letters, on the other hand, are more historically reliable when they describe people, places, and life situations. We first have to interpret Paul's letters within the first century context without imposing later church doctrines and practices.

Locating Paul within the Greco-Roman World

What's missing from the evidence when people normally read the Bible is that all the New Testament documents are written in Hellenistic Greek. In fact, translation committees intentionally try to make the various books of the Bible read like they were written by the same person, ostensibly God. Not only is the Greek of the New Testament not like the Hebrew Bible, each work of the New Testament has its author's own style and vocabulary.

The most glaring fact is that Paul wrote his letters in Greek. Furthermore, he used the standard form of the Greek letter with the identification of the writer and the recipients, a greeting, the body of the letter, and an ending. The function of the letters conforms to the recognized types of letters in the Greco-Roman world.

Not only does Paul write letters according to standard Greek epistolography, Paul's letters contain other evidence of a more sophisticated knowledge of Greek rhetoric. One example is Paul's use of a scholastic literary device called the diatribe. A close parallel to his use of the diatribe can be found in the discourses of Epictetus.

Paul's letters reveal his role within the communities he established and with whom he communicated by his practice of using the language of moral exhortation much like popular Greco-Roman moral philosophers. I will argue that Paul functioned as a household or philosophical advisor to the groups he helped form within the context of the household.

Unless Paul is to be thought to have a dissociative personality disorder, Paul must be constructed as a multicultural person. There's no reason to doubt that Paul was a Jew who received training in Hebrew and the Torah. But we must recognize that Paul was equally at home in Greco-Roman culture. Whether Paul received a formal education in a school such as existed in his hometown of Tarsus, the evidence of his letters is a witness to his level of knowledge of writing in Hellenistic Greek and his understanding of rhetorical and literary forms and popular Greek moral philosophy.

Most likely it is the case that by the time of Paul there was already a practice among Hellenistic Jews to read the Bible in Greek, to interpret the Bible through the lens of Platonism or Stoicism, to observe the principles of Torah through philosophical practice, to replace the models of Greco-Roman moral exhortation with the figures of the Bible, or even to adopt the lifestyle and teachings of Cynics and Stoics.

Multicultural and bilingual people today know what it's like, for example, to speak English outside of the home, perhaps with no recognizable accent, and to behave in ways typical for the dominant culture, but then to switch naturally to their native language at home or with those of the same ethnicity. It's not just the language but the mannerisms and customs of that culture. These people are not bifurcated in their identity but live and act in more than one cultural context. We may imagine Paul in much the same way. When he writes in Greek to people, he is not simply transferring his Hebrew concepts or his

"Jewishness" into a different language but communicating cross-culturally within the structures of that culture.

Stowers has emphasized the role of the concept of self-mastery within the Greco-Roman world and within Paul's writing.[41] My view is that Paul replaces law observance for gentiles with philosophical exercises that bring about the progress leading to mature character. If Paul shared the same views regarding the purpose for circumcision as Philo, then Paul may have considered rigorous philosophical practices a necessity for gentiles. Philo gave these two reasons for circumcision.

> I consider circumcision to be a symbol of two things most necessary to our well-being. One is the excision of pleasures which bewitch the mind. For since among the love-lures of pleasure the palm is held by the mating of man and woman, the legislators thought good to dock the organ which ministers to such intercourse, thus making circumcision the figure of the excision of excessive and superfluous pleasure, not only of one pleasure but of all the other pleasures signified by one, and that the most imperious. The other reason is that a man should know himself (*gnōnai eauton*) and banish from the soul the grievous malady of conceit. For there are some who have prided themselves on their power of fashioning as with a sculptor's cunning the fairest of creatures, man, and in their braggart pride (*alazoneias*) assumed godship, closing their eyes to the Cause of all that comes into being, though they might find in their familiars a corrective for their delusion. For in their midst are many men incapable of begetting and many women barren, whose matings are ineffective and who grow old childless. The evil belief, therefore, needs to be excised from the mind with any others that are not loyal to God (Philo, *Spec.* 1.9–10).[42]

On this basis, Paul may have thought uncircumcised gentile men were more susceptible to desire and pleasure. Paul's letters, especially

---

[41] Stowers, *A Rereading of Romans*, 42-82. See also Stanley K. Stowers, "Paul and Self-Mastery," in *Paul in the Greco-Roman World: A Handbook*, ed. J. Paul Sampley (Harrisburg, PA: Trinity Press International, 2003).

[42] Philo, *On the Decalogue. On the Special Laws, Books 1-3.* trans. F. H. Colson, Loeb Classical Library 320 (Cambridge, MA: Harvard University Press, 1937), 105, 07.

Galatians and Romans, tend to focus on why gentiles do not need to undergo circumcision and then on seeking to persuade gentiles to live a virtuous life through philosophical practices to reach maturity in the same way Jesus did as evidenced by his resurrection.

An Explanation for Paul's Affinity for the Greco-Roman World

Although Paul addresses himself to a gentile audience in his letters and Acts portrays him as such, people still seem to imagine Paul as a Hebrew prophet or a Rabbi who, for the sake of his gentile converts, puts his Hebrew into Greek merely as a concession for the understandability of his readers. Scholars have frequently tried to find in Paul's letters a thorough-going Judaism that can be compared to the later texts of the Mishna and Talmud.[43] But not only are these Jewish texts much later than Paul, they themselves were influenced by Greek culture. While I maintain that Paul considered himself to be an observant Jew and had nothing negative to say about Judaism for Jews—though he, along with the Jerusalem apostles, wanted fellow-Jews to recognize Jesus as a messianic figure whose death might lead to the overthrow of the Roman authorities and institute a national restoration—I wish to emphasize Paul's language when he addresses his gentile audience. When Paul uses the collective "we," I translate that by adding "gentiles" in parentheses. Here is my translation of this crucial text in Romans.

> 5:1 So then, because we *gentiles* have been regarded as upright based on faithfulness, we *gentiles* have rapprochement with God by participation with our Lord, Jesus Christ. 5:2 It is through him we *gentiles* have obtained the entrance into this benefit where we hold steady and we base our boasting in the expectation of *receiving* the splendor of God.

My initial thought in doing this was that Paul thought in these terms only as a rhetorical way of adapting himself to his readers. While translating Galatians, I came across a text that I think may shed more light on why Paul could identify himself so closely with his gentile audience. For ease of analysis, I quote my translation as follows.

---

[43] William D. Davies, *Paul and Rabbinic Judaism: Some Rabbinic Elements in Pauline Theology* (New York: Harper & Row, 1967).

> 4:12 Siblings, I beg you: Become the kind of person I am. After all, I became *a gentile* as you. You have not at all hurt my feelings. 4:13 You are aware that I previously announced good news to you because of a flesh wound. 4:14 Even though my wound tested you, you did not ostracize me or show disgust, but you accepted me as a messenger of God, as though I were Christ Jesus. 4:15 Therefore, where is your receptivity? For I am convinced that–if possible–you would have presented to me your gouged-out eyes.

There are several items in this text that must be accounted for to explain the context of Paul's infirmity.

- Paul has become like the Galatians.
- Their treatment of Paul is not critical.
- Paul gives as a reason for his bringing the good news to them his infirmity of his flesh.
- The Galatians were under some stress about the nature of this infirmity, but they did not react in a way that showed their disgust or rejected Paul.
- Their response was extreme enough that Paul could exaggerate their willingness to remove their eyes and give them to Paul.

The most common assumption has been that Paul had some kind of eye problem. It's thought that this is why the Galatians would have given Paul their healthy eyes, and also why Paul remarks that his handwriting is large (Gal 6:11). In fact, this aside of Paul would be better understood to refer to the length of the letter. I translate this, "Notice I have made the effort to write this long document with my own handwriting" (see discussion on page 27).

An eye problem doesn't explain how it could have been the reason for Paul coming to them, what it has to do with Paul becoming like the Galatians, or how their eyeballs could have helped Paul when that kind of transplant surgery was not possible then and is still not.[44] I suggest

---

[44] Gouging out the eyes is always set in a context of undergoing punishment or torture. Herodotus describes it as a horrible thing the Thracian king did to his sons when they disobeyed him (Herodotus, *Hist.* 8.116). Plutarch reports that a certain

that what could fit the circumstances and language is that in Paul's youth, when he was learning the Greek language and about Greek culture, Paul underwent circumcision reversal surgery. It was this that could account for Paul identifying himself so closely with his gentile audience—he had become as them—and that the disfigurement and perhaps even lifelong injury, which would have become obvious when Paul would have appeared in the nude in public baths, latrines, and perhaps even during athletic participation in his younger years, was a potential source of shame for which the Galatians would even have been blinded so as not to offend Paul.

It is generally recognized that Paul seems to have experience with the language of athletics that goes beyond a shared metaphor with Greco-Roman moral philosophy.[45] Tarsus would have provided him every opportunity to take part in athletics in the gymnasium. In an outdated but beautifully written book, Robert Bird imagines Paul to grow up in Tarsus as a strict Jewish boy who only observed other boys running the racecourse or exercising nude in the gymnasium.[46] Paul's adeptness at Greek letter-writing, knowledge of Greek literary devices, and awareness of technical, athletic terminology suggests that Paul might have spent his youth steeped in the Hellenistic culture of that burgeoning Roman city recently having become the capital of Cilicia. As Robert Hall puts it, "Athletics constituted a chief avenue of social advancement for underclass boys. Greek cities competed with each other to grant citizenship to promising boys and to sponsor them at the games. Since athletes exercised and competed without clothes, this avenue was denied to those who were circumcised."[47]

Even those men who were not circumcised might feel the need to use a method of preventing the glans of the penis from showing. Waldo Sweet lists three types of people who might make use of this method:

Carian, who boasted of being instrumental in the death of Cyrus, was punished for his lies by having his eyes gouged out and molten metal poured into his ears (Plutarch, *Art.* 4.10.4).

[45] Michael Poliakoff, "Jacob, Job, and Other Wrestlers: Reception of Greek Athletics by Jews and Christians in Antiquity," *Journal of Sport History* 11, no. 2 (1984): 58-59.

[46] Robert Bird, *Paul of Tarsus* (New York: Charles Scribner's Sons, 1916), 33-34.

[47] Robert G. Hall, "Epispasm: Circumcision in Reverse," *Bible Review* August (1992).

"athletes, revelers, and the mythological creatures called satyrs."[48] One method was to secure the foreskin of the penis with a thong and even to secure it to one side. This type of infibulation was called *kynodesmē*, "dog leash." Much of the art from ancient Greece depict this practice. I will describe the practice of circumcision reversal below.

It is clear that in the Greco-Roman world, "the aesthetic preference for the longer, tapered prepuce is a reflection of a deeper ethos involving cultural identity, morality, propriety, virtue, beauty, and health. Accordingly, the violation of this ethos by the specter of a deficient prepuce was addressed through individual, political, legal, and medical remedies."[49]

We know about the practice of circumcision reversal among Jews during this period because some Jews were seeking to have this procedure done to engage more fully in Greek culture during the time of the Hasmonean revolt against the Seleucid king Antiochus Epiphanes.

> In those days certain renegades came out from Israel and misled many, saying, "Let us go and make a covenant with the Gentiles around us, for since we separated from them many disasters have come upon us." This proposal pleased them, and some of the people eagerly went to the king, who authorized them to observe the ordinances of the Gentiles. So, they built a gymnasium in Jerusalem, according to Gentile custom, and removed the marks of circumcision (lit. "made themselves foreskinned") and abandoned the holy covenant. They joined with the Gentiles and sold themselves to do evil (1 Macc 1:11–15 NRSV).

We have in this text a precedence for Jews to "make themselves uncircumcised" (1 Macc 1:15). In other words, to make themselves have a foreskin in order that they might engage in athletic exercises, which according to Greek custom, done in the nude. Their actions were

---

[48] Waldo E. Sweet, *Sport and Recreation in Ancient Greece: A Sourcebook with Translations* (New York: Oxford University Press, 1987), 29.

[49] Frederick M. Hodges, "The Ideal Prepuce in Ancient Greece and Rome: Male Genital Aesthetics and Their Relation to Lipodermos, Circumcision, Foreskin Restoration, and the *Kynodesme*," *Bulletin of the History of Medicine* 75, no. 3 (2001): 377.

considered leaving the Jewish covenant and joining with a gentile covenant. In effect, they make themselves to become gentiles.

Josephus also mentions this story in the Maccabean literature. He reports that it was Jason who went to Antiochus and

> informed him that they wished to abandon their country's laws and the way of life prescribed by these, and to follow the king's laws and adopt the Greek way of life. Accordingly, they petitioned him to permit them to build a gymnasium in Jerusalem. And when he had granted this, they also concealed the circumcision of their private parts (*tēn tōn aidoiōn peritomēn epekalypsan*) in order to be Greeks even when unclothed, and giving up whatever other national customs they had, they imitated the practices (*erga*) of foreign nations (Josephus, *Ant.* 12:241).[50]

Josephus does not provide the same judgment as the Maccabean literature against those who took part in the practice. What he tells us is that the participants were unclothed. It is not the case that they were wearing tunics as they may have been doing in Rome according to Dionysius of Halicarnassus (*Ant. rom.* 7.72). Jewish custom was that "they should cover their shame and they should not be uncovered as the gentiles are uncovered" (Jub. 3:31 trans. O. S. Wintermute).[51]

In the Testament of Moses, a document thought to be from the first century CE, there is a prophecy that a ruler will come who will persecute those who practice circumcision. Young men who have been circumcised "will be cut by physicians to bring forward their foreskins" (8:3 trans. J. Priest).[52] The Jerusalem Talmud mentions that "in the time of Bar Coziba, many people had practiced the *epiplasm*" [sic *epispasm*] (y. Šabb. 19:2). The Mishnah requires that the foreskin must be cut to the extent that the corona of the glans is exposed otherwise it is not legitimate (m. Šabb. 19:6).

---

[50] Josephus, *Jewish Antiquities, Volume 5: Books 12-13*. trans. Ralph Marcus, Loeb Classical Library 365 (Cambridge, MA: Harvard University Press, 1943), 123.

[51] James H. Charlesworth, ed., *The Old Testament Pseudepigrapha*, vol. 2 (Garden City, NY: Doubleday & Co., Inc., 1983), 60.

[52] James H. Charlesworth, ed., *The Old Testament Pseudepigrapha*, vol. 1 (Garden City, NY: Doubleday & Co., Inc., 1983), 931.

It wasn't only a matter of Jews appearing to be uncircumcised to participate in athletics or carry out business while enjoying the public baths. Hiding one's circumcision in one way or another became important in the late first century CE when a tax was imposed on Jews. Suetonius explains the situation.

> Besides other taxes, that on the Jews was levied with the utmost rigor, and those were prosecuted who without publicly acknowledging that faith yet lived as Jews, as well as those who concealed (*dissimulata*) their origin and did not pay the tribute levied upon their people. I recall being present in my youth when the person of a man ninety years old was examined before the procurator and a very crowded court, to see whether he was circumcised (*Dom.* 8.3).[53]

Perhaps Suetonius refers not just to hiding one's circumcised penis by wearing clothing but "disguising" its appearance.

From this period, we have a description of the process from the medical work of Aulus Cornelius Celsus (c. 25 BCE–c. 50 CE). Celsus describes the situation in which a male's glans is bare, because of a natural defect or to circumcision. The procedure is easier in the case of a defect in which there is some foreskin. Next, Celsus provides instructions for the circumcised male which requires pulling the existing skin up, cutting around the penis, and lifting the skin into position. Within this context Celsus gives another example of a similar procedure. In this case, the male—the example Celsus gives is of a boy—wants to prevent the foreskin from revealing the glans. The medical term for this is preputial infibulation.[54]

> Some have been accustomed to pin up the prepuce (*infibulare*) in adolescents either for the sake of the voice, or for health's sake. This is the method: the foreskin covering the glans

---

[53] Suetonius, *Lives of the Caesars, Volume 2: Claudius. Nero. Galba, Otho, and Vitellius. Vespasian. Titus, Domitian. Lives of Illustrious Men: Grammarians and Rhetoricians. Poets (Terence. Virgil. Horace. Tibullus. Persius. Lucan). Lives of Pliny the Elder and Passienus Crispus.* trans. J. C. Rolfe, Loeb Classical Library 38 (Cambridge, MA: Harvard University Press, 1914), 349-51.

[54] D. Schultheiss, J. J. Mattelaer, and F. M. Hodges, "Preputial Infibulation: From Ancient Medicine to Modern Genital Piercing," *BJU International* 92, no. 7 (2003).

is stretched forwards and the point for perforation marked on each side with ink. Then the foreskin is let go. If the marks are drawn back over the glans too much has been included, and the marks should be placed further forward. If the glans is clear of them, their position is suitable for the pinning (*fibulae*). Then the foreskin is transfixed at the marks by a threaded needle, and the ends of this thread are knotted together. Each day the thread is moved until the edges of the perforations have cicatrized. When this is assured the thread is withdrawn and a fibula inserted, and the lighter this is the better. But this operation is more often superfluous than necessary (Celsus, *De med.* 7.25.2).[55]

We can only infer that, if this is what Paul implies, he had this procedure done as a boy to participate fully in his training, whether or not formal, in Greek life. We can imagine that, even if the procedure was successful, it would have been temporary as he grew into manhood. The infibulation procedure would have made sure that the foreskin remained in place when he needed it to. It would not be more of a stretch of the imagination to conclude that such procedures would have left him prone to irritation and even infection. Paul would seem to have regretted his decision to have the procedure and advised gentile proselytes who had been circumcised not to reverse the circumcision (1 Cor 7:18). The verb Paul uses is the term used to describe this foreskin restoration surgery, *epispasm*.

An important text is 2 Cor 12:7, the well-known "thorn in the flesh" text. Paul is sufficiently vague in this context about the "weakness" that is the source of torment for him. I suggest that his metaphor of a "thorn" is a play on the word. The Greek word refers to any sharp object. Paul could be referring to the pin (*fibula*) he wears as being an irritant like a thorn stuck in the paw of the fabled lion. Paul says he asked God to remove the ailment. But Paul felt that the persistent wound was an opportunity to depend on God and endure the pain and the shame.

In another context in Galatians we have an obscure reference to what has become known as stigmata, the mystical appearance of the marks of Christ's crucifixion (Gal 6:17). A *stigma* in Greek refers to the pin used in

---

[55] Celsus, *On Medicine, Volume 3: Books 7-8*. trans. W. G. Spencer, Loeb Classical Library 336 (Cambridge, MA: Harvard University Press, 1938), 423-25.

tattooing to mark a slave or a soldier. Once again Paul makes use of a pun to refer to the way the *fibula* is a pin that has designated him as a slave of Christ. The larger context is a concluding remark about circumcision and uncircumcision. Perhaps Paul also connects the word "cross" with "stigma," since the Greek word for cross is another word which refers to a pointed object like a pike used in impaling captives and criminals.

When these texts are re-examined within the context of infibulation, there is a coherence and consistency that provides a better explanation than what is traditionally held. Paul's circumcision reversal was something he came to regret owing to the chronic condition that both caused him pain and shame. For him whether a man was circumcised or "fore-skinned" wasn't the most important issue. It provided Paul with the unique condition of being able to remain a Jew by removing the fibula and to take part in Greco-Roman culture as a gentile. It served as an impetus for Paul to travel beyond Judea to the rest of the Roman Empire with the message that the one true living God was their God as well.

Paul's Distinction When Addressing Gentiles and Jews

As I have said above, I have attempted to make additions to my translations when I have interpreted Paul's address as having to do specifically with gentiles or Jews. Mostly, Paul's letters are to gentiles. When Paul uses the second-person plural, I take him to be referring most closely with the gentiles within the city or region to which he addresses himself. His language is about specific experiences his audience has had. When Paul uses the first-person plural, I take Paul to be including himself within the gentile experience, either rhetorically as adapting himself to his audience or, perhaps, as I've argued above, literally as someone who thinks of himself as both gentile, having undergone reverse circumcision surgery, and Jew by birth and religious practice.

Let me suggest another possibility in Paul's language when addressing or referring to Jews. I take the position that Paul's language of "holy ones" (*hagioi*, traditionally translated "saints") is a way he refers to Jews within a city or region. The two times Paul uses the term to refer to gentiles (Rom 1:7; 1 Cor 1:2), he uses the expression "invited *to be* saints" (*klētois hagiois*, "called saints" or "called to be saints"). The sense of the Greek word is not that it is their name, as may be assumed from the English word "call," but that they have been invited to join the holy people of God. Even if the sense is "referred to as," gentiles are not named as "holy ones." It seems that Paul is consistently calling Jews "holy ones," or as I have translated the Greek with a Hebrew term *qedoshim*.

There is one other peculiar instance. While studying the literary composition of Philippians, I concluded that it is a composite of Paul's correspondence with Jesus-followers in Philippi. I distinguish a section made up of Phil 3:2–4:1 as obviously a letter to gentiles in which he warns them about the Judaizers who want to have Jesus-followers become circumcised to become full proselytes. More controversial will be my decision to take Phil 1:1–2:18; 3:1; 4:2–9; 21–23 as an original letter addressed to Jewish followers of Jesus in Philippi. I have translated the address of Paul as "A letter from Paul and Timothy, devotees of Christ Jesus. We are writing to all of you *Jewish qedoshim* in Christ Jesus, living in Philippi, including your *household* overseers and servers *in the synagogue*" (Phil 1:1). Let me try to say why I think this is right.

Arguably the most important text is Lev 19:2, which from Greek reads, "You shall be holy ones (*hagioi*)," which term in Hebrew is *qedoshim*. Elsewhere in the LXX we find this language, such as Ps 16:3; 34:9. Also in the book of Daniel, "As I looked, this horn made war with the holy ones (*hagious*) and was prevailing over them" (Dan 7:21 NRSV). That this language made its way into the parlance of Greek-speaking Jews is proven by its appearance in the Wisdom of Solomon. Twice the author uses the parallelism of "holy ones" and "elect" (Wis 3:9; 4:15; also 18:1, 5). Frequently, Paul uses this language regarding support for Jewish Jesus-followers in Jerusalem (Rom 12:13; 15:25, 31; 1 Cor 16:1, 15; 2 Cor 8:4; 9:1, 12). Another frequent usage is the reference to "holy ones" in a region, either as greeting them or passing along their greetings (Rom 16:2, 15; 2 Cor 1:1; 13:12; Philem 5, 7). There are two instances that need further explanation.

In 1 Cor 6 Paul talks to the Corinthians about reconciling wrongs committed within the community against each other. After referring to the Roman legal system as "based on the unjust ones (*adikōn*)," he contrasts it with intra-community resolution as "based on the holy ones (*hagiōn*)." It would seem that Paul's choice of wording here is influenced by the number of syllables and similar endings. It's difficult to know how to take the verses that follow. I take Paul to say, "Don't you know that the "holy ones" (the angels) will judge the (future) world? And if the (present) world is to be judged by you, are you incompetent to try trivial cases? Don't you know that we are to judge angels—to say nothing of ordinary matters" (1 Cor 6:2–3 NRSV adapted).

The other difficult instance is 1 Cor 13:33–36.

> As in all the assemblies *i.e. synagogues* of the *qedoshim*, gentile wives should be silent in the *gentile* meetings. ... If there is anything they desire to know, let them ask their husbands at home. For it is shameful for a wife to speak in an assembly. Or did the word of God *i.e. Torah* originate with you *gentiles*? Or are you *gentiles* the only ones it has reached (1 Cor 14:33–36 NRSV adapted).

I take this text as Paul saying that the gentile meetings should follow some of the same customs as the Jewish assemblies. Jewish custom in the synagogue was for women to be separated from the men. Apparently, women were taking part in the table-talk of gentile household meetings, and Paul had his own prejudices about social customs within Roman households. Married women should show deference in public to their husbands.

The further in time one goes in the texts of the first century the less distinct will be Paul's usage. No doubt at some point gentile Christians began appropriating the Jewish language for themselves in the gradual development from Jewish Christian factions claiming other Jews are not legitimate and then to gentile Christians beginning to claim to supersede Judaism altogether. The later literature of Philemon, Ephesians, and Colossians strain my interpretation, though I will still try to claim it for Philemon. The most difficult texts for me are those in which the audience is called "holy ones," but specified as gentiles as in Eph 2:11 ("you Gentiles by birth, called 'the uncircumcision'" NRSV) and Col 2:13 ("you were dead in trespasses and the uncircumcision of your flesh" NRSV). I would take this as evidence of the development from Paul's usage into a later, more generalized usage by his coworkers.

Chapter 4:
Paul as Philosophical Guide
Within Households of Patrons

We know that Paul was someone who traveled between cities in the Roman Empire, stayed at length in certain households, spent his time talking with people about Jesus while working in places as a tentmaker (Acts 18:3), and wrote Greek letters of moral exhortation to the primarily non-Jewish households in cities where he had formed or intended to form a community of people whose shared life centered on Jesus as the means to the fulfillment of their souls. To understand Paul's activity, scholars have focused on certain aspects of Paul's life. Paul is often described as a missionary, but that is an obvious anachronism. It is more likely that Paul patterned his activity on one or more models for achieving his purposes.

We might think Paul's participation in the craft of tent-making could explain his traveling around the empire and finding work within Roman cities. We even have examples of those who plied a trade while also performing the function of a philosophical guide.[56] Ronald Hock has shown that Paul's attitude toward his work reflects an upper-class mentality of one who sees working as enslaving (1 Cor 9:19) and demeaning (2 Cor 11:7).[57] He and others have shown that for Paul to work at a trade within a household shop fits with how a philosopher might engage with people in the publicly accessible shop.[58] That might help to explain how Paul could move around, sustain his life, and have

---

[56] Ronald F. Hock, "Simon the Shoemaker as an Ideal Cynic," *Greek, Roman and Byzantine Studies* 17 (1976).

[57] Ronald F. Hock, "Paul's Tentmaking and the Problem of His Social Class," *Journal of Biblical Literature* 97, no. 4 (1978): 558-62.

[58] Hock, "Paul's Tentmaking and the Problem of His Social Class," 563. For a fuller treatment see Ronald F. Hock, *The Social Context of Paul's Ministry: Tentmaking and Apostleship* (Philadelphia: Fortress Press, 1980).

a connection to a trade conducted within the normal operations of a Roman household.

Scholars continue to try to understand the social context for the meetings of Jews and followers of Jesus.[59] Some have argued that Paul's activities within households and his writing letters of moral exhortation could be compared to the practice of philosophical schools.[60] I interpret Paul's letters within this context and attempt to show Paul's philosophical language.

The Practice of Psychagogy

Paul's activities within assemblies and through his letter writing are best described with the term psychagogy. Psychagogy means the guidance of the soul. A psychagogue is a soul guide or as we call the person today, a spiritual director.[61] Using the term psychagogy seems to stem from German classical scholarship. Two classic works in German describe the practices of ancient philosophy with the language of "soul leading" or "soul guidance."[62] Other scholars have built on this work to

---

[59] Wayne A. Meeks, *The First Urban Christians: The Social World of the Apostle Paul*, 2nd ed. (New Haven: Yale University Press, 2003); John S. Kloppenborg and Stephen G. Wilson, eds., *Voluntary Associations in the Graeco-Roman World* (London: Routledge, 2012); Anders Runesson, "The Question of Terminology: The Architecture of Contemporary Discussions on Paul," in *Paul within Judaism: Restoring the First-Century Context to the Apostle*, ed. Mark D. Nanos and Magnus Zetterholm (Minneapolis: Fortress Press, 2015).

[60] Abraham J. Malherbe, "Paul: Hellenistic Philosopher or Christian Pastor?," *Anglican Theological Review* 68, no. 1 (1986); Stanley K. Stowers, "Social Status, Public Speaking and Private Teaching: The Circumstances of Paul's Preaching Activity," *Novum Testamentum* 26 (1984); Loveday Alexander, "Paul and the Hellenistic Schools: The Evidence of Galen," in *Paul in His Hellenistic Context* (Minneapolis: Fortress Press, 1995); Stanley K. Stowers, "Does Pauline Christianity Resemble a Hellenistic Philosophy?," in *Paul Beyond the Judaism/Hellenism Divide*, ed. Troels Engberg-Pedersen (Louisville, KY: Westminster John Knox Press, 2001).

[61] For a classic description of psychagogy, see Ilsetraut Hadot, "The Spiritual Guide," in *Classical Mediterranean Spirituality: Egyptian, Greek, Roman*, ed. A. H. Armstrong, World Spirituality (New York: Crossroad, 1986).

[62] Paul Rabbow, *Seelenführung: Methodik der Exerzitien in der Antike* (München: Kösel-Verlag, 1954); Ilsetraut Hadot, *Seneca und die griechisch-römische Tradition der Seelenleitung* (Berlin: de Gruyter, 1969).

emphasize that ancient Greek philosophy was not the kind of academic enterprise we might think of today, but it focused on how to live life well.[63] How does a person become the best that a human can be?[64]

Psychagogy has found its way into North American scholarship through the work of Abraham Malherbe of Yale. His small book *Paul and the Thessalonians: The Philosophic Tradition of Pastoral Care*[65] describes psychagogy by comparing the practices of Cynics to that of Paul. Recent work that discusses Paul as a Jewish follower of Jesus within a Greco-Roman context of philosophical groups has appeared mainly in collections of articles.[66] Much of that work comes from the Hellenistic Moral Philosophy & Early Christianity unit of the Society of Biblical Literature. Many of those scholars were colleagues of Malherbe at Yale, were his students at one time, or are students of his students such as

---

[63] Here I refer to the translated works of Pierre Hadot: Pierre Hadot, *Philosophy as a way of life: spiritual exercises from Socrates to Foucault*, trans. Arnold I. Davidson, ed. Arnold I. Davidson (Malden, MA: Blackwell Publishing, 1995); Pierre Hadot, *The Inner Citadel: The Meditations of Marcus Aurelius* (Cambridge, MA: Harvard University Press, 2001); Pierre Hadot, *What is Ancient Philosophy?*, trans. Michael Chase (Cambridge, MA: The Belknap Press of Harvard University Press, 2004).

[64] A leading figure in the application of ancient Greek philosophy to contemporary issues is Martha Nussbaum. Her work that bears directly on this topic is: Martha Nussbaum, *The Therapy of Desire: Theory and Practice in Hellenistic Ethics* (Princeton: Princeton University Press, 1994). Also see the following works along the same lines: Julia Annas, *The Morality of Happiness* (New York: Oxford University Press, 1993); Richard Sorabji, *Emotion and Peace of Mind: From Stoic Agitation to Christian Temptation* (Oxford: Oxford University Press, 2002); Lunette Warren, "Psychagogy in Plutarch's *Moralia* and *Parallel Lives*: The Image of the Ideal Woman" (Ph.D Stellenbosch University, 2016).

[65] Abraham J. Malherbe, *Paul and the Thessalonians: The Philosophic Tradition of Pastoral Care* (Philadelphia: Fortress Press, 1987).

[66] Balch, Ferguson, and Meeks, eds., *Greeks, Romans, and Christians*. Troels Engberg-Pedersen, ed., *Paul Beyond the Judaism/Hellenism Divide* (Louisville: Westminster John Knox, 2001); Fitzgerald, ed., *Friendship, Flattery, and Frankness of Speech*; Fitzgerald, Obbink, and Holland, eds., *Philodemus and the New Testament World*; Fitzgerald, Olbricht, and White, eds., *Early Christianity and Classical Culture*; Sampley, ed., *Paul in the Greco-Roman World*.

Clarence Glad and his published dissertation, *Paul and Philodemus: Adaptability in Epicurean and Early Christian Psychagogy*.[67]

How do philosophical guides practice psychagogy? They first seek to persuade people to abandon conventional wisdom and the continual striving for reputation, wealth, and luxury. Protreptic literature is that which encourages people to take up the philosophical life, to be free from fear and anxiety, to become a virtuous person who will come to know the flourishing and divine life of the sage, in whatever social level or occupation they find themselves.[68] Lucian of Samosata describes his experience of hearing the Platonic philosopher Nigrinus.

> For he (Nigrinus) went on to praise philosophy and the freedom that it gives, and to ridicule the things that are popularly considered blessings—wealth and reputation, dominion and honor, yes and purple and gold—things accounted very desirable by most men, and till then by me also (Lucian, *Nig.* 4).[69]

Lucian's report of the effect of Nigrinus's speech on him reads like a testimony of a conversion experience following a Pentecostal tent meeting.

> When he (Nigrinus) had said this and much more of the same sort, he ended his talk. Until then I had listened to him in awe, fearing that he would cease. When he stopped, I felt like the Phaeacians of old, for I stared at him a long time spellbound. Afterwards, in a great fit of confusion and giddiness, I dripped

---

[67] Clarence E. Glad, *Paul and Philodemus: Adaptability in Epicurean and Early Christian Psychagogy*, vol. 81, Supplements to Novum Testamentum, (Leiden; New York: E. J. Brill, 1995).

[68] On conversion in Greco-Roman groups, including philosophical schools, see the classic work of Arthur Darby Nock, *Conversion: The Old and the New in Religion from Alexander the Great to Augustine of Hippo* (London: Oxford University Press, 1961). Also see David Sedley, "Philosophical Allegiance in the Greco-Roman World," in *Philosophia Togata: Essays on Philosophy and Roman Society*, ed. Miriam T. Griffin and Jonathan Barnes (Oxford; New York: Clarendon Press, 1989).

[69] Lucian, *Phalaris. Hippias or The Bath. Dionysus. Heracles. Amber or The Swans. The Fly. Nigrinus. Demonax. The Hall. My Native Land. Octogenarians. A True Story. Slander. The Consonants at Law. The Carousal (Symposium) or The Lapiths.* trans. A. M. Harmon 14 (Cambridge, Mass.; London, England: Harvard University Press, 2006), 103.

with sweat, I stumbled and stuck in the endeavor to speak, my voice failed, my tongue faltered, and finally I began to cry in embarrassment; for the effect he produced in me was not superficial or casual (Lucian, *Nig.* 35).[70]

Philosophers then seek to help their adherents make progress through teaching and encouragement, advice and reproof. They develop a close relationship in which they can use frank speech to correct destructive behavior and ways of thinking.

Often philosophers use medical imagery to describe the practice of philosophy as a therapy for the ailments of the soul.[71] Philosophers used a variety of methods or exercises of spiritual discipline. These include thoughtful meditation, memorization of precepts, visualization, speaking to oneself, practice of moderation both physical and emotional, the study of logic and rhetoric to persuade oneself and others to the philosophical life, reading of poets and philosophers, and the imitation of examples.

Paul's Philosophical Language and Practice

We come to Paul, who defines himself as the apostle to gentiles. His message is that gentiles are made righteous before God apart from the works of the law.[72] He travels from city to city and often takes up residence within a household and plies his trade as a leather worker.[73]

---

[70] Lucian, *Phalaris. Hippias or The Bath. Dionysus. Heracles. Amber or The Swans. The Fly. Nigrinus. Demonax. The Hall. My Native Land. Octogenarians. A True Story. Slander. The Consonants at Law. The Carousal (Symposium) or The Lapiths.*, 135.

[71] Abraham J. Malherbe, "Medical Imagery in the Pastoral Epistles," in *Texts and Testaments: Critical Essays on the Bible and Early Church Fathers*, ed. W. Eugene March and Stuart Dickson Currie (San Antonio: Trinity University Press, 1980); Martha Nussbaum, "Therapeutic Arguments: Epicurus and Aristotle," in *The Norms of Nature: Studies in Hellenistic Ethics*, ed. Malcolm Schofield and Gisela Striker (New York: Cambridge University Press, 1986); Nussbaum, *The Therapy of Desire*.

[72] The larger issue about Paul's attitude about the Law and Gentiles—often referred to in recent years as the New Perspective on Paul—is summarized in Gager, *Reinventing Paul*.

[73] The study of the role of the household in early Christianity is extensive. See especially Meeks, *The First Urban Christians*; Abraham J. Malherbe, *Social Aspects of Early Christianity* (Philadelphia: Fortress Press, 1983); Carolyn Osiek and David L.

According to Acts, Paul even spends time "dialoguing" in the *schole*, the hall or school, of Tyrannus (Acts 19:9). After Paul forms these household groups into a community of Jesus-followers, he moves on. But he writes letters back to them in which he uses the same language as the philosophical schools to encourage his brothers and sisters to remain faithful.[74] He wants them to continue to imitate him as he imitates Christ, to make progress toward virtue, to become *teleios*, perfect/mature/complete. He gives advice, reproof, examples, lists of virtues and vices. Paul even uses the dialogical language of the philosophical school in the form of the diatribe in Romans.[75] Several times in Romans Paul switches to the singular address and briefly carries on a dialogue with an imaginary discussion partner, just like Epictetus does. Paul would not describe himself as a philosopher, yet he acts like one in the way he forms a community.[76] In typical fashion he emphasizes that he is not like the charlatan or sophist who charges money for instruction and uses guile, deceit and flattery. Instead, Paul depicts himself as the sage who endures great afflictions and difficulties, the *agōn* language of toils and labors being reminiscent of the models of Odysseus and Heracles.[77] Paul is gentle with them and doesn't use harsh criticism

---

Balch, *Families in the New Testament World: Households and House Churches* (Louisville: Westminster John Knox, 1997); Carolyn Osiek, Margaret Y. MacDonald, and Janet H. Tulloch, eds., *A Women's Place: House Churches in Earliest Christianity* (Minneapolis: Augsburg Fortress Press, 2005). For a recent article supporting the view that a household would have enough room for a large gathering of people, see David L. Balch, "Rich Pompeiian Houses, Shops for Rent, and the Huge Apartment Building in Herculaneum as Typical Spaces for Pauline House Churches," *Journal for the Study of the New Testament* 27, no. 1 (2004).

[74] The tradition of Greco-Roman letter-writing, frequently practiced among philosophers, and how it relates to letter-writing among early Christians is thoroughly examined in Stanley K. Stowers, *Letter Writing in Greco-Roman Antiquity*, Library of Early Christianity, (Philadelphia: Westminster Press, 1986).

[75] Stowers, *The Diatribe and Paul's Letter to the Romans*.

[76] Alexander, "Paul and the Hellenistic Schools."

[77] John T. Fitzgerald, *Cracks in an Earthen Vessel: An Examination of the Catalogues of Hardships in the Corinthian Correspondence*, SBLDS, (Atlanta: Scholar's Press, 1988).

like some Cynics.⁷⁸ Yet he uses frank speech as a friend would, rather than be a flatterer.⁷⁹

Paul even uses the technical language of the philosophical schools. We find in Paul's letters words like passion (*pathos* Rom 1:26; 7:5; Gal 5:24; 1 Thess 4:5), desire (*epithymia* Rom 1:24; 6:12; 13:14; 1 Cor 10:6; Gal 5:16f, 24; 1 Thess 4:5), appetite (*orexis* Rom 1:27), duties (*ta kathēkonta* Rom 1:28), prudence (*sōfroneō* Rom 12:3), self-indulgence (*akrasia* 1 Cor 7:4), self-control (*enkrateia* Gal 5:23; *enkrateuomai* 1 Cor 7:9; 9:25), virtue (*aretē* Phil 4:8), self-sufficiency (*autarkeia* 2 Cor 9:8; Phil 4:11; cf. 1 Thess 4:12), "the things that make a difference" (related to the Stoic class of "indifferent": *ta diapheronta* Rom 2:8; Phil 1:10), progress (*prokopē* Phil 1:25), goal (*telos* Rom 6:22; Phil 3:19; *skopos* Phil 3:14), and perception (*aisthēsis* Phil 1:9). Some vocabulary of Paul seems to derive from his use of the Greek version of the Hebrew Bible, but the language is also a part of Greek philosophy and at times Paul uses it that way. The word "righteousness" (*dikaiosynē*) is always translated as "justice" in Greek philosophical texts and is one of the primary virtues. Our word "sin" (*hamartia*) is commonly used to refer to moral faults. Other terms in the New Testament like soul, flesh, and body are also important terms in philosophy.

Paul's practices in guiding and forming people within communities of faithfulness is like that of many of the philosophers of his day. His rhetoric and vocabulary reflect an acquaintance with philosophical literature and teaching, even though it probably came to him through the practice of other Jewish thinkers who had adopted Greek culture.

Paul as a Household Guide

Within the recent generation of scholarship, we have received great help in understanding the social world of early Christianity within the context of the Roman household. So far in this book we have looked at the social location of the meetings within households, the connection

---

[78] Abraham J. Malherbe, "Gentle as a Nurse: The Cynic Background to 1 Thess 2," *Novum Testamentum* 12, no. 2 (1970).

[79] Glad, *Paul and Philodemus*; Clarence E. Glad, "Frank Speech, Flattery, and Friendship in Philodemus," in *Friendship, Flattery, and Frankness of Speech*, ed. John T. Fitzgerald (Leiden: E J Brill, 1996).

between the work of a householder and the household, and the role of a philosophical guide. There is another role within the Roman household that may also fit how Paul functioned within households, that of the household or philosophical advisor.[80] Paul not only wrote letters to households but lived with people in their households. Rather than Paul being a lodger, he may have been sponsored by the householder as his patron.

Paul's Connections with Households

Paul mentions several people who have helped him with living accommodations. At the end of Romans, perhaps within an appended recommendation letter, Paul refers to Phoebe in 16:2 as a patroness (*prostatis*). This is a term synonymous with the Greek *patrōn* (from the Latin *patronus*). For example, Plutarch describes the foundation of Roman society as being divided between patrons (*patrōnas*) and clients (*klientas*). He gives the equivalent Greek terms as *prostatis* ("protector") for the former and *pelatas* ("dependents") for the latter.

> At the same time, he inspired both classes with an astonishing goodwill towards each other, and one which became the basis of important rights and privileges. For the patrons advised their clients in matters of custom, and represented them in courts of justice, in short, were their counsellors and friends in all things; while the clients were devoted to their patrons, not only holding them in honor, but actually, in cases of poverty, helping them to dower their daughters and pay their debts. And there was neither any law nor any magistrate that could compel a patron to bear witness against a client, or a client against a patron. But in later times, while all other rights and privileges remained in force, the taking of money by those of high degree from the

---

[80] To research this I was able to spend a month in Rome visiting museums and traveling to sites like Pompeii, Herculaneum, the villa of Horace, and Ostia thanks to a grant to attend a National Endowment for the Humanities (NEH) classical studies seminar at the American Academy in Rome, "Identity and Self-Representation Among the Sub-cultures of Ancient Rome," led by Eve D'Ambra and Eleanor Leach.

lowlier was held to be disgraceful and ungenerous (*Vit. Rom.* 13.7–9).[81]

In P.Mich.:5:243 (first century CE, Tebtunis) a guild agrees to pay fees and fines under the new "president" (*prostatēs*) at whose home they will meet monthly.[82] P.Mich.:5:322 (mid first-century CE, Tebtunis) is an account of how much beer is delivered to the "president of the guild of priests" (*prostatēs synodou hiereon*).[83] In what capacity Phoebe functioned, it is impossible to tell. She may have served as a benefactor to people; she may have presided over the logistics of meetings; she may have hosted the meetings in her household.[84]

Paul also mentions Gaius who served as "host" (*xenos*) for Paul and the entire assembly (Rom 16:23). While it is the case that this term most often refers to a guest, it is also used to refer to the host. Plutarch, for example, has a character mention his host (*xenos*), Ephebus of Athens (*Quaest. conv.* 8.9.3 [733c]. In the *Dinner of the Seven Wise Men*, Plutarch has Diocles tell Nicarchus on their way to the banquet, "I was the host (*xenos*) of Thales, for he lodged with me (*par' emoi gar katelysen*)" (*Mor.* 146c [*Conv. sept. sap.*]).

When Paul writes to his friends in Philippi, he directs himself to a single person (Phil 4:3). He refers to this person as "dedicated companion (*syzyge*)." Whomever Paul was addressing, the person would have been the one receiving the letter, most likely the householder. Even though the language here is grammatically masculine, early readers of Philippians still thought the recipient could have been a woman; some even thought it could have been Paul's wife.

When Luke writes his second book, Acts of the Apostles, he characterizes Paul in his own way. My own view is that Luke is trying to portray Paul as an Alexander the Great for a sect of Judaism. Just as Alexander brought the gods of Hellenism from Macedonia, across Asia Minor, and to Syria and Palestine, so did Paul retrace his steps to bring

---

[81] Plutarch, *Lives, Volume 1: Theseus and Romulus. Lycurgus and Numa. Solon and Publicola*. trans. Bernadotte Perrin, Loeb Classical Library 46 (Cambridge, MA: Harvard University Press, 1914), 127.

[82] http://papyri.info/ddbdp/p.mich;5;243.

[83] http://papyri.info/ddbdp/p.mich;5;322b.

[84] We compare Phoebe to the example of Ummidia Quadratilla, who was a benefactress of Casinum and whose architectural donations still exist.

the God of Israel (as worshipped by the followers of Jesus) from Palestine and Syria, across Asia Minor, and to Macedonia and Greece. Luke's references to Paul's travels and stays in cities seem to be historically reliable, though whether Paul had as much contact with Jews and synagogues on his travels as Luke writes is doubtful.

Luke has Paul live in Antioch for a year and teach many people (Acts 11:26). Paul then stays for a length of time in Iconium (Acts 14:3), visits various cities, and returns to Antioch for an indeterminate length of time (Acts 14:28; 15:35). On a return trip across Asia, this time to Macedonia, Paul stays for a while in Philippi, eventually in the house of Lydia (Acts 16:15) before being jailed (Acts 16:23). After a miraculous jail escape, Paul spends the night in the jailer's home where the jailer converts, and his household follows suit (Acts 16:33–34). In Athens Paul discourses (*dialegomai*) with various groups of people (Acts 17:17) and conversing (*symballō*) with Epicureans and Stoics in the *agora* (Acts 17:18). He then delivers a protreptic speech on the Areopagus (Acts 17:22–31). Paul stays for some time in Corinth working and living with Aquila and Priscilla (Acts 18:1–3). When he encounters trouble with the local synagogue (Acts 18:6), Paul goes to live next door to the synagogue in the house of Titius Justus (Acts 18:7), where Paul teaches for a year and a half (Acts 18:11,18). Paul returns to Antioch for some time before leaving for another visit to central Asia Minor (Acts 18:23). Luke has Paul return to Ephesus and spend three months living in the house where Jews gathered (Acts 19:8). After a falling out with the local Jewish population, Paul moves out and discourses (*dialegomai*) at the school (*scholē*) of Tyrannus for two years (Acts 19:9–10).

Luke describes a symposium-like event in Troas where Paul had been staying for the past week (Acts 20:1–12). Luke reports that he and others met for a meal on a Sunday. Since they are dining in an upstairs room on the third floor, it is most likely they were staying in a multi-dwelling building like an apartment in an *insula*. One would expect the triclinium in a house to be on a first floor near a kitchen. As is typical for groups who meet for a meal, Paul began delivering a discourse (*dialegomai*) (Acts 20:7). According to Luke's account, Paul lectured for so long through the night that a boy dozed off and fell out of the window to his death three floors below (Acts 20:9).

After Paul's last years of travel, he arrives in Rome and lives by himself in a guest house under guard (Acts 28:16,23). Luke says Paul lived in Rome for two years. The phrase "in his own rental (*en idiw misthōmati*)" seems to suggest that Paul had funds to pay for his lodgings (Acts 28:31).

Paul's Objections to and Acceptance of Support

Before Paul's fateful trip to Jerusalem and his arrest, Luke has Paul give a farewell speech in Miletus to friends coming from Ephesus (Acts 20:17). His great concern seems to be his conduct while he had been with them: "I coveted no one's silver or gold or clothing. You know for yourselves that I worked with my own hands to support myself and my companions" (Acts 20:33–34 NRSV). We know from Paul's letters that this was a common concern of his. To the Thessalonians he had said that he and his companions were not hucksters (1 Thess 2:3), flatterers, parasites (1 Thess 2:5), or sycophants (1 Thess 2:6). These are all traits of charlatans, philosophers who sell themselves by saying whatever a patron wants. Paul goes on to say that they worked hard night and day so that they wouldn't need patronage (1 Thess 2:9).

Paul does make the claim to the Corinthians that he and his coworkers deserve material remuneration (1 Cor 9:11–14). However, Paul says he doesn't want that because it might seem that he did it for the payment rather than for the benefit of others (1 Cor 9:15–18). In 2 Cor 2:17 Paul says he and his coworkers "are not peddlers (*kapēleuontes*) of God's word like so many." This idea goes back at least as far as Socrates and the self-aggrandizing sophists.

> In the same way, those (sophists, *sophistēs*) who take their teachings from town to town and sell them wholesale or retail (*kapēleuontes*) to anybody who wants them recommend all their products, but I wouldn't be surprised, my friend, if some of these people did not know which of their products are beneficial (*chrēston*) and which detrimental (*ponēron*) to the soul. Likewise, those who buy from them, unless one happens to be a physician of the soul (Plato, *Prot.* 313e).[85]

Paul seems to be in a situation in which his activities and acceptance of support could be interpreted negatively. He objects to anyone who

---

[85] John M. Cooper and associate editor D. S. Hutchinson, eds., *Plato: Complete Works* (Indianapolis and Cambridge, MA: Hackett, 1997), 751.

criticizes him for staying in people's homes and teaching. Yet, he still has a need for some support beyond his own leather craft work.

In Phil 4:10–19 Paul explicitly discusses the financial support he has expected and finally received from the Philippians. After he thanks them (Phil 4:10), he tells them he could live without it because he has learned how to be self-sufficient, without dependence on circumstances (Phil 4:11–13). Paul's language is not so much an acknowledgement of patronage but of partnership in the business of spreading God's message. The reciprocity he offers for their financial investment comes from the blessing of God (Phil 4:17–19).

That Paul spent so much time living with people in their houses, refers to some as hosts and patrons, and makes such a point to deny that he is out for personal gain by his teaching suggests to me that Paul knew people had a reason to suspect him. As a Jewish man, he was no doubt bearded. But to the Greco-Roman world a bearded man was an intellectual, perhaps even a philosopher. A man living within someone else's household and teaching people would suggest he was a "salaried" philosopher, whether or not he worked at a craft.

Household Advisors and Intellectuals

The literature on patronage and the role of the household or court advisor and salaried intellectuals is vast.[86] Despite the more commonly negative attitudes toward "salaried" philosophers, we know of many philosophers and other intellectuals, such as poets and rhetoricians, who accepted the patronage of wealthy people. There is also evidence that artistic depictions in Roman households functioned to encourage people to imitate the values promoted by the philosophical life. The figure of the bearded intellectual shows up in family scenes suggesting that this individual was considered to be part of the family.

---

[86] Elizabeth Rawson, "Roman Rulers and the Philosophic Advisor," in *Philosophia Togata: Essays on Philosophy and Roman Society*, ed. Miriam T. Griffin and Jonathan Barnes (Oxford Clarendon Press: New York, 1989); S. L. Mohler, "A Roman Answer to the Salary Question," *The Classical Weekly* 21, no. 14 (1928); Jeremy Tanner, "Portraits, Power, and Patronage in the Late Roman Republic," *Journal of Roman Studies* 90 (2000).

Negative Portrayals of Resident Philosophers

A hundred years after Paul, Lucian of Samosata, a city in northern Syria, would leave his home and the family business to learn Greek, gain an education, and become a well-traveled lecturer of philosophy. He took up writing while in Athens and composed essays and dialogues among which was *On Salaried Posts in Great Houses*.[87] He warns a friend, Timocles, not to sell himself into servitude by becoming a salaried household philosopher. He describes the appeal to a philosopher, especially one who is poor and starving.

> [S]omeone of the company praised this kind of wage-earning, saying that men were thrice happy when, besides having the noblest of the Romans for their friends, eating expensive dinners without paying any scot, living in a handsome establishment, and traveling in all comfort and luxury, behind a span of white horses, perhaps, with their noses in the air, they could also get no inconsiderable amount of pay for the friendship which they enjoyed and the kindly treatment which they received; really everything grew without sowing and plowing for such as they (*Merc. cond.* 3).[88]

Lucian considers their greed, indulgence, and desires to motivate them for pleasure and fame (*Merc. cond.* 7). He paints a picture—he literally does at the end describe a painting in the manner of Cebes—of the worst sort of demeaning life: rising early to greet the householder, joining the patron's entourage trudging through town all day, eating and drinking at symposia late into the night, and being the butt of everyone's jokes (*Merc. cond.* 14–16). Lucian admonishes Timocles to be ashamed to present the appearance that he is one of those lazy flatterers (*Merc. cond.* 24). The wealthy patron does not really want philosophical guidance but to make people think he is intelligent and cultured by having in his escort a bearded man wearing a Greek mantle, obviously an intellectual

---

[87] Earlier Juvenal, writing in Latin, had made some of the same criticisms in *Satire* 5.

[88] Lucian, *The Dead Come to Life or The Fisherman. The Double Indictment or Trials by Jury. On Sacrifices. The Ignorant Book Collector. The Dream or Lucian's Career. The Parasite. The Lover of Lies. The Judgement of the Goddesses. On Salaried Posts in Great Houses.* trans. A. M. Harmon, Loeb Classical Library 130 (Cambridge, MA: Harvard University Press, 1921), 417.

like a philosopher, grammarian, or rhetorician (*Merc. cond.* 25). And it's not just men, Lucian says, but also women who want to have a learned man living in their household on salary (*Merc. cond.* 36). A salaried philosopher can be expected to give a lecture while she's using the toilet or having her hair coiffed (*Merc. cond.* 36).

Later in life Lucian wrote a defense of this work after he took a well-paying job in his old age working for the Roman government in Egypt. Mostly he didn't think it was a fair comparison because everyone works for payment of some sort, and it wasn't just wage-earning that he had criticized. To him a salaried position was no better than working as a slave in a household since the philosopher sells himself into servitude. Lucian offers a defense that a philosopher might make for undertaking a post within a household: "I admired my patron's intelligence and courage and elevation of thought and wished to share the fortunes of such a man" (*Apol.* 9).[89]

Lucian talks about such a household philosopher, Thesmopolis, the Stoic (*Merc. cond.* 33–34). This venerable man with a long, gray beard worked for a wealthy and indulgent woman from an aristocratic family. The story goes that the patroness asked him to take care of her pregnant dog. Thesmopolis had no choice but to tuck the dog inside his cloak where she urinated on him and eventually gave birth. The end of the anecdote is that he was a Stoic who had become a dog (a Cynic, in other words).

Noted Resident Philosophers

Despite the negative attitude of some about philosophers who become advisors to patrons, there are many who are known to have fulfilled their calling in this way.[90] One of the oldest topics in Greek and

---

[89] Lucian, *How to Write History. The Dipsads. Saturnalia. Herodotus or Aetion. Zeuxis or Antiochus. A Slip of the Tongue in Greeting. Apology for the "Salaried Posts in Great Houses." Harmonides. A Conversation with Hesiod. The Scythian or The Consul. Hermotimus or Concerning the Sects. To One Who Said "You're a Prometheus in Words." The Ship or The Wishes.* trans. K. Kilburn, Loeb Classical Library 430 (Cambridge, MA: Harvard University Press, 1959), 203.

[90] My overview here has it's basis in Samuel Dill, *Roman Society from Nero to Marcus Aurelius*, The Meridian Library, (New York: Meridian Books, 1956), 293-94.

Roman philosophy was how a person was "to rule well, whether it be ruling himself or a household or the greatest state or, in short, all mankind" (Dio Chrysostom, *Rec. mag.* 49.3).[91] Kings and others in power "entreat men of cultivation to become their counselors in their most important problems" (Dio Chrysostom, *Rec. mag.* 49.3).[92] Dio Chrysostom goes on to mention Aristotle (384–322 BCE) as the tutor of Alexander (49.4). Tiberius Gracchus (163–133 BCE), a tribune during the Roman Republic, had Gaius Blossius as a resident philosopher (Plutarch, *TG* 8.5). Blossius had been a student of the Stoic philosopher Antipater of Tarsus (2nd cent. BCE). The Stoic philosopher Panaetius (185–110 BCE) is known to have accompanied Scipio on his tour of the eastern Mediterranean. Cicero (106–43 BCE) mentions a certain Laelius remarking to Scipio that he often discussed the nature of the State with Panaetius and with the historian Polybius (*Rep.* 1.34). The philosopher and scholar Alexander (early 1st cent. BCE) is said to have always traveled with Crassus who became governor of Syria (Plutarch, *Crass.* 3.4). Philodemus (110–35 BCE), the Epicurean philosopher from Gadara, appears to have been the resident philosopher of his patron Piso, whose villa at Herculaneum contains a library that includes works of Philodemus. An influential and wealthy friend of Caesar Augustus was Maecenas (68–8 BCE), who was a patron of poets, most notably Horace (65–8 BCE) and Vergil (70–19 BCE). Another friend of Augustus was the Stoic philosopher Arius Didymus of Alexandria (1st cent. BCE).[93] Seneca relates the comfort Arius (Areus) gave to the wife of Augustus, Livia (Julia Augusta), upon the death of her son, Drusus in 9 BCE (Seneca, *Cons. Ad Marc.* 4–5). Seneca also mentions the Stoic court philosopher Julius Canus whom Caligula had sentenced to death (*Tranq.* 14.7). Seneca (4 BCE–65 CE) himself was a tutor of Nero. The Cynic philosopher Demetrius of Corinth (1st cent. CE) was advising the Roman senator Thrasea, who was discussing the nature of the soul with Demetrius and others at his villa before hearing the decision of the Senate for his death (Tacitus, *Ann.* 16.34). The Stoic philosopher Euphrates of Tyre (35–118

---

[91] Dio Chrysostom, *Discourses 37-60*. trans. H. Lamar Crosby, Loeb Classical Library 376 (Cambridge, MA: Harvard University Press, 1946), 297.

[92] Dio Chrysostom, *Discourses 37-60*, 297.

[93] Arius Didymus, *Epitome of Stoic Ethics*, ed. Arthur J. Pomeroy (Atlanta, GA: Society of Biblical Literature, 1999), 3.

CE), "tall and distinguished to look at, with long hair and a flowing white beard" (Pliny, *Ep.* 1.6), was a close friend of Pliny (the Younger) when he was a military tribune in Syria in 81 CE. In a letter Pliny describes his relationship with Euphrates.

> Whenever I have the chance I complain about these duties to Euphrates, who consoles me by saying that anyone who holds public office, presides at trials and passes judgement, expounds and administers justice, and thereby puts into practice what the philosopher only teaches, has a part in the philosophic life and indeed the noblest part of all. But of one thing he can never convince me—that doing all this is better than spending whole days listening to his teaching and learning from him (Pliny, *Ep.* 1.10).[94]

It should not be surprising that most of our literary references are to residential philosophers of the wealthy and powerful. We need to look at a different type of evidence for the presence of intellectuals within the households of less famous people.

Artistic Representations of Intellectuals Promote Philosophical Ideals in Roman Households

Paul Zanker has traced the image of the intellectual through the classical Greek period, through the Hellenistic, and into the Roman age.[95] While statues of intellectual figures in the Classical period focused on the beauty of the human body, in the early Hellenistic period that focus shifted to intense contemplation.[96] Whereas Athenian intellectuals were portrayed as model citizens, the images of third-century intellectuals represented them as poets and philosophers.[97] The statue of Zeno, the founder of the Stoic school, commissioned as a public honorific in Athens, is most notable for the thoughtful seriousness of his furrowed

---

[94] Pliny the Younger, *Letters, Volume 1: Books 1-7.* trans. Betty Radice, Loeb Classical Library 55 (Cambridge, MA: Harvard University Press, 1969), 33.

[95] Paul Zanker, *The Mask of Socrates: The Image of the Intellectual in Antiquity*, vol. 59, Sather Classical Lectures, (Berkeley, CA: University of California Press, 1995).

[96] Zanker, *The Mask of Socrates*, 91.

[97] Zanker, *The Mask of Socrates*, 93.

brow.[98] The seated figure of Chrysippus, another important Stoic philosopher, shows him seated on a simple stone block with an appearance in his face of an intensity to show that thinking is hard work.[99] Sculptures and portrait busts of the main figures of the other schools of philosophy, as well as poets, show similar representative features.

Zanker points out that the practice of men shaving their face first appears with Alexander the Great. At first those who wore beards were considered to be more conservative. The wearing of a beard came to be a way of symbolizing manliness—as opposed to an effeminate-looking hairless face—and one's commitment to morality and to the flow of nature. From the style of one's hair and beard could be determined what school of philosophy a man belonged to.[100]

One might overlook the fact that the busts of philosophers in the Museum of Naples, for instance, come from the homes in Pompei and Herculaneum. The statues and busts of ancestors, rulers, gods, goddesses, and other divinities, as well as philosophers displayed in homes was supposed to remind people of the values they represent and that members and visitors to the home should imitate them. They might be topics of conversation after dinner in the triclinium or while strolling in the garden.[101]

Lucian has his character describe a visit to the home of the Platonist philosopher Nigrinus. As he entered the home, he "found him with a book in his hands and many busts of ancient philosophers standing round about" (Lucian, *Nigr.* 2).[102] Seneca writes that he surrounds himself with "statues of great men to kindle my enthusiasm" (Seneca, *Ep.* 69.9).[103]

---

[98] Zanker, *The Mask of Socrates*, 93-97.

[99] Zanker, *The Mask of Socrates*, 98-103.

[100] Zanker, *The Mask of Socrates*, 109-14.

[101] Zanker, *The Mask of Socrates*, 207.

[102] Lucian, *Phalaris. Hippias or The Bath. Dionysus. Heracles. Amber or The Swans. The Fly. Nigrinus. Demonax. The Hall. My Native Land. Octogenarians. A True Story. Slander. The Consonants at Law. The Carousal (Symposium) or The Lapiths.*, 103.

[103] Seneca, *Epistles, Volume 1: Epistles 1-65*. trans. Richard M. Gummere, Loeb Classical Library 75 (Cambridge, MA: Harvard University Press, 1917), 443.

Zanker discusses a grave relief picturing a family. To the right are three figures: the one in the center is much taller and appears to be bald, while the other two are about the same size and appear to be the sons of the father. A more noticeable and larger figure is a seated, bearded man. Zanker thinks this represents an in-house philosopher.[104]

The villas that surrounded the cities of Pompeii and Herculaneum were not all as luxurious as the Villa of the Papyri. A lesser-known group of buildings, referred to as the villa of T. Siminius Stephanus, contains a workshop (Villa 21) and another building of an equally rustic nature (Villa 20). It was in this building that excavations unearthed a mosaic showing seven philosophers in discussion by a tree.[105] Some say it represents Plato and the Academy; some the seven sages. If it is Athens in the background and the philosophers are in a garden, then perhaps it represented Epicurean philosophers. After all, not very far away from the site is the Villa of the Papyri with an Epicurean library.

---

[104] http://www.smb-digital.de/eMuseumPlus?service=ExternalInterface&module=collection&objectId=698258. Zanker, *The Mask of Socrates*, 189.

[105] https://www.museoarcheologiconapoli.it/en/room-and-sections-of-the-exhibition/mosaics/

Chapter 5:
Philosophy as the Art of Living

For most people, being a philosopher is to be an academic in a philosophy department, to do research and writing in some area of philosophy, and to teach courses on topics like epistemology, metaphysics, and ethics. In recent years it has become more common for some philosophers to point out we have been missing the crucial aspect of ancient philosophy. Philosophy was not just about thinking intellectually but becoming a better human being and living a morally responsible and personally fulfilling life. A training regimen of mental exercises strengthens the person who is committed to living the philosophical life, enabling the person to make progress toward the goal of completeness. The more mature philosopher becomes an example for others and acts as a guide in their development. It is important to understand some of the ways that this movement has developed.[106]

Practicing Spiritual Exercises: Pierre Hadot

More than anyone else, Pierre Hadot (1922–2010) has popularized the notion during the past half century that ancient Greek philosophy is best characterized as a "way of life."[107] Hadot describes how the Stoics considered philosophy to be an art of living rather than a development of theories or interpretation of texts. Students of philosophy were to make a conscious decision to change the course of life and progress toward becoming a completer and more fulfilled human. Yet they are hindered from making progress because of ineluctable desires and irrational fears. To overcome these passions, philosophy devised methods of therapy designed to bring about transformation. For the Stoics, the problems people face have to do with their dependence on

---

[106] One of the earliest scholars to discuss the "leading of the soul" and to use the term psychagogy is Rabbow, *Seelenführung*.

[107] Pierre Hadot was Professor Emeritus of the History of Hellenistic and Roman Thought at the Collège de France.

things outside of their control. They must learn how to think about and respond to their desires and the circumstances of life if they want to achieve the goal of a virtuous, tranquil, free and happy life. It takes a reversal in how one looks at the world. Hadot sums up his brief description: "Such a transformation of vision is not easy, and it is precisely here that spiritual exercises come in. Little by little, they make possible the indispensable metamorphosis of our inner Self."[108]

The difficulty with describing the practice of *askēsis* in antiquity is that we have no definitive guide book that has come down to us. Instead, we have many allusions to the techniques and practices. Hadot points out that we have several lists of Stoic-Platonic spiritual exercises, which have come down to us from Philo of Alexandria. From the work *Who is the Heir of Divine Things* (253), Hadot enumerates research (*zētēsis*), thorough investigation (*skepsis*), reading (*anagnōsis*), listening (*akroasis*), attention (*prosochē*), self-mastery (*enkrateia*), and indifference to indifferent things."[109] The other list appears in *Allegorical Interpretation* (3.18) and includes "reading, meditations (*meletai*), therapies of the passions, remembrance of good things, self-mastery (*enkrateia*), and the accomplishment of duties."[110] Hadot then organizes the spiritual exercises into the following four groups: (1) attention; (2) meditation and memorization; (3) the intellectual exercises of reading, listening, research, and investigation he calls nourishment; (4) finally, the more active and practical exercises of self-mastery, accomplishment of duties, and indifference to indifferent things.

To begin with, the practice of attending to the present moment is foundational in Stoicism. Practicing exercises prepares you for whatever might happen. But you must be attentive to what you experience and be ready to respond rationally and appropriately to any event. Dwelling on the past failures and losses brings sorrow and grief; being overly concerned about what might happen can cause worry and fear. Finally, being in the present means seeing your own place in the cosmos and accepting the providential course of your own life.[111]

---

[108] Hadot, *Philosophy as a way of life*, 83.
[109] Hadot, *Philosophy as a way of life*, 84.
[110] Hadot, *Philosophy as a way of life*, 84.
[111] Hadot, *Philosophy as a way of life*, 84-85.

To be prepared for constantly practicing attention, we need to prepare ahead of time with a routine of meditation focused on how to think about circumstances we might encounter. These might include such things as meditating on experiences of poverty, suffering, or death. Memorization then provides us with rational forms of self-dialogue, precepts, maxims, and sayings. Daily meditation could include time in the morning for anticipating the day and in the evening for examining faults and progress.[112]

The intellectual exercises—reading, listening, research, and investigation—are described as nourishment, a way for you to give yourself food for thought, so to speak. Philosophers would be familiar with the writings of those within their own tradition as well as those of others. Listening and being in dialogue with others would help create new ways to form arguments when faced with adversity.[113]

The final category is the practical exercises designed to instill habitual action. We need to practice recognizing what things neither contribute to our virtue nor cause us vice, what Stoics called "indifferent." Self-mastery would involve learning to act with virtue but avoid vice. Fulfilling duties is the practice of proper behavior.[114]

Hadot goes on to demonstrate how Epicureans also practiced spiritual exercises as therapy. The healing for Epicureans is restoring the soul from worries of life to enjoy existing. People have unnecessary fears and desires. This deprives them of the pleasure of life. Their approach to physics teaches them the gods are not to be feared and death is nothing. Epicureans practice meditation on precepts and are known for their four-fold healing formula, "God presents no fears, death no worries. And while good is readily attainable, evil is readily endurable."[115] Especially characteristic of Epicureans was their practice of friendship within communities: "These include the public confession of one's faults; mutual correction, carried out in a fraternal spirit; and examining one's conscience."[116] Beyond his description of the spiritual exercises, Hadot

---

[112] Hadot, *Philosophy as a way of life*, 85.

[113] Hadot, *Philosophy as a way of life*, 86.

[114] Hadot, *Philosophy as a way of life*, 86.

[115] Hadot, *Philosophy as a way of life*, 87.

[116] Hadot, *Philosophy as a way of life*, 89.

proceeds to discuss more in depth the principles of learning to dialogue, to die, and to read.

The Ancient Philosopher as Spiritual Guide: Ilsetraut Hadot

Ilsetraut Hadot, like Pierre, had a research focus in Neo-Platonism as well as in ancient Greece and Rome.[117] Her contribution to the study of the philosopher as a guide of the soul was her doctoral dissertation at the Freie Universität Berlin in 1965 on *Seneca and the Greco-Roman Tradition of Soul Guidance*.[118] She summarized her research for a book section "The Spiritual Guide."[119]

I. Hadot also points out that philosophy was not just a theoretical practice, but "philosophy was, above all, an education toward a happy life—happy life here and not only in some hypothetical life after death, even if the latter was not always left entirely out of consideration."[120] This became true of the succeeding schools as well.

> All Hellenistic and Imperial schools of philosophy, including the Cynics and Skeptics, regarded guidance toward a happy life as the most important goal of their philosophy. What was understood by happy life could vary considerably in theory, but in all cases it had the practical end of strengthening the individual inwardly against all the vicissitudes of fate and, as far as possible, of making the person self-sufficient. Ancient philosophy was, above all, help with life's problems and spiritual guidance, and the ancient philosopher was, above all, a spiritual guide.[121]

The theoretical aspects of philosophy were secondary and were the foundation for the primary goal of moral progress and living a happy

---

[117] Ilsetraut Hadot is now Professor Emerita since 1977 from Le Centre national de la recherche scientifique (The National Center for Scientific Research).

[118] Hadot, *Seneca und die griechisch-römische Tradition der Seelenleitung*. For a helpful review of her book, see Hans Dieter Betz, review of *Seneca und die griechisch-römische Tradition der Seelenleitung*, *Journal of the History of Philosophy* 9, no. 1 (January 1971): 86-87.

[119] Hadot, "The Spiritual Guide," 436-59.

[120] Hadot, "The Spiritual Guide," 444.

[121] Hadot, "The Spiritual Guide," 444.

life. This required friendly relationships with philosophical guides (leaders of schools called in Greek *kathēgemōn* or *hēgemōn*) and with other students. Plato, for example, engaged students with a dialectical method of dialogue. It was even considered necessary for moral progress to have help of a friend who reflects to us our true nature. A friend who has made more progress can give assistance to the younger or less mature person. Spiritual guides establish their authority by the quality of the lives they live rather than their intellectual prowess or rhetorical abilities. Students as well needed to provide evidence in their lives of making progress to participate as students and in a philosophical friendship.[122]

I. Hadot structures her discussion of "Exercises" around the pair of formulae "learning to live" and "learning to die." In order for one to learn to live, one needs the freedom that comes from learning to die.

> To accustom oneself to not regarding death—one's own as well as that of relatives and friends—as an evil is the necessary precondition for the attainment of that inner freedom that allows one to follow only one's own conscience in all circumstances and to maintain peace of mind in every situation.[123]

To learn to live means overcoming irrational fears and passions to achieve a happy life. Some methods include inuring oneself to physical hardship as a way of preparing for the potentiality of loss. Students are expected to begin with basic dogma of the philosophical school and learn condensed forms of memorable maxims. The student might then widen knowledge to include a study of physics. It is not simply learning about things, "but rather knowledge as *habitus*, the transformation of the individual through knowledge."[124] This development follows stages. First, there is study that provides the student with knowledge to have at the ready in case of unforeseen circumstances. Second is the habitual practice as preparation.

> The philosopher-spiritual guide knows that it is not sufficient to know this and to be familiar with and to have grasped

---

[122] Hadot, "The Spiritual Guide," 444-50.
[123] Hadot, "The Spiritual Guide," 450.
[124] Hadot, "The Spiritual Guide," 452.

intellectually the philosophical proofs that are the foundation for this statement; one must be convinced to such a degree that one's whole inner nature is penetrated by it. In order to achieve this transformation, the spiritual guide uses various pedagogical methods that are supposed to appeal to the emotional part of the soul.[125]

Third, the student studies the branch of physics as a way of understanding how the world works and what is the place of the human in it. Finally, the intended goal is reached, a condition referred to as "greatness of soul."

A crucial part of the process is to learn to examine one's own progress. Philosophical schools often encouraged a twice-daily time for this critique. This required the person to learn to be attentive throughout the day. I. Hadot quotes a relevant text from Epictetus that illustrates the progress that a student makes through attentiveness and self-examination.

> If you wish to stop being irascible, then do not give your habit any further nourishment, do not give it any opportunity of growing. Suppress the first outburst and count the days in which you did not lose your temper: "I used to lose my temper every day, now only every second day, and so forth: every three days, every four days." If you have been able to control yourself for thirty days, bring a thank offering to God. At first the habit of losing your temper will be weakened; in the end it will be completely overcome. "Today I did not give in to melancholy, nor the following day, nor after that for two or three months, but I kept a close watch on myself whenever an inclination that way arose" (Epictetus, *Diatr.* 2.18.12–14).[126]

The spiritual guide might listen to another's faults or even provide criticism. Epicureans followed guidelines on how to apply criticism, to give encouragement, and to recognize the progress of another by their acceptance of criticism.

---

[125] Hadot, "The Spiritual Guide," 452.
[126] Hadot, "The Spiritual Guide," 454.

I. Hadot, like Pierre, mentions the degree to which Christians adopted these forms of spiritual guidance. She concludes with a critique of modern approaches to this discipline: "In conclusion I would be so bold as to ask, 'Has modern spiritual guidance or contemporary psychology, which is so proud of its scientific researches, brought the slightest advance over the millennia-old practice of spiritual guidance?'"[127]

Hellenistic Philosophy as Therapy: Martha Nussbaum

In 1994 Martha Nussbaum published a book that was to be influential to a generation of students and scholars interested in what Hellenistic ethics have to say about how to remedy the human condition in the modern world. She begins with the claim that all the Hellenistic philosophical schools thought of the philosopher "as a compassionate physician whose arts could heal many pervasive types of human suffering."[128] This is dissimilar to the "more detached and academic moral philosophy that has sometimes been practiced in the Western tradition."[129] Until recently, she notes, there has been a dearth of attention paid to Hellenistic ethics despite the importance they have played in the works of influential thinkers over the past millennia.

In the first chapter Nussbaum introduces the concept of philosophy as therapy, explains some key ideas, and then summarizes the book's argument. Generally stated, all the Hellenistic philosophical schools agreed that philosophy was about the "art of human life," that the goal was human flourishing (*eydaimonia*), and that philosophical therapy could alleviate human suffering.[130] Put simply, the medical model will have a way of figuring out what the illness is and its causes, present a picture of what the goal is for a healthy, flourishing, and complete human life, and have a therapeutic methodology.[131]

Some clarification is required concerning several key concepts of Hellenistic ethics. One is the concept of nature. Rather than viewing

---

[127] Hadot, "The Spiritual Guide," 455.
[128] Nussbaum, *The Therapy of Desire*, 3.
[129] Nussbaum, *The Therapy of Desire*, 4.
[130] Nussbaum, *The Therapy of Desire*, 15.
[131] Nussbaum, *The Therapy of Desire*, 28-29.

nature as what exists apart from human interference or as bare instinct like an animal in contrast to a socialized adult human, nature is a value-laden account of what is deemed to be the best of human living, regardless of whether it is part of human social development, though human socialization is something to be mistrusted.[132]

A second clarification is the role of action in this medical model of ethics. Rather than simply theorizing about what is the best life, the medical model insists on a commitment to action and the use of reason to discover what is the disease, what is the cure, and carrying out the proper therapy. It also requires that the philosophical teacher must be involved in the pupil's life and to discover methods that will appeal to all facets of the person to bring about a healthy condition.[133]

Finally, clarification is needed regarding beliefs and emotions/passions. It is important to understand that emotions or passions are not simply feelings but products of thought and reasoning. Passions are irrational in the sense that the beliefs on which they are based are not the product of well-reasoned argument. These beliefs are influenced by the values inculcated by society and can become deep-seated beliefs, requiring intense scrutiny and careful critique.[134]

In chapter four, Nussbaum begins an analysis of the Epicureans by considering "Epicurean Surgery: Argument and Empty Desire." Epicurus sees the human condition as one in which people suffer a painful and stressful disturbance of the soul. Because the causes of this disturbance are false beliefs about the value of objects within the world and the desires for things that produce nothing of lasting value, these causes can be removed by changing the beliefs and desires. To do this, Epicurus must show, first, how to tell the good and healthy from the bad and unhealthy desires. Second, he will need to show how these desires come about from the false beliefs. Finally, he will need to articulate a therapy for changing the false beliefs and removing the desires.[135]

The distinction Epicurus makes between types of desires is to classify one as "empty desires" (*kenai epithymiai*) and the other "natural" (*physikai*). The model for natural desires is a child who has not yet been

---

[132] Nussbaum, *The Therapy of Desire*, 29-32.
[133] Nussbaum, *The Therapy of Desire*, 35.
[134] Nussbaum, *The Therapy of Desire*, 38-40.
[135] Nussbaum, *The Therapy of Desire*, 104-05.

corrupted by the common knowledge and practice of society. An animal can also serve as an example of conduct not influenced by human popular values, such as religious superstition, sexual fantasy, and dreams of wealth and power. These natural desires can be distinguished reliably by the senses apart from what society teaches.

These freedoms from disturbance (*ataraxia*) and from pain are not merely passive but represent the "undisturbed and unimpeded" activity of the human person. To live that kind of life, a person needs philosophical therapy. Society's values are deeply ingrained in people and people have a difficult time discovering how to overcome them on their own. The natural desires people experience are temporary and limited; they ensure the continued health of the person.

This diagnosis of how disturbing desires are based on false beliefs requires a therapy that can cure those beliefs. Epicurus is said to have defined philosophy as "an activity that secures the flourishing life by means of arguments and reasonings."

Nussbaum describes the kind of school people would have entered to follow Epicurus. The students would have represented a broad range of social classes (including slaves), educational levels, ages, and economic statuses, as well as the inclusion of both sexes. People supported the school financially and worked cooperatively to maintain the facilities. The school is something like a modern "gated community," with the central feature being a garden. The students become like a family of friends. The head of the family is Epicurus, who is revered by the community as a hero and savior. His image appears in a variety of places as a way of reminding the students of his teachings and his example. The order of the community is structured as well as its daily life.[136]

Epicureans made use of levels of therapy based on the severity of the problem and responsiveness to treatment. A gentle, mild therapy might be applied. A stronger, harsher treatment might be called for. In difficult situations, the philosopher might need to administer a purgative, a stronger type of reproof and critique. Harsh medicine might be alternated with more pleasant words of encouragement and praise. Finally, the philosophical guide might decide that surgery is necessary, which may comprise a more aggressive disapproval and perhaps even

---

[136] Nussbaum, *The Therapy of Desire*, 117-20.

shaming. For Epicurus all therapy is argumentation, and all argumentation is for therapeutic purposes. The community is the context for the shared life of rehabilitation.[137]

For the doctor-patient relationship, Epicureans had a hierarchy in which the students followed their philosophical guide and might even show reverence for their teacher. Sometimes, a teacher might receive critique from an advanced student or from another teacher. Each one is expected to continue to develop. They showed an extraordinary amount of reverence for Epicurus, depicting him as a hero, a savior, and even a god. Students placed their care in the hands of Epicurus and subsequent Epicurean philosophical guides.[138]

Epicureans concentrated instruction on learning the principal doctrines of Epicurus. One way was to have students memorize the summaries and repeat them daily. By doing this they internalized the teachings, developed a broad grasp of the whole system, and could influence their ways of thinking at a deep, even unconscious, level. Another method of identifying the student's progress was for the student to describe that progress or lack of it. This type of confession revealed to others what was not clear. When this wasn't accomplishing a full disclosure, there was a third method, which was for students or their friends and family to inform the teacher of activity and attitudes that still were not evident to the philosophical community.[139]

Epicureans, Nussbaum concludes, considered the disease of false belief to be an epidemic, and the cure to require urgent care. Epicurus's publication of his writings seems to have been intended to influence a larger audience than just the Garden. The inscription of Diogenes of Oenoanda, presenting a summary of the Epicurean doctrines and methods of therapy for saving the people, was an attempt to reach the masses that would pass by. For the Epicureans, what was most important was the practical benefit of living a better life, free from painful disturbances and focused on achieving *eydaimonia*.[140]

In chapters nine and ten, Nussbaum focuses on Stoic therapy and the Stoic's account of the passions. Stoic literature contains many texts which

---

[137] Nussbaum, *The Therapy of Desire*, 125-27.
[138] Nussbaum, *The Therapy of Desire*, 130-31.
[139] Nussbaum, *The Therapy of Desire*, 131-35.
[140] Nussbaum, *The Therapy of Desire*, 136-39.

develop the medical analogy. The philosopher or philosophical teacher functions like a physician by diagnosing and treating diseases of the soul. The therapy is not so much done to the person, but they prescribe a course of therapy which will bring the person to a healthy state, a state of well-being normative for a human, one which includes self-sufficiency and tranquility.[141]

Each patient is considered having what it takes to follow the course of therapy, since each one possesses practical reasoning. In fact, each person takes control of their own progress toward health, strengthening and toning the soul's fitness.[142] What needs to be cured is the attachment people have to their perceptions about what is good for them and what is bad, and the emotions that result from their desires.[143]

One area of difference for the Stoics is that they are interested not just in the outcome of their therapy for individuals or small communities but for society at large. Their commitment is for the whole of the cosmos, which is made of humans as part of the whole, no matter in which city or region they live.[144]

This begins with highly valuing each human's dignity as a rational being. In fact, Stoics considered women to be included in those who would benefit from the study of philosophy, as seen in the work by Musonius Rufus, *That Women Too Should Do Philosophy*.[145] Not only are humans of both genders, as opposed to animals, encouraged to respect and nurture their human rationality, they are to recognize that the reason they possess is a piece of divinity within them. Seneca, for example, tells Lucilius that he does not need to pray or perform a ritual to make progress in his understanding. Seneca tells him, "The god is near you, with you, inside you. This is what I'm saying to you. Lucilius: a holy spirit is seated within us, a watcher and guardian of our good and bad actions. As this spirit is treated by us, so it treats us" (41.1–2).[146]

One of the fundamental functions of reason is to help us make a choice between what to do and what not to do based on accurately and

---

[141] Nussbaum, *The Therapy of Desire*, 316-17.

[142] Nussbaum, *The Therapy of Desire*, 317.

[143] Nussbaum, *The Therapy of Desire*, 318.

[144] Nussbaum, *The Therapy of Desire*, 319.

[145] Nussbaum, *The Therapy of Desire*, 320-24.

[146] Nussbaum, *The Therapy of Desire*, 322-26.

consistently interpreting the way the world appears to us. The way we think about the way the world appears to us is colored by our acculturation and our own experiences. These are deeply ingrained in our way of thinking and can control what we value and how we feel. The beginning point is a critical self-examination and watchfulness over the way we respond to appearances, in other words, our impulses. Epictetus is reported to have told his young students, "Right from the start, get into the habit of saying to every harsh appearance, 'You are an appearance, and not the only way of seeing the thing that appears.' Then examine it and test it by the yardsticks you have" (*Ench.* 1.5).[147] The philosophical teacher is there to assist. This doctor is, as Chrysippus put it, a "physician of the soul" (Galen, PHP 5.2.224).[148]

Stoics understood their philosophy to have practical value. Seneca makes the statement about philosophy that it "shapes and constructs the soul, orders life, guides conduct, shows what is to be done and what omitted, sits at the helm and guides our course as we waver amid uncertainties" (*Ep.* 16.3).[149] If the philosopher's speaking or writing is not understandable, persuasive, relevant, or beneficial to people in all walks of life, then the philosopher has failed in the mission to help people live the best life.[150]

Stoics commonly held the belief that humans enter the world with an innate sense of what is good and beneficial. There is no sense in which humans are born with innate evil or a propensity to act in evil ways. The Stoic idea of human development (*oikeiōsis*) teaches that a child's orientation is toward self-preservation, while a mature adult has widened that perspective to include the good of the entire world. Therefore, the philosophical teacher can present rational arguments that may move the person forward in their grasp of what is true and what is false in the world. False belief, according to the Stoics, is the conventional wisdom children accept from the surrounding culture. As the source of the disease, the student must examine the reasons for holding certain

---

[147] Nussbaum, *The Therapy of Desire*, 328.
[148] Nussbaum, *The Therapy of Desire*, 328.
[149] Nussbaum, *The Therapy of Desire*, 329.
[150] Nussbaum, *The Therapy of Desire*, 330-31.

opinions, ones that can bring about fear, anxiety, grief, and unhappiness, and present rational arguments to the mind that these are false.[151]

Another sense in which the Stoics regard the human person as valuable is their conviction regarding the nature of the world.

> For the universe is ruled by a virtuous god, whose self-sufficiency the truly virtuous life attempts to emulate. Ethics is in the heavens as well as on earth. Our orientation to virtue is not a purely human response to our needy circumstances but, rather, a piece of divine perfection lodged within us by god's providential design.[152]

This concept also leads to the conclusion that all humans equally share that divinity and can equally think rationally and, to live a virtuous life.[153] But this depends on learning to think rationally about the world, to overcome false beliefs, and to choose what is good.[154]

Nussbaum shows that the Stoics considered the best place to begin philosophical therapy is with the concrete situation of the student. The teacher would need to understand the student's history, experiences, beliefs, struggles, and personal constitution. Even the timing of therapy is a crucial element. In addition, the philosopher would need to know how in each case to apply a philosophical remedy. Stoics were open to reading works from other traditions in their search for proper treatments. The context for this form of education is not a speech given to a crowd or a treatise written for the public. Rather, the setting is one of friends holding a conversation. That's not to say there isn't a place for writing, since Seneca is a good illustration of an intimate conversation being held between two people who love and admire each other.[155]

Nussbaum identifies two crucial procedures for carrying out this personalized education. The first is to approach helping the student by taking concrete cases rather than try to argue from generalizations regarding how one should respond to appearances (what one thinks and

---

[151] Nussbaum, *The Therapy of Desire*, 332-33.

[152] Nussbaum, *The Therapy of Desire*, 333.

[153] Nussbaum, *The Therapy of Desire*, 334.

[154] Nussbaum, *The Therapy of Desire*, 335.

[155] Nussbaum, *The Therapy of Desire*, 335-38.

feels about circumstances whether real or imagined). By using a relevant concrete example, the student might be able more readily to grasp how to think rationally and to witness the consequences. From there the student might extrapolate to the general concept, or it may take many times to develop a capacity for making use of the specific, concrete example in a similar situation.[156]

The second procedure, similar to the first, is to provide the student with examples through telling an interesting story or by relating an example from existing literature. The student might be better able to grasp a concept by hearing about it in another context. For the Stoics, examples are a central part of their philosophical therapy.[157]

It's not enough, however, to do the right thing in many contexts. First, Stoics referred to this as an "acceptable act" (*kathēkon*). The goal is to act as the wise person would act, to engage in a "fully virtuous act" (*katorthōma*). The exempla can show not only what is to be done, but how one thinks about it, responds to it, feels about it, and to imitate that action in one's own life. Also, it is necessary for the student to learn an intense vigilance, since the soul is complex and obscure, capable of hiding one's deepest thoughts. Yet, it is only by going through this process that people can come to know themselves and to find peace and freedom.[158]

For Stoics, an individual cannot seek to be good without promoting the good in others. This type of friendship is central in the relationship of those seeking the philosophical life. Nussbaum quotes an extended passage from Seneca to illustrate.

> I am not your friend, unless whatever is at issue concerning you is my concern also. Friendship makes a partnership of all things between us. Nothing is advantageous or disadvantageous for the individual: we live in common. And nobody can live happily who considers only himself and turns everything into a question of his own utility. You must live for another, if you wish to live for yourself. This fellowship, scrupulously and reverently preserved, which makes us mingle as a human being with human beings and which judges that there is a common law of

---

[156] Nussbaum, *The Therapy of Desire*, 338.
[157] Nussbaum, *The Therapy of Desire*, 339.
[158] Nussbaum, *The Therapy of Desire*, 339-41.

right for the human race, also makes a big contribution to fostering that more intimate fellowship of friendship of which I was speaking. For he that has much in common with his fellow human being has everything in common with his friend (48.2–3)[159]

In contrast to Aristotle, who thought of the Greek city-state (*polis*) as the social boundary, the Stoics thought of all humans as "citizens of the world" (*politēs toy kosmoy*), since all share in the "worldwide community of rational beings."[160]

Stoics value the study of logic, since it is fundamental to reasoning well. Yet much of their focus is on the benefit the student gains from rational dialogue with the self about the nature of appearances. It's necessary, Epictetus thought, for a student to be trained in logic to evaluate critically one's own beliefs.[161]

Nussbaum talks about the Stoics' belief that the study of wisdom will bring about progress in the devoted student. Even beginning the study of philosophy will make life better. This quality of life will also impact the lives of others. It is understandable Stoics have this optimism, since they believe in the fundamental goodness of humans and that all humans have the capacity for rational thought.[162]

Nussbaum begins her chapter "The Stoics on the Extirpation of the Passions" by discussing what the Stoics thought about the end goal of human life. Stoic therapy functions as a way to achieve that goal. The Stoics held that "only virtue is worth choosing for its own sake; and virtue all by itself suffices for a completely good human life, that is, for *eydaimonia*."[163] External circumstances cannot affect virtue. And external goods, such as health, wealth, fame, and fortune, are irrelevant to the virtue of the person and the flourishing life (*eydaimonia*). Likewise, the negative counterparts (sickness, poverty, ignominy, and misfortune) are also ineffective against virtue. Both make up the classification of things

---

[159] Nussbaum, *The Therapy of Desire*, 342.

[160] Nussbaum, *The Therapy of Desire*, 343.

[161] Nussbaum, *The Therapy of Desire*, 348-51.

[162] Nussbaum, *The Therapy of Desire*, 351-52.

[163] Nussbaum, *The Therapy of Desire*, 359.

that are indifferent. The former are considered to be preferred indifferents, while the latter are dispreferred indifferents. Yet they do not play any part in living the virtuous life and experiencing *eydaimonia*.[164]

Since virtues are the disposition of the soul and not the result of virtuous activity, they are not contingent on external circumstances. That doesn't mean the virtuous disposition is inactive itself, but is thought to be "striving or straining,"[165] always aiming at the goal of virtue. This radical detachment is necessary for the Stoic position. This is why it is so important for the Stoics to develop a therapy to extirpate the passions. Nussbaum concludes this section saying, "Thus philosophy is not only a road to *eydaimonia*: practiced at its highest, it is our human end, and the whole of it, not simply a part. *Phronēsis*, wise and virtuous thinking, just is *eydaimonia*."[166]

Next, Nussbaum explores the nature of the passions. Rather than thinking about the passions as some irrational part of the soul, struggling against the mind, bringing out some kind of animalistic nature, Stoics regarded the passions as rational judgments or beliefs, albeit false ones. It is for this reason, then, that "a rational art that sufficiently modifies judgments, seeking out the correct ones and installing them in place of the false, will actually be sufficient for curing … the ills that are caused by the passions."[167]

Passions, therefore, have a cognitive element, as opposed to the appetites such as hunger and thirst. Along with the experience of the passions are feelings that go with them and are part of the judgment or belief and can be determined to be false or true. There are two important qualities about these beliefs. One is that the person ascribes great value to that belief, whether it involves loss or gain. Second, the belief involves something external to the person's control. By removing the belief in the object's desirability, whether real or imagined, one can eradicate those passions along with the destructive feelings.[168]

A judgment for Stoics is an assent to an appearance: first a person is confronted by an appearance that presents itself to the mind as a

---

[164] Nussbaum, *The Therapy of Desire*, 359-62.
[165] Nussbaum, *The Therapy of Desire*, 363.
[166] Nussbaum, *The Therapy of Desire*, 360-66.
[167] Nussbaum, *The Therapy of Desire*, 367.
[168] Nussbaum, *The Therapy of Desire*, 366-72.

proposition; second, the person must either accept the appearance and what it means (assent) or reject it (by accepting the opposite of the proposition). A judgment has three elements that make it identical to a passion. First, the implicit proposition is based on the person's values about what is good and bad. Second, the person over-estimates the goodness or badness. Third, the judgment must have to do with something that is both external and vulnerable.[169]

The Stoics classified the passions, according to Nussbaum, by whether something is good or bad and by whether it occurs in the present or future. The result is four basic passions.

	Present	Future
Good	delight (*hēdonē*)	longing (*epithymia*)
Bad	distress (*lypē*)	fear (*phobos*)

Within each category are many subcategories depending on the situation and the feeling associated with the proposition. The passions are not, however, isolated from each other. Instead, once assent has been given to one passion, the way is open for others to be experienced. In medical terms, this is a chronic illness (*nosēma*) and can lead to a worse condition of infirmity (*arrhōstēma*).[170]

While other philosophical schools spoke of moderating the passions, the Stoics insisted that the passions must be rooted out completely. The wise person is then passion-free (*apathēs*) and self-sufficient (*autarkēs*). If the goal of life is to live in an undisturbed, free, and self-sufficient condition of *eudaimonia*, then not seeking to remove the passions leaves one vulnerable to the exigencies of life and the damage it may bring to one's integrity and dignity as a human person. Therefore, the Stoics held that one could not simply moderate the passions, because they invariably lead to excess.[171]

Not that a person is with no emotional feelings. Apart from these passions that are judgments about propositions based on false beliefs that have associated feelings, there are also feelings that are not based on valuing externals. We call these good emotions (*eupatheiai*). One could think of the future and respond with prudent caution (*eulabeia*) to outcomes classified as dispreferred indifferents. One might feel hopeful

---

[169] Nussbaum, *The Therapy of Desire*, 373-78.

[170] Nussbaum, *The Therapy of Desire*, 386-89.

[171] Nussbaum, *The Therapy of Desire*, 389-98.

and experience rational wish (*boulēsis*). If circumstances turn out positively, one could experience a kind of joy (*chara*), something described as "rational uplift" (*eulogos eparsis*). These sound good, but it must remembered that they are discussed in contexts of austerity.[172]

Exercises Revisited: John Sellars

In 2003 John Sellars (Lecturer in Philosophy at Royal Holloway, University of London) published his revised 2001 doctoral thesis from the University of Warwick, *The Art of Living: The Stoics on the Nature and Function of Philosophy*.[173] Sellars accepts Hadot's basic premises that philosophy is concerned with the quality of a person's life and that a fundamental way to achieve the goal is to practice exercises. Sellars chooses the expression "philosophical exercises" rather than "spiritual."[174] Sellars sums it up,

> Stoic philosophy should be understood as an art (*technē*) grounded upon rational principles (*logoi*) which are only expressed in one's behavior (*erga*, *bios*) after a period of practical training (*askēsis*). Both *logos* and *askēsis* are necessary components of philosophy conceived as a *technē* but neither can be identified with philosophy itself.[175]

Sellars identifies two aspects or functions of the philosophical exercises: habituation and digestion. He summarizes it this way: "In both cases we might say that the function of a spiritual exercise is to accustom or to habituate (*ethizō*) the soul according to philosophical doctrines or principles (*logoi*), to absorb philosophical ideas into one's character

---

[172] Nussbaum, *The Therapy of Desire*, 398-400.

[173] John Sellars, *The Art of Living: The Stoics on the Nature and Function of Philosophy*, Ashgate New Critical Thinking in Philosophy, (Aldershot: Ashgate, 2003). See also John Sellars, *Stoicism*, vol. 1, Ancient Philosophies, (Berkeley; Los Angeles: University of California Press, 2006); John Sellars, *Hellenistic Philosophy* (Oxford: Oxford University Press, 2018).

[174] Sellars, *The Art of Living*, 110.

[175] Sellars, *The Art of Living*, 118.

(*ēthos*) which, in turn, will determine one's habitual behavior."[176] The key to habituation is the repetition of the activity.

A second function is the metaphor of digestion. Epictetus, for example, draws the comparison to sheep. They do not show their shepherds how much they have eaten. Instead, they digest their food and then produce the results, which in their case is wool and milk. Epictetus applies the illustration, "And so do you, therefore, make no display to the laymen of your philosophical principles (*ta theōrēmata*), but let them see the results (*erga*) which come from the principles when digested" (*Ench.* 46).[177] Seneca instructs Lucilius to take time to think about the authors and books he reads. He must allow time to digest what they say. To read something and then talk about it is like eating a meal and then vomiting it. Instead, he should, "Each day [...] after you have run over many thoughts, select one to be thoroughly digested that day" (*Epist.* 2.4).[178]

At this point Sellars reminds his readers what is meant by transforming the soul according to the Stoics, like Epictetus and Seneca. The soul, as all physical objects, contains matter and breath/spirit (*pneuma*). The quality of an object depends on the level of the tension of *pneuma* within it. There are four categories of tension. Inanimate objects contain a type of tension called cohesion (*hexis*). Plants exhibit the tension called nature or growth (*physis*). Third, animals have a pneumatic tension called soul (*psychē*). Finally, rational adult humans may have the tension of a rational soul (*logikē psychē*). Philosophical exercises can increase the tension of the *pneyma* within the soul. A soul with a weak tension is more subject to disturbances and to negative emotions. A soul that has been improved has a stronger pneumatic tension and an increased ability to make correct judgments and not be disturbed by the passions. The result is a "transformation in one's way of life (*bios*)."[179]

Sellars follows the theory that the sections of the *Handbook* can be loosely organized by the typical divisions of philosophy (logic, physics, and ethics). The opening section hints at the tripartite division, though in a reverse order. Here Epictetus makes the important separation

---

[176] Sellars, *The Art of Living*, 120.

[177] Sellars, *The Art of Living*, 121.

[178] Sellars, *The Art of Living*, 122.

[179] Sellars, *The Art of Living*, 126.

between those things which depend on us ("are up to us") and those that do not. The three areas that depend on us, Sellars suggests, correlate to the three *topoi* of philosophy. The first is "opinion," the forming of judgments, which is the domain of logic. The second is "impulse," the decision to act or not to act, which is the division of ethics. The third is "desire and aversion," which requires an understanding of the nature of the cosmos and to live harmoniously with it and relates to the category of physics.[180]

Sections 2–29 are about philosophical exercises designed to bring about actions related to an understanding of physics. These sections contain exhortation, encouragement, and advice on how to prepare for and to respond appropriately to life events. The way to do this is to accept that you are part of a larger cosmic system of causes and effects and to align your will with the will of the cosmos. We will act in accordance with nature unless something external causes us to have desires and to act in ways contrary to nature. The exercises are designed to overcome those desires and actions through an understanding of and conformity with the nature of the cosmos.[181]

Sections 30–41 contain ethical exercises concerned with controlling one's impulses so that the person performs only "appropriate actions (*kathēkonta*)." It is in this way that the aspiring philosopher "will be able not merely to *say* how the sage should act but also to *act* as the sage should act."[182]

A third section covers 42–45 and contain exercises related to logic. They have to do with judgment (*hypolēpsis*) and assents (*sygkatatheseis*). When we notice something, we receive an impression (*phantasia*) of it. We need to make a judgment based on principles of logic whether our impression is "adequate," or whether we have added to the impression some unwarranted value or belief. We should only give our assent to those adequate impressions, which will impact how we act.[183]

---

[180] Sellars, *The Art of Living*, 134-36. This division is laid out elsewhere in the *Discourses*, such as 3.2.1–2.

[181] Sellars, *The Art of Living*, 136-39.

[182] Sellars, *The Art of Living*, 141.

[183] Sellars, *The Art of Living*, 141-42.

The theme of sections 46–52 seems to focus on the philosophical life: how the philosopher should act, how to tell someone is making progress, and how to train oneself in the philosophical life.[184] The final section, Section 53, contains maxims the student should learn.[185]

---

[184] Sellars, *The Art of Living*, 143.
[185] Sellars, *The Art of Living*, 143-44.

Chapter 6:
The Hellenistic Context of Paul

Many have attempted to survey the life of Paul, and I have read many of them.[186] Scholars far more knowledgeable than I am have worked out detailed analyses of the places and events appearing in the narration of Acts and mentioned by Paul in his letters. Some are more certain of the historicity of Acts than others. I only want to talk about the Hellenistic context of Paul's formation and the way it impacted the language he used in his writing.

Hellenistic Context of Paul's Formation

Paul's references to his birth and upbringing are located in contexts in which Paul is defending himself against those who thought he wasn't Jewish enough. That he does this should cause us to consider the degree to which people took him for a Hellenist. As we have seen, the evidence from Paul's letters is that he not only is an able communicator in Greek, but that he also has some knowledge of Greek epistolography and rhetorical style.

Paul's Formative Years

There's no reason to doubt that Paul was born in Tarsus of Jewish ancestry (despite the tradition cited by Jerome that his family was from the Galilean town of Gischala [Jerome, *Comm. Phlm.* 23–24]), was circumcised, and reared as an observant Jew. That Paul only calls himself Paul in his letters should cause us to doubt that he had been named after

---

[186] My earliest introduction to the historical study of the New Testament was F. F. Bruce, *New Testament History* (New York: Doubleday, 1991; repr., London: Nelson, 1969). My professor at Wheaton also published a conservative approach to the history of Paul: John McRay, *Paul: His Life and Teaching* (Grand Rapids, MI: Baker Academic, 2003). Another scholar who has contributed much to the study of Paul's life: Jerome Murphy-O'Connor, *Paul: A Critical Life* (Oxford; New York: Oxford University Press, 1997).

the great king of Israelite history and most prominent Benjaminite, Saul (*sha'ul* in Hebrew, *Saulos* in Greek), as Luke has it in the beginning of Acts. Luke's change of Paul's name is a clever twist on the similarly spelled names in Greek and is most likely another element in Luke's narrative plot to move the story of the early church from Jerusalem—and Jewish language and culture—to Rome. Luke does not say that Saul had another name, Paul, but that Saul/Paul shared his name with Sergio Paul (Acts 13:9). Luke uses that point in the story to make his transition to calling him Paul.

We can only surmise that Paul had some form of education in Greek, if not some formal schooling.[187] Not only that, but Paul's knowledge of Stoic philosophy suggests he attended lectures by Greek philosophers. Tarsus was well-known as a city that produced philosophers. Paul's dependence in his letters on a Greek translation of the Bible, one closely related to the textual tradition that has come down to us, surely means he grew up with a form of Hellenistic Judaism. I argue elsewhere (see p. 32) that Paul may have even chosen to undergo circumcision reversal to participate more fully in Greek life as a Roman citizen in the city of Tarsus.

I suggest that Paul was born into a Jewish family, possibly in Tarsus but not necessarily so. In his late teens, perhaps, he became more interested in Greek life and attempted to reverse his circumcision. It could have been in his twenties when he had a change of heart, moved to Jerusalem, and became something of a Jewish fanatic against those, like the Jesus followers, who were not strictly observant Jews. Perhaps he was in Jerusalem when Jesus was executed and had been approving of it. It might have been the experience of hearing someone like Stephen, the Greek proselyte to Judaism and follower of Jesus, deliver a protreptic speech seeking to persuade people to become followers of this life (Acts 5:20) and way (Acts 9:2) that caused Paul to "convert" to this way of life. For Paul this was not just a prophetic call to a mission and not a change to a different religion. I take it as a change from one sect of Judaism to another.

---

[187] For a recent study of Paul's rhetorical background see Ryan S. Schellenberg, *Rethinking Paul's Rhetorical Education: Comparative Rhetoric and 2 Corinthians 10-13*, Early Christianity and its Literature, (Atlanta: Society of Biblical Literature, 2013).

Luke's Attempt to Present a More Jewish Paul

Over the course of the narrative of Acts, Luke portrays Paul as the second phase of God spreading the Gospel from Jerusalem to Rome, from Judeans to gentiles, and from the role of Peter to the role of Paul. Luke also shows in his composition his own facility with Greek, even at a higher level than Paul, and his knowledge of historiographical style, biography, and narrative fiction. As we have seen above, Luke uses verisimilitude to portray Paul as an Aramaic-speaking Jew (see p. 12). Although Luke says Paul hears the risen Christ speaking to him in Hebrew, Luke is using a relatively common Greek idiom. Therefore, we should not take Luke's portrayal of Paul at face value because of Luke's theological and narrative purposes.

In one instance in Acts Paul says in Greek to a tribune in Jerusalem that he is a Jew and a citizen of Tarsus in Cilicia (Acts 21:39). When he addresses the crowd, Luke has Paul speak to them in Hebrew. However, Paul describes his speech as an *apologia*, a defense speech, a technical term in Greek for a speech given in response to accusations (Acts 22:1). Luke composes Paul's speech having him say that, though he was born in Tarsus, he was reared in Jerusalem and studied Torah and no doubt the oral law as a Pharisee at the feet of Gamaliel. That Luke includes this bit of information only within a speech he composes for Paul, which is intended to bolster Paul's affinity with the Jerusalem residents and is not something Paul mentions in his letters, suggests we should take it with a grain of salt.

Paul Within Judaism

The most extensive description of Paul's formative years appears in his letter to the Philippians (Phil 3:5–6). As I show in the summary of that letter (see p. 135), Paul is listing the advantages he had to demonstrate that these are, in Stoic terms, the things that are indifferent (they are not things that "make a difference" in Paul's usage) to one's moral progress. Paul's list is certainly not meant to be taken as a disparagement of Judaism or a denunciation of his experience as a Jew.

While I accept that Paul remained an observant Jew and engaged in Jewish life, I don't think Paul was attempting to make Jews out of gentiles. He did, however, want them to become worshippers of the God of Israel and to reject the worship of gods and their images. In my translations I have represented places where I think Paul may have in mind the tetragrammaton (see p. 104) by using all uppercase letters for LORD (1 Thess 4:6, 15–17; 5:2; Phil 4:5; Rom 9:28–29; 10:12–14, 16; 11:3, 34; 12:11, 19; 14:4, 6–8, 11; 15:11; 16:2, 8). I don't think Paul considers Jesus to be the LORD (or God, for that matter), but he uses the fact that Jesus is called a lord as a way of fulfilling a biblical text in Rom 10:9 (see p. 215). However, Paul thinks of God in ways that are more Hellenistic. To be like God is not to be like the God of the Bible (in the sense of being transcendent, all-knowing, and pure, for example) and certainly not to be like the gods of Greek mythology, but to be like the god of the philosophers: existing in unperturbed tranquility without desire, fear of loss or fate; wise and just). Paul regards Jesus as a divine being, but I hold that Paul also thought people who lived in the same way as Jesus would also experience an apotheosis to immortality.[188]

Paul's Assemblies

I propose that Paul was not consciously forming gentiles into household groups as a way of imitating the practices of Jewish synagogues. In Greco-Roman society people met in groups in the houses of wealthy people to share a meal, socialize, and carry out business, whether that business was as a burial club, a guild, or a philosophical school. Paul's groups might have looked like a Jewish "gathering," the meaning of the word synagogue, but it would have also looked like a philosophical group. Indeed, Jewish "gatherings" looked like philosophical groups. Philo says as much about synagogues in Alexandria. People regarded them as "schools of temperance and justice" (*Legat.* 312.3)[189] and viewed Jews as "athletes of virtue produced by a philosophy free from the pedantry of Greek wordiness, a philosophy which sets its pupils to practice themselves in laudable actions, by which the liberty which can never be enslaved is firmly

---

[188] M. David Litwa, *We are Being Transformed: Deification in Paul's Soteriology*, Beihefte zur Zeitschrift für die neutestamentliche Wissenschaft und die Kunde der älteren Kirche, (Berlin; Boston: De Gruyter, 2012); M. David Litwa, *Iesus Deus: The Early Christian Depiction of Jesus as a Mediterranean God* (Minneapolis: Fortress Press, 2014).

[189] Philo, *On the Embassy to Gaius. General Indexes*. trans. F. H. Colson, Loeb Classical Library 379 (Cambridge, MA: Harvard University Press, 1962), 157.

established" (*Prob.* 88.1–89.1).[190] The similarity of these meetings is evident in the same Greek word being used of both (*ekklēsia*). I have translated this term not with "church" but with "assembly."[191] In fact, Paul refers to the "assemblies" of Jewish followers of Jesus as synagogues several times (1 Thess 2:14; Gal 1:13, 21; Phil 1:1; 3:6; Philem 2; Rom 16:1). One reason for some of these is that I have concluded that Paul regularly uses the term "holy ones," which I translate as *qedoshim* (see p. 34), as a way of referring to Jews (Phil 1:1; 4:21, 22; Philem 5, 7; Rom 8:27; 12:13; 15:25, 26, 31; 16:2, 15).

Paul's Motivation to Spread the Good News to Gentile Peoples

It is possible Paul was driven to be an apostle or envoy to gentile peoples because of prophecies related to Jews being "a light to the gentiles" (Isa 49:6). I contend that Paul was not focused on fulfilling an apocalyptic scenario but on telling people of non-Jewish ethnicity the "good news" that God had now wiped out the sins of the gentile peoples and would now be the God not only of the Jewish people but also of all people.[192] I assume Paul doesn't expect gentiles to do anything to have God as their god, but expects them to worship only the one God. Paul's language of "grace and peace" encapsulates the two things God offers to a people, and that is (1) benevolence, in the form of providing for the necessities of life like fertility and sustenance, and (2) security or concord, in the form of being safe from dangerous forces.

The Israelites believed the God of Israel would bless a faithful people with fertility and security:

> I will give you your rains in their season, and the land shall yield its produce, and the trees of the field shall yield their fruit. Your threshing shall overtake the vintage, and the vintage shall overtake the sowing; you shall eat your bread to the full and live

---

[190] Philo, *Every Good Man is Free. On the Contemplative Life. On the Eternity of the World. Against Flaccus. Apology for the Jews. On Providence.* trans. F. H. Colson, Loeb Classical Library 363 (Cambridge, MA: Harvard University Press, 1941), 61.

[191] For a discussion on this see Runesson, "The Question of Terminology: The Architecture of Contemporary Discussions on Paul."

[192] I'm trying to avoid the word "nation" in order not to give the impression that God is a national deity and to reject the idea that a political entity like the USA has a God watching over it and needing to be worshipped and appeased.

securely in your land. And I will grant peace in the land, and you shall lie down, and no one shall make you afraid; I will remove dangerous animals from the land, and no sword shall go through your land (Lev 26:4–6 NRSV).

In Paul's view God's favor and security are blessings that all nations may have.

Paul believes God has done this because of the "faithfulness of Christ" (see p. 191). That is what God has freely given. But Paul doesn't leave it there. He writes letters of moral exhortation that first explain why gentile peoples should now turn to God and then how they should conduct their lives in order to attain the goal (*telos*) of life. In fact, I think this *telos* was the same *telos* Paul had as a Jew. It is the telos of the philosophical life, what it means to become a fully formed human and become divine. Paul's use of Greco-Roman moral philosophy wasn't just to provide an ethical system but to provide the means by which the followers of Jesus make progress toward a virtuous and flourishing life.

Hellenistic Context of Paul's Linguistic Concepts

Rather than try to present a detailed description of Paul's travels and a systematic outline of his theology, I want to focus on certain terminology Paul uses that has caused misunderstanding. Words of Paul's letters that are read in English sound the same as the words that appear in the Old Testament. Often the words are interpreted in the same way as they are used in the Old Testament. People have a tendency to forget that they are reading a translation of a Greek text. Even if they know Greek, they might infer that the Greek word is just a token for whatever Hebrew word it translates. Not only is that not the case, the Hebrew Bible and its translation is sometimes interpreted with Greek concepts.

Here is an example regarding language about the new covenant in the Hebrew Bible.[193] Jeremiah describes the making of this new covenant in traditional terms. Yahweh will "cut" a new covenant with the house of Israel and the house of Judah (Jer 31:31, 33). Most translations read, "I will put my law within them." The Hebrew expression, however, is

---

[193] This discussion appeared in an article I wrote: Timothy W. Seid, "The New and Eternal Covenant," *Quaker Religious Thought* 109 (2007).

formulaic in contexts in which God or Moses "gives the law" (Exod 24:12; Lev 26:46; Deut 4:8; 31:9; Ezra 7:6; Neh 9:13; 10:29; Jer 9:13; 26:4; 44:10; Dan 9:10). This Hebrew verb is often translated in these contexts along with a prepositional phrase as "to set before them" (or, literally, "before their face"). The prepositional phrase appearing in Jer 31:33 has as its object a term that when referring to the human body can mean to be "inside" the body. However, in contexts where the prepositional phrase refers to a group it is most often considered being something done "in the midst of" the people. In other words, the Hebrew of Jeremiah simply describes God giving God's law among the congregation of God's people.

The parallel expression in Jer 31:33 is "I will write it on their hearts." This idiomatic expression for memorization occurs elsewhere in the Hebrew Bible (Prov. 3:3; 7:3). A parallel text occurs in Jer 17:1, "The sin of Judah is written with an iron pen; with a diamond point it is engraved on the tablet of their hearts, and on the horns of their altars" (NRSV). All this text means is that God will cause them to remember and obey God's law.

The last phrase of Jer 31:33 repeats the conditions of the Sinai covenant as expressed in Lev 26:12, in which God promises to function as their deity and the people promise to only revere Yahweh as their God. The difference comes in the next phrase in Jer 31:34. Under the Sinai covenant Moses (Deut 4:1, 10, 14; 5:31; 6:1) and the later scribes (Ezra 7:10; Neh 8:8) have the duty of teaching Torah to the people. Families have the responsibility of teaching their children (Deut 11:19). The knowledge of Yahweh is expressed most often in the words, "know that I am Yahweh." Jer 24:7 helps us understand the context of the new covenant language, "I will give them a heart to know that I am the LORD; and they shall be my people and I will be their God, for they shall return to me with their whole heart" (NRSV).

The language of Jer 31:33, therefore, concerns the collective consciousness of the nation, rather than an implanting of innate ideas upon individual souls. The language of "inward mind" belongs to the later development as Jews began translating the Hebrew scriptures into Greek and interpreting them within the context of Greek philosophy.

Sin as Moral Error

A central term for Christians is sin. In the Hebrew tradition "trespass" refers to going beyond the boundaries of God's moral code. We think of sin as being something humans do that offends God and causes God to be wrathful against the offense. In philosophical terms, this Greek word has to do with making an error or mistake. People are confronted with a situation in which they have to judge what response they make. When they misjudge and act in a way contrary to what is the best way for them to act, they have made an error in judgment. They made the wrong choice. The effect of that error is to diminish their progress toward the goal of spiritual and moral maturity. It is taking a step backwards.

Salvation and Destruction as Progress and Regress

One of the most important words in Christian literature is also a word found frequently in philosophical texts. It is the word salvation (*sōtēria*; verb *sōzō*). It also occurs often with its opposite, destruction (*apōleia*; verb *apollymi*). In literature from Plato to Epictetus, salvation/destruction language is used to describe the salutary effects of progress in virtue and the degradation of progress through the commission of moral error.[194]

In the *Theaet.* 153, Plato has Socrates discussing the basic principle of active and passive forces in the world. What is not in motion in the world leads to decay and destruction (*apollymi*). The opposite, that which is in motion, is what brings about preservation (*sōzō*). Socrates applies this to the body and to moral progress.

> And what about the condition of the soul? Isn't it by learning and study, which are motions, that the soul gains knowledge and is preserved (*sōzetai*) and becomes a better thing? Whereas in a state of rest, that is when it will not study or learn, it not only fails to acquire knowledge but forgets what it has already learned (*Theaet.* 153b–c)?[195]

Epictetus is reported to have said in *Diatr.* 4.1 about the death of Socrates,

---

[194] For a further description about how this functions in moral philosophy, see Glad, *Paul and Philodemus*, 78-81.

[195] Cooper and Hutchinson, eds., *Plato: Complete Works*, 170.

The Hellenistic Context of Paul

Did he think it a bit of good luck? Impossible! No, he regards what is fitting (*dikaiō*), and as for other considerations, he does not so much as look at or consider them. For he did not care, he says, to save (*sōsai*) his paltry body, but only that which is increased and preserved (*sōzetai*) by right conduct and is diminished and destroyed (*apollytai*) by evil conduct (*Diatr.* 4.1.163–164).[196]

An interesting text that frequently uses the salvation/destruction language in the context of moral progress is *The Tabula of Cebes*. This Cynic/Stoic allegory of life reads like Bunyan's *Pilgrim's Progress* and may have even influenced Bunyan's writing. An old man describes to visitors to a temple in Thebes a tablet portraying multiple enclosures with gates through which people pass. He compares learning about the meaning of the tablet with the riddle of the Sphinx.

Thus, if anyone does not understand these things he is destroyed by her [Foolishness], not all at once, as a person devoured by the Sphinx died. Rather, he is destroyed (*apollymi*) little by little, throughout his entire life, just like those who are handed over for retribution. But if one does understand, Foolishness is in turn destroyed (*apollymi*), and he himself is saved (*sōzō*) and is blessed (*makarios*) and happy (*eydaimōn*) in his whole life (3.3–4).[197]

As people are guided on their way into the first enclosure, they meet female figures who personify Opinion, Desire and Pleasure. The old man explains, "Some of these women lead to salvation (*sōzō*), while others by deception lead to destruction (*apollymi*)" (*Ceb. Tab.* 6.2).[198] Salvation language continues through this description of how people can avoid deception and vice so they may experience the best sort of life. Although the *Tabula* relates *eydaimonia* with the present life, at one point that life is described in terms reminiscent of the realm of the gods (*Ceb. Tab.* 17.1–

---

[196] Epictetus, *Discourses, Books 3-4. Fragments. The Encheiridion.* trans. W. A. Oldfather, Loeb Classical Library 218 (Cambridge, MA: Harvard University Press, 1928), 301.

[197] John T. Fitzgerald and L. Michael White, *The Tabula of Cebes*, Texts and translations 24; Graeco-Roman Religion 7, (Chico, CA: Scholars Press, 1983), 65.

[198] Fitzgerald and White, *The Tabula of Cebes*, 69.

3). It is "beautiful, grassy, and brilliantly lit" and the name of the place is "the dwelling place of the happy. For all the Virtues and Happiness spend their time here (*Ceb. Tab.* 17.3)."[199]

Trust and Faithfulness rather than Belief and Faith

There are several terms related to the larger concept of constancy and allegiance. Typical words appearing in early Christianity are terms like endurance and perseverance. Subsumed within that concept is the Hebrew concept of obedience, the doing of what one hears. A more difficult term to explain fully is the Pauline term faith. This Greek term *pistis* can refer to belief but also to faithfulness and loyalty. A growing consensus takes Paul's expression commonly translated as "faith in Christ" to refer actually to the "faithfulness of Christ."[200] Where Paul uses this expression (Rom 3:22, 26; 4:16; Gal 2:16, 20; 3:22), he is referring to Christ's endurance and constancy as our exemplar, who by his constancy achieved the goal as evidenced by his resurrection and also removed God's wrath from against the gentile peoples.

Endurance has to do with how one remains constant in faithfulness to God during trials, persecution, and suffering. The experience of pain in itself is not efficacious, but what is beneficial is the endurance of suffering.[201] It requires the person to be submissive to God's will in the universe and live in accordance with it.

Paul described the way of life as followers of Jesus with the same imagery as philosophers used. Paul used athletic imagery to illustrate

---

[199] Fitzgerald and White, *The Tabula of Cebes*, 89. Note 58 discusses the view of some who take this to be a description of the Islands of the Blessed and Elysian Fields, while others take it to refer to this life (pg. 149).

[200] Jouette M. Bassler, David M. Hay, and E. Elizabeth Johnson, *Pauline Theology* (Minneapolis: Fortress Press, 1991); Richard B. Hays, *The Faith of Jesus Christ: An Investigation of the Narrative Substructure of Galatians 3:1-4:11*, Dissertation series / Society of Biblical Literature, (Chico, CA: Scholars Press, 1983). A recent translation, the NET Bible, created by evangelical scholars maintains the "faithfulness of Christ" idiom. http://net.bible.org.

[201] Martin Hengel, *The Atonement: The Origins of the Doctrine in the New Testament* (Philadelphia: Fortress Press, 1981); Sam K. Williams, *Jesus' Death as Saving Event: The Background and Origin of a Concept*, Harvard Dissertations in Religion, (Missoula, MT: Published by Scholars Press for Harvard Theological Review, 1975).

the training of the soul. Scholars refer to the *agon* motif as the language of the philosopher's struggle to endure the trials of life.[202]

To reach the goal, according to the philosophers, a person needs to be making progress toward the goal. We are more apt to think of Christian theological language as being past tense, what Christ did for us, or future tense, what will happen to us after death or at the second coming of Christ. Some traditions have recognized the present tense language of the New Testament that describes how followers of Jesus are being changed and transformed. I find the philosophical term in Phil 1:25 "I know that I will remain and continue with all of you for your progress (*prokopē*) and joy in faith."

Perfection and Blessedness

Goal of Perfection

Greco-Roman moral philosophers often discussed the goal of life.[203] There are a cluster of terms in the New Testament that come from the same root. You may know the term telos. The telos of something is its goal, aim, or outcome. In some contexts, the term telos can have a temporal meaning referring to the end. In some contexts, the early Christian authors used *telos* language to refer to the goal of life. 1 Pet 1:9 "for you are receiving the outcome (*telos*) of your faith, the salvation of your souls." Paul used a synonym in Phil 3:14 "I press on toward the goal (*skopos*) for the prize of the heavenly call of God in Christ Jesus."

A related term refers to the state of having reached the telos, the goal. There are several forms of this sort including the verb form. Normally these terms are translated in our English Bibles with forms of the word "perfect." These terms do not describe some state of flawlessness as much as they do the condition of having achieved the goal, to be complete. In human development terms, we call this maturity. In English we get our word "adult" from the Latin form. Paul says in 1 Cor 14:20

---

[202] Fitzgerald, *Cracks in an Earthen Vessel*; Abraham J. Malherbe, "The Beasts at Ephesus," *Journal of Biblical Literature* 87, no. 1 (1968); Abraham J. Malherbe, "Antisthenes and Odysseus, and Paul at war," *Harvard Theological Review* 76 Ap (1983).

[203] Brad Inwood, "Goal and Target in Stoicism," *The Journal of Philosophy* 83, no. 10 (Oct. 1986).

"Brothers and sisters, do not be children in your thinking; rather, be infants in evil, but in thinking be adults (*teleioi*)."

Eudaimonia

We saw in the *Tablet of Cebes* that the final destination of the travelers of life was to arrive at the meadow where they discovered the woman named Happiness, in Greek *Eudaimonia*. Here is one of the most important terms for understanding the goal of life. At the top of the scale or ladder of nature is *eudaimonia*. It is the state in which God, or the gods live. It is a blessed state of divine existence.[204] Traditionally the term has been translated as "happiness." Most commonly today classicists will use the expression "human flourishing." In Aristotelian terms, it is that which humans achieve for its own sake and not as the means to something else. It is the ultimate expression of human living and flourishing.

Eudaimonia appears in the texts of the Greek Church from the second century on. Note especially the experience of Justin Martyr in his *Dialogue with Trypho*.

> But straightway a flame was kindled in my soul; and a love of the prophets, and of those men who are friends of Christ (*oi Christou philoi*), possessed me; and whilst revolving his words in my mind, I found this philosophy alone to be safe and profitable. Thus, and for this reason, I am a philosopher. Moreover, I would wish that all, making a resolution similar to my own, do not keep themselves away from the words of the Savior. For they possess a terrible power in themselves and are sufficient to inspire those who turn aside from the path of rectitude with awe; while the sweetest rest is afforded those who make a diligent practice of them. If, then, you have any concern for yourself, and if you are

---

[204] In a review of Martha Nussbaum's *Therapy of Desire*, Diskin Clay argues for a more theistic view of the term *eudaimonia*: "The problem of representing the Greek concept of happiness (*eudaimonia*, literally being favored by divinity) by the current term "flourishing" is that it expunges from the record of ancient philosophy the aspiration—shared by Platonists, Aristotle, Epicureans, and Stoics (and indeed some Hellenistic kings)—to come to resemble the divine—*homoiōsis theō*." Diskin Clay, "Deep Therapy," *Philosophy and Literature* 20, no. 2 (1996).

eagerly looking for salvation, and if you believe in God, you may—since you are not indifferent to the matter—become acquainted with the Christ of God, and, after being initiated (or "having become complete" *teleiō genomenō*), live a happy life (*eudaimonein*) (*Dial.* 8.1–2).[205]

We do not find this term in the New Testament, but we do find the synonymous term blessedness (*makarios*). The early Christian authors developed the Greek concept of heaven as the abode of God to describe the future state of blessedness. Until the Hellenistic period, the Hebrew concept did not depict God as residing in heaven or that heaven was a place where the dead might go. The Hebrew's concept of the underworld was like the Greek concept of Hades. For the Greeks, heaven was the abode of the gods, where the immortal ones existed.[206] Only in rare situations would a human achieve divinity and be translated to heaven or the Isle of the Blessed. Heroes and sages could achieve such a thing. What we find described in the New Testament is the belief that Jesus achieved such a state and that the followers of Jesus can also achieve immortality through resurrection. The early Greek church continued the belief that the Christian experience after death was not just the human spirit living for eternity in heaven with God but in fact a participation in divine life.[207] The goal of the human life is the attainment of this goal by the end of life and the resurrection to immortality is a participation in the divine life with Jesus.

---

[205] Justin Martyr, *Dialogue with Trypho*. trans. Marcus Dods and George Reith, The Ante-Nicene Fathers: Translations of the Writings of the Fathers Down to A.D. 325 (1885-1887), 532.

[206] Werner Jaeger, "The Greek Ideas of Immortality," in *Immortality and Resurrection; Four Essays by Oscar Cullman, Harry A. Wolfson, Werner Jaeger, and Henry J. Cadbury*, ed. Krister Stendahl (New York: Macmillan, 1965).

[207] Emil Bartos, *Deification in Eastern Orthodox Theology* (Eugene, OR: Wipf & Stock, 2006); Michael J. Christensen and Wittung Jeffery A., *Partakers of the Divine Nature: The History and Development of Deification in the Christian Traditions* (Grand Rapids, MI: Baker Academic, 2008); Stephen Kharlamov Vladimir Finlan, *Theosis: Deification in Christian Theology* (Eugene, OR: Pickwick Publications, 2006).

Moral Progress and the Scale of Nature

A common way in Greco-Roman philosophy to describe the place of humans in the world is the scale of nature.[208] Every object in nature belongs to a particular group based on similar characteristics. As we ascend this ladder, subsequent objects bear characteristics of the preceding but have more advanced features. A rock or a stick, for instance, has the quality of movement from outside itself, but it is inanimate—it doesn't have a soul. An animal can also be moved, but it can also move itself and it has a soul, but it doesn't have rationality. Humans have movement, have a soul, and also share an aspect of the highest order of being by having reason or logos. Humans, however, are plagued by debilitating passions like fear and desire, and often live a troubled existence because of dependence on outward circumstances and fate. The highest order of being is god or the gods. A god is an immortal being, pure rationality the Stoics would say, who dwells in perfect tranquility, not dependent on anything.

When a human is born, the infant is like an animal, whose basic instinct is self-preservation and acting on its impulses. As a person develops, he or she is to learn to judge the appearances affected by the impulses to do what is virtuous. Gradually the person can moderate or even extirpate or remove the passions. Reason becomes dominant, and the person learns to live according to nature, to be self-sufficient, to be self-controlled, and to be tranquil and happy. The goal of the human is to move up the scale of nature to achieve a godlike state and even to become immortal after death. Heroes like Heracles (Hercules) attain such a state through their endurance or through a noble death. Philosophers who advance to such a level of perfection are referred to as a sage and are thought to attain a divine status.

Cicero, for instance, in *De Amicitia* writes about Scipio, "If the truth really is that the souls of all good men after death make the easiest escape from what may be termed the imprisonment and fetters of the flesh, whom can we think of as having had an easier journey to the gods than Scipio?" (*Amic.* 14). Seneca portrays the uncertainty of most

---

[208] Brad Inwood, *Ethics and Human Action in Early Stoicism* (Oxford: Clarendon Press, 1985), 18-27.

philosophers about life after death, but includes the possibility of a divine existence for the great-souled (*magnus animus*) person:

> Let great souls comply with God's wishes, and suffer unhesitatingly whatever fate the law of the universe ordains; for the soul at death is either sent forth into a better life, destined to dwell with deity amid greater radiance and calm, or else, at least, without suffering any harm to itself, it will be mingled with nature again, and will return to the universe (Seneca, *Ep.* 71.16).[209]

Epicurus concludes his *Letter to Menoeceus*:

> Exercise thyself in these and kindred precepts day and night, both by thyself and with him who is like unto thee; then never, either in waking or in dream, wilt thou be disturbed, but wilt live as a god among men. For man loses all semblance of mortality by living in the midst of immortal blessings (Diogenes Laertius, *Lives*, 10.135 [Epicurus]).[210]

The Epicurean poet Lucretius then wrote of Epicurus in Book Five of his *De Rerum Natura*:

> Who is able with mighty mind to build a song worthy of the majesty of nature and these discoveries? Or who is so potent in speech as to devise praises fit for his merits, who by his own intellect winning and gaining such treasures, has left them to us? None will be found, I think, of the sons of mortal men. For if we must speak as this very majesty of nature now known to us demands, he was a god, noble Memmius, a god he was, who first discovered that reasoned plan of life which is now called Wisdom, who by his skill brought life out of those tempestuous billows and that deep darkness, and settled it in such a calm and in light so clear. ... But good life was impossible without a

---

[209] Seneca, *Epistles, Volume 2: Epistles 66-92*. trans. Richard M. Gummere, Loeb Classical Library 76 (Cambridge, MA: Harvard University Press, 1920), 83.

[210] Diogenes Laertius, *Lives of Eminent Philosophers, Volume 2: Books 6-10*. trans. R. D. Hicks, Loeb Classical Library 185 (Cambridge, MA: Harvard University Press, 1925), 659.

purged mind; which makes him seem to us with better reason a god, from whom even now spreading abroad through great nations come sweet consolations of life to soothe our minds (Lucretius, *De rerum natura* 5.1–21).[211]

Fundamental to living life well is to make progress (*prokopē*) toward a goal (*telos* or *skopos*). That goal is bound up in one word, the Greek word *eudaimonia*. While most texts translate the word as "happiness," more recent classicists have constructed expressions like "the human flourishing life." Seldom do classicists want to understand *eudaimonia* with its theological implications. Although the meaning of words is not a construct of their etymology, it is important to realize that within that term is the word *daimon*, the word for a divinity: *eudaimonia* is a "good divine state." *Eudaimonia* or its synonym "blessedness" (*makarios*) describe the condition of the gods.

The classic description of *eudaimonia* occurs in Aristotle's *Nichomachean Ethics*. Aristotle puts "happiness" in this theological context.

> For this reason also the question is asked, whether happiness is to be acquired by learning or by habituation or some other sort of training or comes in virtue of some divine providence or again by chance. Now if there is any gift of the gods to men, it is reasonable that happiness (*eudaimonion*) should be god-given, and most surely god-given of all human things inasmuch as it is the best. But this question would perhaps be more appropriate to another inquiry; happiness seems, however, even if it is not god-sent but comes as a result of excellence and some process of learning or training, to be among the most god-like things; for that which is the prize and end (*telos*) of excellence seems to be the best thing and something godlike and blessed (*makarion*) (*Eth. nic.*1.9 [1099b]).[212]

---

[211] Lucretius, *On the Nature of Things*. trans. W. H. D. Rouse. Revised by Martin F. Smith, Loeb Classical Library 181 (Cambridge, MA: Harvard University Press, 1924), 379, 81.

[212] Aristotle, *Complete Works of Aristotle: The Revised Oxford Translation*, ed. J. Barnes, Bollingen Series. 2 vols. (Princeton, NJ: Princeton University Press, 1983), 2:1737.

Maturation and Cosmopolitanism

A more technical term for the progress a person makes going up the scale of nature is the Stoic term *oikeiosis*.[213] As people mature, they recognize their place in the world differently. As an infant, they are concerned with self-preservation. The more mature they become the more they recognize themselves as a citizen of the world, a cosmopolitan. No matter what one's ethnicity, nationality, gender, or social class, the mature person sees him or herself as interrelated to all of life. From this grows a sense of altruism. The phrase in Paul's letter to the Philippians is "think about the things of others" (Phil 2:4). Jesus acted out of that sense of altruism, which Paul describes in the second chapter of Philippians.[214] After exhorting the mature among the Philippians in 3:15 to think the way Christ thought and imitate his own example, he contrasts the Philippians with the enemies of Christ. These enemies are characterized as nothing other than people who are not virtuous people: "Their end (*telos*) is destruction; their god is the belly; and their glory is in their shame; their minds are set on earthly things" (Phil 3:19 NRSV). In contrast to them, these mature people have a "citizenship in heaven" (Phil 4:20 NRSV). Paul goes on to say that Jesus will "transform the body of our humiliation that it may be conformed to the body of his glory" (Phil 3:21 NRSV).

Self-Mastery

To make progress a person must achieve self-mastery (*enkrateia*).[215] A more literal translation of the word would be something like "empowerment." The bad emotions, the passions, are those impulses that are part of nature or learned responses which cause us to become fearful, selfish, angry, lustful, and so on. When we develop self-control, when we become empowered, we form the habit of right ways of thinking and acting healthy for us and lead us toward the goal of the

---

[213] Troels Engberg-Pedersen, *The Stoic Theory of oikeiosis: Moral Development and Social Interaction in Early Stoic Philosophy*, Studies in Hellenistic Civilization, (Aarhus, Denmark: Aarhus University Press, 1990).

[214] Troels Engberg-Pedersen, "Radical Altruism in Philippians 2:4," in *Early Christianity and Classical Culture* (Leiden: E J Brill, 2003).

[215] Stowers, "Paul and Self-Mastery."

divine state of life. Paul uses the technical term in 1 Cor 9:25 "Athletes exercise self-control (*enkrateuetai*) in all things; they do it to receive a perishable wreath, but we an imperishable one" (NRSV).

Self-Sufficiency

One of the most important attributes of divine life is to not depend on any material thing or circumstance of life for the condition of one's soul. This is referred to as self-sufficiency (*autarkeia*). Epictetus put it as not being dependent on anything outside of one's own power or control. That has nothing to do with how one relates to God in some atheistic way. To be self-sufficient doesn't mean you defy God. Paul attributes his self-sufficiency to God, as in 2 Cor 9:8, "And God is able to provide you with every blessing in abundance, so that by always having enough of everything (*pasan autarkeian echontes*; lit. "having all self-sufficiency"), you may share abundantly in every good work" (NRSV). Paul uses another form of the word in Phil 4:11, "I have learned to be self-sufficient (*autarkēs*) in whatever circumstances I encounter" (trans. mine).

The positive outcome one achieves when one is empowered and self-sufficient is to no longer live in worry or fear about the circumstances of life, whether that is impoverishment, disease, injury, loss, or even death. When we use the word peace, we often think of the Hebrew context of *shalom*. Paul, however, doesn't simply translate a Hebrew word into Greek. He sometimes uses the Greek word *eirēnē* to refer to the Greek concept of tranquility. Paul speaks to this with philosophical language in 1 Thess 4:10–12 "But we urge you, beloved, to do so more and more, to aspire to live quietly (*hēsychazein*, "tranquilly"), to mind your own affairs, and to work with your hands, as we directed you, so that you may behave properly toward outsiders and be dependent on no one" (NRSV).

OVERVIEW OF PAUL'S LETTERS

Chapter 7:
First Thessalonians

The story in Acts 17 of Paul and his fellow-travelers coming from Philippi to Thessalonica and then Paul going on to Athens fits with the details Paul mentions in 1 Thessalonians. They had difficulty in Philippi and came to Thessalonica (1 Thess 2:2). When they left Thessalonica, they traveled to Athens and, out of concern for their friends in Thessalonica because of persecution (1 Thess 1:5; 2:14; 3:1–3), they sent Timothy to visit them (1 Thess 2:17–3:3). Paul writes this letter to them upon the return of Timothy (1 Thess 3:6).

Other than Acts 17 there is no evidence for a Jewish community in Thessalonica during this period. The author of Acts depicts Paul preaching for three days arguing with the Jews in the synagogue "explaining and proving that it was necessary for the Messiah to suffer and to rise from the dead" (Acts 17:2–3 NRSV). Acts portrays the Jews as becoming jealous, forming a mob, and creating a riot in the city (Acts 17:5). Even when Paul left, they are supposed to have tracked Paul down in the next city and harassed him there (Acts 17:13). None of these fits with the context of Paul's letter to these gentiles who were convinced by Paul to abandon their pagan practices, accept the one God of Israel, and to follow Paul's example of the virtuous life in imitation of Jesus.

In this letter, Paul praises them for their actions and character which have been a great example in the region (1 Thess 1:3, 7–9; 2:14). Paul reinforces his claim that he and his collaborators spoke and acted appropriately during their time there (1 Thess 1:4–5; 2:3–12). The bulk of the letter contains Paul's moral exhortation for continued progress, warnings about misbehavior, and assurances about the future.

Letter Opening (1:1)

Paul identifies himself and his companions, Silvanus (Acts calls him Silas) and Timothy, as the senders of this letter (1:1). Rather than using the common term "church," I have chosen "assembly" to show that this is not a special term for a religious gathering but is a meeting which is gathered together for some purpose. Here we are to think of the group as residents of the city of Thessalonica. Most likely the group is a single household or a group that gathers at the house of the most prominent householder, the one with the largest space available. The householder "converted"—changed allegiance from whatever religious and philosophical practices he followed—and his family, extended family, and his circle of friends and clients, were also persuaded. The group would be gathered, perhaps after sharing a meal, to listen to the letter-carrier read Paul's letter to them and perhaps clarify questions.

The language of being "in God" or "in Christ" refers to the ancient concept of lineage and descent (1:1). The fictive kinship language imagines God as the Father, whose life-giving seed produces his son, Jesus, and in turn, the followers of Jesus are in God. Rather than a mystical relationship, it refers to the patrilineal descent in the same way a descendant could be said to have taken part in something an ancestor did because they existed within the seed of their ancestor.

The greeting within a letter was typically formulaic. I think the primary divine qualities here are the benevolence and the concord that God now gives to gentile peoples (see p. 81).

What the casual reader of the Bible might not realize is that there are many important ancient manuscripts that contain a variant for 1:1. These manuscripts include the common phrase from other letters of Paul: "from God our Father and the Lord Jesus Christ." The decision of text critics to exclude this phrase is based on the principle that it is more difficult to understand why any scribe would leave out the phrase than it is that scribes might include it. Also, more than one texttype has the shorter reading, meaning that the variant wasn't limited to one region. It may seem insignificant to discuss this, but I want to illustrate that scribes had a hand, so to speak, in not only copying but also adding text. Scribes might make simple corrections to spelling and grammar or make changes for the purpose of harmonizing similar texts. Some altered texts that might have misleading implications or that seemed not to fit with their theology. Even without textual evidence scholars might speculate that some biblical passages seem out of place or reflect a later period. I have made that judgment regarding certain texts of Paul's letters and have indicated those in my translations with brackets.

Gratitude for Progress (1:2–3)

Paul begins his letter on a positive note by praising the followers of Jesus in Thessalonica (1:2). Because of their great progress Paul can be grateful for the time and effort spent visiting Thessalonica in their initial visit. I take Paul's reference to prayer as something he and others did consistently but periodically as they gathered for a time of prayer, perhaps even as part of his own attendance at synagogue worship. Again, I substitute a different word for the theologically laden term "work." Their efforts in spreading the message combined telling others what they had discovered as well as being examples of the way of life they had learned (1:3). This effort was carried out faithfully, lovingly, and with hopefulness. Any difficulties they encountered were endured in the same manner as Jesus endured his own detractors.

Reception of Message at Initial Visit (1:4–10)

Paul retraces the initial encounter he had with this group. For Paul the crucial point of his understanding of the good news for the gentile peoples was the experience they had when they heard the message (1:5). Those who were persuaded to become adherents of the new way had remarkable demonstrations of God's presence in ways similar to what Jewish believers had experienced in Jerusalem.

These new adherents did not just change their thinking but became imitators of the way of life that was described and modeled for them (1:6). Paul notes that their decision brought them joy, an emotion that Stoics identified as a good or beneficial emotion (*eupatheia*). As they progressed in their own practice of this way of life, they began to become guides for people in nearby regions (1:7).

Although Paul may be said to apply attributes of the Stoic conception of the divine (whether Logos, Nature, or Pneuma), he firmly believes that the God to honor is the singular God known by the Jewish people (1:8) and now believed to be available to all people of the world—or, as Paul may have thought more restrictively, to the various ethnic groups that formed the Roman Empire. Paul's simple use of the article may be more emphatic, and so I have included the sense in italic as the *One* God. Paul spells this out by referencing the fact that conversion from one way of life to another involved not only their philosophical practice but their religious activity by no longer observing the ancestral and national gods

(1:9). Jews considered those images, a term more commonly translated as idols, as works crafted by human hands, inanimate objects, and therefore false constructions. The God of the Jews, however, was not portrayed as an image, whether carved in wood, sculpted in stone, or painted in frescoes. Instead, this is a God who is alive, active, and authentic.

Verse ten has characteristics I identify as possibly having been added by a later copyist. The apocalyptic tone comes from a later period when Christians have lost hope in being freed from religious and political persecution. The only thing left to do, in the apocalyptic worldview, is to wait for God to bring about the destruction of the ungodly.

Proper Conduct as Philosophical Guides (2:1–12)

Paul's language in this section is reminiscent of the perennial charge against philosophers for being nothing more than charlatans and parasites out for rewards and fame (2:2–6). As discussed above, those who pass themselves off as teachers of divine wisdom by their flowery speech and works of wonders could be proven to be fakes or charlatans. Sophists were those who would teach anything to anyone for a price regardless of whether it was considered to be true or in the best judgment. Flatterers and toadies would obsequiously follow around the wealthy patron hoping to ameliorate him and to get something for themselves. Parasites would glam onto the person of means and eagerly wait for the next handout. A household advisor was often perceived to be a salaried worker and not free to give the necessary criticism to a disciple or student.

The hortatory address Paul would give would be classed as protreptic speech. This is the exhortation to people to leave their old way of life, whether belonging to a different philosophical school or as one living an "unexamined life" led by popular opinions, false judgments, and perturbed by the passions, and to take up a new way of life. As a household philosophical guide, Paul also devoted himself, along with his companions, to manual labor, most likely positioning himself with the local guild of leatherworkers and tentmakers (2:9–10).

Paul's approach was not that of the harsh Cynic, a caricature of which is the annoying and obstreperous misfit, haranguing people and offering biting criticism. Paul characterizes his approach as applying gentle, mild critique (2:7; 11–12). His words were a gentle salve for the wounded soul rather than a cauterizing trauma. Whether like a "child-minder" or a parent, Paul's approach was to persuade his hearers to a way of life that brings about progress and transformation.

Becoming Followers Brought Adversity (2:13–16)

Paul is glad that the message he brought was received as a divine message (2:13). The way he and his companions conducted themselves convinced the Thessalonians that they were not charlatans just out to dupe people and to profit from them. The authenticity is confirmed by their experience of adversity in the same way the Judeans faced it (2:14).

To me the next few verses (2:15–16) seem like a later addition. This type of anti-Judaism comes from the experience of Jewish Christians who had been expelled from Jewish community life. Its most natural interpretation is that this is a reference to the destruction of Jerusalem in 70 CE.

Constancy in the Midst of Conflict (2:17–3:13)

Paul refers now to his thwarted plans to visit Thessalonica (2:17–18). Paul consistently considers the progress of those to whom he has introduced this new way of life not only his responsibility but also the source of his pride and reason for his joy (2:19–20). Put negatively, if people do not show improvement or they abandon the way of life, then Paul would have to consider his efforts to have been futile. He naturally wants to check on them and to know of their progress. Because he and his companions weren't able to make the trip together, they remain in Athens and send young Timothy alone (3:1–2).

Besides Timothy finding out about the health of the community in Thessalonica, he is to help them become more stable in their constancy and faithfulness by providing moral exhortation (3:3). Through philosophical exercises they would become better able to not be disturbed by circumstances such as violence against them or difficulties that may arise from being ostracized in the community (3:4).

Timothy returned and reported that the Thessalonians were remaining constant in their practice, were committed to each other in a loving friendship, and showed concern for the work of Paul and his companions (3:6). Paul expressed his utter joy at the report and strongly emphasized their desire to make the trip to visit the adherents in Thessalonica (3:7–11).

The doxological prayer of 3:12–13 seems to me to have the characteristics of a later addition. It interrupts the flow of the letter; the wording is florid, exaggerated, and repetitive, and it focuses on apocalyptic themes.

Personal Character & Progress (4:1–8)

Paul turns his attention to philosophical paraenesis: praise for constancy in moral progress and an exhortation to an even greater progress (4:1). As philosophical guides, Paul and his companions presented themselves as models for imitation because they were imitators of those qualities of Jesus that brought about his apotheosis or divinization after his noble death. The metaphor in literal terms is walking, but it is too ambiguous in English. It refers to the manner of life and conduct. It is not the following of moral precepts, though the immature may need that instruction (4:2). Learning to make proper moral judgments about the value of things and actions leads to a consistent manner of life.

The philosophical theme here is self-mastery, the rational control of the passions. One of the strongest biological urges is for sexual gratification. If a person gains mastery in this area, then that person will be strong-willed enough to overcome other desires that will disturb one's disposition (4:3–6). Not only does one hurt oneself when thinking pleasure will be beneficial, but self-centered actions can harm others. In social terms proper behavior takes place within areas of purity and propriety, while wrong actions take place outside of those boundaries and are contrasted as impure or dirty and cause disgust. Those who seek to experience the blessing of the One, True and Living God need to live in purity (4:7–8). While Paul and his fellow Jews observe Torah in order not to trespass the boundaries of what is pure, Paul expects the gentile adherents to attain self-mastery, which brings about the development of one's own self and proper attitudes and behaviors towards others.

Community & Social Values (4:9–12)

A crucial aspect of moral progress and the development of character is the community of friendship. Like-minded people with familial ties, whether a fictive kinship or a real family within a household, bring an accountability through mutual frank criticism and admonishment but also encouragement and praise based on altruistic concerns for the betterment of others.

Paul praises the Thessalonians for exhibiting this loving friendship within their own group and with other groups in the surrounding region (4:9–10). He follows his praise with encouragement to a greater level of care for others. The intended outcome for the practice of self-mastery within a community of friendship is that humans achieve the divine state of tranquility (4:11). Within Greek thought the gods are characterized by tranquility. To be divine is to be unperturbed by needs and passions, without fear, and free from dependence on anything external to themselves.

The philosophical life is not one lived in isolation either by one's self or in a segregated community. It is also important to be active in society and to be reputable in one's relationships (4:11–12). Most often the livelihood of a householder was a part of one's house. Therefore, how one does business reflects on the household and its values. To provide for oneself is to enhance one's self-sufficiency. By this is meant that the person is not dependent for one's peace of mind on external factors. To the degree that one can provide for the common necessities of life, then that person and those within the household, such as family members and clients, are not disturbed by a lack of sustenance and security.

Overcoming the Grief of Death (4:13–18)

Just as important as overcoming the debilitating passion of sexual desire, which Paul has just talked about, is overcoming the despondency of grief. And one of the most difficult sources of grief can be the loss felt over the death of a loved one (4:13). For Paul the way to avoid the pain of grief is to be reminded of the Pharisee's belief in resurrection. In the ancient world the dead were described euphemistically as being asleep (4:14). Corpses were arranged together like a dormitory of sleeping people. Their souls were thought to exist in the shadowy underworld.

Paul is teaching these gentiles about the prophetic Day of Yahweh (4:15–17). We are easily confused by Paul's use of the Greek word *kyrios* to mean lord or master and the use of that word also, in a different context, to translate the Hebrew *adonai*, which was used in place of the sacred name, which we write as Yahweh. Paul is clear when he writes that it is God who will lead the procession. In 5:1 Paul uses the technical expression "Day of the Lord" or "Day of Yahweh." The image is of Yahweh coming in battle to reclaim what is his. In his train follows those who have died. Their corpses are raised from their graves and are joined with those who are still alive to be with God in heaven. Jesus being raised from the dead in Greek terms was an apotheosis, but in Hebrew terms it was a preemptive resurrection. Paul expects this doctrine to be a source of hope and a means of mitigating grief (4:18).

Living in the Light in Dark Times (5:1–11)

Paul continues to instruct his gentile audience about the Jewish belief in the Day of the Lord when Yahweh comes to Zion (5:1–2). He warns them to remain vigilant rather than relax their attention to their moral development. Paul uses metaphors of the unexpectedness of the thief or of a pregnant woman suddenly going into labor to illustrate the need to be constant (5:2–3). He switches to the metaphor of light in the day and darkness as night (5:4–5). The night time is characterized by people being unconscious because they are sleeping or because they are intoxicated (5:6–7). One must be thoroughly protected in the same way that a soldier would wear a helmet and a chest guard (5:8). No matter if a person has already died or remains living, the outcome will be the same. The outcome is not the cataclysm of an apocalyptic war but to be alive with Jesus (5:9–10).

The result of this eschatological lesson of impending doom is not that the Thessalonians should hide together and wait out the remaining days. They are to be providing mutual encouragement to live lives of constancy (5:11). This topic began with a concern about grief and its moral consequences. Paul returns to the topic of mutual moral exhortation and philosophical guidance. Not only are they to maintain their level of growth but be built up; they are to continue to make progress in the structuring of their character.

Culminating Paraenesis (5:12–22)

Paul's paraenesis—his moral advice and exhortation—is not just an appended section to the main content of his letter but the culmination of the topics of the letter. He has responded to some issues on his mind and

First Thessalonians   105

to remind them about their relationship with him. Paul now focuses his attention on what he thinks they need to hear.

Paul's first concern here is the relationship of the household assembly with those who function as philosophical guides (5:12–13). They might be older people but ones notable for their development in the philosophical life. Paul's language seems to imply that these are older people who deserve respect and who are characterized as an older person growing weary with their effort (5:13). The term used to refer to these leaders who have oversight (the participle form of the verb *proistēmi*, which I translate as "director,") is one that can refer to the leader of a philosophical school, whether, for example, the Peripatetic, Athenion (Athenaeus, *Deipn.* 5.47.35), or the associates of Epicurus (Sextus Empiricus, *Math.* 8.177.6).

Paul characterizes the effort as more than just work or labor. It is an extreme effort that can be tiring and wearying (5:12). Paul mentions the intense striving carried out by people in various household assemblies (Rom 6:6, 12). In 1 Tim the language is similar: "Let the elders who *rule* (*proestōtes*, provide philosophical direction) well be considered worthy of double honor, especially those who *labor* in preaching and teaching" (1 Tim 5:17 NRSV).

In Epicurus's *Letter to Menoeceus*, he contrasts the young and the old in connection with the philosophical life.

> Let no one be slow to seek wisdom when he is young nor weary in the search thereof when he is grown old. For no age is too early or too late for the health of the soul. And to say that the season for studying philosophy has not yet come, or that it is past and gone, is like saying that the season for happiness is not yet or that it is now no more. Therefore, both old and young ought to seek wisdom, the former in order that, as age comes over him, he may be young in good things because of the grace of what has been, and the latter in order that, while he is young, he may at the same time be old, because he has no fear of the things which are to come (Diogenes Laertius, *Lives* 10.122 [Epicurus]).[216]

Similarly, Paul wants the younger people to show deference to the older and wiser members of the household assembly. Their effort to provide

---

[216] Diogenes Laertius, *Lives of Eminent Philosophers, Volume 2: Books 6-10*, 649.

philosophical direction is a tiring work but beneficial to the less mature. Coincidentally, Epicurus is writing about the fear of the future, which has also been Paul's concern in the preceding section.

There are two sides to the practice of moral exhortation. The positive side praises a person and encourages continued good practice. The negative side is called blame, as in warning, rebuke, admonishment, and censure for bad behavior. This often requires frank criticism (*parrēsia*), which can either be mild, with minor offenses, or harsh, with prolonged and recalcitrant behavior. In this context Paul is specifically referring to the admonishment that comes from a superior to an inferior (5:14).

Since Paul frames the relationship of the household assembly in terms of siblings and uses the expression *philadelphia* "brother love" (4:9), it is helpful to draw comparisons to Plutarch's work "On Brotherly Love." He discusses the case in which a brother has done wrong, and the other brother should

> ... turn to him and rebuke him somewhat sharply, pointing out with all frankness his errors of commission and of omission. For one should neither give free rein to brothers, nor, again, should one trample on them when they are at fault (for the latter is the act of one who gloats over the sinner, the former that of one who aids and abets him), but should apply his admonition as one who cares for his brother and grieves with him (Plutarch, *Frat. amor.* 483.B.3).[217]

Paul reiterates showing respect for one's philosophical guide (5:13). As elsewhere, I translate the usual term for love within the context of the social structure of friendship. The term for "friend" in Greek means "a loved one." The terms for love are often synonymous, though early Christian texts more often use the *agapē* terminology, which I interpret as a self-sacrificial love.

Paul finishes his remarks about the relationship with superiors with an instruction regarding peace (5:13). We may surmise that he is urging

---

[217] Plutarch, *Moralia, Volume 6: Can Virtue Be Taught? On Moral Virtue. On the Control of Anger. On Tranquility of Mind. On Brotherly Love. On Affection for Offspring. Whether Vice Be Sufficient to Cause Unhappiness. Whether the Affections of the Soul are Worse Than Those of the Body. Concerning Talkativeness. On Being a Busybody.* trans. W. C. Helmbold, Loeb Classical Library 337 (Cambridge, MA: Harvard University Press, 1939), 275.

the neophytes and the more mature guides to get along with each other and not cause conflicts.

Paul gives an example of the types of behaviors that require action. In the first example he repeats the need for admonition. The type of behavior is disorderly (*ataktos*) (5:14). Rather than assume this means what we think of when we use the English word disorderly, we need to look at how the word is used in moral contexts. If we look at its usage in a text like Plutarch's *On Moral Virtue*, we find that the quality of disorderliness, in Platonic terms, is opposed to the order of the intelligent and rational part of the soul, "whose natural duty it is to govern and rule the individual." The other part is "the passionate and irrational, the variable and disorderly (*atakton*), which has need of a director" (Plutarch, *Virt. mor.* 442.A.5).[218] Plutarch describes in more detail the control of disorderliness.

> This, then, is the natural task of practical reason: to eliminate both the defects and the excesses of the passions. For wherever, through infirmity and weakness, or fear and hesitation, the impulsion yields too soon and prematurely forsakes the good, there practical reason comes on the scene to incite and kindle the impulsion; and where, again, the impulsion is borne beyond proper bounds, flowing powerfully and in disorder (*ataktos*), there practical reason removes its violence and checks it. And thus by limiting the movement of the passions reason implants in the irrational the moral virtues, which are means between deficiency and excess (Plutarch, *Vir. mor.* 444.C.6).[219]

Paul does not seem to refer to disorderly conduct in the sense of trespassing social codes of behavior. It is the frame of mind which is not in keeping with rational thought. The reasoning mind makes consistent proper judgments about the good.

Paul uses another rare term to describe the less mature people in the household assembly. This term (*oligopsychos*), which I've translated "without a fully developed moral capacity" seems to refer to people with a diminished capacity for rational thought (5:14). They have not yet

---

[218] Plutarch, *Moralia, Volume 6*, 27.
[219] Plutarch, *Moralia, Volume 6*, 39.

developed a strong mind for making good judgments about virtue and vice. They need to be coaxed toward consistent thought.

The third phrase of this series calls on people to provide care, support, or assistance for those who have a weakness in their character (5:14). The medical analogy would be that a person's constitution is compromised and needs to be brought back to health. The therapy needed is to provide the care and support required in order for the patient to be brought back to a state of healthiness. In the same way, the member of the household assembly, who has had difficulty with some form of vice, needs supportive attention to overcome the negative impulses.

A fourth phrase in the series seems to encompass the previous injunctions (5:14). In any of these ways in which someone has not become mature and fully developed in their thinking and moral capacity, they should be shown patience. They bring change about by consistent behavior over time in order for a person's way of thinking to adapt. Paul says that treating someone bad—we might think of getting angry with the person or shaming them—is not an effective way to bring about change (5:15).

The type of paraenesis Paul continues with in 5:16–22 is something often called "miscellaneous," but it is what scholars call *gnomai* in Greek and *sententiae* in Latin. These brief maxims touch on a variety of topics beginning with joy. In several other places Paul also enjoins his readers to adopt a joyful attitude and be glad (2 Cor 13:11; Phil 2:18; 3:1; 4:4). To be in a state of continuous joy requires a person to achieve a level of mental discipline in which circumstances do not disturb one's equilibrium. Just as the first maxim is maintained always, so the second one is to be done ceaselessly. It is by a constant recognition of God's providence that one can experience continuous joy. Third, Paul enjoins the members of the household assembly to be grateful in every circumstance of life. God wants this for people, and the more they carry out these three maxims the happier a person will be in life.

Since the verb in 5:19 is most often used for quenching or extinguishing fire, it is important to remember that *pneuma* is perceived as being an element composed of both air and fire. This *pneuma* pervades all and is the active force in the world. The *pneuma* is God's life-giving power, and that fiery breath should not be diminished or repressed in the human person.

Perhaps in 5:20 Paul has in mind the type of prophecies he has mentioned which should remind a person not to grieve the death of loved ones or to be complacent about one's manner of life.

In 5:20–21 Paul includes the typical contrast between virtue and vice. Every thought and decision must be examined. What is good and virtuous must be embraced (*katechō*). Every form of evil and vice must be shunned (*apechō*).

Closing (5:23–28)

Paul closes this letter in the usual way. He gives a blessing for their continued purity (5:23). He addresses his readers with a request for their prayers for him and his companions (5:25), wishes for them to greet each other affectionately (5:26), and that the letter is read to all the household assembly (5:27). Paul concludes with a final benediction (5:28).

Chapter 8:
Galatians

It seems unnecessarily cumbersome to think Paul wrote a letter to a region or province about which we have no information in Acts at all. That is the conclusion of those that propose Paul wrote to a region of northern Asia Minor where people could be called ethnically Galatian. There's little reason to suggest Paul couldn't have been addressing himself to followers of Jesus who inhabited cities in central Anatolia like Derbe and Lystra. In that case, the Jerusalem council of Acts 15 would describe the same event as Paul talks about.

The Galatians would have heard about Paul's activities against the Jesus movement (1:13–14). Perhaps they also heard about Paul's change of heart that Paul was now a follower of Jesus and a promoter of the movement. When he first visited the area, the people in these cities in the Galatian region were, what we might call, pagans. It's fair to assume that native people to this region of central Anatolia were worshippers of Cybele, the mother goddess. When Paul was there, he felt like they treated him well despite his physical injury. They acted as though they were blind to his condition, perhaps because they were accustomed to men who had disfigured genitals: It was a ritual practice for male worshippers of Cybele to castrate themselves. They responded to Paul's protreptic speeches and became followers of Jesus.

Since his visit he has learned that a rival group of Judaizing missionaries have moved into the Galatian region. They are being successful in persuading these gentile followers of Jesus to become full proselytes to Judaism. This means, in effect, becoming Judean citizens who, to be protected and blessed by God's covenant relationship with the Israelite people, will learn how to follow Torah, take part in synagogue worship, fulfill their obligations to the Temple in Jerusalem, and for the males to become circumcised. Paul seeks in this letter to reinforce his teaching that gentiles need not become Judeans to live as people in covenant with the One, True, and Living God. In fact, to become circumcised would have a negative effect in that it would mean ignoring what the death of Christ has achieved for the gentiles.

Letter Opening (1:1–5)

Despite the common mistake of mirror-reading—assuming that a person makes a claim about something because others claim the opposite—it seems like Paul quickly wants to address a major concern. Paul claims an authority and authenticity for the message he has brought to gentiles. His authority and authenticity stem from his direct encounter and experience of Jesus and not second-hand from anyone else, whatever authority they might be understood to have (1:1). Paul names himself as God's envoy (*apostolos*), the messenger appointed and given the task of traveling throughout the realm to announce this favorable decree to all the inhabitants. Paul includes all of his companions as the senders of this letter (1:2).

The naming of the recipients of this letter is unique because it is addressed to the various household assemblies existing in a province in eastern Asia Minor (1:2). Paul must be able to include these various cities because of a common experience. These assemblies are connected by their common culture. Paul visited these cities, and the Judaizing group has come to the same group of people in that area.

Paul includes his usual form of greeting (1:3). I suggest that a later editor has added to Paul's mention of Jesus. The effect of the addition is its wordiness, floridness, and apocalyptic context. The generation of believers in the late first century was experiencing a heightened opposition from the Romans and had a greater concern for their own insularity and purity as regards the dominant culture (1:4). Within that context there is a greater focus on Jewish eschatology and the end of the age (1:5).

Distortion & Desertion in Galatia (1:6–12)

Paul begins the body of his letter to the household assemblies in the cities of Galatia with admonishment. Usually a letter will begin with some praise. Here, Paul starts with critique. Because Paul later will connect their actions with the work of magic (3:1), this expression of amazement (1:6) may also be put into the context of wonderment.

That some of his followers are being talked into becoming full-fledged Judeans through circumcision has apparently become a major concern of Paul. It is not that in doing so they would be abandoning God. They would be leaving or deserting Paul. Jewish proselytes and God-fearers worshipped the same God as Paul is preaching, though to ignore or abandon his message and undergo circumcision would be an affront to Christ. Paul had traveled north to several cities in this part of central Anatolia, established groups among them, and soon after leaving is finding out that they are going against what he taught them. Rather than being communities marked by peaceful comradery, these visitors are distorting his message and disturbing the development of the individual members of the households (1:7). Paul puts his assessment of the situation in the strongest of terms. Not even the appearance of an angel with a different message than his should be accepted (1:8). Anyone who contradicts the terms of his message should suffer the consequences of a curse. Perhaps Paul is again referring to the magical practice of putting a curse on someone. Within the context of Jewish practice, he may simply express his desire for the readers—and for God—to treat them as accursed (1:8–9). These Judaizing interlopers have wanted these pagan gentiles to become proselytes to experience God's blessing rather than God's curse. Paul turns that around and may be saying that they themselves should be the ones to experience God's curse.

It would seem that Paul assumes or knows that part of the argument of the Judaizers is that he is not authoritative as an apostle who had direct connections with Jesus and, therefore, he is subordinate to the message and requirements coming directly from the apostolic authority in Jerusalem (1:12). Paul seems also to be sensitive to the typical accusation that someone is acting inappropriately for personal gain by promoting a course of action that would especially please people (1:10). Paul would have objected strenuously to any of these typical terms used against an opponent: sophist, charlatan, toady, parasite, or a flatterer.

Paul will reinforce his claim that he has apostolic authority because he received direct insight from Jesus as to the good news to impart to the gentile peoples. Paul's point in verse 12 is not that he had an epiphany of Jesus, but that he had an epiphany of the message which he received from Jesus. That he had been vehemently opposed to the Jesus movement will be presented as an argument that his transformation was genuine.

Circumstances of Calling (1:13–24)

To convince the Galatians that they should not believe what the Judaizers are saying about him, Paul rehearses his story of how he went from being an opponent of the Jesus movement to be a proponent. The dramatic change in his way of life supports his contention that something powerful must have happened.

Whatever we make of Paul's description of his former life and the change that came about, there is nothing here to support the idea that Paul is describing anything like a conversion experience. There is no change from one religion to another or even from one philosophical school to another. Paul was already a Hellenized Jew who interpreted his Judaism in terms of Stoic practices. The only change is that he came to believe that Jesus experienced apotheosis, which meant that he was God's teacher of wisdom. That gentiles, who accepted the message that the one, true, and living God was now their God because of the faithfulness of Jesus in his death, experienced signs of God's presence and blessing convinced Paul that gentiles throughout the Roman Empire needed to hear this message. Because of his unique relationship with gentiles, Paul was just the right person to travel to Roman cities, make connections with households, function as a philosophical guide, and work to establish a network of friendship to help them make progress in their development.

Paul reminds them of his story. He juxtaposes his former way of life in Judaism with his present way of life in Judaism. Not that the former way of life was Judaism and now it's Christianity. That's not at all what he says. As an arm of the Judean administration in Jerusalem, Paul vociferously and violently went after this Jesus movement among Jews in Judea and beyond (1:13–14). We may ask why Jews in the city of Jerusalem and in Judea would have been so antagonistic toward the Jesus movement. Paul is not clear about that at all, and neither is Luke in the book of Acts. I suspect it had something to do with the Jesus movement being connected to the northern area of the Galilee. These northerners were diminishing the central role of Jerusalem, the Temple, and the ruling body in Jerusalem. They should allow nothing to minimize the superiority and centrality of Jerusalem, its Temple, and its leadership.

Paul's argument here is that the message he brings and his authority for bringing it results from a direct commissioning from God (1:15–17). After all, that's what it would take to change someone so drastically. However, if Luke's narrative in Acts can be trusted, Paul was to some extent in contact with the disciples from the early days of the Jesus movement in Jerusalem. Luke connects Paul's first contact with the outgrowth of the Hellenistic Jews like Stephen (Acts 7:58–8:3). Paul may have been persuaded by Stephen. Based on what Paul describes here in Galatians, we could even imagine Paul to have had a similar experience as Lucian describes his character in his work Nigrinus, who was so moved by the protreptic speech of Nigrinus that it opened his eyes and filled him with joy (see p. 40). It is easy for us to assume Paul is talking about the same experience as Luke describes (Acts 9:1–9). However, whenever the Greek word "to reveal" (*apokalyptō*) functions as a transitive verb, the object is in the dative case ("to reveal to" 1 Cor 2:10; 14:30; Eph 3:5; Phil 3:15) or with the preposition *eis* ("to reveal unto" Rom 8:18) and not with the preposition *en* as it is here. What Paul describes here is that God chose Paul to disclose the good news to the gentiles and for them to see the outcome of the message in Paul. Yet, Paul says in 1 Cor 9:1 that he "saw Jesus our Lord." This reference coincides with what he describes later in 1 Cor 15:8 when he lists himself as the last one that Jesus "was seen by." Paul does not, however, provide us more detail about the circumstances of seeing Jesus.

The main point Paul is trying to make is that when he came to realize he needed to spread the news of what the death of Jesus meant for the gentile peoples, he did not even discuss it with anyone let alone go to Jerusalem to talk it over with the apostles (1:16–17). That Paul says he returned to Damascus must imply that he was in Damascus before leaving, which would coincide with Luke's narrative. However, Luke includes nothing about Paul going to Arabia (1:17). It remains a mystery what Paul might refer to. Perhaps he went to some locale within the region of the Nabatean kingdom. There was a very short distance between Damascus and the area called Arabia. Some suggest Paul traveled all the way to Mt. Sinai in the south because he draws a parallel to Mt. Sinai later in Galatians. Others think Paul traveled across Arabia to Babylon where there was a large concentration of Jews in the eastern region. We can't even be certain about the time frame Paul gives us (1:18). Are the three years he mentions inclusive of his visit to Arabia and

Damascus or are they the time Paul spent after he returned to Damascus? The text is unclear.

Paul intends to impress his readers that there was such a long period before he traveled to Jerusalem. When he left Jerusalem, he was on his way to Damascus to target Jews who were not being loyal to the leadership of Jerusalem. Paul now returns to Jerusalem to talk to the main leader, whom Paul refers to by his Aramaic name, Cephas. We can only assume that Cephas represented the more Judaizing faction in the Jesus movement. That's not to say—and this is important—that Peter, James, and others were not also Hellenistic Jews in the sense that for them Judaism was interpreted and practiced within the framework of Greco-Roman moral philosophy. Not only was Paul's trip to Jerusalem a long time coming, but it was also only about a fortnight. Paul adds that James was the only other person he met (1:19).

What Paul doesn't explicitly mention is whether he was alone or with anyone else. In the Acts account (Acts 9:23–29)—and told from Paul's perspective in 2 Cor 11:32–33—Paul makes a narrow escape from Damascus and tries to unite with the disciples in Jerusalem. According to Luke, it is Barnabas who takes Paul under his wing, brings him to the apostles, and explains the message that Paul has been spreading. Paul tries to talk with Hellenistic Jews, but they seem to be hostile to Paul (Acts 9:29).

Calling Endorsed in Jerusalem (2:1–10)

Before ever meeting with the apostles in Jerusalem, Paul writes that he spent fourteen years in his first expeditionary trip to Cyprus, to central Anatolia (1:21), and back again to Antioch (Gal 2:2; Acts 13:1–14:28). It was during this time that he first brought his message to those in the Roman province of Galatia. The initial catalyst for his life's purpose was an epiphany of Jesus, a revelation that convinced him that Jesus had been raised from the dead—he had experienced apotheosis (2:2). The outcome of his noble death was that God was now including the gentile peoples and overlooking their sins. Because of this he felt called to share this news with the inhabitants of the Roman provinces, the various ethnic groups of people comprising nations other than the nation of Judea.

According to Luke in the book of Acts, Paul had been living and teaching in Antioch for some time after his return from his tour of Anatolian cities (Acts 14:28). During this time a faction from Judea arrived in Antioch and brought a more nationalistic approach to the message about the inclusion of the gentiles: circumcision was a requirement. A delegation was chosen and sent to talk to the leading men of the Jesus movement in Jerusalem. The Acts account only mentions Paul and Barnabas by name. Along with them were "some others" (Acts 15:2). Paul singles out Titus as one of those who accompanied him to Jerusalem (2:1).

Our knowledge of Titus is limited by the fact that he is never mentioned by name in the book of Acts. In addition, there is a great deal of conjecture passed along in literature about Titus: he was from Crete; he was educated in philosophy and poetry; he was somehow related to Luke; he and Timothy were the same person. All or none of that may be true. What we know is that Titus was an uncircumcised Greek man, a convert to a worshipper of the one God and a follower of Jesus, and an important asset to Paul in his life's work.

The account in Acts portrays Paul as attending a public conference with the leading authorities in the Jesus movement in Jerusalem (Acts 15:2–3). Paul would seem to downplay that for his argument that he is an independent and authoritative representative of the movement to bring the message of Jesus to the gentile peoples. His evidence for the acceptance of his message is that Titus was not compelled to be circumcised (2:3). He specifies that Titus was not just a part of the delegation, but that Titus was present, "alongside of" (*syn*), him.

Paul's description of the events preceding the meeting match well the narrative in Acts 15. The attempt by the Judaizing group to persuade gentiles to be circumcised is couched in terms of espionage (2:4). Paul makes it a matter of protecting freedom from those who would take it away. Luke uses similar language in his speech of Peter to the council (Acts 15:7–11). He asks, "Now therefore why are you putting God to the test by placing on the neck of the disciples a yoke that neither our ancestors nor we have been able to bear?" (Acts 15:10 NRSV).[220] The freedom here is not the freedom of Christianity over Judaism as in the supercessionism model but that individuals from the gentile peoples

---

[220] For a brief discussion see page 184.

need not become full-fledged citizens of Judea to have the forgiveness and blessing of the living God.

For what it's worth, Paul continues, he had a complete agreement from the Jerusalem authorities (2:6–8). A dual-pronged mission was accepted. Paul and Barnabas would spread the message to the gentile peoples while James, Cephas, and John would be responsible for those of the Judean nation (2:9). In Paul's diatribe with Cephas in 2:14–21 he will spell out the distinction in the message between the two. Paul purports that they only asked them to encourage the Jewish practice of charity: "remember the poor" (2:10). The Acts account includes issues of purity relating to sacrifices to images, sexual immorality, and dietary rules regarding eating meat that has not been properly prepared and drained of blood (Acts 15:20; 28–29).

Diatribe against Cephas in Antioch (2:11–21)

According to Paul, after the Jerusalem council, Peter—he calls him Cephas—came to Antioch (2:11). He describes a situation in which Peter is having meals with gentiles. Some people come to visit, whom Paul understands to be from James and representing a pro-circumcision faction, what I refer to as Judaizers. Peter loses his nerve and stops joining the gentile group for meals (2:12). Other Jewish believers in Antioch, even Barnabas, go along with Peter (2:13). This is the context for Paul inserting in his letter a diatribe with Peter representing an inconsistent person. I take the censure of 2:14–21 as the whole of Paul's speech; not just verse 14, as translations seem to show.

Paul's diatribe opens with a rhetorical question that points out Peter's character as inconsistent (2:14). When Paul refers to gentiles in this context, he is using the term as a trope. A Jewish term of derision for gentiles is a "sinner." Here Paul typifies a gentile as someone who is ethically inconsistent (2:15). By characterizing Peter as a Jew in this diatribe, he parallels his usage of the Jewish teacher who is his imaginary interlocuter in the diatribe in Rom 2:17. Paul points out the paradox of someone who advocates something but acts oppositely. Peter's actions are inconsistent because his actions are siding with those who want gentiles to be like Jews, but he is acting like a hypocrite and being inconsistent like the worst sort of person.

Paul points out that he and Peter are born as Jews/Judeans and thus should have by nature a propensity to do right (2:15). They would regard the nature of gentiles as ones prone to sinfulness. However, what they both have realized is that being God's covenant people, having God's laws, and making sacrifices for trespasses has not always meant that they have been pleasing to God and have maintained God's blessing (2:16). What they believe is that the faithfulness of Jesus Christ through his endurance of suffering and execution has made available God's forgiveness and blessing, which is demonstrated by Jesus's resurrection and the signs of the presence of God's Holy Spirit. Jews remain God's covenant people, but it doesn't prevent God's judgment, which is clear in the Roman occupation of Judea.

Paul's argument is that those who have experienced the presence of God's Spirit have become an extension of Jesus as the son of God. Through this participation they have retroactively undergone the experience of Christ being crucified, dying, and having sharing in the resurrection life of Jesus. Because death releases a person from contractual obligations, those Jews who have experienced God's Spirit by being followers of Jesus are no longer dependent on law-keeping for their standing before God but share in a new life as participants in the extension of Christ's divine sonship blessing (2:19).

Paul addresses his interlocuter in verse 17. Does Peter's inconsistent behavior mean that Christ causes it? Paul responds with the typical diatribe response, "No way" (*mē genoito*), just as he does in his letter to the Romans. When we act inconsistently, we make ourselves into transgressors blessing (2:18).

The concept of participation in Christ has to do with the ancient idea that a man has present within his seed all of his descendants. The actions of an ancestor can be thought to have also been done by a descendant through their participation in that ancestor. When a person receives God's Spirit by joining with Jesus, they share in the generative force of the divine life. Paul can say that his life force is not his own, but that it is the life force of the son of God blessing (2:20). Jesus acted benevolently in the sacrifice of his life, and that faithfulness was rewarded by resurrection through which Jesus was known to be God's Son. If he were now to advocate that the way for gentiles to be right before God was by the keeping of Torah through circumcision, then the result would be rejecting the benefit of the death of Christ blessing (2:21).

Invective against Galatians: Inconsistency (3:1–7)

Paul continues the theme of inconsistency. He begins this section of admonishment by addressing them with an exclamation about their ignorance blessing (3:1). It's the same expression used by Luke in his story of Jesus walking with his disciples to Emmaus (Luke 24:25). Rather than concluding that Paul must have known Luke's Gospel, it is more probable that the expression "Oh foolish" (*ō anoētoi*; I render this "Oh senseless") derives from the usage in Aesop's *Fables*.[221]

Paul next uses language suggestive of the use of magic, perhaps related to the practice of putting someone under a spell by giving them the "evil eye."[222] Paul would have been familiar with Anatolian folklore involving Cybele, for example.[223] Instead of receiving a curse, Paul had blessed them with his vivid portrayal of Jesus's crucifixion. He puts a rhetorical question to them in 3:2. What brought about the indications of God's presence spreading throughout the world? Did anyone experience signs and wonders after a circumcision? No, it was when they heard Paul telling them about what Jesus had done and that God was the God of all nations.

Paul adds that it's not only their beginning that proves his point but also their progress in their moral development toward maturity. The issue here is not that of the Reformation focus on works vs. faith. The presence of God's Spirit initiated their beginning; it had to do with *pneuma*. Their progress toward completion (*epiteleō*), the *telos* of the philosophical life, would not be accomplished by their flesh, by which Paul means the act of circumcision (3:3–4).

Paul puts the same question to the Galatians another way. Did God provide God's Spirit to you and perform wonders at your circumcision or was it when you responded with allegiance to the message (3:5)? A

---

[221] It appears in Fable 40 and 128. E. Chambry, *Aesopi fabulae*, Paris: Les Belles Lettres, 1:1925; 2:1926: 532–533, 536–538, 545–546, 556–557, 561, 564–565. See Steve Reece, "'Aesop', 'Q' and 'Luke'," *New Testament Studies* 62, no. 03 (2016). The expression also occurs in Philo, *On Dreams*, 2.181.2 and Plutarch, *Apophthegmata Laconica*, 224.E.7.

[222] Susan Eastman, "The Evil Eye and the Curse of the Law: Galatians 3.1 Revisited," *Journal for the Study of the New Testament* 24, no. 83 (2002).

[223] Birgitte Bøgh, "The Phrygian Background of Kybele," *Numen: International Review for the History of Religions* 54, no. 3 (2007).

comparison proves the point and concludes Paul's argument. In the same way that Abraham showed his faithfulness and was considered to be upright (Gen 15:6), so also are those who act faithfully and consistently the descendants of Abraham (3:6–7).

Abraham and the Gentile Peoples (3:8–14)

Paul explains to his gentile audience, based on the Greek Bible, how they are descendants of Abraham (3:8–9). The scripture predicted what was now happening among the gentile peoples (Gen 12:3). The promise to Abraham was that all the nations, every ethnic group, would be blessed because they originate in the seed of Abraham—they are also his descendants—and they participate in Christ whose faithfulness was also recognized by God by raising him from the dead (3:9).

Paul states further that those gentiles who attempt to be righteous before God by becoming circumcised to keep Torah are also under the curse for not doing all of it (3:10). He quotes from Deut 27:26 in the Greek Bible that says that the requirement is to continue to practice all the law's commandments, otherwise there is a curse. One may object that the Hebrew Bible does not include this implication to always keep everything in Torah, but Paul seems to make use of a Greek translation with the text that has come down to us. Paul's conclusion is that gentiles should not seek to be made upright by performing circumcision because of scripture that emphasizes faithfulness (3:10). The Hab 2:4 text says that the upright people are those who live their lives based on faithfulness. Practicing circumcision is not an aspect of living faithfully (3:12).

Instead, Paul creates an argument that says gentiles are not cursed by Torah because Christ was cursed for our benefit by undergoing crucifixion (3:13). The logic of Paul's thought starts with the experience of phenomena by gentiles associated with the spread of God's presence throughout the world through God's Pneuma, to the Pneuma of Christ raised from the dead by God because of Christ's faithfulness, and ultimately to Jesus being a Jew and a direct descendant of Abraham. Paul turns it around to go from Abraham's blessing, to Jesus, to those who receive the Pneuma because of the faithfulness of Christ (3:14).

Promise to Abraham Not Superseded by Law (3:15–18)

Paul creates another argument, one that turns on the multiple meanings of the Greek term *diathēkē*, "a covenant, testament, or will." The principle is that when any agreement, such as a will, is made there can be no changes made to it or a revocation of one's willingness to abide by it (3:15). The originating agreement was the promise made to Abraham regarding his seed (3:16). Paul takes advantage of the fact that the term is in the singular even though the term is a collective noun. Paul interprets this to refer to Christ. Paul concludes that Torah came much later and could not cancel the Abrahamic covenant with its promise to his seed (3:17). The inheritance, which I translate with the term "patrimony" to emphasize the concept of the seed of the male, is a promise that cannot be changed or canceled by the requirements of Torah.

Diatribe on the Benefits of God's Moral Code (3:19–25)

Paul expects an objection by using the style of the diatribe. The context would suggest we are to imagine Paul responding to questions from a Jewish person.[224] The interlocuter asks, if God's promise was secured through a covenant, then why did God give the Israelites the Torah (3:19)? Paul's response has given scribes a problem, since there are several differing variants in the textual tradition. Text critics reason from concluding that scribes would have been trying to soften Paul's language about transgressions. My theory is that scribes would have been more anti-Jewish and taking the position that Paul has done away with the Jewish law. The reading of Papyrus 46 seems to suffer from a case of haplography. I reconstruct the exemplar of P46 in this way.

ti oun o nomos
tōn praxeōn
charin etethē
achris ou elthē

Because of the similar endings in lines three and four, the scribe's eye dropped to line four and skipped line three. At some point *praxeōn*

---

[224] Paul used Peter as his interlocuter in chapter two. In Rom 2:17 Paul identifies his imaginary interlocuter as a caricature of a Jewish teacher who is boastful but lacks consistency.

("deeds") was changed to *parabaseōn* ("transgressions"). The interpretation in that case would be like the argument of the book of Hebrews in that the Law did not have the capability of preventing trespasses. The reason for the Law, as I reconstruct the text, is that it provided people with precepts for ethical behavior. This would be considered an elementary stage of moral development before one reaches that faculty for judgment about right and wrong actions based on a perception of the value of what is good and what is bad.

The traditional reading of verse 19 does not seem to fit Paul's recognition that the Law was put into force by angels (3:20). The rest of the context continues to be clouded by the choice of the language of enslavement and inferiority. We will see that there is a more consistent reading of this argument of Paul.

Paul anticipates another objection by his Jewish imaginary interlocuter. Now he asks if Torah opposes the promises (3:21). Paul responds with his usual exclamation in his diatribes, "No way!" In Paul's view the ethical precepts of the law identified what to do and what not to do and the consequences for one's trespass. Following moral precepts brings about moral behavior but does not train the mind to develop moral judgments and do not bring about a person's progress. The precepts functioned like a governess (*paidagōgos*, "child-minder") who makes sure a child behaves (3:24). This is not, however, the function suggested by modern translations with terms like "imprisoned" (3:22 NRSV). The function of the law was to protect and guard, to form a hedge that prevents trespass (3:23). The Abrahamic promise would eventually be fulfilled in one who would be regarded as faithful and in death for others be made alive. Because of Christ's faithfulness God has regarded as upright those who have become his followers and have experienced God's Pneuma (3:24). Just as a child who grows to be a responsible adult no longer needs a governess, so also does the morally mature person no longer need to focus on moral precepts (3:25).

Jews & Gentiles Benefit Together in Christ Jesus (3:26–4:7)

Paul has completed the diatribe and changes his form of address to the second-person plural. Paul's worldview is based on the concept of patrilineal descent through the seed of the ancestor. Jesus was "in" Abraham and is the "seed" that has by his faithfulness been made God's son by resurrection (Rom 1:4). Since Jesus is God's son, then those who are his followers are, in a sense, "in" Christ (3:26). Through this participation all become God's sons, God's offspring, and share in resurrection and immortality (3:27).

Paul does not say in these next sentences, as is commonly held, that there is a category of Christian that does away with ethnic groups, social status, and gender roles. These are subsumed by participation in Christ as the seed of Abraham and the beneficiaries of the Abrahamic promise (3:28–29).

Paul picks up on the metaphor of the role of the young man in a household. He will someday be the heir to the estate, but as long as he is underage, he is subservient to the people who will one day serve him (4:1–2). In this sense, humans were at one time in the world's history "bound by basic ethical precepts (*stoicheia*)" (4:3). At the crucial moment in time, God had Jesus be born into the world (4:4).[225]

Paul's language is enigmatic. I suggest that he is subtly distinguishing between the meaning of Christ for Jews and for gentiles. On the one hand, the expectation is the redemption of Jerusalem and Judea for the Jewish people. On the other hand, the gentiles are now adopted as also being God's children (4:5). Because Jews and gentiles are alike God's children, God's Pneuma has infused their souls (4:6). On the one hand, Jews cry out to God with the Aramaic, "*abba*."[226] On the other hand, gentiles cry out to God with the Greek, "*ho patēr*." God now recognizes his children as full beneficiaries (4:7).

Inconsistency of Religiosity for Gentiles (4:8–11)

Paul switches his focus with a strong transition. He balances the next two sentences. On the one hand, before Paul's visit to the cities of the Roman province of Galatia, the gentiles there were living in ignorance of the one God and acted as the slaves of the gods in their homes, in the temples, and in their religious festivals (4:8). On the other hand, their

---

[225] The language of being sent into the world was common expression for birth. It need not infer a high Christology in which God sends God's Son from heaven to enter the world below.

[226] Against the earlier Christian tradition, the consensus is now that Abba was not the equivalent of the American English term "daddy." In this context, Paul would not have used the Greek *ho patēr* but something like *ho pappas*.

condition changed when they heard Paul's message about the new relationship with God because of the death and resurrection of Christ (4:9). Paul makes a play on the word by saying that it is not so much that the gentiles now recognize God, but that God has now recognized the gentile peoples.

Paul's question is how they can revert to the kinds of "impotent and worthless" practices that required servile duty (4:10). He is not here criticizing Jewish customs and rituals in themselves. Paul has compared their former practice of pagan ritual duty, by which they gained nothing, and their current scrupulous attempts to follow Jewish practices as if that will change their relationship to God. He will have wasted his time and effort if they ignore his message and become Jewish proselytes anyway (4:11).

Exhortation to Progress and not Reversion (4:12–18)

Paul's terse language presents us with problems. I take Paul to mean that he wants the gentile converts from the cities of Galatia to imitate him in their progress toward living a full and divine life (4:12). He repeats this goal in 4:19, which is literally rendered "Christ is formed in you" (NRSV). In other words, they develop to become like Christ. This process is one in which the neophyte practitioner lives by the same principles as the sage-like example, who has achieved a completed level of development characterized by a kind of divine life. The philosophical guide, the psychagogue, seeks to be that example for those making progress. Paul puts himself forward as an example to follow as he seeks to achieve his own goal of godlikeness as Christ.

The reciprocity he calls for is based on his claim that he became like these gentiles (4:12). It makes sense to me that this has something to do with what he says in the next sentence. He says in 4:13 that the reason he came to tell them the good news about God's acceptance of gentile peoples because of the death of Jesus was because of a "weakness of the flesh" (4:13). I have argued above (see p. 32) that this is Paul's way of subtly referring to his lifelong injury because of his attempt to reverse his circumcision. Paul could fully engage in the life of the Roman city and appear as a gentile by inserting a pin through the skin overlapping and covering the end of his penis. Paul's language hints that this procedure caused disfigurement and pain (4:14). Despite this, the gentile people of those cities in Galatia did not respond negatively. In fact, they ignored his condition as though blinded and treated him as though he were Christ Jesus (4:15). Now, however, they are turning their backs on him when he is not there and are going along with the Judaizers (4:16–18).

Synkrisis of Hagar and Sarah (4:19–5:1)

In the language of psychagogy, a philosophical guide relates to a convert as a child to whom one has given birth. Paul calls them *tekna* (lit. "my children") (4:19). Similarly, Epictetus praises the Cynic, who typically would not marry and have a family, who treats all as his family.

> Man, the Cynic has made all mankind his children; the men among them he has as sons, the women as daughters; in that spirit he approaches them all and cares for them all. Or do you fancy that it is in the spirit of idle impertinence he reviles those he meets? It is as a father he does it, as a brother, and as a servant of Zeus, who is Father of us all (Epictetus, *Diatr.* 3.22.81–82).[227]

Paul wishes he could speak with a milder censure (4:20). Paul could feel that he is too strong in his letter writing, but he might be considered too weak in person (2 Cor 10:9). To the Thessalonians Paul wrote, "we chose to be gentle with you, in the same way a nurse cares for children in her charge" (1 Thess 2:7).

Paul explains his perplexity. He asks, "Explain to me, you who want to be *Judean citizens* under *Judean* law, do you not listen to Torah?" (4:21). With the literary device of comparison (*synkrisis*), Paul matches up the two representative characters from the Torah (4:22). Paul characterizes Hagar as a bondmaid with whom Abraham, in a moment of distrust of God's promise for him to have a son with Sarah, chose to make pregnant and have a son, Ishmael. On the other hand, Sarah, Abraham's freewoman, ultimately gave birth to a son, Isaac, by which God's promise was fulfilled (4:23). The expectation of Paul's audience would be to associate the gentile peoples with Hagar and Ishmael and the Jewish nation with Sarah and Isaac. As I read it, Paul boldly turns this on its head so that Hagar represents the servitude of proselytes won over by the Jerusalem Judaizing faction. At another level, Paul aligns present

---

[227] Epictetus, *Discourses, Books 3-4. Fragments. The Encheiridion*, 159.

day Jerusalem, which, as the capital of Judea, is occupied by the Romans (4:25). Metaphorically, the residents of Jerusalem are her children. Conversely, Sarah is made to represent a mother who is an "above Jerusalem (*hē de anō Ieroysalēm*)" (4:26). Traditionally, this language has been understood as reflecting the same traditions of Hebrews, "the heavenly Jerusalem" (Heb 12:22) or the apocalyptic language of Revelation in which a new Jerusalem descends from heaven (Rev 3:12; 21:2,10). I suggest that the Greek word *anō* to describe a city functions in the sense of a geographical location to the north. Herodotus, for example, uses *anō* with *boreas* "north" in the context of Syria and Cappadocia (Herodotus, *Hist.* 1.72.7). When describing the location of the Panionium, he refers to the north and the south as above and below (Herodotus, *Hist.* 1.142.2). Josephus regularly uses this language for northern or upper Galilee and southern or lower Galilee. In fact, Diodorus refers to the area of Seleucia as *anō Syrian*, "upper Syria" (Diodorus Siculus, *Bib. hist.* 29.47.5). Therefore, I translate 4:26 as "Now the upper/*northern* Jerusalem *i.e. Antioch* represents the freewoman; she is the mother of us *gentile followers of Jesus*." Paul quotes from the Greek of Isa 54:1 to refer to the size of the gentile peoples being larger than that of those who are represented by Hagar (4:27).

Paul continues to turn the tables on the Judaizing faction. They are like Ishmael, who was born from Abraham's human choice, and like him they torment those who are the gentiles born of Pneuma (4:29). He again quotes scripture to say that the gentile believers should get rid of the Judaizers from their midst. Paul concludes, "we *gentile followers of Jesus* are not children of the bondmaid *Hagar*, but of the freewoman *Sarah*" (4:31). He then exhorts them to remain steadfast, don't give in to the Judaizers, and maintain their freedom (5:1).

Dire Effects of Judaizing (5:2–12)

Paul now uses his strongest language. If a gentile who has heard the good news about God's acceptance of the gentile peoples and has become a follower of Jesus, succumbs to the false message of the Judaizing faction and becomes circumcised, then Paul says that Christ has been of no benefit to that person (5:2); that person needs to adhere to Torah (5:3); that person is now estranged from Christ by losing what was given for free (5:4). What is most important is the Pneuma of God that accompanied the acceptance of the good news about the faithfulness of Christ by which is achieved uprightness (5:5). What matters most is "constancy (*pistis* "faithfulness") expressed through commitment (*agapē* "selfless love")" (5:6).

Paul exclaims to his audience with an athletic metaphor, perhaps alluding to the stadium found in the cities of Galatia, "You were making good progress like a runner! Who cut you off from no longer being persuaded by the truth?" (5:7). The Judaizers are to Paul like a small amount of yeast that gets into the dough when making a flat bread (5:9). Paul trusts that his audience will choose wisely (*phroneō*) and make the right decision about their actions (5:10). As for the Judaizers, Paul reveals his animosity toward their activity. They will get what's coming to them (5:10).

I find the prevailing interpretation of 5:11 difficult to understand. When was Paul ever "preaching circumcision" to gentiles? He went after Jewish followers of Jesus. Why would any Jews be against Paul making proselytes among gentiles? It seems to me that Paul is referring to accusations he is against Jews continuing to be circumcised and follow Torah. His objection is that he is not anti-circumcision for Jews, so why is he still being chased after?

After interjecting his frustration with the opposition he encounters, Paul concludes that Jesus dying on a cross at the hands of the Romans should not be a reason for Jews to be against his message (5:11). It is not a rejection of Judaism but an inclusion of the gentiles.

Again, Paul interjects with a harsh statement. Paul goes to the extreme of expressing his wish that the Judaizers, who are causing so much trouble about cutting off the foreskin, would go the full extent of cutting off their genitalia (5:12). The making of eunuchs by castration would have brought to the minds of the people in the cities of Galatia those priests of Cybele called Galli who self-castrated themselves to become eunuchs.

Liberty Does Not Mean Libertine (5:13–15)

Paul's good news to the gentile peoples is two-fold. The first part has to do with the reasons Paul thinks the one, true living God has opened access to the gentile peoples to be part of God's people because of the faithfulness of Christ in death (5:13). The signs of God's presence, God's

Pneuma, outside of Jerusalem and Judea was demonstrated when gentiles became followers of Jesus. They did not need to become Torah-observant Judeans by circumcision to be right with God. The second part of Paul's message is that, while gentile adherents need not be Torah-observant, they need to become ethical and develop fully as godlike people (5:14).

Paul tells the gentile adherents of the cities of Galatia that the freedom they have been given not to be required to undergo circumcision does not mean that it gives them freedom to act in any way they might want (5:13). The context suggests that the libertinism Paul is most concerned about is a kind of selfishness contrary to altruism and even a cosmopolitanism. In the households where they follow Jesus and worship the one God, they should not act selfishly but serve each other in loving friendship (5:14).[228] Paul considers that the fundamental principle of Torah is expressed by the one commandment to "love your neighbor as yourself" (Lev 19:18). A neighbor is anyone that you come into contact with, anyone you become near to. Paul is thinking about the household group and how they relate to each other. His dining metaphor in 5:15 might be an allusion to the central activity in which the household shares a meal together and engages in discussion. Their conversation should not be a chance for taking a bite out of someone else and hurting them to where they want to leave the group and discontinue the process of their development.

Progress in Divine Life based on Right Living (5:16–26)

Paul gives his moral advice for the gentile adherents to live their lives in harmony with Pneuma. A person will have physical impulses, but Paul wants them not to bring those impulses to their completion (*teleō*): they are not to act on the physical impulses (5:16). Bodily impulses tend to desire what it perceives to aid its own preservation. In fact, these are not beneficial. Pneuma is contrary to those desires (5:17). The bodily impulses can be strong enough to cause a person to make mistakes about

---

[228] Elsewhere I argue that the terminology for "love" (*agapē*) is related to the relationship of friendship (Gk. *philia*; Lat. *amicitia*). The social bonds of friendship included responsibilities and reciprocity.

what is the best thing to do. One's choices should be guided by Pneuma rather than rely on a moral code (5:18).

Paul now presents a list of vices and virtues. The actions of the physical impulses are obvious (5:19–21). People who act this way are characterized by engaging in improper sexual activities or by living in a way that promotes vulgarity and lewdness. When someone desires certain things or wants a particular thing to happen, they might sacrifice to an image of a deity or an ancestor or they might engage in magical practices. Both are ways are mistaken attempts to get what one wants. Someone might also want what other people have, whether that's wealth, beauty, fame, or status, and that can lead to conflicts (hostility, rivalry, dissension, factionalism) and negative emotions (strife, jealousy, rage, envy). Another way people try to get their desires is by cozying up to a patron, act like a toadying parasite, and attend their dinner parties where they get drunk and engage in revelry.

Apparently, Paul had already warned them about these behaviors and is now repeating his admonishment (5:21). These are characteristics of those who are not making progress in their moral development and, consequently, will not be among those who live a divine life or be raised to the divine realm.

By contrast, those whose conduct is guided by Pneuma exhibit these virtuous outcomes (5:22–23). Rather than using people to get what they want, they form relationships based on selflessness and seeking good for the other. Rather than seeking to experience pleasure for oneself, they feel the positive emotion of joy. Rather than be at odds with others, they get along with others without conflict through mutual reciprocity. Rather than be short-tempered, they have a long fuse. Rather than selfish, they are benevolent and generous. Rather than disloyal or untrustworthy, they display a constancy of allegiance. Rather than be manipulative and dominating, they have a gentleness about them. Finally, rather than be morally incontinent and lacking self-mastery, they are not moved by their passions but have self-control. To live this way is not at all incongruent with any moral code. Paul may hint here that the Jewish practice of Torah-observance was considered being a rigorous application of the philosophical life (5:23).

Paul imagines here that those who are connected to Christ and participate in him were, in effect, with him on the cross when his body was executed (5:24). The physical impulses of our bodies and the mistaken choices that are made based on them have been put to death. Paul uses the technical language for these impulses, the passions (*pathēma*) and desires (*epithymia*).

If our flesh died with Christ, then it follows that we live by being animated with Pneuma. And if we are empowered by Pneuma, then we should be guided in our thoughts and behavior by Pneuma (5:25). In sum, Paul says, we should "not over-emphasize status, challenge one other, feel the need to have what others have" (5:26).

Mutual Critique and Moral Therapy (6:1–6)

In Paul's attempt to form communities within households in the cities of central Anatolia, he describes how people should act in the previous section and now in this section how they should relate to each other. Paul's language is that of the practice of frank criticism. Clarence Glad defines this as "a stochastic method used by friends in the art of therapeutic healing of souls, comparable to the methods used by physicians in the art of healing."[229] The purpose of providing each other with critique is to maintain progress toward the goal of maturity in a divine way of living. When someone makes an error in judgment and it is detected, then the more advanced person can provide a gentle critique in a way that restores the person and provides for their progress (6:1). This psychagogy requires that it is not done out of a sense of moral superiority but is performed out of a sense of care for others. The moral code of Christ, that of loving others like you do yourself, is like the standard of friendship in which a friend is another self (6:2). Feeling pride is not negative in 6:4 but is the sense of satisfaction in making progress. Carrying each other's burden, as 6:5 is usually translated, has more to do with it than just listening to each other's woes. It was with similar language to Paul's in 6:5 that the Stoic philosopher, Cleanthes, who was described as being an ass, said that "he alone was strong enough to carry (*bastazō*) the load (*phortion*) of Zeno" (Diogenes Laertius, Lives 7.5.170).[230] Within the structure of the household, the one who

---

[229] Glad, *Paul and Philodemus*, 110.

[230] Diogenes Laertius, *Lives of Eminent Philosophers, Volume 2: Books 6-10*, 277.

teaches, specifically the household guide like Paul, should receive a compensation (6:6).

Good Choices Lead to Good Outcomes (6:7–10)

Paul argues from the natural world that a seed that is planted will always produce the right plant (6:7). Good seeds produce good crops. Seed from a crop that is not resistant to insects and bad weather will produce a crop that will rot in the field (6:8). As in the natural order, so also in human experience, whether in education or in ethics. When humans choose to do what is selfish, then the outcome will not be beneficial but lead to moral decay. When people live a good life, one in keeping with the Pneuma, then the outcome is a divine quality of life (6:9).

Paul exhorts his readers to have the patience and tenacity of a farmer. Through constant care, a good harvest is produced. Likewise, it is through the habituation of right choices that progress is made. Therefore, Paul encourages the members of the various household groups in Galatia to continue to do what is good for all people but especially to the members within their households (6:10).

Summation of Paul's Argument & Exhortation (6:11–15)

The concluding section of Paul's letter functions like a peroration and even a recapitulation of his letter. In it he compares the actions and motivations of the Judaizers over against his own position. In v. 15 he sums up what he considers to be the most important point.

Paul's self-referential statement in 6:11 about the writing of the letter has been taken to mean that Paul wrote with large letters because he had poor eyesight because of some kind of eye disease that was his weakness (see p. 27). The plural of *gramma* need not refer to individual letters but can refer to the whole of the document made up of letters. Herodotus, for example, uses the plural when he writes, "Darius wrote a letter (*grammata*) to Megabazus" (*Hist.* 5.14.1).[231] A letter of recommendation (P.Oslo 2.55) refers to the letter carrier as "the one handing to you these

---

[231] Herodotus, *The Persian Wars, Volume 3: Books 5-7.* trans. A. D. Godley, Loeb Classical Library 119 (Cambridge, MA: Harvard University Press, 1922), 13.

characters of mine (*tauta mou ta grammata*)."²³² Diogenes is, of course, referring to "this letter of mine" for Theon that he is sending to Pythagoras. Paul is referring to the size of the roll on which he has written the letter in his own handwriting.²³³ What he has to say is so important that he wants to emphasize the great effort he has made to write to them.

As Paul has been saying, the Judaizers are not so much concerned with the gentiles they want to be circumcised but act selfishly out of fear of reprisals against themselves. In this way they are not fulfilling the commandment of love but take pride in the number of foreskins that can be excised (6:12–13).

In contrast, Paul refuses to take any credit for the response to the message he brought them (6:14). In fact, the way of life Paul presents is one in which society's values are considered of no consequence. In the language of the Stoics, things such as fame, wealth, status, or ancestry are considered indifferent to one's character and virtue. Paul places circumcision and uncircumcision in this same category of indifferents. They are not anything (6:15). What does matter, in Paul's view, is becoming a new creature, a renewed person.

Closing (6:16–18)

Paul pronounces a blessing on those gentile adherents that go along with (*stoicheō*) the code (*kanōn*) he has laid out (6:16). This is the language Musonius Rufus uses to refer to the philosophical life. He is said to have talked to a king of Syria about the necessity for a king to study philosophy.

> [He] must know what is good for a man and what is bad, what is helpful and what harmful, what advantageous and what disadvantageous, inasmuch as it is plain that those who ally themselves with evil come to harm, while those who cleave to good enjoy protection, and those who are deemed worthy of

---

²³² Samson Eitrem and Leiv Amundsen, eds., *Papyri Osloenses*, vol. 2 (Oslo: Dybwad, 1931), 55.

²³³ Reece lists those who have interpreted Paul to refer to the length of the letter. Steve Reece, *Paul's Large Letters: Paul's Autographic Subscriptions in the Light of Ancient Epistolary Conventions* (London: Bloomsbury T&T Clark, 2017), 233-38.

help and advantage enjoy benefits, while those who involve themselves in things disadvantageous and harmful suffer punishment. But to distinguish between good and bad, advantageous and disadvantageous, helpful and harmful is the part of none other than the philosopher, who constantly occupies himself with this very question, how not to be ignorant of any of these things and has made it his art to understand what conduces to a man's happiness or unhappiness (Musonius Rufus, *Diatr.* 8.7–17).[234]

When Musonius finished his argument for why a king should attend to the philosophical life, the king offered to reward him. In typical fashion for a philosopher, Musonius rejected any offer of reward and said, "The only favor I ask of you is to remain faithful (*stoichein*) to this teaching, since you find it commendable, for in this way and no other will you best please me and benefit yourself" (Musonius Rufus, *Diatr.* 8.135–137).[235]

Paul wishes peace on the gentile adherents. In addition, Paul wishes for mercy on "the Israel of God" (6:16). As Paul has done throughout his letter, he distinguishes the two groups.

Once again Paul refers to the Judaizers who have been causing him trouble. On page 4 I have argued that the stigmata he refers to here is a reference to the circumcision reversal surgery he had done in his youth (6:17). A stigma is the pin used to prick the skin when tattooing. The pin he would have to wear was a sign of his calling. It was the reason he felt obliged to bring the message to the gentile peoples.

Finally, Paul wishes that his gentile adherents experience the favor of God which Jesus has made available to them (6:18).

---

[234] Cora E. Lutz, "Musonius Rufus, 'The Roman Socrates'," in *Yale Classical Studies*, ed. Alfred R. Bellinger (New Haven: Yale University Press, 1947), 61.

[235] Lutz, "Musonius Rufus," 67.

Chapter 9:
Philippians Correspondence

From Paul's letter to the Philippians we get some indication of what has been happening. Paul is writing to the Philippians along with Timothy and sends greetings from other associates with him (1:1). Paul wants to develop among the Philippians a pattern of moral thinking that puts the needs of others as more important than personal desires (2:1–4). This is the way Jesus thought (2:5–11), and it's the way of thinking that leads people to a mature and deep contentment with circumstances and a tranquility that enables them to cope with any difficulties of life (4:8–9).

Paul is in an unnamed city and being held in custody at a praetorium (1:13), and there are followers of Jesus who are part of the administrative center (4:22). Paul has both support and opposition to his teaching (4:15–18). He mentions that the Philippians were involved in his early ministry (1:5), and they have recently provided Paul with financial support delivered to him by Epaphroditus (4:18), though I take this section to have been a separate letter of thanksgiving on that occasion.

I take the two recommendation sections of Philippians as possibly having been separate correspondences. Paul knows that the Philippians have heard that Epaphroditus had become ill while bringing their support to Paul (2:26). Paul desires to send Timothy and Epaphroditus to the Philippians to learn about their condition (2:23–25). As soon as the officials free him from incarceration, he plans to visit the Philippians (2:24).

Acts tells us the story of Paul first visiting Philippi (c. 49 CE). Before making the trip from Asia Minor to the Greek mainland, Paul meets Timothy (Acts 16:1), who becomes his associate and fellow-traveler (Acts 16:3), along with Paul's coworker, Silas. When Luke begins to chronicle the events of making the sea-voyage, he uses the language of "we," suggesting that he also accompanied Paul and Timothy at this point.

Luke accurately describes Philippi as "a leading city of the district of Macedonia and a Roman colony" (Acts 16:12 NRSV). Philip, the father of Alexander the Great, founded this Macedonian city. The city became a Roman colony and a favorite retirement city for Roman soldiers. After Augustus became emperor, he renamed the city *Colonia Augusta Iulia Philippensis*. The city was wealthy because of the gold mines in the area and the main roads passing through the city.

Luke's story begins on the Sabbath (Acts 16:13), probably early on Saturday morning, when Paul and his companions look for a Jewish gathering place ("synagogue") to worship. They have to go outside of the city gate next to a river where the Jews of the city had a place of prayer (the common designation in Greek for a Jewish synagogue but not necessarily a building). One would have to guess that a minimum number of Jewish men were present, but Luke only mentions that Paul takes up a conversation with a group of women. Luke says one of them is named Lydia. Apparently, she is a widowed woman originally from Thyatira, who has continued the household business of dyeing cloth purple (Acts 16:14). Although she is a gentile, she is a worshipper of the One God of the Jews. Paul would have found her an interesting conversation partner, not only because of her practice of Judaism but also because they would have shared a common interest in the production and market of textiles. Lydia accepted Paul's message about Jesus, and she and her household were all baptized. She impressed upon Paul and his friends to stay with her in her home (Acts 16:15).

On another Sabbath visit to the place of prayer, Paul meets another woman. She is a slave who is being used as a fortune-teller (Acts 16:16). As so often happens in Luke's stories, those who are possessed recognize the power of God in the followers of Jesus. She began chasing Paul and his companions, yelling "These men are slaves of the Most High God, who proclaim to you a way of salvation" (Acts 16:17 NRSV). Out of annoyance, Paul exorcizes her demon (Acts 16:19). That Paul had destroyed her masters' source of revenue irritated them. They grabbed Paul and Silas and brought them to the magistrates in the Agora claiming, "These men are disturbing our city; they are Jews and are advocating customs that are not lawful for us as Romans to adopt or observe" (Acts 16:20–21 NRSV). After receiving a beating, Paul and Silas are dumped into a holding cell (Acts 16:22–24). Paul and Silas hold a midnight vigil of prayers and hymns at which time an earthquake frees all the prisoners (Acts 16:25–26). The jailer is so impressed that Paul and Silas did not escape that he accepts their message along with all the others in his house (Acts 16:27–34). When the magistrates learned that Paul and Silas are both Roman citizens, they apologize for their incarceration and set them free (Acts 16:35–39). Before leaving Philippi, Paul, Silas, and the others visit in Lydia's household assembly, where they exhort them how properly to conduct their lives as followers of Jesus (Acts 16:40).

We don't know for certain when Paul wrote this letter or from where he was writing as a prisoner. Traditionally, there are two candidates based on evidence from Acts. Rome has been considered a likely candidate with Caesarea as a second possibility. Nothing in Philippians suggests these places other than Paul's mention of the praetorium (1:13) and the people working at the imperial headquarters (4:22). Both imprisonments were late in Paul's career. Many scholars feel that Philippians seems to come from an earlier time in Paul's experience. The mention of frequent travel between where Paul is being held and Philippi implies to some that where Paul is being held and Philippi must be close enough to traverse more quickly than would have been Rome or Caesarea.

There are other possibilities for the place of writing. Paul's letters refer to many occasions in which he had a run-in with the law, which might have landed him in jail (1 Cor 11:23; 6:5). One place that is a favorite candidate is Ephesus. Some have taken 1 Cor 15:32 as evidence that Paul was imprisoned in Ephesus and even made to be part of gladiatorial games. Paul writes from Ephesus to the Corinthians,

> And why are we putting ourselves in danger every hour? I die every day! That is as certain, brothers and sisters, as my boasting of you—a boast that I make in Christ Jesus our Lord. If with merely human hopes I fought with wild animals at Ephesus, what would I have gained by it (1 Cor 15:30–31 NRSV)?

However, in an important article by Abraham Malherbe shows convincingly that Paul's language is not literally about gladiatorial competition but the struggles that a philosopher faces from adversaries.[236] This conforms to the experience Paul describes in Philippians. That's not to say Paul wasn't also imprisoned in Ephesus. He wrote again to the Corinthians about his conflict in Ephesus.

---

[236] Malherbe, "The Beasts at Ephesus."

> We do not want you to be unaware, brothers and sisters, of the affliction we experienced in Asia; for we were so utterly, unbearably crushed that we despaired of life itself. Indeed, we felt that we had received the sentence of death so that we would rely not on ourselves but on God who raises the dead. He who rescued us from so deadly a peril will continue to rescue us; on him we have set our hope that he will rescue us again, as you also join in helping us by your prayers, so that many will give thanks on our behalf for the blessing granted us through the prayers of many (2 Cor 1:8–11 NRSV).

According to Acts 19 Paul spent a considerable amount of time living in Ephesus. After teaching in a synagogue for three months and then experiencing conflict, Paul moved his teaching from the synagogue to a school, "the lecture hall of Tyrannus" (Acts 19:9 NRSV). The language suggests philosophical dialogue. Paul taught here for two years.

Acts 19 tells the story of two different controversies at Ephesus. The first involved itinerant Jewish exorcists (Acts 19:13–20). Paul was a hero with the locals after this adventure. Subsequently, we're told that Paul planned to go to Macedonia, which surely would have included Philippi (Acts 19:21). He sends Timothy, while he himself stays in Ephesus and then really gets himself into trouble (Acts 19:22–23).

To whatever degree Paul's teaching is a synthesis of Hellenistic philosophy and Jewish thought, he remains a monotheist and a critic of idolatry and polytheism. Some merchants fear Paul's success might impact their sale of Artemis figurines (Acts 19:24–27). Some rabble rousers make trouble for Paul and he is under threat of bodily harm. Two of Paul's associates, Gaius and Aristarchus, are dragged into the theater (Acts 19:29). When Alexander, a local Jew, tries to give a defense, they shout him down (Acts 19:33–34). It's not until the town clerk speaks to the crowd that they restore order (Acts 19:35–41). In fact, that's the primary concern, that social order is restored so that the Romans don't get wind of rioting in Ephesus and respond with a military presence. Paul finally leaves Ephesus for Macedonia and Greece, which undoubtedly would include Philippi (Acts 20:1–3).

However, we're not able to say with any certainty that Paul wrote to the Philippians from Ephesus–or from Rome or Caesarea. In fact, some scholars argue that Philippians does not have a single place and time of authorship. They consider Philippians to be a compilation of three or more letters from different times in Paul's life.

Scholars have long recognized a structural disunity to Philippians.[237] Although it is possible that Paul wrote a single letter over time in which his purposes, and perhaps audience focus, changed, I will present the correspondence as having been edited into a single letter in order to copy and publish the correspondence as a single papyrus roll.

I may be alone in my interpretation that Paul uses the term *hagios* (lit. "holy ones;" commonly translated as "saints") to refer specifically to Jewish adherents (see p. 34). Therefore, I take the first letter of the composite as a letter written specifically to the Jewish adherents in Philippi. If we accept the story in Acts, then this could be the household of Lydia and her social network of clients and friends.

I also take 4:2–9 to have been a part of the first letter. It seems that 4:1 is a closing of a letter, and 4:2 lacks a coordinating conjunction. I would take Euodia and Syntyche to be members of the same household group (4:2). Perhaps even the reference to an individual in 4:3 is to Lydia herself.

Within the first letter, Paul quotes what seems to be an early hymn to Jesus (2:6–11). The two recommendation letters, one for Timothy (2:19–24) and for Epaphroditus (2:25–3:1), would seem to allude to the hymn in how Timothy and Epaphroditus exemplify the characteristics of Jesus. This may have caused the editor to insert these commendatory letters following the hymn.

I take 3:2–4:1 as containing a letter Paul wrote to gentile adherents in Philippi. They are to be wary of Judaizers who might come to Philippi as they did elsewhere. In this section Paul does not indicate that he is no longer a Jew but that any status or achievements are indifferent to one's virtue, as the Stoics taught.

Finally, the section in 4:10–20 forms a distinct unit focused on a single topic of the financial support Paul received from the group in Philippi. It would seem to have been written some period after earlier letters when Paul was still needing help from his followers in Philippi while he was jailed and waiting for a hearing.

---

[237] For an overview of the issues and a review of the literature to date, see David E. Garland, "The Composition and Unity of Philippians: Some Neglected Literary Factors," *Novum Testamentum* 27, no. 2 (1985).

I would take the closing of Philippians to belong to the letter to the Jewish adherents. Once again, we have the language of the holy ones as in the opening section of that letter.

Letter Opening to Jewish Adherents [Doc 1.1] (1:1–2)

Paul identifies himself as the sender along with Timothy (1:1). Rather than think of the Greek term *doulos* in the context of the English word "slave," I take it to be within the context of religious devotion. They serve God in their lives as devotees. As discussed above, I take the language of "holy ones" to be a way of indicating Jewish adherents. Within the household there were positions known by the terms Paul uses. Persons in charge would be an overseer, and those who perform menial tasks around the house, perhaps serving meals, I call servers.

With his typical form, Paul wishes that his audience would experience God's benevolence and the concord or security God provides. It is from the one God, the Father and Creator, that blessing comes. Paul includes Jesus, but here *kyrios* should be taken in its sense of "master" or "lord."

Personal Development [Doc 1.1] (1:3–11)

This friendly letter begins with Paul expressing his connection to the Jewish adherents in Philippi. He is grateful to God and prays for their continued blessing (1:3–4). Paul remembers the first time he met with them. They were the among the earliest converts across the Aegean (1:5). He begins his theme of their progress in personal or moral development. When they first embraced the way of life Paul described, it was a good work that they started in their transformation (1:6). Paul then uses goal language (*tel-*) that refers to the outcome of that progress. On the one hand, God is working within people to bring them to completion (perfection or maturity) until time runs out. On the other hand, Paul says "I press on toward the goal (*skopos*, a synonym for *telos*) for the prize of the heavenly call of God in Christ Jesus" (3:14 NRSV). In 3:15 Paul says, "as many as are perfect" (*teleios*). When one becomes a follower of Jesus, the infant stage is meant to be followed by progress towards the culmination in a mature and completed human person to be achieved before death (or Christ's return). Paul is confident God will do this for those who follow Jesus's example. Day by day the transformation continues, and Paul is confident that God will bring them to full maturity in the wholeness of their humanity right up to the day Jesus returns.

The term Paul uses to refer to his cognition in 1:7 is more than just thinking. Central to the theme of this letter is *phronēsis*. It is often translated as prudence; it is a type of practical wisdom exercised in forming proper judgments.[238] Plutarch credits Zeno of Citium with defining prudence as effecting virtue.[239] In the case of justice (*dikaiosynē*), prudence is the decision about what is due someone. In 1:7, Paul says that it is the just (*dikaios*) thing to do to have this affection for them. With temperance or moderation (*sōphrosynē*), prudence is the right thing to choose and what to avoid. Paul will discuss this topic with the Philippians. Also, fortitude (*andreia*) is the prudential decision about what to endure. This will be another theme of Paul's.

Paul gives the reason for his affection (1:7). He feels that the Philippians are supporting him during his incarceration and are, in effect, his co-defendants when he goes before a magistrate to give his defense speech (*apologia*) (1:7–8). His is a gut-wrenching (*splanchnon*) type of affection, the kind that Christ Jesus has shown (1:8).

Paul expresses his desire for the personal and moral development of the Philippians. He wants them to develop the capacity for knowledge (*epignōsis*, a synonym for *epistēmē*) and discernment (*aisthēsis*) so they can form proper judgments about what is the best thing to do (1:9–10). In this way they will make progress toward complete maturity characterized by being genuinely with no cause for blame (1:10).

Paul uses the language of examining moral options and determining what is the best course of action (Rom 2:18; 12:2; 2 Cor 13:5; Phil 1:10). His language (*dokimazō*) is also that of moral philosophers (e.g. Epictetus, *Diatr.* 2.12.21). It is the evaluation of what to do in a certain situation to determine what is beneficial for progress or what might hinder progress.

A unique doctrine of the Stoics is the category of indifferents (*adiaphora*). These are the things that do not contribute to or take away from progress in virtue. Zeno, the founder of Stoicism, lists these "indifferents," first the preferred and then the dispreferred, as "life, health, pleasure, beauty, strength, wealth, fair fame and noble birth, and

---

[238] For the classic discussion see Aristotle, *EN* VI.5,1140a24–1140b30.

[239] Plutarch, *On moral virtue* 441A.

their opposites, death, disease, pain, ugliness, weakness, poverty, ignominy, low birth, and the like" (Diogenes Laertius, *Lives* 7.102 Zeno).[240] Paul refers to "the things that make a difference (*diapheronta*)" (1:10). Epictetus uses this same language:

> What then? Are these externals to be used carelessly? Not at all. For this again is to the moral purpose an evil and thus unnatural to it. They must be used carefully, because their use is not a matter of indifference, and at the same time with steadfastness and peace of mind, because the material is indifferent (*adiaphoron*). For in whatever really concerns (*diapheron*) us, there no man can either hinder or compel me. The attainment of those things in which I can be hindered or compelled is not under my control and is neither good or bad, but the use which I make of them is either good or bad, and that is under my control (Epictetus, *Diatr.* 2.5.6–10).[241]

At the outset, Paul is encouraging the Philippians to think prudently about their attitudes and actions to one another. It will be something that puts the other person's needs before one's own.

Metaphorically, Paul writes that they are filled to the brim with the harvest of their right actions (1:11). Fruit as the effect of right living is a commonplace in Greek philosophical texts. One philosopher wrote, "The happiest person is the who harvests from himself the fruit of righteousness, which is happiness (*eydaimonia*, "the divine flourishing life")" (Atticus, *Fragmenta* 4.17.4). Epicurus is quoted as saying, "The greatest fruit of righteousness is to be undisturbed (*ataraxia*)" (Clement of Alexandria, *Strom.* 6.2.24). This quotation from a letter of Seneca (a Roman Stoic writing in Latin, a close contemporary of Paul), which he has written to a pupil, contains the metaphor of fruit and includes many of the concepts we've already discussed.

> I grow in spirit and leap for joy and shake off my years and my blood runs warm again, whenever I understand, from your actions and your letters, how far you have outdone yourself; for

---

[240] Diogenes Laertius, *Lives of Eminent Philosophers, Volume 2: Books 6-10*, 209.

[241] Epictetus, *Discourses, Books 1-2*. trans. W. A. Oldfather, Loeb Classical Library 131 (Cambridge, MA: Harvard University Press, 1925), 233-35. See also Chrysippus, *Fragmenta moralia*. 140.10; Marcus Aurelius, *Meditations* 6.32.1.

as to the ordinary man, you left him in the rear long ago. If the farmer is pleased when his tree develops so that it bears fruit, if the shepherd takes pleasure in the increase of his flocks, if every man regards his pupil as though he discerned in him his own early manhood,—what, then, do you think are the feelings of those who have trained (*educaverunt*) a mind and molded (*formaverunt*) a young idea, when they see it suddenly grown to maturity (*adulta*)?

I claim you for myself; you are my handiwork. When I saw your abilities, I laid my hand upon you, I exhorted you, I applied the goad and did not permit you to march lazily but roused you continually. And now I do the same; but by this time I am cheering on one who is in the race and so in turn cheers me on.

Hence it is that the larger part of goodness is the will to become good. You know what I mean by a good man? One who is complete (*perfectum*), finished (*absolutum*),—whom no constraint or need can render bad. I see such a person in you, if only you go steadily on and bend to your task and see to it that all your actions and words harmonize and correspond with each other and are stamped in the same mold (Seneca, *Ep.* 34.1–2).[242]

One might object that Paul's language is about his relationship with God. To compare his ideas with philosophers like the Stoics might seem incompatible. Yet, for a Stoic like Epictetus (and others), his language includes theological expression.

…I have one whom I must please, to whom I must submit, whom I must obey, that is, God, and after Him, myself. God has commended me to myself, and He has subjected to me alone my moral purpose, giving me standards for the correct use of it (Epictetus, *Diatr.* 4.12–14).[243]

Paul's focus on theology should not obscure his moral exhortation and the practices he encourages of his followers.

---

[242] Seneca, *Epistles, Volume 1: Epistles 1-65*, 243.

[243] Epictetus, *Discourses, Books 3-4. Fragments. The Encheiridion*, 425.

Effects of Paul's Incarceration [Doc 1.1] (1:12–24)

Paul attributes the progress (*prokopē*) of the adherents in their moral development to his incarceration (1:12). He is not making a point about the advancement of evangelization. Paul is referring to the same thing he does in 1:25: "your progress (*prokopē*) and joy resulting from a faithful life." The indication of the progress of adherents around him is that they have greater boldness to talk to people because Paul is being recognized as jailed because of the new message he is bringing (1:14). Wherever he is being held, there is a provincial headquarters there (1:13).

Paul introduces a comparison (*synkrisis*) in verse 15 with the normally untranslated particle *men*. He distinguishes two groups, both of which are talking to people about the good news of Christ. The difference is their motivation. It would seem that they are vying for power or status among the followers of Jesus. Paul doesn't attribute to them anything wrong in what they are saying but thinks they are envious of him (1:15). By being more vocal and public, they hope that Paul will have a more difficult time in jail and will lose followers (1:17). Yet, those who understand that he is in jail for the cause and will be able to present a defense speech to a broader group, they are working with Paul.

Paul expresses his joy that people are joining him in telling others about the good news (1:18). He is confident that their efforts will lead to his release (1:19). Rather than referring to prayer requests being made, Paul may refer to someone writing a request (singular), or, in other words, a petition. The Greek word for a *libellus* was *enteuxis*, though Paul's word *deēsis* is used. Plutarch tells of Cato saying that they should seek to secure their safety (*sōtēria*) but should not make a petition (*deēsis*) because they had done no wrong (Plutarch, *Cat. Min.* 64.7.2).

There is a similarity between how Paul talks about his imprisonment, his defense, and release (1:20–24) and that of the widely known case of Socrates. Epictetus uses similar language and context to talk about Socrates.

> Later on, when he had to speak in defense of his life, he did not behave as one who had children, or a wife, did he? Nay, but as one who was alone in the world. Yes, and when he had to drink the poison, how does he act? When he might have saved his life, and when Crito said to him, "Leave the prison for the sake of your children," what is his reply? Did he think it a bit of good

luck? Impossible! No, he regards what is fitting, and as for other considerations, he does not so much as look at or consider them. For he did not care, he says, to save his paltry body, but only that which is increased and preserved (*sōzetai*) by right conduct (*dikaiō*) and is diminished (*meioutai*) and destroyed (*apollytai*) by evil conduct (*adikō*). Socrates does not save his life with dishonor, the man who refused to put the vote when the Athenians demanded it of him, the man who despised the Tyrants, the man who held such noble discourse about virtue and moral excellence; this man it is impossible to save by dishonor, but he is saved by death, and not by flight (Epictetus, *Diatr.* 4.162–165).[244]

Epictetus goes on to quote Socrates to the effect, "If I save my life I shall be useful to many persons, but if I die I shall be useful to no one" (Epictetus, *Diatr.* 4.168).[245] Socrates, however, decides that his death would do more good than escaping and staying alive.

Paul expresses his hope that he will be brave at his trial and not act shamefully, perhaps by begging or saying whatever he needs to be released (1:20). He might exaggerate a bit at this point by saying that the outcome of his trial might lead to his execution. In Stoic fashion he downplays death as an advantage (*kerdos*) for him (1:21). Remarkably, Plato uses this exact language in the *Apology*.

> I was convicted because I lacked not words but boldness and shamelessness and the willingness to say to you what you would most gladly have heard from me, lamentations and tears and my saying and doing many things that I say are unworthy of me but that you are accustomed to hear from others (Plato, *Apol.* 38.d).

> What has happened to me may well be a good thing, and those of us who believe death to be an evil are certainly mistaken (Plato, *Apol.* 40.b).

---

[244] Epictetus, *Discourses, Books 3-4. Fragments. The Encheiridion*, 301.
[245] Epictetus, *Discourses, Books 3-4. Fragments. The Encheiridion*, 303.

> If it [death] is a complete lack of perception, like a dreamless sleep, then death would be a great advantage (*kerdos*) (Plato, *Apol.* 40.d).[246]

For Paul death is a better option because he would be with Christ in heaven and experience the fullness of what he has worked for in his own life (1:23). Yet, Paul chooses, not what might be the gain or advantage for himself but, what is best for his followers (1:24).

This attitude toward death is notable among the Stoics. I find a good example of that in Seneca's Letter 4.

> No man can have a peaceful life who thinks too much about lengthening it, or believes that living through many consulships is a great blessing Rehearse this thought every day, that you may be able to depart from life contentedly; for many men clutch and cling to life, even as those who are carried down a rushing stream clutch and cling to briars and sharp rocks.
>
> Most men ebb and flow in wretchedness between the fear of death and the hardships of life; they are unwilling to live, and yet they do not know how to die. For this reason, make life as a whole agreeable to yourself by banishing all worry about it. No good thing renders its possessor happy, unless his mind is reconciled to the possibility of loss; nothing, however, is lost with less discomfort than that which, when lost, cannot be missed. Therefore, encourage and toughen your spirit against the mishaps that afflict even the most powerful (Seneca, *Ep.* 4.4–6).[247]

So then, Paul assures his readers that he will present a defense and not be silent at his hearing. He will endure the present circumstances and be courageous when he speaks. Unlike those adherents who speak about Jesus for their own benefit, Paul will carry on for the benefit of his followers. His motivation is that they will continue to make progress in their moral development (*prokopē*), that they will experience the good emotion of joy (*chara*), and that they will feel good about how Paul has represented the movement (1:25–26).

---

[246] Cooper and Hutchinson, eds., *Plato: Complete Works*, 35.

[247] Seneca, *Epistles, Volume 1: Epistles 1-65*, 15-17.

Responsible Community Behavior [Doc 1.1] (1:27–30)

Paul is in trouble with the civic authorities and has been jailed. He knows that his followers in Philippi are also struggling with opposition that can have repercussions within the city. Yet, he encourages them to act appropriately as citizens. Traditionally, the term Paul uses (*politeuō*) is translated as though it is a metaphor and refers to behavior. This would seem to be a rather unique usage. Paul could refer to their behavior as citizens in Philippi (1:27).

This could be another way in which we see Paul as having been influenced by Stoicism. To be a good citizen was viewed as one of the duties (*kathēkonta*). Epictetus lists these as "citizenship, marriage, begetting children, reverence to God, care of parents" (Epictetus, *Diatr.* 3.7.25).[248] The household group is both its own association but also a part of the larger civic organization as well as their being citizens of the world. Paul wants to know that they will continue to act appropriately and respectably.

In a circle of relationships there is a closer connection than civic duty, and that is friendship.[249] This is at the heart of Paul's line of thought beginning with 1:27. Paul uses technical terminology (*mia psychē* "with one soul") from Greek philosophy in the context of friendship. Aristotle provides an early and influential discussion in which he alludes to a commonly understood characteristic of friendship as a "single soul" (Aristotle, *Eth. nic.* 9, 1168b7). Likewise, Plutarch writes "in our friendship's consonance and harmony…it must be as if one soul (*mias psychēs*) were apportioned among two or more bodies" (Plutarch, *Amic. mult.* 8 [96f3]).[250] To Posidonius, the Stoic philosophy of the first century

---

[248] Epictetus, *Discourses, Books 3-4. Fragments. The Encheiridion*, 57.

[249] For an excellent and readable overview see Anthony A. Long, "Friendship and Friends in the Stoic Theory of the Good Life," in *Thinking about Friendship: Historical and Contemporary Philosophical Perspectives*, ed. Damian Caluori (New York: Palgrave Macmillan, 2013).

[250] Plutarch, *Moralia, Volume 2: How to Profit by One's Enemies. On Having Many Friends. Chance. Virtue and Vice. Letter of Condolence to Apollonius. Advice About Keeping Well. Advice to Bride and Groom. The Dinner of the Seven Wise Men. Superstition.* trans. Frank Cole Babbitt, Loeb Classical Library 222 (Cambridge, MA: Harvard University Press, 1928), 67.

BCE and a native of Syria, is attributed the position (along with Hecato) that friendship "exists only between the wise and good, by reason of their likeness to one another. And by friendship they mean a common use of all that has to do with life, wherein we treat our friends as we should ourselves" (Diogenes Laertius, *Lives* 7.1.124 Zeno).[251] Friendship is further characterized by the lengths one will go for a friend. In response to the question of why to have a friend, Seneca writes, "In order to have someone for whom I may die, whom I may follow into exile" (*Ep.* 9.10).[252] It is within this context that we should read Paul. Each person within the group should make progress in their moral development, but they cannot do this alone but within their community of friendship. Within this relationship they love each other if they not only treat one another as they would themselves but put the interests of the other before themselves. Paul will show that this is the example that Jesus provides as praised in a hymn he quotes and in the lives of Timothy and Epaphroditus.

If his friends in Philippi are making progress, then Paul says they will learn to overcome the emotion of fear (1:28). He doesn't say much about who their opponents are. Paul may simply refer to those who are antithetical to the philosophical life. There are reasons to think Paul is not talking about heretics whose destiny is Hell, as it is traditionally interpreted. Paul makes use of a typical salvation/destruction (*sōtēria apōleia*) dichotomy in Greek philosophy between a person whose moral health is being healed (*sōzō* "save") by the therapeutic effect of a virtuous life and the person in decline (*apollymi* "destroy") because of the errors of their ways.[253] The antithesis of their lives is a sign of their moral regress. The quality of the lives of his friends in Philippi indicates their moral health and progress (1:28). For Paul to credit God is not that different from the doctrine of the Stoics. They perceive God as equivalent to the Pneuma, Logos, and Nature that permeates the Cosmos. But it is the active principle that energizes and gives life that is the deity responsible for progress in virtue.

If we take the traditional view about Christian suffering, then verse 30 makes obvious sense. Paul would seem to say that Christians are

---

[251] Diogenes Laertius, *Lives of Eminent Philosophers, Volume 2: Books 6-10*, 229.

[252] Seneca, *Epistles, Volume 1: Epistles 1-65*, 49.

[253] For a full discussion see page 199.

doomed to suffering. However, if we interpret the next sentence within the larger context, then it may further explain Paul's purpose. The followers of Jesus have the responsibility to trust in him and remain firm in their allegiance. They also are responsible to experience the emotion or passion of moral struggles. What is this struggle (*agōn*)? The so-called "agon motif" refers to the struggles of the philosopher. Paul says that they have seen this struggle in him, and they are now hearing in his letter the struggle he is having (1:30). Those who try to live a moral life, Paul says, will "deal with hardships (*paschein*) for (*hyper*) him" (1:29).

It's the struggle Musonius Rufus talks about in Discourse 7. His argument is that people should not be reluctant to experience hardships for the sake of virtue and goodness, since people who want what is bad are willing to experience difficulties getting what they desire. They "for (*hyper*) no honorable reward endure (*paschontas*) such things, while we for the sake of (*hyper*) the ideal good … are not ready to bear every hardship" (Musonius Rufus, *Diatr.* 7.7–11).[254] He concludes by saying:

> How much more fitting, then, it is that we stand firm and endure, when we know that we are suffering (*kakopathountes*) for some good purpose, either to help our friends or to benefit our city, or to defend our wives and children, or, best and most imperative, to become good (*agathoi*) and just (*dikaioi*) and self-controlled (*sōphrones*), a state which no man achieves without hardships (Musonius Rufus, *Diatr.* 7.36–42).[255]

The issue here for Paul is not belief and heresy or salvation and hell-fire (1:28). It is the consistent life of moral progress, the constancy of allegiance, and experiencing hardship for the sake of the cause (1:29).

Mutual Unselfish Relationships [Doc 1.1] (2:1–11)

Paul knows that moral progress is not something achieved privately and alone. He has been discussing the hardships that may be encountered by engaging publicly with people about their need to change from accepting the prevailing social values to be committed to a path that leads to becoming all that a human can be. The household to which he has addressed this letter is made up of people with familial

---

[254] Lutz, "Musonius Rufus," 57.
[255] Lutz, "Musonius Rufus," 59.

relationships as well as friendly connections. They need each other to provide encouragement, support, and commitment (2:1). Central in their relationship needs to be a selfless altruism. Paul once again uses the language of friendship when he describes them as having the same soul (2:2). It is not just that they think alike but that they form the same moral judgments (*to hen phronountes*). Rather than treat each other based on social status, they should have a mutual and reciprocal attitude that the other person is more important (2:3). Paul will present an example for how they should think about the value of others. The death of Jesus is a prime example for Paul about how to regard others. It's not that Jesus's act is the originating example, but that the attitude and actions of Jesus are the principle example of the qualities that Paul wants to see in the interactions of the Philippians (2:5).

The mature person who Paul hopes they will be is based on the idea that humans progress from an early stage in which self-preservation is most important to a fully developed level in which they have come to recognize their place within the world and their relationship to it. The commonly used illustration of this is found in the writings of the Stoic philosopher Hierocles (fl. second century CE). After arguing that animals and human infants demonstrate a guiding principle of self-preservation (so humans will tend to do good because it is the most advantageous), he proceeds to discuss the ways in which more advanced humans recognize their place in the world (*oikeiōsis*) (Hierocles, *Elements of Ethics* 9.2).[256] In his treatise *How Should One Behave toward One's Relatives*, Hierocles illustrates the relationship a person has with others in the form of concentric circles.[257] The inner circles begin with oneself and proceed out to include one's family, relatives, city, ethnic group, citizens, and ultimately all of humanity. One should then work to bring the outer circles into the closer relationship of the next inner circle.[258] Hierocles goes further in his treatise *How Should One Behave toward One's*

---

[256] For the text, translation, and commentary see Hierocles, *Hierocles the Stoic: Elements of Ethics, Fragments, and Excerpts*, ed. Ilaria Ramelli. trans. David Konstan, Writings from the Greco-Roman World 28 (Atlanta: Society of Biblical Literature, 2009).

[257] Hierocles, *Elements of Ethics, Fragments, and Excerpts*, 91.

[258] Hierocles, *Elements of Ethics, Fragments, and Excerpts*, 91.

Country to say that a person should put the needs of the larger group before one's own.

> ...a person who wishes to save himself more than his country, in addition to doing what is unlawful, is also senseless, since he desires things that are impossible, whereas one who honors his country more than himself is both dear to the gods and is furnished with rational arguments. It has been said, nevertheless, that even if one does not count himself in the whole, but rather reckons himself individually, it is appropriate for him to prefer the safety of the whole to his own, because the destruction of the city renders the safety of the citizen impossible (Stobaeus, *Flor.* 3.39.35).[259]

This aspect of progress is also represented by the so-called *scala naturae* (see p. 90). On the one hand, this ladder represents the natural order in which humans near the top are thought to share with the divine the use of reason. On the other hand, this ordering represents the development of humans in their use of reason and attainment of the ultimate goal of a flourishing life (*eudaimonia*) lived in virtue.

Plato begins with the highest order of being and the potential of humans.

> But he who has seriously devoted himself to learning and to true thoughts, and has exercised these qualities above all his others, must necessarily and inevitably think thoughts that are immortal and divine, if so be that he lays hold on truth, and in so far as it is possible for human nature to partake of immortality, he must fall short thereof in no degree; and inasmuch as he is forever tending his divine part and duly magnifying that daemon who dwells along with him, he must be supremely blessed (Plato, *Tim.* 90.C).[260]

Cicero provides later confirmation of the ubiquity of this view, notwithstanding some differences of opinion about the nature of the soul and what constitutes happiness.

---

[259] Hierocles, *Elements of Ethics, Fragments, and Excerpts*, 69,71.

[260] Plato, *Timaeus. Critias. Cleitophon. Menexenus. Epistles.* trans. R. G. Bury, Loeb Classical Library 234 (Cambridge, MA: Harvard University Press, 1929), 247.

> [T]he soul of man, derived as it is from the divine mind, can be compared with nothing else, if it is right to say so, save God alone. Therefore if this soul has been so trained, if its power of vision has been so cared for that it is not blinded by error, the result is mind made perfect, that is, complete reason, and this means also virtue. And if everything is happy which has nothing wanting, and whose measure in its own kind is heaped up and running over, and if this is the peculiar mark of virtue, assuredly all virtuous men are happy (Cicero, *Tusc. Disp.* 5.39).[261]

The outcome of such a development is the capacity of the one who has made progress to determine what is good and what are the right choices to make, even if that might mean the dispreferred indifferents of pain or even death. This is how Epictetus discusses it.

> What is it, then, that disturbs and bewilders the multitude? Is it the tyrant and his bodyguards? How is that possible? Nay, far from it! It is not possible that that which is by nature free should be disturbed or thwarted by anything but itself. But it is a man's own judgements that disturb him. For when the tyrant says to a man, "I will chain your leg," the man who has set a high value on his leg replies, "Nay, have mercy upon me," while the man who has set a high value on his moral purpose replies, "If it seems more profitable to you to do so, chain it." "Do you not care?" "No, I do not care." "I will show you that I am master." "How can you be my master? Zeus has set me free. Or do you really think that he was likely to let his own son be made a slave? You are, however, master of my dead body, take it." "You mean, then, that when you approach me you will not pay attention to me?" "No, I pay attention only to myself. But if you wish me to say that I pay attention to you too, I tell you that I do so, but only as I pay attention to my pot" (Epictetus, *Diatr.* 1.19).[262]

It is for this reason that a person who has made progress and can view other humans as a fellow-citizen and even a friend, has the capacity even

---

[261] Cicero, *Tusculan Disputations*. trans. J. E. King, Loeb Classical Library 141 (Cambridge, MA: Harvard University Press, 1927), 465.

[262] Epictetus, *Discourses, Books 1-2*, 129.

to die for the good of others in a noble cause. Jacob Klein reaches this conclusion in his study of Stoics and *oikeiōsis*.

> Such a reconstruction is consonant with the prominent place given to the *oikeiōsis* doctrine in even cursory allusions to Stoic ethical theory, and it supplies the Stoics with the ethical foundation they need: one that makes the end for each creature consist in the functions appropriate to it in virtue of the kind of creature it is. Under this interpretation, the Stoics are no longer saddled with the burden of explaining how narrowly egoistic motivation is supplanted in human beings by rational motivation of a fundamentally different character. Instead, they are building an inductive case for an analysis of teleological functioning that applies throughout the *scala naturae*.[263]

It is within this framework that the author of 4 Maccabees describes the endurance of the Jewish patriots who withstood the attempts of Antiochus Epiphanes to force them to act contrary to their own moral judgements based in Torah. Their faithfulness in death is an example of reason having mastery over the passions (4 Macc 1:7–8; 18:1–2). Further, their deaths were considered a ransom (*antipsychos*) for sin (4 Macc 17:21) and an atonement (*hilastērion*) for the nation (4 Macc 17:22). They are extolled for their reward by which "they now stand before the divine throne and live the life of eternal blessedness" (4 Macc 17:18 NRSV).

It would seem that, when Paul wanted to provide the Philippians with an example of the practical wisdom that is selfless and altruistic, he has at hand this hymn (2:6–11). Scholars differ on how to arrange the lines to reconstruct the poetry. Here I am adapting the lines as Jerome Murphy-O'Connor has suggested, though the translation is completely my own. I also follow him in his suggestion that extended lines might give evidence of someone adding a gloss (explanatory phrase) to complete the meaning.[264]

How we understand Paul's use of the word "form" (*morphē*) in verse 6 needs to be balanced with its opposite in verse 7. In verse 7 Jesus renounces his status. The term usually translated as "empty" is

---

[263] Jacob Klein, "The Stoic Argument From Oikeiōsis," in *Oxford Studies in Ancient Philosophy*, ed. Victor Caston (Oxford University Press, 2016), 194.

[264] Murphy-O'Connor, *Paul: A Critical Life*, 225.

misunderstood by putting it in terms of a container that has its contents poured out. It's not this idea but one of being stripped of status and value. The result is Jesus takes the "form" of a slave. One wouldn't say that there is an ontological entity that is a deity and one that is a slave. Becoming a slave is a matter of giving up one's status in society rather than an ontological transformation. Verse 6 refers to the divine role that Jesus subsumed as a wise teacher. In the same way that Jesus did not grasp and hold on to his status as god-like person but gave up his freedom when he was arrested, so he did not maintain his own rights as a human but debased himself to be executed in the most humiliating of ways.

As a result of his willing "demotion," God recognized the death of Jesus as a noble death: he endured the suffering of execution and did it for the benefit of others (2:7–8). The hymn includes the exact phrase (2:8) as appears in the 4 Maccabees account of the martyrs, "They vindicated their nation, looking to God and enduring torture even to death (*mechri thanatou*)" (4 Macc 17:10 NRSV).

Paul uses a term not appearing much elsewhere, but he knows from his Greek Bible where it is used to refer to the divine realm, "you are exalted beyond all gods" (Ps 96:9 LXX). What Jesus received was, in a sense, a promotion to the highest rank, which Paul puts in terms of receiving a name (2:9). It would not seem that Paul should be taken literally here. It's not the specific name of Jesus or the title of lord. It is the glory and fame he received which transcends all others. It's because of this that all bow with respect and that all would profess Jesus Christ as Lord (2:10–11).

Consistent Practice Produces Moral Health [Doc 1.1] (2:12–18)

The outcome Paul desires from the Philippians based on them putting into practice a form of life based on selfless thinking that sacrifices for others and following the example of Jesus is, literally, "to work out your own salvation (*tēn eautōn sōtērian katergazesthe*)" (2:12 NRSV). These terms are used together in an interesting text for comparison.

In the tragedy, *The Children of Herakles*, Macaria, a daughter of Heracles, volunteers to be a sacrifice to Persephone to save the city from the military attack of Eurystheus, king of Mycenae. Macaria speaks.

Is it not better to die than to win a fate I do not deserve? The other course might more befit someone else who is not as illustrious as I.

Lead me to the place where it seems good that my body should be killed and garlanded and consecrated to the goddess! Defeat the enemy! For my life is at your disposal, full willingly, and I offer to be put to death on my brothers' behalf and on my own. For, mark it well, by not clinging to my life I have made a most splendid discovery, how to die with glory (Euripides, *Heracl.* 526–534).[265]

In the end Eurystheus tells the city of Athens that, if they go ahead and execute him, his spirit will benefit them by protecting them from the children of Heracles. He says to the Athenians, "Why then do you hesitate if you can *secure safety* (*sōtērian katergasasthai*) for the city and for your descendants" (Euripides, *Heracl.* 1045)?[266]

Paul uses this language and tradition of a noble death within a philosophical context. Salvation terminology in the context of moral progress refers to the therapeutic effects produced by the healing of the soul. Paul can both say they produce the salutary effects of moral progress, but also that it happens because of God's activity (2:13). Stoics could have said the same thing by attributing to God—or Pneuma or Nature—the active force of change in the soul.

In Plato's work, *Theaetetus*, he has Socrates drawing a parallel between the action necessary to strengthen and improve the body and the same effect needed for the soul (see also p. 84). Rest and idleness spoil the body, but the body "by exertion and motion it can be preserved (*sōzetai*)" (Plato, *Theaet.* 153.b).[267] Socrates then concludes, "Isn't it by learning and study, which are motions, that the soul gains knowledge and is preserved (*sōzetai*) and becomes a better thing" (Plato, *Theaet.* 153.b)?[268] As early as Plato and during the time of Paul and later, Greco-

---

[265] Euripides, *Children of Heracles. Hippolytus. Andromache. Hecuba.* trans. David Kovacs, Loeb Classical Library 484 (Cambridge, MA: Harvard University Press, 1995), 59.

[266] Euripides, *Children of Heracles. Hippolytus. Andromache. Hecuba*, 111.

[267] Cooper and Hutchinson, eds., *Plato: Complete Works*, 170.

[268] Cooper and Hutchinson, eds., *Plato: Complete Works*, 170.

Roman moral philosophy used the language of salvation in moral contexts to describe the improvement of the soul by the exercise of the mind in making proper moral judgments. This is the context in which Paul is urging the Philippians to practice their way of thinking in a way that improves the soul.

It is clear in this section that Paul expects an ongoing practice that brings about moral progress. Within the community there needs to be a focused and deliberate process of mutual and reciprocal psychagogy "without bickering and quarreling" (2:14). Paul concludes this section with a flourish of metaphorical language. His exhortation is for them to be constant and consistent in their actions so that he would be proud of what they have accomplished, and he will not feel like his efforts were useless.

Recommendation Letter for Timothy [Doc 2] (2:19–24)

Letters of introduction or recommendation usually have a specific form. There is an opening identifying the sender and the recipient along with a greeting and some wish for good health. Next, the person being introduced, who is the person carrying the letter, is mentioned and reasons are given for the recommendation. The sender will ask for this favor, promise to return the favor in some way, and provide a reason for having sent the person. After expressing appreciation, the sender wishes the recipient well and closes with a salutation.[269]

In this section of Philippians, the commendation of Timothy is not written as though it would be carried by Timothy but for an expected visit by Timothy. If this had been a letter Paul sent ahead of a visit by Timothy, then the editor has left off the opening of the letter. Paul writes that the purpose of the letter is that he hopes to send Timothy so he can know how things are in Philippi (2:19). He repeats his intentions at the end and hopes that he can visit Philippi soon (2:23–24).

The body of the letter introduces Timothy and why Paul is commending him to them. For Paul, no one is like Timothy (2:20). Timothy is an example of someone who has the qualities Paul exhorts in 2:4 and was exemplified by Jesus as the hymn shows. Timothy will have concern for "the things" of the Philippians, what is best for them, and

---

[269] Stowers, *Letter Writing in Greco-Roman Antiquity*, 153-65.

not use them for his own purpose (2:21). Those who pretend to be a friend but are only out for their own gain is a common trope in Greco-Roman moral philosophy.

Paul then commends Timothy as being trustworthy. He reminds them of their experience of Timothy (2:22). To Paul, Timothy was more like a son in the way they traveled around and talked to people about the good news. Letters of recommendation might contain language of the relationship of the person to the sender. In this case, Paul uses the language of kinship as a metaphor.

Recommendation Letter for Epaphroditus [Doc 3] (2:25–30)

This section of Philippians closely fits the style and formula for a letter of recommendation. The editor has not included the opening to maintain the flow of the composite document. Epaphroditus is introduced and given a string of epithets: brother, coworker, fellow soldier, apostle, and minister (2:25). The reason for sending him is that he had been experiencing a near-fatal illness. Paul is aware that they know of his illness (2:26) and is sending not only a report of his recovery but, it would seem, the man himself (2:28).

Paul then asks that they treat him well (2:29). He is deserving of their hospitality because his bad condition was somehow directly related to helping Paul. This sense of self-sacrifice (2:30) is expressed with the same language as in the hymn with the phrase "to the point of death" (2:8). At the point of the writing of this, Paul had yet to receive any support from the Philippians. It may be that Epaphroditus was working to earn wages in order to help Paul in his situation. Rather than supposing he had an illness, perhaps he was involved with dangerous work, injured himself, and thereby became "weak" in his body.

Inserted Letter Closing [Doc 1.2] (3:1)

The sentences in 3:1 seem like the ending of a letter. It is introduced by an idiom, which used in this way, indicates the last or final things in the sequence of topics. It functions in the same way as 2:18 in its call to rejoice.

The second sentence of 3:1 may or may not have followed the preceding sentence in its original context. If it did, then it would seem to be an apology for telling them to rejoice a second time. In what sense doing this is a preventative is difficult to see. In whatever context this appeared, it would have contained a repetition of something Paul had written previously. He says it is not a problem for him to write again, but it is a way of making sure they get the message.

Letter to Gentile Adherents [Doc 4] (3:2–4:1)

It is not too far-fetched to think Paul is addressing gentiles beginning at 3:2. Whether or not I'm right will depend on how much it helps explain what Paul has to say. This paraenetic letter begins with a warning. That Paul gives a warning in the context of circumcision would suggest that he is directing his attention to gentile men.

Paul uses repetition to identify of whom the gentile men should be aware. It would seem that he is making a pun by calling this group *katatomē* in verse two and then using the term *peritomē* in verse three. To get across the pun I've translated the first term as "Excision" and the second as "Circumcision." I take it that Paul is addressing a similar topic as he did in his letter to the Galatians.

It's not surprising that Paul is the harshest when talking about the Judaizing group of Jewish followers of Jesus. I take Paul's first term "dog" to refer to these Judaizers in a way that exaggerates their behavior (3:2). Dogs often appear in contexts related to blood. Theocritus (third century BCE) in *Idyll* 10 has Milon use a proverb, "It's dangerous for a dog to taste guts." Aesop tells the story of a man who is told that his dog bite can be cured if he drops blood on a piece of bread and has the dog eat it. The man rejects the suggestion believing that all the dogs in the city will then want to bite him (Aesop, *Fab.* 64). Aeschylus uses the phrase, "As a dog hunts a wounded fawn, we also track the blood-drops" (Aeschylus, *Eum.* 247). Paul would have been familiar with the story of Naboth, "In the place where dogs licked up the blood of Naboth, dogs will also lick up your blood" (1 Kgs 21:19 NRSV; 3 Kgdms 20:19 LXX). The second epithet, literally "evil workers," is equally puzzling, since it is not a common expression. Perhaps Paul equates the performance of circumcision on a gentile follower of Jesus with someone doing something bad.

As I have argued elsewhere (see p. 32), Paul adapts himself to his gentile audience not only rhetorically, but perhaps even as someone who had circumcision reversal surgery and came to consider himself something of a biracial person or of having dual citizenship. In this way, he can write to gentiles with the "we" as one who shares in their experience (3:3). Maybe Paul has in mind anyone who is a follower of Jesus by which that relationship becomes more important than one's position or status.

Paul responds to the Judaizing faction by boasting that there is a better way of thinking of cutting off the flesh. I take Paul to mean that pride in the customs of one's heritage does not lead to progress in the moral life (3:3). The advantages of what is external does not make a difference in one's virtue. In what follows Paul gives a Jewish version of the categories of one's birth, upbringing, power, and status (3:5–6). He does not mean that he considers his Judaism to be of no worth, but it is not what makes him an upright man.

Paul affirms that he is an observant Jew and blameless of any wrongdoing regarding Torah (3:6). He also acknowledges that he is righteous as a Jew (3:9). We should not infer a pejorative meaning like "self-righteous." This also happens when people read Luke's statement of Jesus answering the question why he eats with tax collectors and sinners: "Jesus answered, 'Those who are well have no need of a physician, but those who are sick; I have come to call not the righteous but sinners to repentance" (Luke 5:31–32). Christians feel duty bound to insert a word to make it say "self-righteous." The clear implication is that those Jews who observed Torah were "righteous" and not in need of repentance.

Paul's list is like what we find in speeches of praise. It was common in encomia to recount a person's heritage (ethnic background, country of birth, famous ancestors, parentage), upbringing (education, achievements), and their accomplishments that indicate the quality of their character. Paul seems to take those things that the Judaizers might be proud about and beat them at their own game. While Paul values these, when it comes to one's moral development, they are not significant at all (3:7–8).

Paul's categories can be compared to the Stoic "indifferents." For example, Epictetus lists the things external to us and not under our control as "our body, our property, reputation, office…" (*Ench.* 1.2).[270]

---

[270] Epictetus, *Discourses, Books 3-4. Fragments. The Encheiridion*, 483.

Elsewhere, he imagines a scene in which God tests a young Stoic on his progress.

> When you come into the presence of some prominent man, remember that Another looks from above on what is taking place, and that you must please Him rather than this man. He, then, who is above asks of you, "In your school what did you call exile and imprisonment and bonds and death and disrepute?" "I called them things indifferent." "What, then, do you call them now? Have they changed at all?" "No." "Have you, then, changed?" "No." "Tell me, then, what things are indifferent." "Those that are independent of the moral purpose." "Tell me also what follows." "Things independent of the moral purpose are nothing to me." "Tell me also what you thought were the good things." "A proper moral purpose and a proper use of external impressions." "And what was the end (*telos*)?" "To follow Thee" (Epictetus, *Diatr.* 1.30.1–5).[271]

If Paul were questioned in the same way, he would say that whatever advantages he had because of his upbringing are nothing compared to following Jesus (3:7). The *telos* for Paul is the same. Followers of Jesus are helped by the example of Jesus, who is perhaps the only person to have achieved the level of being a sage because of his faithfulness to God in his death for the benefit of others. Consequently, he experienced apotheosis. Therefore, Paul figures that those who follow his example will also achieve the same (3:12).

It's not that martyrdom is the only way. It's not so much the manner of death but the quality of life at death. Cicero, the politician, rhetorician, and philosopher, wrote over a hundred years earlier, about the destiny of the soul. He disagreed with Stoics, who considered the soul to dissipate into the universal soul, and the Epicureans, who believed the soul to be extinguished at death. In his work *On Friendship*, he wrote in praise of Scipio about his own more Platonic concept of the soul's destiny after death. Cicero has Laelius espouse the view, "that human souls were of God; that upon their departure from the body a return to heaven lay open to them, and that in proportion as each soul was virtuous and just would the return be easy and direct" (*Amic.* 1.4.13). He goes on to say,

---

[271] Epictetus, *Discourses, Books 1-2*, 201.

"If the truth really is that the souls of all good men after death make the easiest escape from what may be termed the imprisonment and fetters of the flesh, whom can we think of as having had an easier journey to the gods than Scipio?" (*Amic.* 1.4.14).[272]

We must always remember that Paul's language is not about being restored to life from the state of being dead (3:11). It is a graphic image of corpses out from among whom the resurrected person rises. More precisely, the image is of the dead existing in the underworld out of which they rise. This is the language describing the ascension of Jesus after having, "descended into the underworld" (Eph 4:9).

Paul imagines the philosophical life as a runner who exercises and trains to reach a pinnacle of performance (3:12). The goal is not to end the race—to die before others—but to be the best one can be, the excellence of what it means to be a human. In verse twelve Paul uses the language of perfection in the sense of completeness and full maturity (*teleioō*). Paul has not reached this level yet, but he eschews the "indifferent" advantages and strives to reach the goal. Paul's words "pursue, press on" (*diōkō*, my trans. "sprint") and "mark, goal" (*skopos*) in verse fourteen are the same words used by Epictetus in a similar context. Those things indifferent to the pursuit of virtue are external to us or outside of our control. Epictetus says,

> First, therefore, we ought to have these principles at command, and to do nothing apart from them, but keep the soul intent upon this mark (*skopon*); we must pursue (*diōkein*) none of the things external, none of the things which are not our own, but as He that is mighty has ordained; pursuing without any hesitation the things that lie within the sphere of the moral purpose, and all other things as they have been given us (*Diatr.* 4.12.15).[273]

Paul calls the goal the award determined by the judge in the competition (*brabeion*) (3:14). He uses this word again in his correspondence with the Corinthians, "Do you not know that in a race the runners all compete, but only one receives the prize (*brabeion*)? Run in such a way that you

---

[272] Cicero, *On Old Age. On Friendship. On Divination.* trans. W. A. Falconer, Loeb Classical Library 154 (Cambridge, MA: Harvard University Press, 1923), 123.

[273] Epictetus, *Discourses, Books 3-4. Fragments. The Encheiridion*, 427.

may win it" (1 Cor 9:24 NRSV). He continues the metaphor, "Athletes exercise self-control in all things; they do it to receive a perishable wreath (*stephanon*), but we an imperishable one" (1 Cor 9:25 NRSV).

The same metaphor is used in 4 Maccabees.

> Truly the contest (*agōn*) in which they were engaged was divine, for on that day virtue gave the awards and tested them for their endurance. The prize was immortality in endless life. Eleazar was the first contestant, the mother of the seven sons entered the competition, and the brothers contended. The tyrant was the antagonist, and the world and the human race were the spectators. Reverence for God was victor and gave the crown to its own athletes. Who did not admire the athletes of the divine legislation? Who were not amazed? The tyrant himself and all his council marveled at their endurance, because of which they now stand before the divine throne and live the life of eternal blessedness (4 Macc 17:11–18) NRSV).

This is the context from which Paul uses this metaphor to talk about what is possible for the follower of Jesus. Again, it's not martyrdom but endurance and virtue that receive an award of divine blessedness with God.

Paul follows up the description of his way of life with a section of moral exhortation. He first addresses the mature (*teleioi*), the ones who have progressed to a level of complete maturity in the moral life (3:15–16). These are the ones Paul works more closely with in the group's leadership. They function as the philosophical guides. He encourages them to support his point of view and to maintain their level of progress (3:16).

Paul urges the rest of the group, the brothers and sisters, to join in the practice of imitation of him and others like him (3:17). That Paul seems to address a less advanced group of people may be supported by the ancient practice of imitation being primarily for the less mature. The Stoic philosopher Panaetius (185–110 BCE) is known to have modified the practice to focus on individual proclivities.

> [Panaetius] also appears to attach much more importance to the individual nature of human beings. Whereas in the doctrine of the ancient Stoa, everyone had to strive for the same ideal,

embodied by the sage, Panaetius succeeds in differentiating the people: each person should hold on to his own peculiar talents (as far as they are not vicious), instead of imitating the personal characteristics of others. Even more, the same action can be appropriate for one person, but not for another, so that one needs a great deal of self-knowledge to determine what should be done. It is clear, then, that the final goal can be reached in many different ways.[274]

Seneca refers to philosophical guides as ones who provide "a helping hand" (*Ep.* 52.2).[275] He continues to discuss the types of students with reference to Epicurus. Praise is given for those who do not need help but find their motivation from within themselves. There is another level of students "who need outside help, who will not proceed unless someone leads the way, but who will follow faithfully" (*Ep.* 52.3). That second level is considered excellent. Seneca says of this, "Nor need you despise a man who can gain salvation only with the assistance of another; the will to be saved means a great deal, too" (*Ep.* 52.4). The third type is one that requires more compulsion. They "do not need a guide as much as they require someone to encourage and, as it were, to force them along" (*Ep.* 52.4).[276] Though they all may reach the goal, the best type is the one who needs less attention.[277]

Paul gives a counter-example (3:18). These are not false teachers of some sort. They represent the stereotype of the vice-ridden person. Those who are not good examples but provide a bad influence are considered enemies (*echthros*). For example, Diogenes Laertius writes about the famous Stoic philosopher Zeno, who applied "to all men who are not virtuous the opprobrious epithets of foemen (*echthrous*), enemies (*polemious*), slaves, and aliens to one another, parents to children, brothers to brothers, friends to friends" (*Lives* 7.1.32 Zeno).[278] Epictetus concurs, "And this is the nature of every being, to pursue the good and

---

[274] Geert Roskam, *On the Path to Virtue: The Stoic Doctrine of Moral Progress and its Reception in (Middle-) Platonism* (Leuven: Leuven University Press, 2005), 42.

[275] Seneca, *Epistles, Volume 1: Epistles 1-65*, 345.

[276] Seneca, *Epistles, Volume 1: Epistles 1-65*, 345.

[277] For more discussion on the types of students in the Epicurean school, see Glad, *Paul and Philodemus*, 137-52.

[278] Diogenes Laertius, *Lives of Eminent Philosophers, Volume 2: Books 6-10*, 145.

to flee from the evil; and to consider the man who robs us of the one and invests us with the other as an enemy (*polemion*) and an aggressor, even though he be a brother, even though he be a son, even though he be a father; for nothing is closer kin to us than our good." (*Diatr.* 4.5.30).

When Paul says, literally, "their end is destruction" in 3:19, he is not referring to eternal damnation. The Greek words for salvation (*sōtēria*) and for destruction (*apōleia*) can be found as early as Plato and among later moral philosophers to talk about the progress and regress of the soul. This concept appears in the following quotation from Epictetus along with the theme of imitating an example.

> You are no longer a lad, but already a full-grown man (*teleios*). If you are now neglectful and easy-going, and always making one delay after another, and fixing first one day and then another, after which you will pay attention to yourself, then without realizing it you will make no progress, but, living and dying, will continue to be a layman throughout. Make up your mind, therefore, before it is too late, that the fitting thing for you to do is to live as a mature man (*teleion*) who is making progress (*prokoptonta*) and let everything which seems to you to be best be for you a law that must not be transgressed. And if you meet anything that is laborious, or sweet, or held in high repute, or in no repute, remember that now is the contest (*agōn*), and here before you are the Olympic games, and that it is impossible to delay any longer, and that it depends on a single day and a single action, whether progress is lost (*apollytai*) or saved (*sōzetai*). This is the way Socrates became what he was ("became perfect" *apotelesthē*), by paying attention to nothing but his reason in everything that he encountered. And even if you are not yet a Socrates, still you ought to live as one who wishes to be a Socrates (*Ench.* 51.1–2).[279]

Paul also criticizes them as gluttonous; literally, "God is their belly (*koilia*)" (3:19). It is not, however, a reference to overeating. It is a typical way to describe the vice-ridden person. For example, Epictetus compares Socrates to the way humans normally think of themselves, "This is what it means for a man to be in very truth a kinsman of the

---

[279] Epictetus, *Discourses, Books 3-4. Fragments. The Encheiridion*, 535.

gods. We, however, think of ourselves as though we were mere bellies (*koiliai*), entrails, and genitals, just because we have fear, because we have appetite, and we flatter those who have power to help us in these matters, and these same men we fear" (*Diatr*. 1.9.26).[280] Likewise, Seneca depicts the person who lives in seclusion and in selfishness out of fear as "not living for himself; he is living for his belly (*ventri*), his sleep, and his lust,—and that is the most shameful thing in the world" (*Ep*. 55.5).

The last phrase of verse nineteen continues the phronetic language regarding how to think or apply practical wisdom. Paul uses similar expressions elsewhere (Rom 8:5–7; cf. Col 3:2). The distinction is between a lower form of thinking that is associated with the earth or flesh and a higher form of thinking that is spiritual and heavenly, a divine way of living. This is the goal of the Christian life, according to Paul, as it was the goal of the philosophical life. Epicurus writes to a disciple, Menoeceus,

> Exercise thyself in these and kindred precepts day and night, both by thyself and with him who is like unto thee; then never, either in waking or in dream, wilt thou be disturbed, but wilt live as a god among men. For man loses all semblance of mortality by living in the midst of immortal blessings (Diogenes Laertius, *Lives* 135.5 Epicurus).[281]

The Socratic schools encouraged this type of practice. Daily meditation was a way to develop the mind so that one could cope with life and rise above the vicissitudes of human experience. For people in the Greco-Roman world, this was the life of the gods.

Those whose lives are filled with vice, Paul shows in 4:19, are ones whose values are earthly. Paul now contrasts this with a political metaphor. He tells his audience their allegiance is to a political entity (*politeuma*) in the heavens (3:20), whose values transcend the customs and opinions of humans. The world to which they belong is larger than the local way of life.

It is common knowledge that the Stoics believed in the "brotherhood of man," in being a cosmopolitan or "citizen of the world." As Epictetus

---

[280] Epictetus, *Discourses, Books 1-2*, 71.

[281] Diogenes Laertius, *Lives of Eminent Philosophers, Volume 2: Books 6-10*, 659.

describes it, quoting either Poseidonius or perhaps Chrysippus, that concept goes far beyond a humanistic and altruistic way of thinking.

> Well, then, anyone who has attentively studied the administration of the universe and has learned that "the greatest and most authoritative and most comprehensive of all governments is this one, which is composed of men and God, and that from Him have descended the seeds of being, not merely to my father or to my grandfather, but to all things that are begotten and that grow upon earth, and chiefly to rational beings, seeing that by nature it is theirs alone to have communion in the society of God, being intertwined with him through the reason,"—why should not such a man call himself a citizen of the universe? Why should he not call himself a son of God? And why shall he fear anything that happens among men? (Epictetus, *Diatr.* 1.9.4)?[282]

For Paul this concept is part of his thinking as a Pharisee. Belief in the resurrection of bodies means that humans not only live a divine life in the Hellenistic sense of *eudaimonia*, but also participate in the resurrection. As a follower of Jesus, Paul regards Jesus as the one who is returning and will be the judge on the day (3:21).

Verse twenty-one describes the reconfiguring or "reschematization" (*metaschēmatizō*) that Paul believes will occur at the resurrection. The language depicts nothing less than the apotheosis of humans to a divine state. This idea is already present in the Hellenistic Jewish text of 4 Maccabees. The eldest son, who is bound and scourged, then tied to the rack, refuses to eat pork as a demonstration of his virtue. The gruesome scene of torture in which he is both stretched on the wheel and being burned alive culminates in the description of his fortitude, "but as though transformed (*metaschēmatizomenos*) by fire into immortality, he nobly endured the rackings" (4 Macc 9:22 NRSV). He then calls on them follow his example: "'Imitate me, brothers,' he said. 'Do not leave your post in my struggle or renounce our courageous brotherhood. Fight the sacred and noble battle for piety'" (4 Macc 9:23–24 NRSV).

The metaphor in 4:1 seems to be of the winner of a race, who is cheered and whose head is wreathed with a garland. Paul's frequent

---

[282] Epictetus, *Discourses, Books 1-2*, 63, 65.

reference to the judgment of Christ suggests he held the belief that the achievement of those to whom he ministered would bring him a great reward in heaven. The psychagogue not only has a responsibility for those who are guided but also a reward for their growth and progress.

Practice of Virtue & the Tranquil Life [Doc 1.3] (4:2–9)

I take this section to be a closing of the main letter which began the collection. Paul's letters, as letters normally did, end with a section in which he mentions various people. We have Paul in 4:2 addressing two women, Euodia and Syntyche, and an anonymous person whom he calls "co-yoked" (*syzyge*). What follows is some miscellaneous paraenesis and a virtue list.

The situation of Euodia and Syntyche has traditionally been taken to be one of disharmony. The literal expression "to think the same thing" refers to being in agreement, but more aptly means "forming the same moral judgment." Josephus, for example, uses this exact idiom to refer to the Essenes' ethical judgment regarding marriage, "to adopt the same view" (*B.J.* 2.160).[283] It is only "mirror reading" that causes us to jump to the conclusion that the women must not be getting along with each other. But nothing in the context suggests they have a conflict between them. Paul has used this expression in Philippians to encourage the community to have unanimity in the moral life regarding seeking the benefit of the other (2:2–3). This climaxes in the plea for them to think (or form the same moral judgment) as Christ Jesus did when he debased himself for the benefit of others (2:5–11). The most we could say is these two women, who have served so faithfully, have a difference of opinion regarding some aspect of the moral life. My speculation is that they are wealthy women who have shown some sense of superiority over others in the assembly by their actions.

Paul addresses a single person in verse three as a "dedicated companion." Since the term here is literally "co-yoked one" and when used in the feminine can refer to a wife, some ancient authorities speculated that Paul is here addressing his wife, perhaps Lydia in whose home the church was founded. The argument against this is a problem

---

[283] Josephus, *The Jewish War, Volume 1: Books 1-2*. trans. H. St. J. Thackeray, Loeb Classical Library 203 (Cambridge, MA: Harvard University Press, 1927), 385.

of grammar. The expression is grammatically masculine. Why this was not a problem for Greek scholars of the second and third centuries C.E. is baffling. Whoever it is it is most likely the householder, Paul's patron in Philippi. Some have suggested this exhortation to a single individual must be Epaphroditus.

An aspect of hortatory letters is to include brief gnomic sentences as we have in 4:4–7). Often the sentences seem not to have any relationship of thought or theme. The term I've translated as "amiability" (*epieikēs*; other trans. read "gentleness, moderation") in 4:5 only occurs here in Paul's undisputed letters and only a few times elsewhere (1 Tim 3:3; Titus 3:2; Jas 3:17; 1 Pet 2:18). We can compare Paul's usage to those writing within a similar context. Musonius Rufus, for example, in a discussion on exile says that a person who has this quality, whom he calls a "reasonable person," should not consider moving one's residence to live elsewhere as banishment. This kind of person, Musonius goes on to say, "does not value or despise any place as the cause of his happiness or unhappiness, but he makes the whole matter depend upon himself and considers himself a citizen of the city of God which is made up of men and gods" (Musonius Rufus, *Diatr.* 9.19).[284] Similarly, Epictetus notes that an ill-tempered person does us a favor by exercising our good-nature and amiability, our capacity for coping with such a person (Epictetus, *Diatr.* 3.20.12). Even disease is not a reason to lose one's composure, but instead Epictetus depicts the amiable person as saying, "I will show its character, I will shine in it, I will be firm, I will be serene, I will not fawn upon my physician, I will not pray for death" (Epictetus, *Diatr.* 3.20.14–15).[285] The same goes for any circumstances of life: "Everything that you give I will turn into something blessed, productive of happiness, august, enviable" (Epictetus, *Diatr.* 3.20.15).[286]

Because the phrase at the end of 4:5 is part of the same verse as what precedes, it's easy to think Paul must mean, "be a certain way because Jesus is coming soon, and he'll punish you for misbehaving." Instead, the phrase is probably a separate, unrelated word of encouragement. Paul may not even be referring here to the second coming of Christ. Although the expression "the Lord is near" occurs in the Hebrew Bible,

---

[284] Lutz, "Musonius Rufus," 69.

[285] Epictetus, *Discourses, Books 3-4. Fragments. The Encheiridion*, 121.

[286] Epictetus, *Discourses, Books 3-4. Fragments. The Encheiridion*, 121.

there are other instances where the expression is intended to give comfort by the close presence of God (Pss 34:18; 119:151; 145:18). Here, the phrase may have more to do with the context that follows.

The disturbed state of mind Paul writes about in 4:6–7 is not a particular concern of Hebrew literature. The tranquility of the soul or mind is of paramount importance to the philosophers of Paul's day. Plutarch, for example, writes of this in his work *On Tranquility of Mind*. Every day, he says, is as much a day for celebration as a festival day, "For the universe is a most holy temple and most worthy of a god. ... Since life is a most perfect initiation into these things and a ritual celebration of them, it should be full of tranquility and joy" (*Tranq.* 477.D).[287] While some people only take delight in the celebrations of a festival and otherwise live in sadness due to the burdensome and unending cares of life, they ought to receive admonition and "remember the past with thankfulness, and meet the future without fear or suspicion, with their hopes cheerful and bright" (*Tranq.* 477.F).[288]

Phil 4:6–7 are grammatically one sentence. (Our earliest Greek texts show virtually no word or sentence divisions either by spacing or punctuation.) The reasoning is that, rather than being overly concerned about our circumstances, we should trust in God's providential care. The result is a tranquility or serenity that overcomes the mind's natural inclination to imagine the negative potential consequences of our circumstances.

Our English translations of 4:7 seem to suggest the meaning that God's peace is something humans cannot understand. The point of the sentence is that God's peace prevails over our minds (*noys*) and protects our way of feeling and thinking so that we are not perturbed by bad emotions.

In 4:8, Paul refers to the philosophical practice of daily meditation. He uses the same term (*logizō*) as Epictetus for making a rational account of one's thoughts and actions. A standard for meditation, which Epictetus quotes in part (*Diatr.* 3.10.2), was the Golden Verses of Pythagoras:

---

[287] Plutarch, *Moralia, Volume 6*, 239.
[288] Plutarch, *Moralia, Volume 6*, 241.

> Never suffer sleep to close thy eyelids, after thy going to bed, till thou hast examined by thy reason all thy actions of the day. Wherein have I done amiss? What have I done? What have I omitted that I ought to have done? If in this examination thou find that thou hast done amiss, reprimand thyself severely for it; And if thou hast done any good, rejoice. Practice thoroughly all these things; meditate on them well; thou ought to love them with all thy heart. 'Tis they that will put thee in the way of divine virtue (40–46).[289]

Epictetus suggests this form of meditation.

> [A]s soon as you get up in the morning bethink you, "What do I yet lack in order to achieve tranquility? What to achieve calm? What am I? I am not a paltry body, not property, not reputation, am I? None of these. Well, what am I? A rational creature." What, then, are the demands upon you? Rehearse your actions. "Where did I go wrong?" in matters conducive to serenity? "What did I do" that was unfriendly, or unsocial, or unfeeling? "What to be done was left undone" in regard to these matters? (*Diatr.* 4.6.34).[290]

Seneca refers to this form of meditation on virtue:

> Hence, you must be continually brought to remember these facts; for they should not be in storage, but ready for use. And whatever is wholesome should be often discussed and often brought before the mind, so that it may be not only familiar to us, but also ready to hand (*Ep.* 94.26).[291]

Phil 4:9 is the language of a teacher with a pupil. They learned from Paul through his teaching, through what he passed along to them, and through observing his life. They were then to put that example into their own daily practice. The result is the tranquility or serenity that is a divine

---

[289] Florence M. Firth, *The Golden Verses of Pythagoras and other Pythagorean Fragments* (London: Theosophical Pub. House Ltd., 1923), 3.

[290] Epictetus, *Discourses, Books 3-4. Fragments. The Encheiridion*, 359.

[291] Seneca, *Epistles, Volume 3: Epistles 93-124*. trans. Richard M. Gummere, Loeb Classical Library 77 (Cambridge, MA: Harvard University Press, 1925), 29.

quality of life. In Epicurus's *Letter to Menoeceus*, he summarizes the philosophical practice that achieves the goal.

> So we must exercise ourselves in the things which bring happiness, since, if that be present, we have everything, and, if that be absent, all our actions are directed toward attaining it. Those things which without ceasing I have declared unto thee, those do, and exercise thyself therein, holding them to be the elements of right life (Diogenes Laertius, *Lives*, 10.122–123 Epicurus).[292]

Gratitude for Financial Support [Doc 5] (4:10–20)

Throughout Paul's letters, he expresses a concern about the support he receives from his communities. On the one hand, he defends the right of people to receive an exchange of goods for ministry they perform. On the other hand, he adamantly opposes any suggestion that he is only performing his work because people are paying him to do it. A common theme of Greco-Roman moral philosophy is the salaried philosopher who is not legitimate but a sophist, charlatan, or parasite (see p. 48).

Paul is quick to say that he is not discussing financial obligations the Philippians might have to him because he has something lacking in his ability to cope with life's circumstances. He takes this time to discuss another essential aspect of the philosophical life, what is commonly referred to by the technical term self-sufficiency (*autarkēs*). This is not a humanistic concept but one in which the person depends on God's providential care in the world. The person is not dependent on the circumstances of life for virtue, freedom, or happiness. Seneca emphasizes that this self-sufficiency—he uses the Latin term *contentum* from which we get our word contentment—does not mean we are emotionless: "our ideal wise man feels his troubles, but overcomes them" (Seneca, *Ep.* 9.3).[293] The self-sufficient person is also not a loner but desires friendship for the purpose of supporting each other in virtue. The mature person lacks nothing even though "the sage may love his friends

---

[292] Diogenes Laertius, *Lives of Eminent Philosophers, Volume 2: Books 6-10*, 649.

[293] Seneca, *Epistles, Volume 1: Epistles 1-65*, 45.

dearly, often comparing them with himself, and putting them ahead of himself" (Seneca, *Ep.* 9.18).[294]

Paul's language about self-sufficiency is in line with that of the Greco-Roman moral philosophers. Wealth itself is something indifferent to progress in virtue. Being poor is not virtuous, nor is having wealth evil. No matter what the circumstances, Paul can say he has taught himself how to maintain his spiritual equilibrium despite poverty or wealth. In a work titled, *On Self-Sufficiency*, preserved from the third century BCE Cynic philosopher, Teles of Megara, we get one of the earliest descriptions of this essential component to the philosophical life. He discusses this issue of how to handle both poverty and wealth. He concludes that "both situations possess the same character, and whoever can handle much reasonably can also do the same with the opposite" (2.15H).[295]

Paul's language in 4:15–20 is filled with allusions to financial relationships and a social contract of giving and receiving. Some scholars assume a formal contract referred to as *societas*. Much of Paul's language, however, can be understood within the relationship of friendship rather than patronage and reciprocity. To whatever degree we might find these formal relationships in this section, Paul seems to change the reciprocity to something more intimate than payment for services rendered.

Paul takes the language of economic reciprocity and uses it as a metaphor in 4:17. The question is what kind of "fruit" does Paul expect. Is it "profit" Paul expects that will be credited to their account? I take it to refer to the accounting Paul expects to take place at the final judgment. According to Paul, everyone will be judged according to their deeds (Rom 2:6). The standard is "doing good" (Rom 2:7) as opposed to being "self-seeking" (Rom 2:8) or doing evil (Rom 2:9). Each one of us, Paul says, "will give an account" (Rom 14:12) before God's (Rom 14:10) or Christ's (2 Cor 5:10) place of judgment for what we do in life.

In 4:19 Paul clarifies that God provides for what humans need rather than for what they desire. Self-sufficiency is possible because humans can have all they need to fulfill the goal of human existence without satisfying all their desires.

---

[294] Seneca, *Epistles, Volume 1: Epistles 1-65*, 53.

[295] Edward N. O'Neil, ed., *Teles (The Cynic Teacher)*, Texts and Translations (Missoula, MT: Scholars Press, 1977), 15.

Assorted Closings (4:21–23)

I take the closing as the closing to the base letter with which the editor began. One reason this fits is that this letter began with a reference to *qedoshim* (1:1), and now they are referred to that way again (4:21, 22). My theory means that Jewish followers of Jesus were members of the imperial residence.

Chapter 10:
Philemon

My interpretation of Paul's letter to Philemon will be colored by my claim that when Paul uses the Greek word *hagioi* ("holy ones") to refer to people he is using an idiom for Jews that I am translating with the Hebrew transliteration *qedoshim* (see p. 34). Therefore, Philemon should be regarding as a Jewish follower of Jesus (and Apphia is most likely the wife of Philemon) whose group meeting in his home constitutes a synagogue, which we know could be called an *ekklēsia*.

It has been generally recognized that the letter to Philemon is connected to the Lycus Valley of Asia Minor, specifically Colossae and Laodicea. In the Colossians letter, considered not to be a genuine letter from Paul, it provides us, nevertheless, with a cross reference from v. 2 to Archippus in Colossae (Col 4:17). Onesimus also shows up in Colossae as "the faithful and beloved brother, who is one of you" (Col 4:9 NRSV). Epaphras, whom Paul mentions in the closing (v. 23) is also associated with Colossae (Col 1:7; 4:12). Also, Aristarchus and Mark (v. 24) are mentioned in the closing of Colossians (Col 4:10). Finally, a Demas and a Luke (v. 24) are also referred to in connection with Colossae (Col 4:14), the Luke being called "the beloved physician" (Col 4:14 NRSV).

Evidence supports a large population of Jews in the cities of the Lycus Valley.[296] There's nothing to say that Philemon, Onesimus, and others named in the letter are not Jewish. I recognize that my interpretation goes against most scholarship.

The main issue of Paul's letter has to do with restoring the relationship between Philemon and Onesimus. Philemon and Apphia would seem to be patrons of the assembly, what we could call a synagogue, and, therefore, from a well-to-do class within the city. When Paul arrives, he hopes to secure lodging with them (v. 22). I have argued

---

[296] Ulrich Huttner, *Early Christianity in the Lycus Valley* (Leiden; Boston: Brill, 2013), 67-72.

elsewhere (see p. 44) that Paul connects himself loosely with patrons of households by living with them and often carrying on his craft.

What is more contentious is the relationship of Philemon and Onesimus. At odds is Onesimus being called a slave and a "brother by nature" (v. 16 NRSV). How are we to reconcile this? Perhaps Onesimus could be thought of as having been a useless, younger brother, who was not much more than a slave in the household. One could imagine that Onesimus owed money to his brother and placed himself in some sort of voluntary servitude. Callahan has some valid arguments for Onesimus not being regarded as a fugitive slave.[297] Paul is not restoring a slave but restoring the brothers by paying what Onesimus owed to his brother (vv. 18–19). Paul vouches for the change in Onesimus (v. 11).

Letter Opening (vv. 1–3)

Paul writes this letter from his confinement (v. 1). Epaphras is also named as confined with him (v. 23). Others are with Paul (Timothy, Mark, Aristarchus, Demas, Luke) as well as Onesimus. Paul makes a pun from names. Philemon's name means "friendly, affectionate." Paul calls him "beloved, dear friend" (v. 2). When he first mentions the name of Onesimus, whose name means "useful," Paul makes the play on words, "to you non-beneficial (*achrēston*) and now to you and to me most beneficial (*euchrēston*)" (v. 11).[298] Paul also names a woman named Apphia, supposedly the wife of Philemon, and Archippus.

Paul also addresses himself to the assembly that meets in the house of Philemon (v. 2). Because Paul refers to the assembly as "holy ones," which I understand to refer to Jews as *qedoshim*, this assembly could also be called a synagogue. To these people Paul gives his typical blessing (v. 3)

Praise & Gratitude for Philemon (vv. 4–7)

Paul begins with a friendly expression of gratitude for Philemon and of praise. He remembers in his prayers what he has heard about

---

[297] Allen Dwight Callahan, "Paul's Epistle to Philemon: Toward an Alternative Argumentum," *The Harvard Theological Review* 86, no. 4 (1993).

[298] Paul may be making a further play on words by using terms reminiscent of the alternative spelling of Christ (*Christos*) and Chrestus (*Chrēstys*) (see p. 6).

Philemon (v. 4). The characteristics are his love (*agapēn*) and constancy (*pistin*) (v. 5). Paul hopes that Philemon will continue to progress in his character (v. 6). He has personally received joy and encouragement because of their friendship (v. 7).

Request for Restoration of Onesimus (vv. 8–20)

As Paul sometimes does, he begins the main part of his letter by saying he could insist on what he needs to have done because of his status, but he wants people to carry out his requests because they want to. He could use frank criticism (*parrēsian*) in his guidance but chooses a milder approach (vv. 8–9). As I showed above, Paul makes a play on Onesimus's name as one who contributed little to Philemon but now, he has made improvement and provides a good benefit (vv. 10–11). Paul seems to say in verse twelve that Onesimus is the letter carrier since Paul has sent him back. He emphasizes the usefulness of Onesimus by saying he wished he could have him be his own helper while he was in jail (v. 13). If Paul had kept Onesimus with him, it would mean Philemon had no choice than to do Paul this favor (v. 14). Paul juxtaposes the separation of Onesimus being away for a short time to Philemon receiving him back in a much greater sense (v. 15). Paul calls Onesimus a "slave" (*doulos*), but he doesn't call him Philemon's slave. He is clear that Onesimus is a brother by kinship (*en sarki*, "in flesh") (v. 16).

Paul expects that because of the social bonds of friendship, Philemon must accept the person sent from his associate or partner as though it were that person himself. To reject him would be to reject the person who was the sender (v. 17). Paul goes even further to say that he himself will settle any of the debts of Onesimus (v. 18). In effect, Paul swears that he will be responsible even though Philemon is already in Paul's debt (v. 19). Paul finishes with another play on names by using the form of the name of Onesimus as a "benefit" (*onaimēn*) (v. 20).

Assurance & Need for Lodging (vv. 21–22)

Paul expresses his trust in Philemon that he will comply with Paul's request to him (v. 21). Even though Paul has said he is in confinement, he expects to be released and travel to visit Philemon. So, Paul requests that they might provide him with a guest room in the household of Philemon (v. 22).

Closing (vv. 23–24)

The individuals Paul mentions in his closing are all connected with Colossians (see introduction above). They are Paul's coworkers and ostensibly making sure Paul has what he needs while he is incarcerated. Paul is much less concerned about his situation than he expressed in his letter to the Philippians (Phil 1:20–24).

Chapter 11: Romans

Paul says little in this letter about his circumstances. He apparently is writing this letter ahead of his planned visit to Rome after he travels to Jerusalem with financial assistance collected for Jewish followers of Jesus (15:22–29). He expects to spend some time with them before continuing on to Spain. By doing this, Paul will have achieved his goal of bringing the good news of God's acceptance of the gentile peoples to the world of the Roman Empire. It's understandable he would want to journey to the center of the western empire from his visit to what he would have considered the center of the eastern empire.

In my view, Rom 16 is a separate letter. Like Phil 2:19 and Phil 2:25–30, the last chapter of Romans is a recommendation letter for Phoebe. I conjecture that it was written by Paul from Corinth not to Rome but to Ephesus. Maybe it became attached to Paul's letter to Rome because both letters were correspondences from Corinth. The occasion of the letter fits the sequence of events in Acts 20 where Paul spends time in Greece before returning to Jerusalem (Acts 21:17).

It is often thought that Paul wrote to the Romans to ameliorate the conflict in the community of Jesus-followers because of the expulsion of Jews from Rome and their subsequent return. In that view, the assembly in Rome had become mainly gentile. Paul wants to encourage the gentile followers of Jesus to be accepting of the Jewish Jesus-followers. In the reading I adopt, informed by Stowers, there is no reason to assume a mixed audience of the letter. Paul addresses himself to gentile readers.

Letter Opening (1:1–7)

As usual, Paul identifies himself as the sender of the letter and will name the recipients. What is unusual is that Paul expands the opening to introduce himself, his motivations, and the content of the message he has been spreading across the eastern Roman Empire. He states that the focus of his life's work is to bring God's message to gentiles.

Rather than tell his story about how he chased down the Jews, who had become followers of Jesus, before he had an epiphany of the risen Christ, he refers to himself as one who God had invited to become a spokesperson for God's message to the gentile people (1:1). In his letter to the Galatians he said he had been destined to this from birth (Gal 1:15). There is nothing to suggest in his language that he no longer considers himself a Jew and has now become a Christian. As a Jew he is calling the non-Jewish people to worship the God of Israel, the one true living God. This God has invited the gentile peoples to be part of the people of God with no need to become full proselytes through acts that would make them Judeans. For Paul it was clear that a change occurred because of the death of Jesus. Not only did the Jewish followers of Jesus receive the signs of God's presence in Jerusalem, but gentiles did too. And not only in Jerusalem, the locus of God's presence in the Temple, but throughout the Roman world. It must be that God no longer was only the God of the chosen nation but the God of all nations. Yet, it was not only a matter of being God's people but of becoming those who, like Jesus, would live a divine life and have the same experience as Jesus in resurrection. Because Jesus achieved this, those who follow Jesus in the quality of his life could too.

Paul bases his brief introduction to the theme of his letter on the dual traditions about the "son of God" language in Jewish tradition and Hellenistic culture. When a person was inaugurated as a king of Israel and received the anointing, they considered him to become God's son (Ps 2:6–7). The Greeks also had a tradition of divine humans: gods and goddesses taking on human form or humans that become divine either as heroes or sages. On the one hand, Jesus was a descendant of David (1:2–3). But the power of his role as a son of God came about because of his being brought back from the realm of the dead (1:4). Not that Jesus came back to the land of the living because he was the second person of the Trinity, but he came back because he had become God's son through the culmination of his life and in his faithfulness in death. His resurrection declared him as a son of God (1:4).

Paul has named no co-senders of this letter, but he refers to them in 1:5. He and his companions received their calling to "bring about a faithful obedience among all the gentile peoples." The recipients of his letter in Rome are gentiles, and so Paul delivers God's invitation to them (1:6).

In the letter's address, Paul makes the astounding claim that these gentiles are the "beloved of God" (1:7). This is what Paul says further on, "And God shows love to us *gentiles*, because, while we were still *gentile* sinners, Christ died for our benefit" (5:8). While I attempt to discern when Paul is speaking to gentiles, I also make the claim that Paul uses the term "holy ones" (*hagioi*, "saints") to refer to members of the Judean nation who are the *qedoshim* (see p. 34). When Paul addresses gentiles, he refers to them as "called *to be* saints" (Rom 1:7; 1 Cor 1:2). I argue that the one time Paul addresses "saints" in Phil 1:1 is the opening of a letter Paul wrote to Jewish followers of Jesus in Philippi, which is one of the letters that forms the edited composite of Philippian correspondences.

Paul expresses his wish that the gentile people in Rome would experience the favor and the peace of God's blessing (see p. 81). It is an archaic notion and one that is based in superstition, but it was the way people in antiquity understood fate. What's important to notice here is that Paul indicates that those residents of Rome—whatever ethnic origin or national identity—may also now be provided for by the God of all nations.

Occasional Remarks (1:8–17)

Paul begins with some remarks that delineate the type of letter he is writing and his relationship to them. Paul shows his care for them as friends and praises them (1:8–12). He hopes that he might travel to Rome to visit with these followers of Jesus (1:13). He acknowledges the mutual benefits they will have by seeing each other's constancy of life (1:12). Paul says he has tried to visit them, but his plans had been thwarted (1:13). The fruit he hopes to have is the positive outcomes in the quality of life they live. Further on in the letter (6:21–23) he discusses the difference in their lives before they decided to live a moral life and describes the change that has come about. The outcome or result is referred to figuratively as fruit (*karpos*). On the one hand, moral error brings shame and corruption (6:21).

> But now, since you have been manumitted from moral error, and have become devoted to God, you have your benefit (*karpos*) of sacred separation: the goal (*telos*) is unending life. For the payback of moral error is death, but the graciousness of God is unending life by participation in Christ Jesus our Lord (6:22–23).

Paul is not then referring to making converts, as might be thought, but of having a positive effect on their moral development (1:13). In the next sentence he uses the expression "to report good news" (*euaggelisasthai*) (1:15). But its meaning goes beyond our notion of evangelism, as in making converts. It includes not only his efforts to make gentiles aware of the change in their status before God but also to encourage their moral behavior and their progress toward a mature state of being. It is in this sense that Paul can refer to the power of the message (1:15). Within this context Paul uses the language of salvation in the sense of therapeutic benefits that the moral life brings (1:16). His use of the present participle shows that he means that those who have a constancy of life and faithfully committed to living a quality life, experience a wellness of soul.

Paul says in 1:16 that Jews first experienced the signs of God's presence when they became followers of Jesus. After that gentiles also experienced the power of God's presence in the world. Paul's point will be that God's justice is demonstrated by God's fairness in being not only the God of the Judean nation but of all nations (2:11; 3:21–22). God's decision to do this is based on the faithfulness of Jesus in his steadfastness when he was tortured and executed (1:17). He was faithful and just, and those who are just will live faithful lives in the constancy of their character.

Against Pagan Idolatry & Practices (1:18–32)

Paul begins his arguments in his letter with an invective against idolatry. It makes the most sense to see this in the context of Paul writing to gentiles who are not being required to become proselytes through circumcision and Torah observance. They are to be worshippers of the God of Israel and, therefore, must no longer practice pagan worship of images. Paul is writing as an observant Jew who finds idolatry abhorrent. His invective is not a call to observe the strictures of Torah but is a rational argument based in human experience. What he writes here is so similar to the Wisdom of Solomon, I can't imagine that Paul is not reflecting those ideas. He would have known it to be a part of the Bible in Greek.

The author of Wisdom turns to the topic of idolatry in chapter 12. He had started his prayer to God at chapter nine. He reminds God how God detested the unholy, ruthless, and even cannibalistic practices of the nations that existed in the land before the people of God entered (Wis 12:3–5). The author includes the common notion that God had given the nations an opportunity to repent, but they were despicably evil and accursed (Wis 12:10–11). God is shown to be just in God's actions with great forbearance. The nations were foolish to accept "as gods those animals that even their enemies despised" (Wis 12:24 NRSV). He states:

> all people who were ignorant of God were foolish by nature; and they were unable from the good things that are seen to know the one who exists, nor did they recognize the artisan while paying heed to his works; but they supposed that either fire or wind or swift air, or the circle of the stars, or turbulent water, or the luminaries of heaven were the gods that rule the world (Wis 13:1–2 NRSV).

The author denounces their failure to recognize God. "Yet again, not even they are to be excused; for if they had the power to know so much that they could investigate the world, how did they fail to find sooner the Lord of these things" (Wis 13:8–9 NRSV). He points out the foolishness of those who put more faith in a carved wooden image when embarking on a sea voyage than in the God who has control over the wind, the sea, and the waves (Wis 14:1–4). He connects idolatry with sexual immorality: "For the idea of making idols was the beginning of fornication, and the invention of them was the corruption of life" (Wis 14:12). With a flourish the author concludes his depiction of the horrors of idolatry.

> For whether they kill children in their initiations, or celebrate secret mysteries, or hold frenzied revels with strange customs, they no longer keep either their lives or their marriages pure, but they either treacherously kill one another, or grieve one another by adultery, and all is a raging riot of blood and murder, theft and deceit, corruption, faithlessness, tumult, perjury, confusion over what is good, forgetfulness of favors, defiling of souls, sexual perversion, disorder in marriages, adultery, and debauchery. For the worship of idols not to be named is the beginning and cause and end of every evil (Wis 14:23–27 NRSV).

With similar language Paul rails against the gentiles and their idolatrous ways. They deserve God's wrath since God's presence is obvious in the world (1:19–20). Instead, they foolishly fashioned images of animals to worship instead of the one who created them (1:21–23). Paul agrees that God allowed gentiles to persist in their sin (1:24–26).

Paul describes same-sex acts as an outcome of their wrong thinking about worshipping the Creator rather than the objects of creation. What Paul refers to is not simply the engagement in same-sex acts. He bases his opinions on his cultural prejudices regarding what it is to be a female and a male and the purpose of sexual intercourse.[299] For Paul the problem with female same-sex acts is that females should engage in sex for procreation. Because there is no fertilization that takes place, the act does not result in the natural outcome of genital penetration (1:26). Likewise, males are not producing offspring either in their sex act. In addition, the male being dominated and penetrated is acting like a woman, which society considered shameful (1:27). We can conclude if a culture no longer views sex as only for procreation and does not view the role of the female as something shameful, then Paul's tirade against same-sex acts is no longer relevant in modern society.

For a third time Paul repeats the expression "God gave them over" (1:24, 26, 28). This time God gave them over to a wrong way of thinking about "appropriate actions" (*kathēkonta*) (1:28). Paul uses this Stoic terminology within the context of cognitive judgments about what is right and wrong. Paul's vice list in 1:29–31 names all sorts of wickedness, though interestingly enough, not one of them has to do with sexual immorality. What the list represents is the very many ways that people act in order to get the things they desire to make themselves happy. They are ignorant to the reality that those things will not bring them happiness and fulfillment (1:32).

Censure of the Inconsistent Judge (2:1–29)

What we lose in translations is that Paul switches to the singular address at 2:1. Paul uses a literary device called speech-in-character.[300] It

---

[299] Stowers, *A Rereading of Romans*, 94-97.

[300] Stanley K. Stowers, "Romans 7.7-25 as a Speech-in-Character (προσωποποιία)," in *Paul in his Hellenistic Context*, ed. Troels Engberg-Pedersen (Minneapolis: Fortress Press, 1995); Stanley K. Stowers, "Apostrophe, prosopopoiia and Paul's Rhetorical Education," in *Early Christianity and Classical Culture*, ed. John T. Fitzgerald, Thomas

represents how a teacher might engage in dialogue with a student. Here, the discussion partner is imaginary and represents a particular characteristic. The dialogue includes the interlocuter raising objections and responding to questions. In this way it has an elenchic function, a Socratic method of questioning a student to guide the student toward a different view than the one they began with. Stowers provides two examples of similar diatribal apostrophes.[301] In his discussion about *The Happy Life*, Seneca turns to a character representing a hypocritical judge.

> But as for you, have you the leisure to search out others" evils and to pass judgement upon anybody? "Why does this philosopher have such a spacious house?" "Why does this one dine so sumptuously?" you say. You look at the pimples of others when you yourselves are covered with a mass of sores. This is just as if someone who was devoured by a foul itch should mock at the moles and the warts on bodies that are most beautiful (*Vit. beat.* 27.4).[302]

Paul has not been describing the human condition and is not now focusing on the inability of Jews to be righteous by law keeping. What he has been doing is describing the primary problem with gentiles, which is idolatry. Paul anticipates the objections someone would raise who would say they are not a sinner like other people are. He castigates such a person for their inconsistent behavior. They shouldn't think they are so innocent, shouldn't be so intolerant of others, and be so stubborn (2:4–5).

Stowers argues that the apostrophe beginning at 2:1 is not a castigation of a hypocritical and arrogant Jew.[303] I think Paul turns to a Jewish interlocuter at 2:1. But there's no reason to assume it is only based it on a prejudice about Jews. My reason is that the function of the diatribe

---

H. Olbricht, and L. Michael White, Supplements to Novum Testamentum (Leiden; Boston: Brill, 2003).

[301] Stowers, *A Rereading of Romans*, 13.

[302] Seneca, *Moral Essays, Volume 2: De Consolatione ad Marciam. De Vita Beata. De Otio. De Tranquillitate Animi. De Brevitate Vitae. De Consolatione ad Polybium. De Consolatione ad Helviam.* trans. John W. Basore, Loeb Classical Library 254 (Cambridge, MA: Harvard University Press, 1932), 177.

[303] Stowers, *A Rereading of Romans*, 13. Stowers, "Paul and Self-Mastery," 535.

is for the gentile audience to listen in on Paul's discussion with someone who thinks they should circumcise gentile followers of Jesus. After talking about how corrupt the gentile peoples are for their history of practicing idolatry, Paul turns to one who would (proudly) agree with him about the condition of the gentiles. After Paul addresses this person (2:1–5), he gives a brief speech about how God judges fairly both Jews and gentiles (2:6–16) and returns to his interaction with the interlocuter at 2:17 at which time he is labeled as a Jew.

I compare this to Paul's diatribe in Galatians chapter two. One might even say that no such incident occurred, but Paul creates a narrative setting for his castigation of Peter to let his gentile audience hear him talk to a fellow Jew. It is in this context that Paul overtly calls what Peter did a hypocrisy (Gal 2:13). Others seem only to take Gal 2:14 as relating Paul's conversation. I think Gal 2:15–21 is Paul's speech to Peter. The "we" section is Paul including himself with Peter and others as Jewish followers of Jesus. After the typical "God forbid" of diatribe in Gal 3:17, Paul then talks about his own experience. The change comes at Gal 3:1 when Paul directs his speech to his audience.

What I have tried to show in my translation of verse four is Paul's choice of the word *chrēstos* ("beneficence, kindness"). I have speculated elsewhere (see p. 6) that the title of Jesus might have originally been the name Chrestus. If that were the case, then Paul would make a pun: God's beneficence—or God's Christ—brings them to a change of heart.

In Paul's view, the other nations of the world are no longer separated from God and they should worship the one God and no other gods and images. God provides the blessing of fertility and security. The requirement for living a fulfilled, happy life—a divine quality of life—and to experience endless life with God is to develop one's character and being into that sort of human. By becoming a follower of Jesus, one seeks to imitate his life to share in the same experience of divinification and life with God. For the Jesus movement, that means both Jews and gentiles. That's not to say that the same way of thinking doesn't also apply for practicing Jews. Their form of philosophical practice would also lead to the same end. Paul says as much in 2:6–10. What he describes in those verses is the common Greek thought about the afterlife.

In fact, Plato relates a judgment scene in the story of Er at the end of the Republic. Er had died in battle. When they discovered his body days later, his body had not putrefied. Before they burned his body on the pyre, he came back to life and told the story of what he had been experiencing in the afterlife.

> He said that, after his soul had left him, it traveled together with many others until they came to a marvelous place, where there were two adjacent openings in the earth, and opposite and above them two others in the heavens, and between them judges sat. These, having rendered their judgment, ordered the just to go upwards into the heavens through the door on the right, with signs of the judgment attached to their chests, and the unjust to travel downward through the opening on the left, with signs of all their deeds on their backs (Plato, *Resp.* 614b–c).[304]

Paul says something similar. God will judge people based on their actions (2:6–8). Paul quotes a line from Ps 62:12 from his Greek scriptures (Ps 61:13 LXX) in verse six. However, he uses it for his own purpose by reinterpreting it within this context about the afterlife. For those who live a good life, their reward is unending life (*zōēn aiōnion*). This expression is not a Hebrew idiom but seems to come from the dialect of Hellenistic Greek used by people like the Maccabean authors, Philo, Jesus-followers, and Plutarch. The former share a Hellenistic Jewish context. But Plutarch uses this expression to say that the lot of God is "a source of happiness (*eudaimon*) in the eternal life (*tēs aiōniou zoēs*)" (Plutarch, *Is. Os.* 1 [351e]).[305] The opposite reward of God's anger is because of those who are selfish and unjust. In reverse or chiastic order, Paul repeats in the negative that those who lead lives of vice will have difficulties (2:9). Those who lead a life of goodness will be praiseworthy and peaceful (2:10). Perhaps he does this because in the first instance he refers to the afterlife, while in the second he refers to the present life.

Paul's unusual coinage of the noun "partiality" (*prosōpolēmpsia*) based on the Greek Bible's translation of the Hebrew expression for "receive the face" (*labein prosōpon*) implies that God is not taking in the ethnic differences in the way people look (2:11). God treats humans all the same. The point Paul makes is that it is not enough for anyone to know

---

[304] Cooper and Hutchinson, eds., *Plato: Complete Works*, 1218.
[305] Plutarch, *Moralia, Volume 5: Isis and Osiris. The E at Delphi. The Oracles at Delphi No Longer Given in Verse. The Obsolescence of Oracles.* trans. Frank Cole Babbitt, Loeb Classical Library 306 (Cambridge, MA: Harvard University Press, 1936), 9.

what the right thing is to do. What matters is whether the person does the right thing.

Paul's argument to his fictitious Jewish opponent is the same one made in the book of James. There we have the same topic.

> Therefore rid yourselves of all sordidness and rank growth of wickedness, and welcome with meekness the implanted word that has the power to save (be a restorative to) your souls. But be doers of the word (God's commandment), and not merely hearers who deceive themselves. For if any are hearers of the word (Torah) and not doers, they are like those who look at themselves in a mirror; for they look at themselves and, on going away, immediately forget what they were like. But those who look into the perfect law, the law of liberty, and persevere, being not hearers who forget but doers who act—they will be blessed in their doing (Jas 1:21–25 NRSV).

James seems to make a pun on the word "word" (*logos*). In Stoic terms the *logos* is implanted in the soul (Jas 2:21). Then James also uses it in the Hebrew sense of *logos* (*dabar*) as "commandment." To a Hellenistic Jew the Torah is God's wisdom and *logos*. God's Torah is implanted in the soul. In Exod 34:28 the expression is literally "the ten words." James continues to elaborate on which "word," in the sense of "commandment," he is talking about.

> You do well if you really fulfill the royal law according to the scripture, "You shall love your neighbor as yourself." But if you show partiality, you commit sin and are convicted by the law as transgressors. For whoever keeps the whole law but fails in one point has become accountable for all of it. For the one who said, "You shall not commit adultery," also said, "You shall not murder." Now if you do not commit adultery but if you murder, you have become a transgressor of the law. So speak and so act as those who are to be judged by the law of liberty. For judgment will be without mercy to anyone who has shown no mercy; mercy triumphs over judgment (Jas 2:8–13 NRSV).

For James this is a discussion for Jewish followers of Jesus. Perhaps the original document existed as a letter from a Jew to Jews in the diaspora (fictively). Either way it supports reading this section of Romans as intra-Jewish.

Paul refers to the gentiles in the third-person to his Jewish discussion partner (2:14). He is trying to convince his opponent that gentiles can make proper moral judgments with their mental faculty apart from laws and precepts (2:14–15). What is important is the manner of life and not one's ethnic identity.

I take 2:16 as another example of a later apocalyptic gloss. The previous verse concludes with each person's self-reflective consciousness determining the correctness or incorrectness of their moral decisions. Yet 2:16 changes that to mean God judges rather than the person's mind judges their actions. It seems an awkward attempt to insert a later apocalyptic context.

Again in 2:17 Paul addresses his Jewish discussion partner. He exaggerates his fictional character with extreme language regarding his boast of having a premier status before God, advanced knowledge, and the role of teacher (2:17–20). Paul's character represents the inconsistent person. He is not saying that all Jews are boastful, arrogant, and hypocritically inconsistent. The strawman Paul sets before his gentile audience represents those Jewish followers of Jesus who have tried to get gentile followers to be circumcised and follow Jewish law. Paul is insulting this kind of person by portraying the Judaizer as inconsistent (2:21–25).

Paul works backward in his argument. His conclusion is that gentiles who live up to the standard of Torah have a greater claim to being upright people than the Jew who does not keep Torah consistently (2:26–29). Paul characterizes the fictive Judaizer as one who knows Torah but doesn't consistently practice it.

Fictive Dialogue on being a Jew (3:1–4:22)

I take 3:1–4:22 to be Paul's conversation with his Jewish interlocuter. Paul has told him—in front of his gentile audience—that being a circumcised, observant Jew is no better than gentile pagans if the person doesn't practice what the law says. Perhaps the one commandment that Paul thinks the Judaizer doesn't fulfill is to love your (gentile) neighbor. Paul treats his imaginary interlocuter as an inconsistent, hypocritical, arrogant person. Paul presents him now as being overwhelmed by

Paul's attack. He acts as though he is rethinking his position and questions his own relationship with God. Paul will assure him that God is still faithful to God's covenant. The dialogue ensues and is peppered with speeches.

There are many words that in Hebrew have a particular meaning within their cultural context, but the Greek word that translates the Hebrew bears another meaning within their Greek cultural context that may or may not have much to do with the meaning in Hebrew. The Hebrew term *zedakah* is translated with the English word "righteousness." But the Greek word used to translate that term is *dikaiosynē*, which is normally understood in Greek thought as "justice." Christian theology has understood Romans to be talking about God's righteousness and how God imparts God's righteousness to the believer. If we understand Paul's language within his Greek context, we discover a consistent and coherent argument about God's justice or fairness in relation to gentiles and Jews. The related Greek word *dikaios* may have the meaning of a just or fair person, but Paul also uses it in the sense of the right-behaving person.

The objection is raised in 3:1, if gentiles can fulfill the law apart from becoming a full proselyte what is the benefit of being the covenant people of God? Paul responds that Jews were given Torah (3:2). The interlocuter asks whether God's covenant faithfulness is done away with because some Jews have been unfaithful (3:3). Paul forcefully rejects that idea (3:4). The Jewish discussion partner responds by questioning whether God is unjust to punish transgressors if God's justice is proven by people's inability to behave properly (3:5). Paul interrupts his dialogue with two "asides" to his audience. In 3:5 Paul may refer to his rhetorical device. He forcefully responds in 3:6 and rejects the idea God shows a lack of justice by inflicting wrath on nations. It's accepted that God will judge the world, God acts justly, therefore God is just when God judges transgressions resulting in God's wrath.

Paul's second aside to his audience expresses his frustration that Judaizers attack him as acting as a gentile—I take the expression "sinner" as a term for gentiles (Gal 2:15)—and encouraging gentiles not to become proselytes because their error results in something good (3:7–8).

Paul moves the dialogue in the manner of elenchus. Plato portrayed Socrates as taking his interlocuter from saying one thing to having him say the opposite by the end. Paul's Jewish interlocuter began at the point of questioning the value of being Jewish. Now he wonders if Paul means that Jews are superior (3:9a). Again, Paul forcefully rejects the false conclusion (3:9b). Paul's point is that Jews and gentiles are equals before God. He first shows by his quotation that both Jews and gentiles are susceptible to the power of the inclination to do what is wrong (3:9b–18). This quotation is not an argument for human depravity but to make his point that people sin.

Paul explains to his Jewish interlocuter what this all means (3:19–26). Gentiles who observe Torah by being circumcised will not automatically be good people but will only realize what the wrong is. God's fairness in treating Jews and gentiles equally has come about because of the faithfulness of Christ. The gentile peoples did nothing to bring about God's change of mind by acquitting (*apolytrōsis*) them of the "previously committed sins" (3:25) based on Christ's faithfulness in his execution. His death is considered an "expiatory sacrifice" or "atonement" (*hilastērion*) (3:25) for the gentile peoples whose past sins had been overlooked. These concepts need some unpacking.

Within the Hebrew context these terms might bring up concepts like the redemption of the Israelites from bondage to Egypt and the "mercy seat" of the Ark of the Covenant over which the High Priest made atonement on Yom Kippur. But the context of the death of a human for the benefit of others comes from Greek culture.[306] We find this language in Hellenistic Judaism in the account of Eleazar and the mother and her seven sons in 4 Maccabees. Their deaths were regarded as a ransom (*antipsychos*), the price paid for redemption, and an atonement (*hilastērion*) (4 Macc 17:21–22). The result for the Jewish nation was freedom from bondage to the Seleucid regime. Jewish followers of Jesus hoped that his death would also bring about the redemption of Jerusalem and freedom from Roman tyranny. Because of gentiles receiving the signs of God's presence apart from becoming proselytes Paul has concluded that God considered the death of Christ a ransom and an expiation for the sins of the gentile peoples. It does not require "faith in Christ" as an assent to Christ's deity or messianic role. Although the Gospel of John will use the language of believing in Jesus, this is not Paul's language. He uses the expression *pistis christou*. That he means the "faithfulness of Christ"

---

[306] See Williams, *Jesus' Death as Saving Event*. Hengel, *The Atonement*.

(subjective genitive) rather than "faith in Christ" (objective genitive) is supported not only by the context but also Paul's use of the same idiom in 4:16: "faith(fulness) of Abraham" not "faith in Abraham."[307]

The dialogue resumes at 3:27. Paul has the Jewish interlocuter first inquire about the Jewish pride of place in God's eyes. Paul replies that simply having pride in having Torah is not possible (3:27b). Paul explains that faithfulness, allegiance, or constancy is what is needed (3:27–28). Paul gets the interlocuter to admit that God is the God of gentiles too (3:29). God is the one god of all nations, Paul declares (3:30). The principle of faithfulness applies to both Jew and gentile. Those who are circumcised are upright people through their faithfulness to God's covenant. The gentile males with an intact penis are considered upright "by means of the faithfulness of Jesus." Again, the interlocuter objects by asking if this means God's covenant with Israel in Torah is invalidated. Paul forcefully rejects the idea and claims that Torah is established by this (3:31).

I take 4:1 as the interlocuter's question. He had asked about the basis for boasting in 3:27. Paul denied there was. Now Paul has the interlocuter introduce the topic of Abraham into the discussion. It seems like Paul's interlocuter is meant to appear to catch Paul on this one. Surely, Abraham has a basis for boasting since his uprightness was based on his actions (4:2). Paul has tricked him with this one because Paul will argue that when the event happened in Gen 15:6 Abraham was uncircumcised! His first line of reasoning is based on reciprocity. If you do something good and get a reward for it, it is not a gift but something you deserved (4:4). This means that, if a person performs a deed required by Torah, then God's blessing is an obligation of the covenant. What Paul is saying is when Abraham (or Jesus or a gentile) trusts God, God's consideration of the person as upright based on faithfulness is a gift of God (4:5).

Paul's second line of reasoning is based on Ps 32 (31 LXX) (4:6–8). His choice of this couplet seems to be based on the repetition of the term "reckon" in the Hebrew Bible (*ḥsb*) as well as the Greek Bible (*logizomai*) in both the Genesis text and the Psalm. He may have been influenced by the type of argument found in later rabbinic texts called *gezerah shawah*. First, Paul asks the interlocuter if, in the case of the Psalm, the

---

[307] Hays, *The Faith of Jesus Christ*. Stowers, *A Rereading of Romans*.

"happiness" or "blessedness" is something experienced only by someone like David who is circumcised or also upon one whose penis is intact (4:9). I infer here that Paul has the interlocuter not able to respond. Paul then asks about Abraham, whether he was "regarded" while circumcised or in an intact condition (4:10a). Again, I infer that Paul expects the reader to catch the silence of the interlocuter because it's Paul's voice that draws the conclusion.

Abraham was regarded as faithful while he was still intact (4:10b). Because of this Abraham is the ancestor of those gentile peoples whose men have intact penises and who are "regarded" as upright based on the faithfulness of Christ (4:11). He is also the ancestor of the Jewish nation of circumcised males who not only have Torah but faithfully follow its commandments and maintain the covenant (4:12).

Paul now gives another speech to his interlocuter (4:13–22). He continues to use the argument that beneficence is given freely but a payment or reward is given as a transaction of what is due (4:13–16). When Abraham was said to be regarded as upright because of his faithfulness, he wasn't obeying God's commandment since the Torah had not yet been given, and he was not yet a circumcised man (4:16). Paul is trying to explain why God can consider an uncircumcised gentile an upright person based on the principle of faithfulness. The faithfulness of Christ exemplified in the type of death he died brought about this change. The gentile peoples are considered being the descendants of Abraham just as the Israelites (4:18). Abraham was regarded as upright based on his faithfulness before he was circumcised. His argument seems to be that gentiles are not able to be upright through the path of the Judaizers (4:14). For the gentile, the Law is only a way to know when they transgress. To receive the promise of the beneficence of God, gentiles are regarded upright based on faithfulness, the faithfulness of Christ (4:16).

Gentile Inclusion (4:23–5:11)

I take it that Paul now switches back to address his audience of gentile followers of Jesus living in Rome. Paul begins to include himself with the use of the first-person plural. There is not a separate category of people other than those belonging to the Jewish nation and those belonging to the rest of the nations, the gentiles. We cannot force into the text a third group we call Christian. My view is that Paul formed groups of Jesus-followers from gentiles not affiliated with a synagogue. His groups were centered in households and were socially constructed as a philosophical group. Paul refers to them as "assemblies of the gentiles" (16:4). In Acts Luke portrays Paul as arriving in cities and seeking out the local synagogue or, less technically, the "gathering place" (*synagōgē*) of Jews in the city. I consider Luke to be among those in the latter half of the first century who wanted to make the basis for the Jesus movement to be more closely connected to the texts and traditions of Judaism. Paul clearly addresses his audience in the letter as gentiles (11:3) and says that his focus is on speaking to gentiles (1:5,13; 15:16,18). Rom 11:3 is usually translated with the conjunction "now" (*de*), which makes it sound like the adverb referring to a present change in address. It does not mark a strong transition and is often a way of marking a new sentence or thought.

I have argued above (see p. 32) that Paul may not just be identifying and adapting himself with his gentile audience when he writes in the first-person plural, but he may consider himself to be both a Jew by birth and practice and a gentile because of a circumcision reversal surgery that left him scarred for life. To clarify that Paul is talking about the inclusion of the gentiles when he uses the first-person plural, I have added "gentiles" in italics. The test is whether this reading helps to make Paul more coherent and if this way of reading remains consistent.

Paul's audience of gentiles has been listening in on his fictive conversation with a Jewish interlocuter. Based on that discussion he can now tell them what this means for them. Viewed this way we can list the characteristics and the things that have resulted for the gentile peoples.

- They now believe in God (4:24). As pagans they previously worshipped the gods. In 1 Thessalonians Paul describes the gentile followers of Jesus as ones who began worshipping the one God having turned away from their idolatry.
- Because the gentile peoples did not share in the covenant of God and have the sacrifices, their sins had gone undealt with. In this way Jesus's death was for the transgressions of the gentile peoples (4:25).
- Jesus being raised by God from the realm of the dead in the underworld became the means by which gentiles have an

example to follow which will bring about their complete maturity as capable humans, something Paul calls being upright in this context based on the language about Abraham (4:25)
- The gentile peoples have "peace" with God (5:1). Paul says, "we were enemies" (5:10), which was the language about the gentile peoples. Ephesians describes the gentiles as "aliens from the commonwealth of Israel, and strangers to the covenants of promise, having no hope and without God in the world" (Eph 2:12 NRSV). They are told that "he is our peace; in his flesh he has made both groups into one and has broken down the dividing wall, that is, the hostility between us" (Eph 2:14 NRSV).
- Paul uses language of separation and inclusion to talk about the gentile condition. Because of Jesus the gentiles have an "entrance" (5:2).
- Paul's expectation is that following Jesus will be the way for gentiles to progress in their character to the culmination of a divine quality of life and to be with God and share God's divinity and immortality. Paul's language here is not apocalyptic but the "expectation of *receiving* the splendor of God" (5:2). He describes this progress in 5:3. He also mentions this in the phrase "saved by his life" (5:10). This is the language of the therapy of the soul and the healing effects of learning to form proper judgements about right and wrong.
- Paul refers to this group as ones who were "weak, helpless," "ungodly, impious" (5:6), "sinners" (5:8), and "enemies" (5:10). These are all terms used to describe the gentile peoples.

It is in this context that Paul discusses the concept of the noble death for the benefit of others (5:7–8). It's not that it happens rarely (*molis*), but that a person barely is able to make that sacrifice (5:7). Although there are examples in Greek literature of a person offering to be executed ritually to the gods for the safety of the city in view of an impending attack, most often the noble death has to do with people whose death comes about in battle or for resisting evil. It's not that Jesus committed suicide by letting himself be executed because he knew his death would be beneficial for others. And it's not the death of any person but the death of the noble, innocent victim. Paul describes this heroic action as having "courage (*tolmaō*) to die" (5:7).

Comparison of Adam & Jesus (5:12–21)

Paul has been talking to his audience of gentile followers of Jesus about the faithfulness of Abraham and the faithfulness of Jesus. Paul continues in this way of thinking and uses the figure of Adam within biblical history with which to compare Jesus. Paul is not talking about Adam to introduce the origins of human sinfulness and the remedy of Jesus paying the penalty for original sin. Paul's argument is not ontological but literary-historical. Because it functions like a formal comparison (*synkrisis*), the function is an encomium on Jesus.[308]

Paul makes use of the story of human civilization in the Bible, but he does it in a way typical of the moral philosophers of his day. Seneca is a case in point. He begins with the beginning of human existence: "But the first men and those who sprang from them, still unspoiled, followed nature, having one man as both their leader and their law, entrusting themselves to the control of one better than themselves" (Seneca, *Ep.* 90.4).[309] Seneca describes that time as "that age which is maintained to be the golden age" in which Posidonius held that "the government was under the jurisdiction of the wise" (Seneca, *Ep.* 90.5).[310] The idyllic world was shattered "when once vice (*vitiis*) stole in (*subrepentibus*) and kingdoms were transformed into tyrannies" and then "a need arose for laws; and these very laws were in turn framed by the wise" (Seneca, *Ep.* 90.6).[311]

In the narrative of the Bible, the first person to commit an error is Adam (5:12). According to the Genesis story, Adam and Eve lived an idyllic life in the paradise ("garden, grove, orchard") of Eden. In the first creation story, God creates the first humans in God's image (Gen 1:26–27). In the second creation story, the Lord God provides for all the needs of the humans as well as providing two special trees: the tree of life and the tree of the knowledge of good and evil (Gen 2:9). We must be expected to infer that the fruit of the tree of life would sustain their perpetual existence since their removal from Eden was to prevent them

---

[308] It would not be considered a well-constructed *synkrisis* because the subject being praised should be compared to another subject that is well-regarded.

[309] Seneca, *Epistles, Volume 2: Epistles 66–92*, 397.

[310] Seneca, *Epistles, Volume 2: Epistles 66–92*, 397.

[311] Seneca, *Epistles, Volume 2: Epistles 66–92*, 399.

from eating of the tree of life because they would "live forever" (Gen 2:22 NRSV). To eat from the tree of the knowledge of good and evil would mean having divine wisdom (Gen 3:22). The effect of eating from that tree is that "the eyes of both were opened, and they knew that they were naked" (Gen 3:5, 7). When God warns the man about not eating this tree, God tells him, in effect, he would become mortal and succumb to death (Gen 2:17). The narrative of Genesis seems to suggest that humans had long life-spans until after the flood but die they did.

Paul introduces the personification of sin (or moral error, as I translate it). Throughout his succeeding arguments he often pictures sin as a character. In these situations, I have transliterated the Greek term for sin as Hamartia. Hamartia comes into the world at the dawn of creation (5:12–13). Hamartia rules (5:21; 6:14,18), dominates (6:6,12), and enslaves (6:17,20). The adherents of Jesus have been manumitted from Hamartia (6:22) and released from their "marital" ties to Hamartia (7:1–6).

Ref.	Adam	Christ
5:15	sin	gift
5:15	Many died because of	Benevolence for many
5:16	condemnation	vindication
5:17	Death ruled	Life rules
5:18	Offense brings Condemnation	Upright action brings life-giving acquittal
5:19	Disobedience causes many to become sinners	Obedience makes many to be upright
5:20	Error increased	Graciousness exuded
5:21	Sin ruled causing death	Grace rules resulting in unending life

The table above shows the comparisons Paul makes. In 5:16 he even uses the feature common in *synkrisis*, the *men/de* construction ("on the one side ... on the other side"). The section concludes by saying the "unending life" that was available from the tree of life is now made possible through imitation of the life Jesus (5:21).

Dialogue with Recalcitrant Gentiles (6:1–23)

At chapter six Paul addresses his audience more directly. Paul continues to use diatribal style of objections and questions from his gentile readers. Stowers notes that "the first-level audience only overhears 'Paul the apostle' speaking to others in 2:1–4:22" but then "in chapters 6–8 he speaks directly to them as one who identifies with their experience."[312]

Paul anticipates their objection in 6:1. The guilt of the sins of the gentile peoples has been graciously overlooked, and God has invited them to be among God's people. Paul has them ask the nonsensical question that might be raised by those who are recalcitrant. If the moral errors of the gentile peoples brought about such an outpouring of God's graciousness, what difference does it make if people continue to live their lives the same way (6:1). For Paul's audience of Jesus-followers, it makes a big difference.

Paul responds in 6:2 with his usual denial of the suggestion. He then draws the analogy of their experience in participation with Christ when he died, when he was planted within the earth, and when God raised Christ out from those who died (6:3–5). To be "in Christ" means to have gone through the experiences he had (6:5). Paul uses this as a motivation for persuading his audience to live a vice-ridden life of self-mastery (6:6). The followers of Jesus have cut themselves off from their former life, they planted themselves within the cosmic element of water (an act which could lead to death) and were brought out to a new condition of life having left the rest behind. By analogy a person who has died is no longer bound to his former existence whether that be as a slave or as someone who died as a penalty for wrong-doing (6:7). Paul's persuasion here is not so much an attempt to get his audience to accept some ontological claim about a spiritual reality but a way to get them to make a choice to become people who live a new and flourishing life (6:8–10). To whatever degree Paul may imagine the existence within an afterlife or some apocalyptic event, he is emphasizing that their present way of life is his greatest concern (6:11–14).

Paul may not here use the technical language of self-mastery, but he uses a different vocabulary to talk about the same thing. While Greco-Roman moral philosophers might not use a term like *kyrieuō*, "to lord over," like Paul does in 6:14, the author of 4 Maccabees does in a context about self-mastery.

> If, then, reasoning appears to hold the mastery over the passions (*pathōn*) which stand in the way of temperance, such as gluttony

---

[312] Stowers, *A Rereading of Romans*, 291.

and lust (*epithymias*), it surely also and manifestly has the rule (*kyrieuō*) over the affections which are contrary to justice, such as malice; and of those which are hindrances to manliness (*andreias*, "courage"), as wrath, and pain, and fear (4 Macc 1:3–4).

This language of self-mastery developed metaphors in the classical age of Greece of citizens ruled by authorities.[313] The soul or the self, however that is defined, through the mental faculty and reasoning controls the emotions or passions that are prompted through impulses to want what it values at the moment as something to give pleasure or gratification without a proper judgment about the value of things. Paul uses the language of self-mastery: *enkrateia, enkrateuomai* "self-control; show self-control" (Gal 5:23; 1 Cor 7:9; 9:25); *akrasia* "lack of self-mastery" (1 Cor 7:5); *sōphoneō* "show self-control" (12:3); *autarkeia, autarkēs* "self-sufficient" (1 Cor 9:8; Phil 4:11).[314] Stowers sums up this section of Romans to say that Paul has argued the Jewish Law was not meant for gentiles as a means "to produce sinlessness and unconflicted self-mastery. Only identification with Christ in his death and new life, and God's spirit, can bring about sinlessness and self-mastery."[315] The view that Paul takes may seem to moderns as Christian language or perhaps Jewish. A philosophical purist might balk at the idea that Paul's system of thought has anything to do with Stoicism. What Paul exhibits is a greater eclecticism that combines his training in a philosophical world of "middle" or Roman Stoicism reflective in the type of Hellenized Judaism because of his interpretation of what the death and resurrection of Jesus means for the gentile peoples.[316]

The result of this way of thinking is for them to consider themselves completely cut off to the former way of live by the popular values of Greco-Roman society where they lived a life directed by moral error. Their present life is to be a renewed life characterized by a divine quality of self-mastery. In Stoicism the goal was the extirpation of the passions. For the early Stoics the only morally good person was the sage who

---

[313] Stowers, "Paul and Self-Mastery," 525.

[314] Stowers, "Paul and Self-Mastery," 534.

[315] Stowers, "Paul and Self-Mastery," 536.

[316] Stowers, "Paul and Self-Mastery," 539.

thoroughly achieved this goal, while later Stoics recognized progress in the development of the wise person. Paul expects his adherents to stop committing moral errors and be ruled by their passions. For Stoics self-mastery was not a battle between two or three parts of oneself but "an inner conflict between two tendencies."[317]

Paul does seem to think of a divided self that is similar to Platonic thought.[318] Stowers puts it succinctly.

> …in the Platonic tripartite soul, the spirited passions can listen to reason and be persuaded, but the appetites (for which he uses *epithymia*) are a many-headed wild beast. It appears that Jews in the first century found congenial a basically Stoic approach to the soul with some key Platonic modifications.[319]

He goes on to make this distinction: "Above all, the claim that true beliefs about the divine were the foundation for proper ethical behavior made a Stoic framework congenial in ethics, even though Jews and Christians favored a Platonic cosmos because it had a transcendent god."[320]

Plato describes his concept of the soul in the *Republic* (588c) by presenting the image of a beast made up of various forms of animals like a Chimera or Cerberus. This single beast has many heads of beasts that are both wild and tame. Another beast is a lion (largest) and a third is a human being (second to the largest). These three are shrouded in the body of a human. For this person to act as though it is beneficial to be unjust, the person would feed the multi-form beast and the lion while starving the "man within the man" (*anthrōpou ho entos anthrōpos*) (589b). If the person considers that justice is the best course of action, then the person would need to care for this inner man to make him the strongest. For the chimera he would need to care for the tame beasts and restrain the actions of the wild ones, especially their influence on the lion so they all get along with each other. Based on this concept of the soul, Socrates tells his interlocuters how one should treat people who think wrongly.

---

[317] Stowers, "Paul and Self-Mastery," 529.
[318] Stowers, "Paul and Self-Mastery," 538-40.
[319] Stowers, "Paul and Self-Mastery," 533.
[320] Stowers, "Paul and Self-Mastery," 533.

> Then let's persuade him gently—for he isn't wrong (*hamartanei*) of his own will—by asking him these questions. Should we say this is the original basis for the conventions about what is fine and what is shameful? Fine things are those that subordinate the beastlike parts of our nature to the human—or better perhaps, to the divine; shameful ones are those that enslave the gentle to the savage (*Resp.* 589c)?[321]

Socrates gives another example of someone becoming wealthy by unjust means. The analogy is selling a child into slavery in order to become rich. Socrates asks his interlocuters, "How, then, could he fail to be wretched (*mochthērotatō*) if he pitilessly enslaves the most divine part of himself to the most godless and polluted one and accepts golden gifts in return for a more terrible destruction…" (*Resp.* 589e–590a)?[322]

The Hellenistic Jew of Alexandria, Philo, interprets the Bible in Greek primarily within a Platonic view of the world and human psychology and ethics. An important point of comparison with Paul is Philo's description of the outcome of the soul that is given over to sin and vice.[323] Philo speaks of the dominance of the appetites and passions of the soul as its death. In the context of the Garden of Eden and the curse of death, Philo writes "the death of the soul is the decay of virtue and the bringing in of wickedness … the soul becoming entombed in passions and wickedness of all kinds" (*Legat.* 1.105).[324] Emma Wasserman notes that Philo's language about the struggle in the soul uses "analogies drawn from slavery, warfare and imprisonment."[325]

In 6:12–14, Paul talks about this aspect of the person as being allowed to dominate and get the person to follow the appetite for what is wrongfully perceived as being what might bring pleasure or happiness (6:12).

---

[321] Cooper and Hutchinson, eds., *Plato: Complete Works*, 1197.

[322] Cooper and Hutchinson, eds., *Plato: Complete Works*, 1197.

[323] Emma Wasserman, *The Death of the Soul in Romans 7: Sin, Death, and the Law in Light of Hellenistic Moral Psychology* (Tübingen: Mohr Siebeck, 2008). See also Dieter Zeller, "The Life and Death of the Soul in Philo of Alexandria: The Use and Origin of the Metaphor," *Studia Philonica Annual* 7 (1995).

[324] Philo, *On the Creation. Allegorical Interpretation of Genesis 2 and 3.* trans. F. H. Colson and G. H. Whitaker, Loeb Classical Library 226 (Cambridge, MA: Harvard University Press, 1929), 217.

[325] Wasserman, *Death of the Soul in Romans 7*, 73.

He describes the person as a tool or weapon in the hands of the controlling part to bring about wrong-doing (6:13). Instead, these gentile followers of Jesus should allow the divine part of themselves be in control to do good. If these gentiles continue to think law-keeping will make them good, they should realize that they no longer need to be under the condemnation of the judgment of their inability to become good based on law-keeping (6:14). God has graciously acquitted the gentile peoples apart from the requirements of the Torah.

Again, at 6:15 Paul has his recalcitrant gentile followers raise an objection. If God is so gracious, why worry about being good (6:15a)? Paul responds with his usual emphatic denial (6:15b). This time his analogy is of the slave market. Whoever offers themselves as slaves, obeys the one to whom they have given themselves (6:16). Their choice leads to necessary consequences. If they give themselves to the unruly part of themselves, it will bring dire consequences. If they give themselves to obey the part of themselves that wants what is good, then it will lead to uprightness (6:16). Paul is grateful that they have remained faithful to the type of teaching he offers and are no longer bound to live a life of vice but one of uprightness (6:17).

After another aside (6:19a), Paul continues this line of argument. He suggests that they should apply the same consistency to their upright behavior. Before their actions led to a state of ritual impurity, their upright behavior leads to the opposite, a state of purity or sacredness (6:19b). When they used to be bound to their impropriety, they were free from any responsibility to act properly. Paul infers that the opposite is true. They are free from doing wrong, so they should be upright in their actions (6:20).

Paul continues to address the recalcitrant gentile followers of Jesus in 6:21. He asks what they got out of their vice-ridden lives. Because Paul's voice continues in the text, it seems he imagines they are too ashamed to respond. He tells them. They feel shame (6:21b). Acting in that way ultimately leads to death. Then the opposite is also true. The goal or ending point (*telos*) of moral behavior is unending life (*zōēn aiōnion*) (6:22). This is the consequence of God's graciousness through their participation in Christ.

Paul concludes this thought with the metaphor of soul-death. The recalcitrant person who continues to choose vice rather than do what is good will get the payback of being dead inside (6:23). In contrast, the person who maintains the progress of their moral character lives a divine and flourishing life of blessedness. There is no reason to inject an apocalyptic future judgment into the text as is often done.

No Legal Duty to the "Husband" for Gentiles (7:1–6)

Paul returns to his point that gentiles who have become followers of Jesus and participants in Christ's death and resurrection are no longer duty-bound to adhere to the Law of Moses. Paul is not specific in his analogy about the legal loophole about death releasing someone from legal responsibility. Therefore, I take his comment in 7:1 to be a generic comment about his audience's knowledge about how law works. His discussion here is not so much explanatory but hortatory. Paul wants to convince the gentile adherents in Rome to solidify their relationship with Christ and to be fully committed to moral progress. He imagines them to have been married to the personification of sin, Hamartia (7:2). But now that they have, in effect, died, they are no longer wedded to Hamartia but are free to be joined to Jesus (7:3–6).

Soliloquy of the Gentile Soul's Inner Person (7:7–8:2)

In this section we have the unusual situation in which we find a switch to a first-person singular. A facile assumption would be that Paul is now revealing his own inner struggles. Readers from Augustine to modern times have taken this as Paul telling his own story of his inability as a Jew to obey Torah and do what is right. When we read this section within the larger framework of Paul's literary and philosophical context—and not just assume an apocalyptic setting—we discover a different sort of reading.[326] The test is whether this reading fits the context, whether it is coherent and consistent, and whether it answers more questions than it raises in comparison with the traditional interpretation. Stowers and Wasserman show that the language and

---

[326] My reading is dependent on Stowers and Wasserman to the extent I understand their positions. Where I diverge is my own interpretation. For further elucidation see Stowers, *A Rereading of Romans*, 258-84; Stowers, "Romans 7.7-25 as a Speech-in-Character (prosopopoiia)."; Emma Wasserman, "The Death of the Soul in Romans 7: Revisiting Paul's Anthropology in Light of Hellenistic Moral Psychology," *Journal of Biblical Literature* 126, no. 4 (Winter 2007); Wasserman, *Death of the Soul in Romans 7*, 76-116.

rhetoric in this section can be better understood within the philosophical tradition of Platonists and Stoics about the conflict within the soul about moral choices and actions as often seen in discussions using the example of Medea from the play of that name by Euripides.

Paul has given hints in his previous dialogues with his imaginary interlocuters as to the identity and characteristics. In this section Paul seems to relate the inner monologue of a gentile whose "inner person," the reasoning part of a platonically conceived tripartite soul, bemoans the conflict over choosing what is right and doing it. We might imagine that this is a gentile who becomes aware of the Jewish Torah and accepts that it contains precepts that should be adhered to. Paul continues his personification of sin, which I have depicted by using the Greek word like a proper noun, Hamartia.

The dialogue begins with a question and the usual strong denial (7:7). The question is whether Torah is to be equated with Hamartia. The principle is that there is no infraction of morality without a moral code; you can't break the law if there is no law to be broken. So, did the giving of the Law of Moses bring about the condition of people being sinful?

The response of the gentile Inner Person is filled with sexual innuendo. The picture is of Hamartia as a seductress. To use the Semitic idiom in Greek of "knowing" has a sexual connotation (7:7). The Inner Person experiences conflict with the part of the soul that feels desire. By becoming aware of the commandment not to desire someone else's wife, it is as though the unruly part of the soul responds with heightened interest. Hamartia sees the response and begins her enticement (7:8).

Before this period within the life of this gentile, there was no Torah and no moral code that purported to be God's rules for right and wrong. But when the knowledge came about, it was then that Hamartia came to life (7:9). The result for the Inner Person was that the passions within the soul dominated the reasoning faculty and the soul was deadened by the overpowering of immorality (7:10). Again, it was as though the seductress Hamartia was deceptive in the way she offered pleasure in the moment, but in the long run it led to the deadening of the Inner Person within the soul (7:11).

In 7:12–13 Paul recapitulates what he has said so far. Torah is not to be equated with sin; it is in fact "sacred, just, and good" (7:12). If Paul were talking about the failure of the Law to bring about the righteousness of Jewish people, then it is incongruent that he would acknowledge that there is nothing wrong about Torah in itself. He goes on to say that it was not Torah, which is personified in the Bible as Sophia ("wisdom"). The blame goes to Hamartia. Her identity is revealed because of Torah, that which Paul says was good (7:13).

Paul now alludes to the Medean struggle of the conflicted soul. Along with the dualism of soul and body is the dualism of spirit and flesh. Torah is God's wisdom, therefore it is an aspect of God's active principle, the Pneuma that animates life. The problem for the Inner Person is that it functions within tension with the other faculties of the soul and acts within the flesh of the body. Hamartia is not only a seductress but also a dominatrix (7:14). The Inner Person claims that, despite its best efforts, it is not in control (7:15). We might infer that the reason it is not in control is that this gentile has not yet been given the tools of philosophical training to habituate himself to making proper choices about the good. Paul does not tell his audience all they need to do is believe in Jesus and then they will choose good. Paul culminates his explanations in his letters about the relationship of the gentile peoples with God by laying out a program for moral development.

Paul has the Inner Person make three statements. First is the admission that the Inner Person is not in control (7:15). Second, the action that is done is not what is wanted but what is detested (7:15). Third, the mind or self is not to blame but the desires and appetites of the body, without the training of the soul, which overpower the reasoning faculty (7:17).

Because these three admissions are repeated in the following section and because the Inner Person is explicitly referred to (7:22), I take it that the voice now switches at 7:18. It is now the gentile person whose Inner Person has been speaking. This gentile person represents those in Paul's audience whom he is trying to persuade towards philosophical practice. Without that training Hamartia will continue to be effective in dominating the soul and deadening their ability to make the proper choices and to make progress in their moral development.

First, the gentile person repeats that he or she is not in control of the choices being made (7:18). Second, he or she cannot do the good thing but ends up doing the opposite (7:19). Third, it is Hamartia responsible since this person has no training to develop the capacity to rule over the passions (7:20–21). If Paul were not reiterating these points to show that the gentile person is identified with the "inner person," then Paul would seem to be redundant for no reason.

It seems even a stronger case at 7:22 to say that it is no longer the "inner person" speaking but the person whose "inner person" has been speaking when that person refers to the "inner person." To take it this way makes better sense of the *syn* prefix to the verb *synēdomai* "to delight together." The mental conflict is depicted in 7:23 as a battle between the body and the mind whose outcome for the recalcitrant and untrained person is to become a prisoner of war under the command of Hamartia.

The defeated person, Paul's imaginary recalcitrant and untrained gentile, admits defeat to the power of the passions and appetites within the soul, "I am a miserable person!" (7:24). Parallels to this text provide a literary and philosophical context for Paul's language. Seneca, for example, has Medea in an apostrophe (aside) talk to herself.

> Why delay now, my spirit? Why hesitate? Has your powerful anger already flagged? I regret what I have done, I feel ashamed. What have I done, poor woman (*misera*)? Poor woman (*misera*)? Whatever my regrets, I have done it (Seneca, *Med.* 990).[327]

When Epictetus refers to Medea, he is discussing the conflicted soul and has his imaginary interlocuter decry his perplexity over a divided mind.

> Do you at this moment desire what is possible in general and what is possible for you in particular? If so, why are you hampered? Why are you troubled? Are you not at this moment trying to escape what is inevitable? If so, why do you fall into any trouble, why are you unfortunate? Why is it that when you want something it does not happen, and when you do not want it, it does happen? For this is the strongest proof of trouble and misfortune. I want something, and it does not happen; and what creature is more wretched (*athliōteron*) than I? I do not want something, and it does happen; and what creature is more wretched (*athliōteron*) than I? (*Diatr.* 2.17–18).[328]

---

[327] Seneca, *Tragedies, Volume 1: Hercules. Trojan Women. Phoenician Women. Medea. Phaedra.* trans. John G. Fitch, Loeb Classical Library 62 (Cambridge, MA: Harvard University Press, 2018), 401.

[328] Epictetus, *Discourses, Books 1-2*, 333.

In Plato's description of the inner person of the tripartite soul, the "man within the man" (*anthrōpou ho entos anthrōpos*) (*Resp.* 589b), he has Socrates exclaim, "How, then, could he fail to be wretched (*mochthērotatō*) if he pitilessly enslaves the most divine part of himself to the most godless and polluted one and accepts golden gifts in return for a more terrible destruction…" (*Resp.* 589e–590a)?[329]

Paul has his gentile character in dramatic fashion call out for rescue from the condition of soul-death due to the overwhelming attack of the appetites and passions against the "inner person" (7:24). He then has this dramatis persona have the epiphany that gratitude is owed to God for providing the circumstances in which a gentile may now overcome the passions by the training that one gets by being a follower of Jesus and to be empowered by God's Pneuma. The conclusion within this exclamation continues in chapter eight. The second-person singular requires that we see 8:3 as the climax.[330] The gentile character now says to the "inner person" that it now has freedom from the domination of Hamartia and the condition of soul-death.

The God-given Moral Capacity for Freedom to Live as God's Offspring (8:3–39)

Paul now returns to his gentile audience of Jesus-followers to explain what this all means for them. Gentiles are no longer bound to their fleshly desires and appetites and doomed to experience the death of their souls as incapable of doing good without proper training (8:3). Gentile followers of Jesus have a new status as participants of Jesus by their adoption as offspring of God (8:14–17). Nothing can separate the gentile peoples from God's love because of Christ's death for them (8:31–39).

The point of Paul's apostrophes and analogies is to say that God has brought about for the gentile peoples what Torah alone was not able to accomplish (8:3). Without philosophical training and a proper exemplar,

---

[329] Cooper and Hutchinson, eds., *Plato: Complete Works*, 1197.

[330] Those Christians dependent on the King James translation will be supported in their interpretation that it is Paul admitting to himself that his Judaism failed to make him righteous before God. This is because the manuscript tradition on which the KJV is based has the direct object in the first-person singular. Modern textual criticism recognizes the better quality of textual reading and the more difficult reading supplied by the variant in the second-person singular.

humans are at the mercy of the appetites and desires of the soul that work in conjunction with the fleshly body. Those who follow the example of Jesus are able to live a moral life.

Paul constructs a battle narrative in which God observes Hamartia killing the pagan people who are too weak to defend themselves. Just as Homer has Zeus or Hera send their divine offspring in human form to affect the human world, so Paul depicts God sending his own divine offspring in human form to defeat Hamartia (8:3). The outcome of the battle is that the pagan people have been enabled to fulfill the standard of God's Torah (8:4).

What has been established is that, when people make judgments about right and wrong based on the desires and appetites of their baser selves, they choose to do those things that satisfy those desires and appetites (8:5). This excessive immorality brings about the death of the soul (8:6). The opposite is true. Proper judgment based on God's Pneuma enables people to choose the good and that results in the vitality and serenity of the soul.

Paul warns that those who want to ignore philosophical practice are doomed to moral failure and will not be able to satisfy the moral standard of God (8:8). He then praises those who want to develop self-mastery by being controlled by God's Pneuma which resides within them (8:9).[331]

Rather than experiencing the death of the soul because of extreme immorality, those who experience Christ are enlivened to a higher quality of life (8:10). It is not only in this life that one can experience the divine life, but God will "immortalize" those in whom God's Pneuma resides (8:11).[332]

Paul has used a variety of metaphors in which a person is in some servitude to a dominant person. We shouldn't be surprised that two of these are wives and slaves, since women were treated as duty-bound

---

[331] The sentence at the end of Rom 8:9 seems out of place. The expression "have the spirit of Christ" is unusual for Paul. To me it fits a late first-century editor who is experiencing the separation of Jewish followers of Jesus and the synagogue. Their polemic is that only those who "possess the spirit of Christ" belong to the exclusive group.

[332] For the terminology of "corporeal immortalization" and the immortalization of humans see Litwa, *Iesus Deus*.

possessions in antiquity and beyond. Paul's message to these gentile followers of Jesus in Rome is that they should realize that they don't have to consider themselves to be duty-bound to the parts of their souls that work with the flesh of their bodies to fulfill desires and appetites. They value only what preserves the body and satisfies or gives pleasure (8:12). Paul warns again that allowing the baser impulses to have free reign leads to the condition of extreme immorality and the death of the soul (8:13).

The most dramatic proof for the earliest followers of Jesus was that Jews and gentiles alike experienced inexplicable indications that something out of the ordinary occurred when people heard about Jesus and decided to become followers. This may have been the same experience described by Lucian as the switch to a different philosophical school (see p. 40). The fact that the experience was shared by both Jews and gentiles meant that God treated all people of the world in the same way. Paul can say then that anyone who experiences God's Pneuma and are "led" or "guided" (*agō*) deserve the same label as Jesus as a "son of God" (8:14). Gentiles should not consider this turning from idolatry to the worship of the one God as a relationship of servitude and fear like a new slave might feel when becoming part of a new household. On the contrary, gentile peoples, specifically those who have become followers of Jesus, have been adopted into God's offspring (8:15). Although it is difficult if not impossible to prove, I take this idiom here and in Gal 4:6 (see p. 124) the combined call of Jews and gentiles, first the Aramaic term and then the Greek. I take the expression in 8:16 then, not as "the spirit itself" but "the same Pneuma." The same Pneuma that causes Jews to cry out "Abba" is the same one that causes gentiles to cry out to God "*Patēr*!" Both are now God's offspring. Paul then goes one step further: Offspring are heirs of the father which means being co-heirs with God's son, Jesus (8:17). The way this is actualized for the followers of Jesus is by their imitation of the pattern of Jesus, which is to endure the hardships of the upright person leading to the reception of honor or divine majesty (*doxa*) through immortalization (8:17).

Although the context of the 8:18–26 is adoption rather than birth, Paul paints a picture of the world as a pregnant woman who groans and moans (8:22–23; 26) with the final birth pangs. He treats the current difficulties in the world as the precursor to the disclosure of the "sons of God" (8:19). Paul's language is both apocalyptic and otherworldly. God is moving the world toward the resurrection which will make clear what God has been doing regarding the gentile peoples. The expectation is, as Litwa puts it, a corporeal immortalization.[333] It is not the soul's release from the body but the body's release of mortality, i.e. corruption and decay (8:21, 23). The language of *doxa*, normally translated as "glory," is nothing less than humans receiving the divine majesty of immortality (8:21, 29–30) as "sons" of God (8:19, 21, 29).

We might surmise that in 8:26 Paul has in view his own compassion and intercession for the Judean nation in Rom 9–11. Paul will express his heartfelt yearning and requests to God on behalf of his fellow-citizens and ethnic kin (10:1). At 8:26 he seems to say that the cosmic birth pangs are beyond human capacity for prayer and even God's spirit only groans in anticipation (8:26). I take this as the context because of my attempt to give a consistent interpretation to the term "saints, holy ones" as referring to Jews as *qedoshim* (see p. 34). Paul returns to gentiles by using the language of those who have been "called, invited" (8:28, 30). Rather than reading 8:28 as expressing confidence that whatever happens to a person will somehow be okay, as it is interpreted in popular Christianity, Paul seems to have in mind the big picture, the grand narrative, of what God will accomplish in the world by bringing all humanity together.

Paul brings his discussion about the inclusion of the gentiles to a close with a flourish in 8:31–39. He eloquently and with a rhetorical style encourages his gentile readers/hearers that they should be confident that there's nothing that could happen that could change their status before God as accomplished by Christ's death.

Paul's National Loyalty and Premise of God's Promise (9:1–13)

Beginning in chapter nine Paul's rhetorical style and focus change to a more personal discussion regarding the status of the Jewish nation in God's plan for humanity.[334] Paul has been assuring his gentile readers of their new relationship with God based on the faithfulness of Jesus. He continues to talk to the gentile adherents but moves his focus from arguing for their inclusion to their need to acknowledge the continuing status of the Jewish nation. Paul has made himself clear that God's

---

[333] Litwa, *Iesus Deus*, 145.

[334] Stowers enumerates the ways in which Paul's style in the letter becomes more personal. Stowers, *A Rereading of Romans*, 291.

covenant with the Jewish nation still continues and that gentiles need not become Jews or adopt the Jewish legislation to be part of God's people. As long as Judea remains occupied by the Romans, we can expect Jews to regard their nation as in need of repentance and a renewal so that God will bring them the blessing of God once again. Those who recognize Jesus as an innocent martyr in the line of the Maccabean martyrs are expecting God to remove the Romans just as God did the Seleucids. Paul wants the Jewish followers of Jesus to recognize the message he is bringing to the gentile peoples. To what extent Paul supports the Jewish mission of the apostles in Jerusalem is unclear, since Paul is traveling around the eastern parts of the Roman Empire and talking to household groups consisting solely or mainly of gentiles. Paul's primary theme about God's impartiality continues in Rom 9–11. But Paul flips it around to say that gentiles shouldn't think God has abandoned the Jewish nation.

In the strongest terms Paul expresses his deep loyalty to his ethnic and religious roots (9:1–3). Everything that was given to the Israelites continues to be theirs (9:4). The one whose death has made the inclusion of the gentiles possible is a natural descendant of Abraham (9:5).

Paul argues that God's promises are still in effect despite what it may seem. The Roman occupation is entrenched, and Jews within cities are still antagonistic to those Jews who mingle with gentiles and do not require that gentiles be circumcised and follow Torah. Paul's hopefulness is based on his argument that the gentile inclusion is a fulfillment of the promises made to the Israelites (9:6). His interpretation of the promise to Abraham (9:7–9) and what was said about the sons of Isaac (9:10–13) sees these as being fulfilled in the gentile peoples. What is most important when understanding the promises is that God is the one who makes choices and it is not something anyone does to deserve God's blessing.

Paul seems to have in mind an athletic metaphor throughout this section. It is as though Paul imagines runners who are trying to reach their destinations. Perhaps this is related to the language of those who are sent to bring news to distant places. Paul seems to say in 9:6 that the one bringing the message about God's promises has not "fallen down" (*ekpiptō*). The common translation of "fail" doesn't seem to have parallels. In the next section Paul refers to "desiring" (*thelō*) and "running" (*trechō*)

(9:16). Translators who render the second word as "exertion" seem to read into the text the Lutheran "law versus grace" scheme.

Dialogue on the Choices of God (9:14–33)

Paul raises the objection in place of an imaginary interlocuter who will appear more clearly beginning with 9:19. Paul anticipates someone might think God is unfair if God's choice does not seem to be based on commonly accepted privileges (9:14). Paul reminds his readers that the Bible depicts God as one who shows mercy and compassion on those whom he chooses (9:15). Here Paul uses the athletic imagery suggested above. God's choice is not like a foot-race. The outcome is not based on how zealous someone is or the way they run (9:16). God's impartiality and fairness are not based on human values but on God's mercy and justice.

Since God is viewed as controlling the course of history, even Pharaoh is considered being someone God chose for a particular purpose (9:17). Bad things happen, but out of them good things come about. If some people receive something good for no clear reason and others seem to be recalcitrant, it is the effect of God's choices (9:18). Paul is not constructing theology here but explaining why gentiles are experiencing God's special presence while it would seem that God continues to allow Rome to occupy the land of Judea because of the lack of repentance.

Paul once again turns to his Jewish discussion partner signaled by the switch to the singular. He wants to know why God makes these choices that seem to be arbitrary (9:19). Whatever the interlocuter means by his questioning, Paul takes it to be the equivalent of the absurdity of a clay pot complaining to the potter about his choice of making a pot (9:20). Paul shapes the metaphor by imagining a potter who has a lump of clay and makes from the same lump one object to be used for something like worship and another object made for everyday use (9:21).

Paul again interrupts his dialogue to return to addressing his gentile audience with an explanation about the meaning of the metaphor of the lump of clay, the different objects made from it, and the choices God makes. I take it that the "objects of wrath" (9:22) and the "objects of mercy" (9:23) represent the same lump of clay and both refer to the gentile peoples. Paul quotes Exod 9:16, which says that God wanted to show (*endeiknymi*) God's power (*dynamis*) through Pharaoh (9:17). Regarding the "objects of wrath," Paul writes that God wants to show (*endeiknymi*) God's power (*dynamis*) (9:22). The "objects of mercy" are ones that Paul says are characterized by wealth (*ploutos*), which is also the terminology Paul uses regarding the inclusion of the gentiles as being their riches (*ploutos*) (11:12). In the former case the gentile peoples, including Egypt and its Pharaoh, experienced God's patience in not punishing them for their sins in God's wrath. Because of the faithfulness of Christ this same lump of clay has now become "objects of mercy" to receive God's "divine majesty" ("glory," *doxa*) (9:23).

Paul tells his gentile audience that those gentiles, who have turned to God as followers of Jesus, are among those, who along with those Jews who have joined the national restoration movement of Jewish Jesus-followers, are those whom God has called (9:24), which Paul will refer to as the remnant (11:5). Paul amasses quotations from the Bible to support the idea that there are other nations that God will choose, and that there is a subset of people who remain faithful to God (9:25–29).

Paul asks or, perhaps, imagines his interlocuter raising the question about what all of this means (9:30). Paul uses his athletic race metaphor to line up two teams. It would seem that the team that gets the prize was not even competing. The team which was in pursuit did not get the prize (9:31). Paul's principle is that God views gentiles as upright based on the faithfulness of Christ. The interlocuter wants to know why Paul thinks that some Jews are not regarded by God as upright even though they have observed Torah (9:32a). Paul thinks the current state of the Jewish nation results from people who are more committed to doing right things than they are to being committed to God (9:32b). Paul may think the way Jews show faithfulness is by supporting and joining the sect of Jesus-following Jews. As a national restoration movement, it requires a renewed commitment to God through repentance. Paul seems to imply that Jesus and his humiliating execution has become an issue that has caused a problem for Jews and "tripped" them up (9:33).

Israel's Role in the Good News to Gentiles (10:1–21)

Paul continues writing to his gentile audience about the homeland of his ancestry. Although Paul is deeply committed to the non-Jewish people of the Roman Empire and wants them to embrace his message about God, he also wants them to understand his ongoing commitment to his ancestral people and their land. He has deep feelings for the future of Judeans and prays for them (10:1). Rather than interpret Paul according to Christian theology as wanting Jews to abandon their religion and become Christians, Paul would more natural be referring to the "deliverance" of the nation from the Roman occupation (10:1). Whether there is evidence of any particular wrong-doing by the Jewish people, that God has allowed the homeland to be occupied means that God has temporarily withdrawn God's blessing. A national restoration movement like the one promoted by the Jewish followers of Jesus hopes that the death of Jesus will bring about their freedom in the same way as the martyrs of the Maccabean period. One way Paul would want for Jews to show their repentance would be to become followers of Jesus and undergo baptism. Paul would also want them to approve of his mission to the gentiles and their inclusion in the people of God apart from becoming proselytes. In addition, Paul's moral psychology seems to be that there is more to becoming the right person than following rules and precepts.

Paul is positive in his assessment of the Jewish people's zeal for God. However, he thinks something is missing in their understanding (10:2). Maybe Paul's only criticism is that most Jews are not accepting his mission to the gentiles (10:3). He might think Jews who do not accept his mission are forsaking their role as a "light to the gentiles" (Isa 42:6; 49:6).

It is crucial to understand that Paul does not say that Torah observance is finished in 10:4. For Paul the *telos*, the goal or culmination, of the Bible is the coming of Christ. To say that Christ brings uprightness to everyone could mean that God considers the Jewish people to be upright based on God's covenant, but the death of Christ includes gentiles.

Paul's quotations would seem to mean that the "message" (*rhēma*) in 10:8 has to do with the covenant within the context of Deut 30. The nearness of the covenant is expressed vocally with the mouth and genuinely from the heart (10:9). Paul interprets that message to refer to his mission to the gentiles regarding the faithfulness of Jesus. The *hoti* ("that, because") that begins verse nine is not causal but signals the indirect speech with the content of the announcement made to a gentile. Verse nine switches to the second-person singular. Paul describes what happens when a gentile changes their way of life and becomes a follower of Jesus (10:9). The person vocally gives their profession that shows their commitment to Jesus and to live a life that shows their genuineness that they are convinced God is the one who raises the upright person from the underworld (10:10). By doing this, the person no longer participates in pagan customs and rituals and changes to a different lifestyle (12:1–2).

I take the designation of Jesus as "lord" or "sovereign" (*kyrios*) in 10:9 not to be the equivalent of saying that Jesus is the One whose name in Hebrew is read as *Adonai* and translated in Greek as *Kyrios*. How to translate objectively *kyrios* is immensely difficult since it is such a polyvalent term. Jesus is considered being a divine sovereign because of his resurrection. The God that gentiles turn to by rejecting pagan deities and idolatry is none other than the *Kyrios* of the Greek Bible. Paul may very well be equivocating in the sense that the gentile belief in Jesus as *kyrios* is the same as Jews worshipping *Kyrios*, the God of Israel. Paul can say that there is no difference in their relationship to the *Kyrios*. The benefit for the gentile peoples of God including them is that God "bestows riches" (10:12). In antiquity a nation's God provides benevolence through food and fertility and safety from invading nations. Although Paul uses the words of the prophet Joel, he reinterprets the context to mean that the gentile peoples are not to be destroyed in judgment but be among those who experience deliverance (10:13).

The identification of whom Paul refers to with his pronouns in this next section is difficult. My translation includes indications of my interpretation. Paul picks up on the previous quotation from Joel to begin his list of his interrogatives. How, Paul exclaims, are gentiles able to invoke the name of Yahweh without first believing that Yahweh is the God to call out to (10:14)? How are gentiles supposed to believe that Yahweh is God unless someone tells them about Yahweh? How are they supposed to hear about Yahweh unless Jews tell the gentile peoples about Yahweh (10:14)? Finally, how are Jews supposed to tell the gentile peoples about Yahweh unless God sends them (10:15)? At this point Paul expects his audience to get the point. God has sent Jews to be a light to the gentile peoples. Paul's proof is the quotation from Isa 52:7. The problem for Paul is that he thinks most Jews have not been obedient so that gentiles hear (10:16–17).

216   Rewriting Paul

Paul continues his rhetorical flourishes with a repetition of "But I ask" (10:18–19). The first question is whether gentiles have heard. Paul answers with Ps 19:4 to say that the voice of Jews has proceeded far out into the diaspora (10:18). The second question is whether Israel has understood its role. Paul uses Deut 32:21 to say that the Jewish people are to be made jealous because of the gentile peoples (10:19). He uses Isa 65:1 to say that God has become known to the gentiles even though they weren't looking (10:20). Paul then names Israel explicitly as being disobedient and opposed to God's inclusion of the gentile peoples (10:21).

Foot Race Metaphor to Cause Competitive Jealousy (11:1–16)

Paul continues the theme of God causing Israel to become jealous because of God's involvement with another nation (10:19). He does this within a context of a metaphor with language alluding to a foot race.[335] It will be helpful to compare this with a text of Philo, *On Joseph*.

> Athletes mightily proud (*mega phronountes*) of the strength and muscle and robustness of their bodies, hoping for undoubted victory, have often failed to pass the test and been excluded from the arena (*mē dokimasthentes*), or if admitted, have been vanquished (*hēttēthēsan*), while others who despaired of taking even the second place have won the first prize and worn the crown (Philo, *Ios.* 138).[336]

Paul also warns a gentile, who thinks he is the clear winner of the contest, as one who should not be proud or boastful (*phroneō*) (11:20). While Philo refers to the one who has lost the contest as having been vanquished, Paul uses a similar term for the defeat (*hēttēma*) of Israel (11:12) in this metaphorical contest.

Paul begins this metaphor with language about the expulsion (*apōtheō*) of a nation (11:1–2). Paul knows of biblical texts that use this language in the Greek translation (1 Sam 19:22; Ps 93:14). Within Paul's metaphor the concept of rejection seems to imply the disqualification of a runner. Paul states adamantly that Israel has not been disqualified. His

---

[335] See Stowers, *A Rereading of Romans*, 312-16.

[336] Philo, *On Abraham. On Joseph. On Moses*. trans. F. H. Colson, Loeb Classical Library 289 (Cambridge, MA: Harvard University Press, 1935), 205, 07.

evidence is that he, and others like him, have accepted God's plan for the inclusion of the gentile peoples. Paul repeats that God has not disqualified the Israelite nation (11:2). He draws attention to the story of Elijah in which he despaired of the waywardness of his fellow Israelites and that he was the only one who has remained loyal (1 Kgs 19:10, 14). Paul quotes the response of God that Elijah is not alone but one of 7,000. So, Paul sees himself as one of many who make up a remnant of people. These are people God has selected based on God's own graciousness and not as a reward for fidelity (11:15–16). It's important for Paul to stress that neither Jews nor gentiles should be arrogant or boastful about their status as worshippers of God.

Although Paul's metaphor has a contestant trip rather than slip, Paul and his readers might have recollected the story in Homer's *Iliad*, Book 23, of the athletic contests fought at the funeral of Patroclus. After the chariot racing, boxing, and wrestling events, Ajax ("the Lesser," son of Oileus), Odysseus, and Antilochus line up for a foot race (*Il.* 23.740–780). As they came around to the last part of the course, Odysseus, struggling behind Ajax, prayed to the goddess Athene. Athene responded by giving Odysseus his second wind, so to speak. At the finish line, Athene caused Ajax to slip on the remains of the butchered bulls. Athene had hindered (*blaptō*) Ajax from completing the race ahead of Odysseus.

Paul further describes the hindrance Israel received, causing them not to obtain what it sought. It was God who caused them not to be responsive but to be calcified or become recalcitrant. Their senses no longer allow them to respond properly to God (11:7–10).

Paul asks and answers his question. Israel has stumbled, but they are not out of the race: they have not fallen down (11:11). Rather than interpret *paraptōma* with the usual word "transgression," in this context it has the sense of a misstep. One would assume that the misstep must refer to whatever waywardness led God to allow the Romans to occupy Judea. The result for the gentile peoples was God's impartial justice that forgave the millennia of sin and turned the gentile peoples from enemy nations to be reconciled as included nations of God's people in the world (11:12). In Paul's understanding, the reason for this was to cause the Judean nation to become jealous and do whatever was necessary as a national restoration. One aspect of this for Paul would be their acceptance of the inclusion of the gentiles based on their atonement through the death of Jesus. Paul highlights the magnitude of the outcome of the completion on the part of Israel (11:12).

Paul repeats this for his gentile readers. He values his role as the envoy sent to the gentile peoples, but an important result will be that some of his co-ethnics will join his so-called "Apostolic Judaism," those Jews who belong to a Jewish sect following Jesus (11:13–14). Rather than a "salvation" that turns them from Jews into "born again" Christians, it is part of a national restoration movement to rescue them from Roman occupation. Paul repeats his argument that, if the present outcome of Israel's temporary "loss of ground" means the inclusion of the other nations of the world (Paul may have limited his thinking to the other nations or provinces that made up the Roman Empire), the re-inclusion of Israel will result in the final resurrection (11:15).

Paul changes his metaphor from a footrace to an argument about the nature of the source and what derives from the source. If part of a batch of dough is taken from a batch that has been consecrated, then the source of the consecrated portion is also consecrated (11:16). In the same sense, Paul argues, a root—and maybe he is not thinking literally of a tree—of a family that is sacred, like a priestly family, then the offshoots/offspring are also sacred.

Dialogue with a Boastful Gentile (11:17–24)

Again, Paul uses the second-person singular with an objection from an interlocuter (11:17). This person represents the type of attitude Paul is warning against. This is the attitude of gentiles who become arrogant regarding the current condition of Judea and consider themselves to be special. Paul admonishes this representative caricature for boastfulness or, as I have translated it, a triumphalism (11:18). It is a boastfulness that sees oneself as superior to someone else.

Paul's agricultural metaphor depicts a farmer who takes a cutting from an olive tree growing out in a field somewhere, brings it back to his olive grove, and grafts it into his tree. The shoot takes hold as a vascular connection takes place and it absorbs what the root of the tree draws up from the ground (11:17). Paul imagines this new, grafted branch of becoming arrogant of its placement while other pruned branches, supposedly pruned in order for new branches to have more nourishment, lay dormant on the ground. Paul reminds his arrogant gentile interlocuter that the tree has not been turned upside down to favor the new branch, but the new branch still depends on the original root system (11:18).

Paul has his interlocuter speak. It is as though the new grafted-in branch boasts, "The farmer pruned all of those old branches for the express purpose of including me as the scion of the desirable cultivar!" The gentile boasts that God has caused some Judeans to become "pruned" so that this new branch might, shall we say, supersede the old (11:19). Paul affirms that some Jews have been "pruned" because of their infidelity to God. He quickly warns the gentile that the status of the gentile is also based on fidelity. The gentile should not be boastful but fearful (11:20). We could imagine Paul's argument in another context. A parent kicks out their wayward child. An adopted child should expect that, if the parent kicks out their biological child for being bad, the parent will certainly not hesitate to kick out the wayward adopted child. The same goes for branches on a tree (11:21).

Paul expands on his metaphor and its lesson to the gentile. God may be benevolent, or God may be severe. The obedient experience God's benevolence, but the disobedient may experience God's severity (11:22). But the obedient person who becomes disobedient will experience God's severity just as the disobedient person who becomes obedient will experience God's benevolence (11:23). If that is true about a grafted-in branch—or an adopted child—then it's even more likely the case with the regrafting of the pruned, natural branch; or the natural child who is included back into the family (11:24).

God's Plan for the Ages to be the God of All (11:25–36)

In this section Paul concisely sums up what he has been explaining in his letter. Paul wants his gentile readers to understand fully something that is difficult to contemplate. He calls it a mystery (*mystērion*). Insiders understand the enigma, but outsiders are oblivious to the deeper meaning. Paul has been concerned that gentiles might be arrogant and boastful that God's attention has turned to them (11:25). He wants to explain the situation so they won't focus too much on their own inclusion. What people might not understand is that God has temporarily caused some Jews to be insensitive to God's plan to include in the people of God the gentile peoples (11:26). At that point, Paul declares that the entire nation of Judea will be delivered. The meaning of Paul's quotations is rather ambiguous. One might even take Paul to mean that in the future a deliverer will lead Israel in a national restoration.

Paul wants his gentile adherents to have a proper understanding of the relationship between God and Israel. The inclusion of the gentile peoples has some Jews at odds (*echthroi*) with God. However, they remain God's chosen nation and God's beloved people (11:28). In no uncertain terms Paul declares that God is with no regret about calling Israel to be God's people and of giving to them, as we might assume Paul means, the covenant, Torah, and the sacrifices (11:29).

Paul reminds the gentiles that for millennia they had been disobedient through their pagan practices, but God showed them mercy through the disobedient condition of the Judean nation (11:30). Likewise, the Jewish people will be shown mercy when they experience God's deliverance (11:31). Both groups have gone through times of disobedience, which means God has showed God's mercy to all peoples of the world (11:32).

Paul reaches his highest pitch by extolling the beauty of the nature of God and the mind of God (11:33). He substantiates his claim by quoting several texts (11:34–35). He then concludes with a doxology repeating prepositions to say that God is everything (11:36).

Personal Transformation and Community Formation (12:1–21)

Paul has established for his gentile audience what God has done for them and why they need to take full advantage of their new relationship to God. Paul has not expected them to adopt a different cultural identity of the Jewish people, their ritual practices, or the ethical prescriptions of the Torah. Paul does, however, expect them to become people who live a better quality of life and move toward attaining full human maturity as God's divine offspring. Paul does this with a program of philosophical practices.

Paul likens their change of a new way of life to a sacrifice (12:1). The image of placing the body on a funeral pyre represents those parts of the soul in league with the body and flesh, the appetites and desires, when allowed to be in control, bring death to the soul. Rather than give way to them, Paul wants them to carry out such a figurative ritual so that reason/rationality (*logikos*) and the mind (*nous*) gain ascendancy (12:1–2).

Paul touches on the two primary problems humans face in society that prevent them from experiencing a flourishing life. First, humans are formed within society to value the wrong things. Without careful thought, humans may think the way to be happy and fulfilled is to subvert fate that might bring harm to a person. If one accumulates wealth, stores up food, becomes powerful, and gets whatever one desires, then the pain of loss, fear, and desire is averted. However, when misfortune strikes, the person loses their equilibrium over what they cannot control. Second, humans are not prone to question their way of thinking and they accept things the way they are. The philosopher as a "physician of the soul" helps people to think properly and re-evaluate what they consider being the best way to live. Martha Nussbaum put it this way:

> For if the diseases that impede human flourishing are above all diseases of belief and social teaching, and if, as they hope to show, critical arguments of the kind philosophy provides are necessary and perhaps even sufficient for dislodging those obstacles, then philosophy will seem to be necessary, perhaps even sufficient, for getting people from disease to health.[337]

This is precisely what Paul wants for the household group(s) in Rome. They are to stop thinking the system of values (*syschēmatizō*) with which they were socialized will help them (12:2). Instead, they are to undergo a process of transformation (*metamorphoō*) by changing the way they test what is good and bad. Examining how one thinks and what one does leads to the best sort of actions.

Plutarch describes the person who is given to having vice as a companion using similar language to Paul.

> In such a state do envy, fear, temper, and licentiousness put a man. For by day vice, looking outside of itself and conforming its attitude (*syschēmatizomenē*) to others, is abashed and veils its emotions, and does not give itself up completely to its impulses,

---

[337] Nussbaum, *The Therapy of Desire*, 34.

but oftentimes resists them and struggles against them (Plutarch, *Virt. vit.* 2 [100f]).[338]

Plutarch goes on to describe the benefits of changing one's way of thinking.

> Where, then, is the pleasure in vice, if in no part of it is to be found freedom from care and grief, or contentment or tranquility or calm? For a well-balanced and healthy condition of the body gives room for engendering the pleasures of the flesh; but in the soul lasting joy and gladness cannot possibly be engendered, unless it provide itself first with cheerfulness, fearlessness, and courageousness as a basis to rest upon, or as a calm tranquility that no billows disturb (Plutarch, *Virt. vit.* 3 [101b]). [339]

The Stoics would say one is to live in accordance with nature. In the same way, Paul encourages his readers to live by God's will (12:2). The outcomes will be those actions that are good, pleasant, and reflect the mature state of progress in the moral life ("perfect, complete" *teleios*).

Paul turns to the household and the relationships among the people. We can expect there to be differing social levels within the household. Along with this are the variety of ways in which the various people contribute to the group. Paul recognizes that some roles and functions might be considered specialized and some might be more menial. Whatever the role or function, people should not treat the more menial jobs as any less important, and everyone should carry out their work faithfully.

The opening lines to this section (12:3–8) read like Paul is cautious to approach the topic gently. He does not want to use harsh criticism but mildly encourage them (12:3). To interpret Paul's language here as pertaining to a lack of humility and a haughty attitude of arrogance seems to me to read modern concerns into the text. Paul chooses several terms related to practical wisdom (*phronēsis*). It is language having to do with critical thinking and judgment. I take it that Paul is saying not to go overboard in one's critical thinking (*hyperphroneō*) about roles and

---

[338] Plutarch, *Moralia, Volume II*, 99.
[339] Plutarch, *Moralia, Volume II*, 99.

functions but to make an assessment (*phroneō*) by thinking sensibly (*sōphroneō*).

It would be odd to interpret Paul as saying that the roles and functions people have is based on various degrees of "faith" God has given to people. God has graciously endowed people with capabilities for a variety of roles and functions. Paul's point seems to be that, no matter what that is, each person should be responsible to do their best (12:3; 6–8).

Paul compares the people functioning within the group with the limbs of the body and their varieties of functions. In much the same way as Paul discusses this topic with the Corinthians (1 Cor 12:4–31), he differentiates among the various roles and functions. Just as the human body has many limbs that do different things with varying levels of importance, so the group has people who do different things, and some may be considered more important than others (12:4–6).

Paul gives two examples of roles in which he mentions a higher status role coupled with a lower status role. The person who is regarded to have the endowment (*charisma*, usually translated as "gift") as a "prophet," an interpreter of the message and will of God, is a special person (12:6). Paul contrasts this person with a household servant who provides for people's needs such as serving the food at a meal (*diakonia*, usually translated as "minister") (12:7). Both people should show the same level of allegiance. Again, the teacher has a specialized role. But the person who has a knack for lifting the spirits of people ("encourager," *parakaleō*) should also be faithful in the work (12:8).

Next in 12:8 Paul links three roles with the same grammatical construction (noun followed by a prepositional phrase with *en*). It would be difficult to know just how these roles were understood. The first one might refer to someone who divides up what the group has and distributes it among people. The second one might refer to a household manager. The third might refer to acts of charity or almsgiving.

In the next section (12:9–18) Paul switches to a paraenetic style. Paraenesis has been defined as a "concise, benevolent injunction that reminds of moral practices to be pursued or avoided, expresses or implies a shared worldview, and does not anticipate disagreement."[340] These brief injunctions provide words of wisdom in a compact form. Many of them are couplets (12:11–12 contain three lines) in a proverbial style of repeating in the second sentence a similar or opposing view. Paul quickly touches on important aspects of interpersonal relationships. The bond of love and friendship among the group should be real and not faked (12:9). In a typical fashion of holding close what's good and shunning what's bad, Paul has the strong language to "abhor" vice and to "cling" to virtue (12:9). The connection among the group should be a "sibling friendship" (*philadelphia*). Paul uses a term from psychagogy when he asks them to provide guidance (*proēgeomai*) to one another (12:10). The next sets have to do with the practice of endurance (12:11–12). Paul again refers to the "saints" (*hagioi*), which I am interpreting as a way within Hellenistic Judaism to refer to Jews as *qedoshim* (see p. 34). If the term just referred to holy people generally, it is more difficult to understand why it's coupled with an injunction regarding foreigners. It makes more sense when we infer that Paul is telling gentiles to take part in programs of raising money to help Jews in Jerusalem. Paul describes this more fully at the close of the letter (15:25–29). Paul wants them to guard their language in response to people who harass them (12:14). When someone in the group is joyful, share in the joy; if they are sad and crying, then cry along with them (12:15).

Paul returns to how to relate to people of differing social levels. With the same phronetic language, Paul tells them not to show deference to high-born people but to associate with people of a lower status (12:16). When encountering people who treat them badly, Paul wants them not to respond in an equally bad way (12:17). In contrast, Paul wants the household group(s) to live peacefully with their neighbors within the city (12:18).

Paul goes more fully into the topic of vengeance. He quotes from biblical texts to say that any sense of retributive justice should be left to God and the natural course of events (12:19). The meaning of the proverb Paul adapts is difficult to interpret (Prov 25:21–22). It most likely is an example of what Paul concludes in 12:21. If someone wrongs you and

---

[340] James Starr, "Was Paraenesis for Beginners," in *Early Christian Paraenesis in Context*, ed. James Starr and Troels Engberg-Pedersen (Berlin: Walter de Gruyter, 2004), 79.

becomes an enemy, be willing to show them the hospitality of your home. Paul might consider that the "fiery coals" are God's vengeance, or it may mean that the person will feel pangs of regret and remorse for their actions.

Civic Duties (13:1–14)

Paul's discussion of civic duties is in keeping with the context of moral exhortation and paraenesis. The points he makes are not too dissimilar from the way Epictetus describes government in the following lengthy quotation.[341]

> Govern us as rational beings by pointing out to us what is profitable, and we will follow you; point out what is unprofitable, and we will turn away from it. Bring us to admire and emulate you, as Socrates brought men to admire and emulate him. He was the one person who governed people as men, in that he brought them to subject to him their desire, their aversion, their choice, their refusal. "Do this; do not do this; otherwise I will throw you into prison." Say that, and yours ceases to be a government as over rational beings. Nay, rather, say, "As Zeus has ordained, do this; if you do not do so, you will be punished, you will suffer injury." What kind of injury? No injury but that of not doing what you ought; you will destroy the man of fidelity in you, the man of honor, the man of decent behavior (Epictetus, *Diatr.* 3.7.33–36).[342]

When Epictetus discusses the existence of the gods and their relationship to humans, he says that a "good and excellent" person should look into this before "he subordinates his own will to him who administers the universe, precisely as good citizens submit to the law of the state" (Epictetus, *Diatr.* 1.12.7).[343]

---

[341] For a complete analysis of how Paul's views compare to Epictetus, see Niko Huttunen, *Paul and Epictetus on Law: A Comparison*, The Library of New Testament Studies, (London: T & T Clark, 2009).

[342] Epictetus, *Discourses, Books 3-4. Fragments. The Encheiridion*, 59, 61.

[343] Epictetus, *Discourses, Books 1-2*, 89, 91.

Cicero summarizes the Stoic teaching about natural impulses for social and political relationships. From the impulse to love our children "is developed the sense of mutual attraction which unites human beings as such; this also is bestowed by nature. The mere fact of their common humanity requires that one man should feel another man to be akin to him" (Cicero, *Fin.* 3.63).[344] Cicero explains that the Stoics consider the universe to be governed by divine will and that gods and humans make up the organization of a city or state. Because humans are members of society together "it is a natural consequence that we should prefer the common advantage to our own" (Cicero, *Fin.* 3.64).[345] According to Cicero, Stoics held that a person should fulfill their civic duties.

> For just as the laws set the safety of all above the safety of individuals, so a good, wise and law-abiding man, conscious of his duty to the state, studies the advantage of all more than that of himself or of any single individual. The traitor to his country does not deserve greater reprobation than the man who betrays the common advantage or security for the sake of his own advantage or security. This explains why praise is owed to one who dies for the commonwealth, because it becomes us to love our country more than ourselves (Cicero, *Fin.* 3.64).[346]

Paul is not only interested in the development of each person and their relationship within the household group, Paul also provides guidance on how to behave within the context of the Roman city. Assuming no situation we might imagine, such as knowing that his audience engages in anti-government actions or Paul wanting anyone reading his letter to know he is not anti-Roman, Paul's treatment of civic duties is in keeping with the larger context of his paraenesis.

Paul encourages his audience to be law-abiding, respectful, and honorable citizens. He takes the view that those who are in power should be regarded as God's agents for maintaining order within a society (13:1–2). If someone breaks the law, they should expect those in authority to arrest, adjudicate, and penalize the offender (13:3–4). The fear of

---

[344] Cicero, *On Ends*. trans. H. Rackham, Loeb Classical Library 40 (Cambridge, MA: Harvard University Press, 1914), 283.

[345] Cicero, *On Ends*, 285.

[346] Cicero, *On Ends*, 285.

punishment is not the only reason to be law-abiding. For anyone to have peace of mind, they would need to avoid the fear that would come from doing anything that would bring recriminations (13:5–6).

Paul understands that the glue that holds society together is the reciprocity of benefits. Governmental officials provide benefits to cities and do such things as create and maintain roads. A reputable person pays tribute in exchange for what the city receives. Tolls are paid when traveling. Rather than repay the beneficence of a patron, what is due is respect and honor (13:7).

For Paul, the language of friendship (*philia*) is expressed by the language of love (*agapē*), no doubt influenced by the dialect of, or usage of, the Greek translation of the Hebrew Bible. The bond within the household community and its relationship to others is that of a loving friendship. Paul interprets Torah for his gentile audience within this context. Paul has said to reciprocate to the one where an obligation is due. He turns this on its head to say the obligation is to have affection and show deference for the other person (13:8). The ancillary benefit of this is that the gentile who does this fulfills the Jewish law, since the commandments are subsumed by the command to love one's neighbor, by which is meant any person one comes near to (13:9–10).

To me, 13:11–14 reads like a late first-century scribal interpolation. First, this pericope seems to interrupt the flow of Paul's paraenetic language. The grammar within the pericope is unlike Paul's: Verse 11 contains a participial construction in the first phrase and an infinitival phrase in the second. Also in verse 11, Paul doesn't have a pronoun before the noun it modifies. And in verse 14, Paul doesn't tend to have a noun in the genitive appear before the noun it modifies. The vocabulary is unusual for Paul. These words and phrases are *hapax legomena* (words only appear once in Paul's letters): "sleep" (*hynos*), "rise from sleep" (*ex hypnou egerthēnai*), "nearer" (*engyteron*), "put away" (*apothōmetha*), "works of darkness" (*ta erga tou skotous*); "weapons of light" (*ta hopla tou phōtos*); "provision" (*pronoia*); "provision of flesh" (*tēs sarkos pronoian*). The tone of the pericope is terse, florid, and doxological. It also is more apocalyptic in tone than the rest of Romans. Instead of Paul's language of progress and formation, this text has the apocalyptic tone of imminence of danger. The picture is of people who are asleep and need to wake up to the reality of the end. Salvation is a deliverance from cataclysm rather than Paul's language of the salutary effects of living and walking. The viewpoint is from a time that looks back to the early days when people first became followers of Jesus (13:11). The duality of light vs. darkness and day vs. night is unusual for Paul but common for apocalyptic language (13:12). Even if one accepts this as the language of Paul, one should not think of it as the reason to claim Paul is primarily an apocalyptic prophet and interpret the rest of Paul's paraenetic language as just some miscellaneous thoughts about morality.

Social Duties (14:1–15:13)

A central activity for a community of people meeting within a household is the shared meal. It is not surprising to find that differences of opinion about food could be a hindrance to the social fabric of that organization. Because a shared meal might have meat or wine that came from a temple selling its leftovers, so to speak, those who considered it defiling to consume that meat or wine could only hope to avoid it by solely eating vegetables and drinking some other beverage than wine. Paul considers these people to be weak (*asthenēs*) in the metaphorical sense of being ill and in need of therapy. That therapy is receiving the knowledge by which one becomes convinced about the truth of something. Pagans who grow up believing in gods and divinities would have a difficult time changing the way they think about the reality of those beings in the world. Paul's message is for gentile followers of Jesus to have allegiance only to the God of Israel and to stop worshipping any other deities. For Paul, a strong or robust (*dynatos*) person is one who has the knowledge that these other deities are not real (1 Cor 8:7). Consumption of food connected with pagan sacrifices does not mean a person becomes affected by that deity (1 Cor 8:4–6).

Paul recognizes that within the assembly there will be some gentiles who have not fully adapted their thinking to this new reality and still think food sacrificed to pagan deities will defile them. Others have experienced the therapeutic effect of consistent teaching that has convinced them that there does not exist other deities and therefore food offered in sacrifice does no harm. The assembly is the place where people receive the "therapy" they need to become more mature in their understanding. It is not a place where only the "strong" gather. Paul wants them to get along with each other so that the "weak" will have the influence of the more mature and make progress toward becoming a fully formed person.

Paul uses the language in 14:1 of accepting a person into a relationship known as "friendship." It is the social cohesion that forms the members of the group together for mutual support and care. The reason for bringing in a new and immature person is not to turn the meeting into a debate (14:1). Members of the group should accept each other into friendship and not react negatively to each other (14:3).

Paul first addresses an interlocuter who is one who abstains from eating any meat. The more scrupulous person thinks they are justified in thinking someone who eats meat is doing something wrong. Paul uses an analogy of someone who finds fault with another person's household servant. That would have been a breach of etiquette. It's just as bad to fault another person when God is the one who makes a judgment (14:4). God is the one who also enables a person to do what is right.

Paul equates this way of thinking about food with the way people think about particular days as being more important than other days (14:5). As with the issue of food, Paul does not specifically say whether this has anything to do with Jewish practices. If Paul is referring to the Sabbath, then it would mean that some gentiles did not observe the Sabbath. That he associates observing a specific day with doing so "for the lord" would seem to suggest Paul is referring to a day like the Sabbath or, perhaps, to an early practice of observing the first day of the week as a resurrection day. Paul wants them to consider that both groups are making their choices for a good reason, whether to honor the Lord or out of a sense of gratitude to God (14:6).

Paul again uses his direct address to a single individual but calls out one from each group. He asks why the one who eats condemns the abstainer and the one who abstains rejects the one who eats (14:10). Paul's reason is that God is the one who will make a final judgment (14:10–12). He concludes that members of the assembly should not be making judgments about someone's status in the afterlife (14:13). The most important consideration is what our effect is on the person.

Since Paul uses the singular pronoun in verse fourteen, he has the interlocuter with a robust conscience state his position in no uncertain terms. Paul agrees with the person but says that the problem is with that person's conscience. If the person still can not think the gods are not real, then whether or not the food is untainted doesn't matter. What matters is that the person who thinks it's bad to eat should not eat it. Paul cautions this person not to harm the others' progress by getting them to do something they think is wrong (14:15).

Paul repeats the idea that one shouldn't do something that will have an ill effect on someone else (14:16). What one eats and drinks are not the most important things. Paul might think in terms of the Stoic view of things that are indifferent. What one eats or drinks does not help or impede a person's virtue. Paul's mention of "kingdom (or realm) of God" does not seem to be a reference to an otherworldly or apocalyptic place but the qualities of the divine life (14:17).

Paul adds that the members of the assembly should focus on maintaining peaceful harmony and what contributes to personal formation (14:19). We typically describe this formation with the ambiguous language of "building up" or "edification." This is another metaphor that has to do with the structure of a person's way of thinking. Epictetus uses this within the same context as a medical analogy. When people decide what the right thing to do is and then think they have to stick to it no matter what, Epictetus says that people should be consistent only when their decision was sound and well-formed. Someone suffering from frenzy should not consider themselves to be an active person but should see a therapist (Epictetus, *Diatr.* 2.15.3). Someone who thinks it is nighttime and resolves to continue to act like it is night even when it turns out to be daytime is building on a false premise.

> Do you not wish to make your beginning and your foundation firm, that is, to consider whether your decision is sound or unsound, and only after you have done that proceed to rear thereon the structure of your determination and your firm resolve? But if you lay a rotten and crumbling foundation, you cannot rear thereon even a small building, but the bigger and the stronger your superstructure is the more quickly it will fall down (Epictetus, *Diatr.* 2.15.8–9).[347]

Epictetus stresses that a person needs to be adaptable to circumstances rather than to resolve to keep to one's convictions. The person who has based their judgment on a precept, has applied that precept wrongly in a specific circumstance, and then refuses to adapt, needs drastic

---

[347] Epictetus, *Discourses, Books 1-2*, 309.

measures of therapy (*Diatr.* 2.15.16). Paul's use of the metaphor fits the context of deciding about moral choices that fit the situation. Paul has his interlocuter state a precept that is true but is the wrong application. People need to start with a good foundation for their thinking and then build their moral system properly.

At verse twenty Paul switches again to the second-person singular. He addresses the "strong" person, who has a robust conscience, but tells him that his failure to adapt to the other person is not "building" but "demolishing" his friend's moral structure. Paul has the robust person stick to his precept and respond with the motto, "Everything is pure." Paul doesn't disagree, but he says in this case it is wrong to "trip up" somebody just so one is consistent with one's moral judgement (14:21).

Paul says that people who make a moral judgment and do not end up doing something harmful to themselves are "blessed" or "happy" (*makarios*) people (14:22). While Paul's language may be reminiscent of the Hebrew idiom in the Psalms, a reader of the Bible in Greek would have interpreted this terminology as the equivalent of *eudaimōn*, a "happy" or "flourishing" person. The person who is fully developed in their character is one who experiences *eudaimonia* or *makaria*.

Paul also argues that the "strong" person should adapt and forego their freedom for the sake of the other person because the person with the "weak" disposition would be doing wrong to adapt to the stronger person. If people feel that it is wrong to do a thing but go ahead and do it, that would be committing moral error (14:23).

Paul concludes that the "strong" person, the one whose character is well-developed, should have to be the one to bear the burden of adaptation for the sake of the "weak" person, the one whose character has yet to be fully developed (15:1). This principle of adaptation is a form of altruism that puts the needs of the other person as more important (15:2).

I take the end of this section to be 15:7. It forms an inclusio with the beginning of the section at 14:1. The section begins and ends with the imperative "accept" (*proslambanesthe*) and the idea that people have been accepted by God (14:3) and by Christ (15:7). Between these verses a scribe has included the section 15:3–6.

One reason for this view is that 15:3 interrupts the flow. Much of what follows until 15:14 is doxological and repetitive. Rom 15:6 includes an instance of more formal piling-up of names having to do with God. For me, I think 15:4 reflects a later, more exclusive and supersessionistic attitude within late first-century Christianity and beyond. The scribe is saying the scriptures were written for Christians and, by inference, not for Jews. I take the emphasis to be on "our" (*hēmeteran*). The use of "teaching" (*didaskalian*) to mean what is taught, in other words "learning," seems unusual for Paul. A similar text is 1 Cor 10:11 where the purpose is given "for our warning" (*pros nouthesian hēmōn*). The scribe may have taken the concept from that text. The language of agreeing with one another (*to auto phronein*) in 15:5 may have been borrowed from Phil 2:2; 4:2.

The section 15:8–12 is also an early scribal insertion. The grammatical construction of "has become a minister of circumcision" (*diakonon gegenēsthai peritomēs*) in which the subject of an infinitive in the accusative case has its modifier come after the infinitive is not found elsewhere in Paul. The idiom itself is odd: "minister of circumcision." The language is also unusual for Paul in that it is more messianic than elsewhere. Scholars take texts like 13:11–14 and 15:8–12 and base their apocalyptic and messianic reading of Paul on it.[348] I take those texts to be outliers and perhaps even scribal interpolations early in the transmission history after original copies were no longer extant during the end of the first-century when Jewish Christians were attempting to claim that the ancient scriptures belonged to them rather than other Jews.

Proclamation to the Gentiles and Plans for a Visit (15:14–33)

Paul returns to his paraenesis with the positive acknowledgment of their progress (15:14). He praises them for their full capacity of goodness (*agathōsynē*), knowledge (*gnōsis*), and mutual admonishment (*allēlous vouthetein*). Plutarch uses this language to describe those who respond to correction and make progress in their moral development.

> So also of the erring (*tōn hamartanontōn*): the incurable are those who take a hostile and savage attitude and show a hot temper toward those who take them to task (*elenchontas*) and admonish (*nouthetountas*) them, while those who patiently submit to admonition and welcome it are in less serious plight. And for a

---

[348] For example, Paula Fredriksen, *Paul: The Pagans' Apostle* (New Haven & London: Yale University Press, 2017), xi.

man who is in error to submit himself to those who take him to task, to tell what is the matter with him, to disclose his depravity, and not to rejoice in hiding his fault or to take satisfaction (*agapan*) in its not being known, but to confess it, and to feel the need of somebody to take him in hand and admonish him, is no slight indication of progress (*prokopēs*) (Plutarch, *Virt. prof.* 11 [82a]).[349]

Paul has encouraged the members of the household assembly to accept one another in friendship and not attack one another (14:1; 15:7). I don't think Paul means for them not to make progress in their moral development and just live with each other. Paul does not want them to condemn and reject each other, but that doesn't mean they are not to help each other make progress. They are to build each other and bring about a formation of character (15:2).

Paul recapitulates in 15:5–21 what he has been saying in his letter. He reminds them that the role of being the envoy to the gentile peoples with the message was a gift God gave him (15:15). He imagines that his function is like a priest who brings an offering to God hoping God will be pleased (15:16). Paul is not so much concerned with the quantity of pagan people who turn to God but the quality of their lives. It is as though Paul expects to be before a heavenly tribunal and the quality of his life's work is represented by the people he has influenced (15:17). He mentions the crucial point at which he realized that God had accepted the gentile peoples, when their commitment to the one God was accompanied by "signs and wonders" (15:18–19). His expeditions to the various provinces bringing his message to the gentile peoples has been from as far east as Jerusalem and as far west as Illyricum (15:19). He now wants to travel even farther to the west to Spain after stopping for a time in Rome (15:23). What he likes to do is go to cities where people have not yet heard about what Jesus Christ has done. That way he starts people with a clean and good foundation (15:20–21).

Paul's last topic is to talk about his travel plans (15:22–29). He wants them to know that he has tried to come to visit them, but his plans have

---

[349] Plutarch, *Moralia, Volume 1: The Education of Children. How the Young Man Should Study Poetry. On Listening to Lectures. How to Tell a Flatterer from a Friend. How a Man May Become Aware of His Progress in Virtue.* trans. Frank Cole Babbitt, Loeb Classical Library 197 (Cambridge, MA: Harvard University Press, 1927), 437.

not worked out (15:22). Paul seems to say that he is leaving where he has been staying and has no other plans of where to stay (15:23). He will come to visit them in Rome on his way to Spain, and he may imply that he wants them to provide some support for him and commission him to continue on to Spain (15:24).

Before traveling westward, Paul intends to travel to Jerusalem with some funds collected from the area to give to the poor of Jerusalem (15:25–26). Again, I take his usage of "holy ones" as a way of designating Jews as God's holy people. Paul's attitude is that gentiles have an obligation to Judea because they are sharing in the Jewish inheritance as adopted "sons" of God (15:27). After he has completed his visit to Jerusalem, he plans to make the journey to Rome on his way to Spain (15:28).

Paul has some concerns about his visit to Jerusalem and asks for those in Rome to pray to God on his behalf (15:30). He would seem to fear for his safety because of Jews ("disobedient") who would be antagonistic regarding his message about Jesus to the gentile peoples and be unsure about the reception of his charity (15:31).

Scribal Addenda with Recommendation Letter (16:1–27)

I am persuaded that chapter 16 was not an original part of Paul's letter to Rome. It seems unusual for Paul in a letter to an assembly where he has not visited to pass along so many greetings. The section begins with a recommendation for Phoebe, which would seem to mean she was the letter carrier. For her to carry a letter to Rome doesn't seem likely to me. It is also strange that Prisca, Aquila, and Epenetus would be living in Rome rather than a city like Ephesus, and that they would have an assembly meeting in their home in Rome. Although it is not impossible that chapter sixteen was the end of Paul's letter to Romans, the bulk of it would seem rather to be a recommendation letter for Phoebe sent by Paul from Corinth to Ephesus.

Before analyzing the textual tradition of 16:25–27, I had already considered it to be a scribal insertion. This doxology, in fact, appears in different places in Romans within the textual tradition. Additionally, 16:24 does not appear in modern texts and translations of Romans but as part of 16:20. I am treating chapter sixteen as a compendium of scribal addenda.

Chapter sixteen begins with a recommendation letter (16:1–2) followed by requests for greetings to be passed along to people in the destination city, most likely Ephesus (16:3–16), and several greetings from people with Paul in Corinth (16:21–23). I have identified sections which I speculate were added to Paul's letter (16:17–20; 25–26).

While Paul was staying in Corinth, he must have sent a recommendation letter along with Phoebe. She is identified as belonging to the assembly in Cenchrea, the port city of Corinth (16:2). The destination is most likely to have been Ephesus. On the one hand, he describes Phoebe as a "server" (*diakonos*, "deacon"). I have treated this term elsewhere as representing a menial function of serving food to people. On the other hand, it seems that she is a wealthy woman who has been a benefactor to Paul and others (16:2). Phoebe seems to have been both a wealthy member of the assembly but also someone who served the community in menial tasks. Because I am interpreting the expression "holy one" not as "saint," as if it were a way of referring to "Christians," but with the Hebrew *qedoshim* to indicate a Jewish person, that would mean Phoebe is a Jewish woman.

Elsewhere Paul mentions Aquila and Prisca (a.k.a. Priscilla) as sending greetings from Ephesus to Corinth along with the assembly meeting in their home (1 Cor 16:19). The book of Acts tells the story of Paul going to Corinth and finding Aquila and Priscilla, who had been in Rome during the expulsion of Jews from Rome by Claudius (Acts 18:2). Aquila is identified as a Jew from Pontus and also a tentmaker like Paul (Acts 18:3). Paul stayed with them and worked making tents. After staying there for a long time, Paul took Priscilla and Aquila with him and left them in Ephesus (Acts 18:18–19). While in Ephesus, Priscilla and Aquila heard Apollos, an Alexandrian Jew, speaking fervently and fearlessly in the synagogue about Jesus, but they spent time with him to bring him up-to-date (Acts 18:24–26). That the only information he had access to was the baptism of John goes a long way toward supporting my contention that not much was known about the life of Jesus in the early to middle of the first century.

Paul mentions that Prisca and Aquila were his coworkers and that they "risked their necks" (*tōn eautōn trachēlon hypethēkan*) (16:4 NRSV). The idiom has come into English as meaning to do something dangerous as in risking your life. Compared to two other instances, it seems to mean risking one's freedom (Epictetus, *Diatr.* 4.1.77; Sir 51:26).

Paul mentions a few people about whom we know very little: Epenetus, Mary, Ampliatus, Urbanus, Stachys, Apelles, household of Aristobulus, Herodion ("co-ethnic" rather than "relative"), household of Narcissus, Tryphen, Tryphosa, Persia, Rufus and his mother, Asyncritus, Phlegon, Hermes, Patrobas, Hermas, Philologus, Julia, Nereus and his sister, and Olympas (16:5–15).

It bears mentioning that of his list of particular interest is the couple Andronicus and Junia (16:7). It is only in recent years that scholars have said that the name should be translated with the feminine form Junia. Paul mentions that they were among the earliest followers of Jesus, are his "co-ethnics," and spent time with Paul in jail at some point. Most significantly is that Paul names them as "significant among the envoys (*apostolois*)" (16:7).

Before discussing the scribal insertions, I want to discuss those whom Paul lists as sending greetings to Ephesus (16:21–23). He mentions Timothy as being in Corinth with him and then includes three that he says are "co-ethnics": Lucius, Jason, and Sosipater (16:21).

If this section was from a recommendation letter to Ephesus sent from Corinth, then it makes more sense for Paul to have used a letter writer for that purpose rather than connecting this Tertius to the writing of the whole letter to the Romans (16:22).

Paul mentions his host as Gaius, so we may infer that Gaius is a householder in Corinth, who hosts the meetings of the assembly in his house, and who also is a patron of Paul staying with him there (16:23). Also, in that context Paul mentions Erastus, a city manager, ostensibly of Corinth.[350] Also there is Quartus, the brother of Erastus.

To me the section 16:17–20 does not sound like Paul, has strange grammar and vocabulary, and ends with an apocalyptic statement. Paul doesn't use *skopeō* in the negative sense of "watch out" or "beware." The article that modifies the participle in verse seventeen has eleven words intervening including a prepositional phrase and a relative clause.

We have the coined word *chrēstologia* ("smooth talk") in verse eighteen. I would suggest that there is a play on words with "Christ" (*christos*). I contend that this name might have originally been Chrestus (*chrēstos*) or at least pronounced in a way that the two words were

---

[350] There is some inscriptional evidence of an Erastus in Corinth. See Henry J. Cadbury, "Erastus of Corinth," *Journal of Biblical Literature* 50, no. 2 (1931).

indistinguishable (the iota being pronounced the same as an eta). Also, the Greek word *akakos* ("naïve" or "simple-minded") is not found elsewhere in Paul.

Concerning 16:20, the word "crush" (*syntribō*) is not found elsewhere in Paul, though frequently in the Septuagint, and more significantly in apocalyptic contexts in Rev 2:27, 1 En. 103:7, and T. Ash. 7:3. It is also interesting, if this section of text is related to Corinth, that Paul's use of "Satan" and "to crush under the feet" is used primarily in the Corinthian letters. I claim that Paul is not hurriedly trying to win over as many people to Christ as possible before the end of the age. This addition expresses a later conception about the imminence of the apocalypse.

The final section is 16:25–27. The main problem with this doxology is that scribes seem to have had a problem with where it goes. A few manuscripts omit it altogether (and end with the text found at 16:24). Some place it at the end of chapter fourteen (and omit chapters fifteen to sixteen). Some place it at the end of chapter fifteen. Some place it in two places. The problems may stem from a manuscript of Paul's letters by Marcion in the early second century that excluded chapters fifteen and sixteen.

The main problem with the text itself is that has that expansive, florid style found in later texts. It is interesting that Paul doesn't use "proclamation" (*kērygma*) elsewhere in Romans, but it appears in the Corinthian correspondence. Paul uses "revelation" (*apokalypsis*) and "mystery" (*mystērion*), but not "revelation of the mystery." The idiom "long ages" (*chronois aiōniois*) only appears in deutero-Pauline texts (2 Tim 1:9; Titus 1:2). We don't find the expression "prophetic scriptures" (*graphōn prophētikōn*) anywhere else. The concepts in the doxology are basically Pauline but are doubted as to their genuineness.

APPENDIX ONE:
LETTERS OF PAUL

To the Thessalonians

Letter Opening

¹:¹ Paul, Silvanus, and Timothy. To the assembly of the Thessalonians, who participate in the lineage of God, the Father, and the Lord, Jesus Christ. May you experience benevolence and concord.

Gratitude for Progress

¹:² My companions and I are always expressing our gratitude to God concerning all of you. We mention you at the time of our prayers before God, our Father. ¹:³ We continuously remember your faithful action, loving labor, and hopeful endurance of the kind shown by our Lord, Jesus Christ.

Reception of Message at Initial Visit

¹:⁴ We are assured that you *gentiles in Thessalonica*, who are siblings dear to God, have been chosen. ¹:⁵ It became apparent to us since the good news arrived to you not only in our message but also in the powerful demonstration of God's presence providing absolute proof. In this way you became aware of our purpose among you. ¹:⁶ After accepting our message, you decided with much deliberation and divine joy to adopt our way of life and that of the Lord. ¹:⁷ As a result, you in turn became a model to the adherents in Macedonia and in Achaia. ¹:⁸ This was due to your message about the Lord which circulated not just in Macedonia and Achaia, but wherever your allegiance to the *one* God has become known. Consequently, my companions and I no longer need to broach the topic there. ¹:⁹ In fact, those people are reporting about the nature of our visit to you, the way in which you converted to *the one* God from images to be devoted to the God who is living and real ¹:¹⁰ [and to expect God's Son from the heavens, whom God raised from among the corpses, Jesus, the Deliverer from the approaching wrath].

Proper Conduct as Philosophical Guides

²:¹ You, siblings, are aware first-hand that our visit to you was not without great impact. ²:² Despite the fact that my companions and I had just undergone brutality and disparagement in Philippi, we were emboldened by our God to broadcast frankly to you the good news with great intensity. ²:³ For our *protreptic* speech was not misleading, wrongly-motivated, or deceitful *like sophists*. ²:⁴ Instead, as divinely ordained messengers entrusted with the good news, we speak, not as sycophants, but out of duty to God who tests our motives. ²:⁵ You know we never used flattering speech nor made pretense for the sake of patronage, ²:⁶ as God is our witness. Neither did we seek fame either from you or others. ²:⁷ Rather than rightfully throwing our weight around as Christ's envoys, we chose to be gentle with you, in the same way a nurse cares for children in her charge. ²:⁸ Such is our dedication for you that we were pleased to share with you not only the good news of the *one* God but also our own selves because you became dear friends to us. ²:⁹ You remember, siblings, our hard work. While we toiled incessantly so that we might not burden any of you, we heralded to you the good news of the *one* God. ²:¹⁰ You and God also are witnesses to our devout, just, and blameless behavior to you, the

adherents. 2:11 In the same way you have known how with each one of you, as a father his own children, 2:12 we were exhorting you and encouraging and witnessing that you conduct yourselves worthy of God [the one who calls you into his own kingdom and glory].

Becoming Followers Brought Adversity

2:13 For this reason, we also are continuously grateful to God because receiving the message heard from us about the *one* God, you responded to it not as a human message but as it truly is, a message of God, who is active among you, the adherents. 2:14 You, siblings, experienced the same circumstances as God's assemblies *i.e., synagogues* of Christ Jesus-followers in Judea when you underwent the same difficulties by the hand of your fellow-citizens as they by their fellow-Judeans. 2:15 [those who killed both the Lord Jesus and the prophets and have expelled us; and are being disreputable and antisocial 2:16 preventing us from talking to the gentile peoples with the purpose of restoring them; the ongoing sins have reached its peak and wrath has finally come against them.]

Constancy in the Midst of Conflict

2:17 Now, siblings, my companions and I, though we briefly experienced a parental separation anxiety from you—not being face-to-face but still heart-to-heart—we were all the more eager to make arrangements to see you face-to-face. 2:18 Consequently, we—especially me, Paul—wanted to travel to you several times but it was as though Satan blocked our way. 2:19 For whom other than you represent what we have to look forward to and are our pride and joy [before our Lord Jesus in his coming].

2:20 It is you who are our best and brightest.

3:1 So when we couldn't stand it anymore we decided we would be forlorn in Athens 3:2 and send Timothy, our sibling and companion with regard to the *one* God in the work of the good news about Christ, 3:3 so that he might stabilize and stimulate you with regard to your allegiance that no person should be perturbed by these afflictions; for you know that they are bound to happen. 3:4 When we were with you, we warned you that afflictions would come, and they did. 3:5 It was for this reason that, when I couldn't stand it any longer, I sent to learn about your allegiance for fear that somehow your experience of testing might result in our labor to have become futile. 3:6 Rather, Timothy came to us from visiting you, delivered the good news to us of your faithfulness and love and that you always remember us fondly wishing to see us in the same way we do you. 3:7 On account of this, siblings, we were encouraged about you because of your faithfulness in spite of all of our duress and affliction 3:8 because now we feel restored to life if you remain standing in your allegiance to the Lord. 3:9 How could we express an equivalent gratitude to God for you in exchange for all of the joy we feel because of you before the *one* God of ours. 3:10 We earnestly pleaded night and day that we might see your face and might improve what is lacking in your allegiance. 3:11 Now may God, our Father, and our Lord, Jesus, direct our path to you.

[3:12 Now may the Lord make you increase and abound in love to one another and to all as also we to you, 3:13 so that your hearts may be established unblemished in holiness before God and our father at the coming of our Lord Jesus with all of his holy ones. Amen.]

Personal Character & Progress

⁴:¹ Finally, then, siblings, we entreat and exhort you in the Lord, Jesus, that in the same way you received from us how you should conduct yourselves *and please God*—like you are conducting yourselves—that you might persist more. ⁴:² For you recall the precepts we taught you through the Lord, Jesus. ⁴:³ This is what the *one* God wants, your holiness: to abstain from sexual immorality, ⁴:⁴ each one of you to know to master one's own bodily vessel in holiness and honor, ⁴:⁵ not in lustful passion like those gentiles who do not know the *one* God, ⁴:⁶ not crossing boundaries and cuckolding his sibling. The LORD is the avenger against any of those, just as we said before and sternly warned. ⁴:⁷ For God did not intend us for impurity but holiness. ⁴:⁸ So then the one who disdains this does not disdain a human but God [who gives his holy spirit to us].

Community & Social Values

⁴:⁹ Now concerning sibling friendship, you don't need anyone to write to you, for you have within yourselves the divine knowledge to love each other. ⁴:¹⁰ For you practice this with all the siblings in the whole of Macedonia. We urge you, siblings, to exceed beyond this. ⁴:¹¹ And we urge you to endeavor to live tranquilly, to be attentive to your dealings, and to employ your craft in the manner we directed you, ⁴:¹² in order that you might conduct yourselves with propriety within society and be self-sufficient.

Overcoming the Grief of Death

⁴:¹³ Now I do not want you to be unaware, siblings, about those who are sleeping *the sleep of death*, so that you might not grieve as the rest of those without expectation. ⁴:¹⁴ Since we are convinced that Jesus died and rose again *from the underworld*, so also will God on account of Jesus lead in procession those who have slept. ⁴:¹⁵ We say this by prophetic word of the LORD that we, the living survivors at the coming of the LORD will not precede those who have slept. ⁴:¹⁶ The LORD will come down from the sky with a shout, with the voice of the archangel and with the trumpet of God and the corpses in Christ's lineage will get up first. ⁴:¹⁷ Then we, the living survivors, will be retrieved together with them in clouds to an encounter with the LORD in the heavens. And so, we will always be with the LORD. ⁴:¹⁸ So then encourage one another with this explanation.

Living in the Light in Dark Times

⁵:¹ Now concerning the span of time, siblings, you do not need to have anything written to you, ⁵:² for you know very well that the Day of the LORD arrives like a thief at night. ⁵:³ When people say, "All is well and good," then an unexpected cataclysm occurs, like contractions occur in the womb, and those people will not escape. ⁵:⁴ Yet you, siblings, are not living in darkness so that the Day should overwhelm you like a thief. ⁵:⁵ You all are children of light and children of the daytime. We are neither of the nighttime nor of darkness. ⁵:⁶ Therefore, let us not be lulled to sleep like the rest but let us be watchful and sober. ⁵:⁷ For those who are sleeping are unconscious at night and those being in

a stupor are intoxicated at night. ⁵:⁸ Instead, let us who are of the daytime be sober by being attired with a chest armor of commitment and affection and a helmet of expected deliverance. ⁵:⁹ For God has not designated us to experience catastrophe but to obtain deliverance on account of our Lord, Jesus Christ, ⁵:¹⁰ who died for our benefit, so that whether we are awake or asleep we will be alive together with him. ⁵:¹¹ So then encourage one another and be constructive to each other, just as you are doing.

Concluding Paraenesis

⁵:¹² Now we entreat you, siblings, to show deference to the *philosophical guides* striving among you, who are your directors in the Lord, and who admonish you ⁵:¹³ and to regard them with the utmost respect in loving friendship because of their work. Maintain concord among yourselves.

⁵:¹⁴ Now we exhort you, siblings, admonish the disorderly, encourage those without a fully developed moral capacity, assist the weak-willed, be patient with everyone. ⁵:¹⁵ Be aware that no one pays back bad behavior with bad behavior to anyone but acts with good behavior to one another and to everyone.

⁵:¹⁶ Always be joyful. ⁵:¹⁷ Pray ceaselessly. ⁵:¹⁸ Be grateful in every circumstance; this is God's desire by means of Christ Jesus to you. ⁵:¹⁹ Do not repress your pneuma. ⁵:²⁰ Do not contemptuously ignore prophecies. ⁵:²¹ Examine every attitude and action; keep what is virtuous. ⁵:²² Abstain from every form of vice.

Closing

⁵:²³ May the God of serenity cause you to be completely uncontaminated. May your entire selves be kept blameless in the presence of our Lord, Jesus Christ. ⁵:²⁴ The one who chose you can be relied on to do this.

⁵:²⁵ Siblings, pray for us. ⁵:²⁶ Greet all of the siblings with sacred affection.

⁵:²⁷ I hold you responsible to read this letter to all of the siblings.

⁵:²⁸ May the benevolence of our Lord, Jesus Christ, be with you. Amen.

To the Galatians

Letter Opening

1:1 Paul, an envoy—not sent from a council or on behalf of a single authority but on behalf of Jesus Christ and God, the Father, who raised him from the realm of the dead—1:2 and all of the siblings with me. To the assemblies of Galatia. 1:3 May you *gentiles there in Galatia* experience the benevolence and concord that comes from God, our Father, and the Lord, Jesus Christ, 1:4 [the one who sacrificed himself for the sake of our sins, so that he might rescue us from the current decadent era as God, our Father, desires 1:5 to whom be splendor in eras to come. Amen].

Distortion & Desertion in Galatia

1:6 I am mystified that you *gentiles there in Galatia* are so quickly leaving me, who invited you by the favor of Christ, to join others with a completely different message of good news, 1:7 which is not simply a different form of the message. These people are causing trouble and are wanting to distort the good news about Christ. 1:8 Mark my words: If we—or even an angel from heaven—should announce good news contrary to what we reported to you, let that one experience the results of a curse. 1:9 Let me repeat: if someone is announcing good news to you contrary to what you received, let that one be cursed.

1:10 Now, then, am I responsible to human agency or divine? Am I trying to satisfy the demands of an organization? Were it so, I would not be a devotee of Christ. 1:11 I assure you, siblings, the good news that I have announced is not second-hand from anyone. 1:12 I did not hear it from anyone nor was I instructed, but I got it directly from a disclosure from Jesus Christ.

Circumstances of Calling

1:13 You heard about my former activity within Judean administration, that I was relentlessly attacking God's assembly *i.e., Jewish followers of Jesus in synagogues* and was decimating it. 1:14 I was advancing in Judean administration beyond my peers, since I was a more extreme fanatic for my ancestral traditions. 1:15 However, when God, who selected me from the time of my birth and with favor appointed me, 1:16 deigned to manifest God's son by me in order that I might make the good news known among the gentile peoples, I did not right away discuss it with anyone, 1:17 nor did I travel to Jerusalem to consult with my ambassadorial predecessors. Instead, I journeyed to Arabia and once again returned to Damascus.

1:18 It was only after three years that I made the trip to Jerusalem to consult with Cephas and lodged with him for fifteen days. 1:19 I did not spend time with any other of the envoys except for James, the brother of the Lord. 1:20 What I'm writing to you—I swear before God I'm not lying.

1:21 After that I went to the region of Syria and Cilicia. 1:22 However, none of the Christ-believing assemblies *i.e., synagogues* of Judea knew me personally. 1:23 They only were hearing "the one who attacked us before is now announcing the good news of the faithfulness *of Christ* which he was previously decimating" ¹:²⁴ and they were extolling God because of me.

Calling Endorsed in Jerusalem

²:¹ Fourteen years later I returned to Jerusalem with Barnabas and also brought along Titus. ²:² Now I traveled there because of an epiphany. I explained to them the good news which I declaim to the gentile peoples—I did this in a private session to the ones I considered appropriate—to ensure I am not now nor have been engaged in futility. ²:³ To the contrary, not even Titus, who was present with me, who was a Greek, was compelled to be circumcised.

²:⁴ The reason for the visit was because of the infiltration of pretenders who connived to surveil our liberality, which we have in our participation in Christ Jesus, so that they might impede us. ²:⁵ We did not yield subservience at all, in order that the reality of the good news might continue for you.

²:⁶ Now from those deemed appropriate (whatever they were formerly makes no difference to me; God shows no partiality) they required nothing more from me, ²:⁷ On the contrary, they were recognizing that I had been entrusted with the good news for the fore-skinned in the same way as Peter for the circumcised. ²:⁸ For the one who empowered Peter as the envoy of the circumcised also empowered me for the gentile peoples. ²:⁹ In fact, when recognizing the favor granted to me, James, Cephas, and John—those deemed to be pillars—they extended to me and to Barnabas the right hand of partnership agreeing that we were the envoys to the gentile peoples and they were the envoys to the circumcised nation. ²:¹⁰ The only request was that we remember the poor, which I was also eager to do.

Diatribe against Cephas in Antioch

²:¹¹ Now when Cephas visited in Antioch, I stood up to him because he was wrong. ²:¹² What happened was that prior to the visit of an embassy from James, Cephas was eating together with gentiles. But when the embassy arrived, Cephas was reticent and disassociated himself *from eating with the gentiles* in response to the pro-circumcision faction. ²:¹³ The rest of the Judeans joined in the duplicity so that even Barnabas went along with them in the pretense. ²:¹⁴ When I observed that they were not acting appropriately in line with the reality of the good news, I reprimanded Cephas publicly,

"If you, though claiming to be a best sort of Judean, act like the worst sort of gentile and inconsistently as a Judean, how do you compel gentiles to become Judeans? ²:¹⁵ We were born as Judeans and not sinners born from among the gentile peoples.

²:¹⁶ We are well aware that a *gentile or Judean* person is not made upright by law observance, but only as a result of the faithfulness of Jesus Christ. Even we *Judean followers of Jesus* have committed ourselves to Christ Jesus in order that we may be made upright on the basis of the faithfulness of Christ instead of on the basis of law observance since "all flesh shall not be made upright on the basis of law observance" (Ps 142:2 LXX). ²:¹⁷ Now if we *Judeans*, while

seeking to be made upright through participation with Christ, we ourselves are discovered to be *inconsistent* sinners, then is Christ a cause of sinful behavior? No way! ²:¹⁸ For if I reinforce the things I have destroyed, I make myself into a transgressor. ²:¹⁹ *As a Judean* I have died with regard to law-keeping because of the law's release of duty for those who have died, in order that I might be enlivened with regard to God. In a sense, I experienced crucifixion with Christ. ²:²⁰ So, it's not really me that continues to live but Christ who lives in me. I live my present fleshly existence by means of the faithfulness of the son of God who loved me and sacrificed himself for my benefit. ²:²¹ I do not reject God's favor. For, if it were the case that uprightness is through the agency of being law-keeping Judeans, then Christ died needlessly."

Invective against Galatians: Inconsistency

³:¹ Oh, senseless people of Galatia! Who has befuddled you with a magical spell? I previously described how Jesus Christ had been publicly crucified. ³:² Answer me this question then, "Did you receive *the signs of the presence of* the Spirit by keeping the law *when you were circumcised* or when you were persuaded by what we said?" ³:³ Are you so senseless? Your progress is initiated by the Spirit and now you want to complete your progress by *cutting* your flesh? ³:⁴ Did you experience such things with no effect–if it indeed was for no effect? ³:⁵ So then the one providing the Spirit to you and enacting wonders among you ... did it happen because of you keeping the law *at your circumcision* or because of your faithful response to what you heard? ³:⁶ Abraham "responded faithfully to God and it was credited to him as uprightness" (Gen 15:6 LXX). ³:⁷ Realize then that those who live lives of faithfulness are the descendants of Abraham.

Abraham and the Gentile Peoples

³:⁸ The scripture predicted that God would make upright the gentile peoples based on faithfulness by previously announcing the good news to Abraham, "All the nations will be blessed in you *through your seed in you to all descendants*" (Gen 12:3; 18:18 LXX). ³:⁹ So then, those *who are made upright* based on faithfulness are blessed along with faithful Abraham. ³:¹⁰ For whichever *gentiles* have their basis in law-keeping *through circumcision* are also subject to the curse. For it is written, "Cursed is everyone who does not continue to keep doing everything written in the book of the law" (Deut 27:26 LXX). ³:¹¹ So it is evident that no one is made upright before God by law-keeping because, "the upright will live based on faithfulness" (Hab 2:4 LXX). ³:¹² Now *the requirement of* the law *pertaining to circumcision* is not a product of faithful living. Rather, "Whoever performs them has to live in accordance with them" (Lev 18:5 LXX). ³:¹³ Christ released us from the curse contained in the law by becoming cursed for us, because it is written, "Cursed is each one suspended upon a tree" (Deut 21:23 LXX). ³:¹⁴ In this way Abraham's blessing might be passed to the gentile peoples by

participation in Christ Jesus, in order that we might receive the promise of the Spirit by means of the faithfulness *of Christ*.

Promise to Abraham Not Superseded by Law

3:15 Siblings, let me use a human analogy: when a person's testamentary agreement is established, no one revokes or adds to it. 3:16 So the promises were pronounced to Abraham and to his descendant *as a seed contained within him*. The scripture does not say, "and to descendants," meaning upon many people but upon a single person: "and to your descendant," which refers to Christ. 3:17 So I conclude: The law, which was made four hundred and thirty years afterward, does not revoke a covenantal agreement which had been pre-established by God, resulting in the abolition of the promise. 3:18 For if the patrimony is based on law, then it is no longer based on a promise. Yet, God granted it to Abraham through a promise.

Diatribe on the Benefits of God's Moral Code

3:19 "Why, then, did God give the law?" *a Jew might ask*. I would answer that the law was established on account of its practices until the descendant should come to whom it had been promised. 3:20 It had been instituted through angels by the hand of a mediator. Now the mediator is not representative of only one side, but God is One.

3:21 *He might counter*, "Is the law, then, contrary to the promises?" No way! For if a law had been enacted which was able to restore life, uprightness would surely be based on law keeping. 3:22 On the contrary, the scripture has hedged everyone under the consequence of sin, in order that the promise based on the faithfulness of Christ Jesus might be made available to those who are the faithful. 3:23 Before Christ's act of faithfulness occurred, we were shielded and hedged by law keeping until the effect of Christ's faithfulness should be made apparent. 3:24 In a sense, the law acted like our governess until Christ's act of faithfulness, in order that we might be made upright based on Christ's faithfulness. 3:25 Now that we experience the benefits of Christ's act of faithfulness, we are no longer protected by the governess.

Jews & Gentiles Benefit Together in Christ Jesus

3:26 For all of you are God's offspring through Christ's act of faithfulness participating in Christ Jesus. 3:27 Any people infused into Christ have taken on Christ's characteristics. 3:28 That person is not in the primary category of Judean or Hellene, slave or freedman, male and female. For all of you are one category participating in Christ Jesus. 3:29 Since you are of Christ *by patrilineal descent*, then you are offspring of Abraham, beneficiaries as a result of the promise.

4:1 It's like this: As long as a beneficiary is a minor, he does not differ from a slave though he is the master-to-be of the whole estate. 4:2 Instead he is under guardians and household managers until the father's determination. 4:3 In the same way, when we were *historically* "minors," we were bound by basic ethical precepts. 4:4 However, when the chronological moment had come, God commissioned his son, birthed by a Jewish mother and therefore a Jew by law, ⁴:⁵ for the *dual purpose of restoring those under Torah, the Jewish people,* and for the reception of us, *the gentile peoples,* as adopted children. ⁴:⁶ Because you are full-fledged sons, God commissioned the Pneuma of God's son to infuse your being resulting in crying out: *Jews cry "Abba"* and *gentiles cry "Patēr."* ⁴:⁷ So then, you are no longer someone without legal standing but a full-fledged son. Since you are a son, you are a beneficiary by God's *commissioning* action.

Inconsistency of Religiosity for Gentiles

⁴:⁸ But in one sense, at the time when you *gentiles in Galatia* were in ignorance of God, you *gentiles* were bound by so-called gods *of pagan religious festivals.* ⁴:⁹ In contrast, now that you are giving recognition to God–or, rather, God has recognized you *the gentile peoples*–how can you revert to impotent and worthless ethical practices to which you once again wish to be bound. ⁴:¹⁰ You are scrupulously observing *Jewish* Sabbath days, as well as the months, festival seasons, and special years. ⁴:¹¹ I am disappointed to think my effort among you has been inconsequential.

Exhortation to Progress and not Reversion

⁴:¹² Siblings, I beg you: Become the kind of person I am. After all, I became *a gentile* as you. You have not at all hurt my feelings. ⁴:¹³ You are aware that I previously announced good news to you because of a flesh wound. ⁴:¹⁴ Even though my wound tested you, you did not ostracize me or show disgust, but you accepted me as a messenger of God, as though I were Christ Jesus.

⁴:¹⁵ Therefore, where is your receptivity? For I am convinced that—if possible— you would have presented to me your gouged-out eyes. ⁴:¹⁶ So have I become your enemy by being honest? ⁴:¹⁷ They *the circumcision faction* act eager for you to join them without good intention. They want to ostracize you so that you will be eager to join them. ⁴:¹⁸ To show eagerness in a good way is always a good thing and not just when I am present with you.

Synkrisis of Hagar and Sarah

⁴:¹⁹ My fledgling followers for whom again I experience the pains of childbirth until you mature to be like Christ. ⁴:²⁰ I would like to be present with you at this time and use a different tone because you perplex me. ⁴:²¹ Explain to me, you who want to be *Judean citizens* under *Judean* law, do you not listen to Torah? ⁴:²² There it is written that Abraham had two sons, one from his bondmaid and one from his freewoman. ⁴:²³ On the one hand, the son from the bondmaid had been born as a result of Abraham's flesh *i.e., his personal choice*; on the other hand, the son from the freewoman because of a promise *God made to Abraham.* ⁴:²⁴ Figuratively speaking, these wives represent two types of marital covenants. On the one hand, *the one covenant* from Mount Sinai engenders servitude (this represents *Abraham's relationship with* Hagar). ⁴:²⁵ At another level Hagar stands for Sinai in Arabia. She aligns with the present Jerusalem. For Jerusalem *capital of Judea* is enslaved *to the Romans* with her children *i.e. residents.* ⁴:²⁶ Now the upper/*northern* Jerusalem *i.e., Antioch* represents the freewoman; she is the mother of us *gentile followers of Jesus.* ⁴:²⁷ For it is written, "Rejoice, the infertile

woman who does not give birth; break out and scream, the woman who is not in labor. For the children of the abandoned one will be more than the one who has a husband" (Isa 54:1 LXX). ⁴:²⁸ So then, you *gentiles*, siblings, are children of promise like Isaac. ⁴:²⁹ However, just like then *Ishmael* the one born from flesh *i.e., human choice* tormented *Isaac* the one born from spirit *i.e. God's choice*, so also now. ⁴:³⁰ Yet, what does the scripture say? "Expel the bondmaid and her son. For the son of the bondmaid will not inherit along with the son" (Gen 21:10 LXX) of the freewoman. ⁴:³¹ In conclusion, siblings, we *gentile followers of Jesus* are not children of the bondmaid *Hagar*, but of the freewoman *Sarah*. ⁵:¹ It is for freedom Christ set us *gentiles* free. So, make a stand and do not be harnessed again by a slave's yoke.

Dire Effects of Judaizing

⁵:² Look, I, Paul, say to you that, if you *gentiles* should be circumcised, Christ does not benefit you at all. ⁵:³ I assert again to each person being circumcised that he is obliged to adhere to the entire law code. ⁵:⁴ You *gentile believers* have been estranged from Christ, whoever is made upright by law *i.e., become a Judean by legal status*. You lose what was given to you freely. ⁵:⁵ For we by Pneuma *i.e. God's choice* based on *Christ's* faithfulness anticipate the expectation of uprightness. ⁵:⁶ For those *who participate* in Christ Jesus, whether anyone has a foreskin or not is not what matters, but constancy expressed through commitment. ⁵:⁷ You were making good progress like a runner! Who cut you off from no longer being persuaded by the truth? ⁵:⁸ This persuasion has nothing to do with your calling. ⁵:⁹ A small amount of yeast spoils the mixture. ⁵:¹⁰ I am convinced about you, based on my trust in the Lord, that you will make the right choice. However, the person who is disturbing you will get what's coming to him—whoever he might be.

⁵:¹¹ If I, siblings, still go around proclaiming circumcision *for Jews*, why am I yet being hounded *by those Jews who think I'm not*? Consequently, the cross is no longer a scandal *for Jews, and, thereby, not a reason for Jews not to accept what God has done for the gentile peoples*. ⁵:¹² Wouldn't it be deserving if those *Judaizers* bothering you *about foreskin removal* were to lop off their own genitals?

Liberty Does Not Mean Libertine

⁵:¹³ In spite of the fact that you *gentiles* were invited *by God to join God's people* based on a principle of freedom, you should not in any way use that freedom to act selfishly. Rather, you should be subservient to one another because of your loving friendship. ⁵:¹⁴ For the whole Torah is epitomized in a single commandment, in this one: "You should love your neighbor as yourself" (Lev 19:18 LXX). ⁵:¹⁵ So if you use biting sarcasm and chomp slanderously at each other, make sure you are not devoured by each other.

Progress in Divine Life based on Right Living

⁵:¹⁶ My advice is conduct yourselves in keeping with Pneuma and do not bring to completion physical desires. ⁵:¹⁷ Physical impulses want what is contrary to the Pneuma. Pneuma wants what is contrary to physical impulses. These are antithetical to each other causing you not to be able to simply

perform the actions you want to do. 5:18 If you are guided by Pneuma, you are not restricted by keeping a moral code *like Torah*.

5:19 The actions of the physical impulses are apparent, which *list of vices* include sexual immorality, vulgarity, and lewdness; 5:20 idolatry and magical potions, hostilities, strife, jealousy, rage, rivalries, dissensions, factionalisms, 5:21 envy; drunkenness and partying and vices like these. I am admonishing you just as I did previously that those who practice such vices will not be heirs of the divine realm.

5:22 The fruitful outcomes of the Pneuma are these *list of virtues*: love, joy, peace; patience, benevolence, generosity, faithfulness, 5:23 gentleness, self-control. There is no moral code that is contrary to these virtues. 5:24 Those who belong to *the patrilineal descent of Christ* "have executed the flesh" *i.e., decided to eliminate the power of the physical impulses* with the passions and desires. 5:25 Since we are animated by Pneuma, let us also follow the moral guidance of Pneuma. 5:26 Let us not over-emphasize status, challenge one other, feel the need to have what others have.

Mutual Critique and Moral Therapy

6:1 Siblings, if someone should be anticipated to be hurt by some failure in judgment, you, the spiritually mature, need to apply a moral curative to such a person with gentleness, paying attention to your own impulses lest you too should be affected. 6:2 Evaluate the gravity of each other's situation and in that way completely enact the moral code of Christ. 6:3 For if someone regards themselves as a superior when they are an inferior, they are misguided. 6:4 Each person should examine their own effort and then they will only have their own reason for feeling satisfied and not focus on the advancement of the other person. 6:5 For each person will evaluate their own outcome. 6:6 The person who receives instruction in our message should share with the instructor whatever goods are available.

Good Choices Lead to Good Outcomes

6:7 Do not be led astray. God is not outsmarted. For whatever someone chooses to plant, that is the outcome that is harvested. 6:8 The person who makes choices in line with their own physical impulses will harvest, based on physical impulses, outcomes of decay. On the other hand, the person who makes choices in line with the Pneuma will harvest, based on the Pneuma, outcomes of ongoing life. 6:9 Let us not be remiss in doing what is good, for we will harvest an outcome in our own time when we remain constant. 6:10 So then, whenever we have an opportunity, let us perform good actions toward everyone, and especially to the members of our own committed household.

Summation of Paul's Argument & Exhortation

6:11 Notice I have made the effort to write this long document with my own handwriting.

6:12 Others compel you to be circumcised for appearance sake for the only reason that they do not want to be antagonized for their commitment to the cross of Christ. 6:13 For neither are the circumcised consistent in their keeping of the law *"love your neighbor"* but want you to be circumcised in order to take pride of place for your excised foreskin.

⁶:¹⁴ May I not have pride *in my efforts* other than pride in *the message to the gentiles about* the cross of Christ. It was by means of Christ that I considered society's benefits dead to me and society regarded me as dead. ⁶:¹⁵ For neither is circumcision of any benefit *to one's character* nor having a foreskin. The only important thing is becoming a new person.

Closing

⁶:¹⁶ To whomever *gentiles* conduct themselves by this rule of life, may peace be upon them and also mercy on the Israel of God. ⁶:¹⁷ Finally, do not let anyone make trouble for me, for I display on my body the piercings of Jesus.

⁶:¹⁸ May the favor of our Lord, Jesus Christ, be with your pneuma, siblings. Amen.

Philippians Correspondence

Letter Opening to Jewish Adherents [Doc 1.1]

¹:¹ A letter from Paul and Timothy, devotees of Christ Jesus.

We are writing to all of you *Jewish qedoshim* in Christ Jesus, living in Philippi, including your *household* overseers and servers *in the synagogue*.

¹:² May you experience the benevolence and concord that comes from God, our Father, and the Lord, Jesus Christ.

Personal Development [Doc 1.1]

¹:³ Let me express gratitude to my God for every memory I have of you. ¹:⁴ I pray for you religiously and joyfully make requests on your behalf. ¹:⁵ I do this because you Philippians have been my colleagues in the spreading of the good news from the very first to the present. ¹:⁶ In fact, I am confident that God will be bringing to completion the good work God started within each one of you until the day of Christ Jesus's return.

¹:⁷ Thinking about you all in this way is the right thing to do, since my affection for you is well-deserved. You are caring for me while I am in jail and now support me when I go before the magistrate to give a defense and validation for the good news. All of you in Philippi share as colleagues this opportunity. ¹:⁸ I could call God as my witness how much I long for all of you in such a very visceral way, just like Christ Jesus.

¹:⁹ This is what I hope for you: for your love to steadily increase intellectually and insightfully ¹:¹⁰ for the purpose of you being able to make moral judgments about what is important for proper living so that you might be judged unpretentious and impeccable when Christ returns. ¹:¹¹ May you be overflowing with the expressions of the moral life to be found in Jesus Christ that brings honor and praise to God.

Effects of Paul's Incarceration [Doc 1.1]

¹:¹² I want you to be aware that my current predicament has resulted in the *moral* progress *of people which is the outcome* of the good news. ¹:¹³ Even though I am in prison, it's clear to all the people working in the provincial headquarters and to everyone else in the city that I am being held because of my commitment to Christ. ¹:¹⁴ Also, many of our siblings in the Lord have been emboldened and encouraged to be more vocal because of my detention.

¹:¹⁵ Compare the two: on the one side, some are speaking because of envy and rivalry; on the other side, others are in fact declaring Christ because of good intentions. ¹:¹⁶ The latter act out of love, realizing that the reason for my situation is the defense of the good news. ¹:¹⁷ The former declare Christ contentiously, not sincerely, expecting to make my incarceration more difficult. ¹:¹⁸ What do I care? The only thing that matters is that in any case, whether pretentiously or honestly, Christ is declared, and this makes me happy. You bet I'm glad. ¹:¹⁹ For I realize that what has happened to me will result in my release because of your petition and the assistance of Jesus Christ's Pneuma.

¹:²⁰ I firmly expect and hope that at my trial I will not act shamefully, but in all frankness with consistency I will magnify Christ through my actions, whether I am allowed to live or be given the death penalty. ¹:²¹ As far as I am concerned, to remain living is for the benefit of Christ and to be put to death is an advantage for me. ¹:²² If I remain living in this flesh, this means producing fruit; yet which to pick I can't decide. ¹:²³ I'm pressed between a rock and a hard place. I have a desire to be released and be with Christ—a much better option. ¹:²⁴ Yet, to remain in flesh is a greater necessity for your sake.

¹:²⁵ Since I am persuaded that my life in flesh is better for you, I realize that I will stay alive and stick with you all for your progress and joy resulting from a faithful life. ¹:²⁶ The reason is that your basis for honor is increased in Christ Jesus through my actions when I am present with you again.

Responsible Community Behavior [Doc 1.1]

¹:²⁷ I only ask of you to act appropriately as citizens representing the good news of Christ, so that, whether I arrive and see you or am absent and hear about you, you hold your ground with singular purpose, resolutely cooperating in commitment to the good news.

¹:²⁸ Do not be intimidated in any way by those who are antithetical *to your moral life*. Their conduct is indicative of their moral regress. Your conduct proves your moral progress. This is God's way. ¹:²⁹ You have been given the responsibility for the sake of Christ, not only to give your allegiance to him, but also to deal with hardships for his sake. ¹:³⁰ You are experiencing the same struggle which you perceived me having and now hear me describe.

Mutual Unselfish Relationships [Doc 1.1]

²:¹ If you have mutual encouragement as Christ followers; if you have loving support; if you have spiritual friendship; if you have a deep emotional commitment to each other…. ²:² You'll make me the happiest person in the world if you think alike, love each other in the same way, *act as friends who share the same soul*, have a singular moral purpose. ²:³ Without any sense of competitiveness or vanity, humbly consider one another as more valuable than yourselves. ²:⁴ Don't just keep looking out for your own affairs but focus on what matters in each other's lives. ²:⁵ This way of thinking should be patterned on Christ Jesus:

> ²:⁶ *The one existing in the role of a god,*
> *did not seek to grasp equal status with a god,*
> ²:⁷ *but demoted himself,*
> *taking the role of a slave.*
> *Having been born in the same way as humans*
> *and looking like any other human,*
> ²:⁸ *he debased himself,*
> *choosing to be willing to die [even the death of a cross].*
> ²:⁹ *So God promoted him*
> *and granted him a rank above any other,*
> ²:¹⁰ *so that before Jesus all would show deference [heavenly, earthly and subterranean]*
> ²:¹¹ *and the voice of all acclaim that Jesus Christ is Lord [for the honor of God the Father].*

Consistent Practice Produces Moral Health [Doc 1.1]

2:12 So then, my dear friends, in the same way as you've always listened to me—not only when I'm present with you but even more now in my absence—generate your own moral health with all due diligence. 2:13 For God is the one who energizes you to have the will and way to be what God wants. 2:14 Practice all these principles without bickering and quarreling, 2:15 so that you might be honest and decent people, God's innocent children living in a time of perversity and decadence. Within it you shine like the stars in the universe. 2:16 By your consistent way of life I will have a basis for honor at Christ's day of judgment. The quality of your character will prove that I did not run *the race of life* uselessly or that I labored unprofitably. Quite the contrary. 2:17 Even though my sacrificial actions are like a libation of wine poured out as a sacrifice and ritual for your faithful lives, I am elated and celebrate with you. 2:18 Similarly, be elated and celebrate with me.

Recommendation Letter for Timothy [Doc 2]

2:19 God willing, I hope soon to send Timothy to you. I'm looking forward to putting my mind at ease when I know of your affairs. 2:20 I have no one comparable to Timothy, who will give careful attention to your affairs. 2:21 People usually are concerned only with their own affairs and not the affairs having to do with Jesus Christ. 2:22 You know how valuable he is, because he worked with me in the spread of the good news like a son works with a father. 2:23 Therefore, I hope to send him immediately after I figure out what's happening with me. 2:24 Then I am confident of the Lord's will that I'll come right away too.

Recommendation Letter for Epaphroditus [Doc 3]

2:25 I consider it necessary to send to you Epaphroditus, my brother, co-worker, comrade-in-arms; your envoy and minister of my need. 2:26 My reason for sending him is that he is missing you and feeling distraught, since you have heard he was ill. 2:27 In fact, he was so ill he nearly died. However, God showed him mercy—not just him but me too, so I might not have grief heaped upon grief. 2:28 For this reason I sent him expeditiously, so that when you see him again you might be glad, and I also might be without grief.

2:29 Give Epaphroditus a warm reception and provide a place to such distinguished people. 2:30 Because of his sense of obligation for *supporting* the work we do for Christ, he almost died, risking his life so that he might take up the slack in your ministry to me.

Inserted Letter Closing [Doc 1.2]

3:1 Finally, my siblings, be elated in the Lord. Repeating myself is not tedious to me but for you it is a preventative.

Letter to Gentile Adherents [Doc 4]

3:2 You gentile men need to watch out for the hungry-for-blood dogs. Watch out for the ones who do the dirty deed; watch out for the Excision. 3:3 On the contrary, we are the Circumcision: the ones who serve through God's spirit and have their basis for boasting in what Christ Jesus has done instead of confidence in a fleshly status; 3:4 I, however, do possess the basis for confidence in a fleshly status. If any other man suggests he is confident in the flesh, I can outdo him:

> 3:5 I was circumcised on the eighth day;
> I am from the race of Israel;
> My family is from the tribe of Benjamin;
> I am a Hebrew from a long line of Hebrews.
> When it comes to the Torah, I'm a Pharisee;
> 3:6 When it comes to zeal, I persecuted the *Jewish* followers of Jesus *in synagogues*;
> When it comes to correctness in obedience to Torah, I'm irreproachable;

3:7 Whatever advantages I had I consider them unprofitable because of Christ in my life. 3:8 In fact, I consider every advantage of life to be unprofitable because of the far superior knowledge of Christ Jesus, my Lord. It is because of him I have discounted the value of every advantage of life—and consider them to be a pile of garbage—in order that I might profit from my relationship with Christ. 3:9 I also want to be evaluated by my relationship to Christ: not because I have a right-standing based on God's covenant in the Torah but a right-standing because of the faithfulness of Christ, the right-standing God has brought about based on faithfulness.

3:10 I want to understand experientially what Christ went through—the impact of his revivification and the participation of his painful experiences. 3:11 When I die, I want to handle death in the same way as Jesus, if, somehow, I might reach my destination at the raising up and out from among the corpses.

3:12 It's not as though I have already reached this point or have been made spiritually mature. Instead, I make chase on the possibility I might overtake that for which I also have been overtaken by Christ Jesus. 3:13 Siblings, I do not consider myself to have crossed the finish line. Yet, I focus myself on one thing: by leaving in the dust the advantages I gained previously and stretching myself toward the benefits before me, 3:14 I sprint toward the goal for the judge's award, the ascension invitation of God in participation with Christ Jesus.

3:15 So then, those of you who are mature, let us be thinking along these lines. (And if anyone takes a different point of view, God will show them this is the right way to think. 3:16 In any case, whatever level we've achieved, let's maintain the same standard of life.

3:17 Imitate my example together, siblings, and watch those who conduct themselves in this way, since you have an example in us. 3:18 There are many people who conduct their lives—I've told you about them often, and now say this with tears in my eyes—as moral enemies of what Christ's death on a cross has achieved. 3:19 Their outcome is moral degradation; their god is their bodily appetites; their basis for honor is their shameful behavior. Their moral judgment favors what is terrestrial.

3:20 For us, instead, there exists a celestial citizenship. It is from there we anticipate also a Savior, the Lord, Jesus Christ. 3:21 He will reconfigure our debased body to be conformed to his magnificent body by his energy, empowering him even to subjugate to himself all things.

⁴:¹ So then, my dear and missed siblings, my source of cheer and crowning achievement, this is how you are to be staying steadfast in your allegiance to our Lord, dear ones.

Practice of Virtue & the Tranquil Life [Doc 1.3]

⁴:² I urge Euodia and I urge Syntyche to form the same moral judgments with regard to life in the Lord. ⁴:³ Yes, I request also that you, dedicated companion, give them your assistance. These women have cooperated with me in the spread of the good news, along with Clement and the rest of my co-workers, whose names are listed in God's heavenly roll call.

⁴:⁴ Be glad as people of God continually. Let me say again, be glad!

⁴:⁵ Let everyone take notice of your amiability. Our LORD is close.

⁴:⁶ Don't fret about anything. Instead, in every situation tell God your needs in prayer and petition with gratefulness. ⁴:⁷ When you do this, God's serenity, which overpowers every mental state, will protect your feelings and thoughts as those who participate in the divine life of Christ Jesus.

⁴:⁸ Consequently, dear friends, make it a practice to contemplate these moral qualities: whatever is true, decent, just, sacred, pleasant, auspicious; if something has moral excellence and if it is deserving of praise.

⁴:⁹ Make a spiritual practice of those things you learned, accepted, heard, and observed in my life. If you do this, the God of serenity will be with you.

Gratitude for Financial Support [Doc 5]

⁴:¹⁰ I'm very glad through God's providence that finally you have arisen to the occasion to be attentive to my circumstances. You were attentive in the past but not at an opportune occasion.

⁴:¹¹ Don't get me wrong. I'm not saying I don't have all I need. Personally, I have schooled myself to be self-sufficient in my present circumstances. ⁴:¹² I am experienced in living in abject poverty and abundant wealth. Into each and every circumstance I have been initiated: feasting and fasting; sufficiency and deficiency. ⁴:¹³ I can handle all these circumstances because God empowers me.

⁴:¹⁴ In spite of past circumstances, you have performed well as partners in my difficulty. ⁴:¹⁵ You are aware, residents of Philippi, that during the beginning of my spreading the good news, when I had gone out from Macedonia, no assemblies partnered with me in the relationship of give and take except you alone. ⁴:¹⁶ As a matter of fact, even when I was *still in Macedonia* in Thessalonica, once or twice you dispatched funds to me. ⁴:¹⁷ I don't say this to imply I'm expecting a donation. Rather, I am expecting the ever-increasing effect shown in your lives, which is credited to your heavenly account. ⁴:¹⁸ I have been reimbursed for all I've done, and I am overwhelmed by your generosity. I continue to be completely satisfied ever since I received from Epaphroditus your compensation, like the savory aroma of roasting meat on an altar, an acceptable sacrifice, satisfactory to God. ⁴:¹⁹ The

God to whom I am committed will provide fully for all of your necessities of life through the splendid wealth made available through participation in the divine life of Christ Jesus.

⁴:²⁰ May all reverence be accorded to God, our divine parent, to the final generation of human existence. Amen.

Closing [Doc 1.4]

⁴:²¹ Give my greetings to all the *qedoshim i.e., Jewish followers of Jesus* in Christ Jesus. My siblings here pass along their greetings to you. ⁴:²² All of the *qedoshim* here give their greetings, but most of all those belonging to the imperial residence.

⁴:²³ May the favor of the Lord, Jesus Christ, be present in your lives.

To Philemon

Letter Opening

¹ Paul, a prisoner because of Christ Jesus and Timothy, our brother. ² To Philemon *"the friendly,"* our dear friend and collaborator, to Apphia, our sister, to Archippus, our co-combatant, and to your household assembly *i.e., synagogue*. ³ May you experience benevolence and concord from God, our Father, and the Lord, Jesus Christ.

Praise & Gratitude for Philemon

⁴ I offer gratitude to my God by always remembering you *Philemon* at the times of prayer ⁵ because I hear about your love and constancy, which you have regarding the Lord, Jesus, and among all the *qedoshim i.e., Jewish followers of Jesus*. ⁶ I hope that the constancy of your cooperation might become an energizing force by means of the awareness of every positive effort we achieve for the cause of Christ. ⁷ I have experienced much joy and encouragement due to your friendship because the inner being of the *qedoshim* is put to rest on account of you, brother.

Request for Restoration of Onesimus

⁸ It is for this reason, in spite of the fact that, due to my status within the Christ movement, I could apply frank speech and insist you do what is proper. ⁹ Instead, it is based on our friendship that the plea comes from such a one as me, Paul, the elderly, and now also a prisoner because of Christ Jesus. ¹⁰ I beg you concerning my offspring, whom I engendered during my imprisonment, Onesimus *"the useful,"* ¹¹ who was formerly to you non-beneficial and now to you and to me most beneficial. ¹² I have returned him to you, this one who is my own inner being. ¹³ I really wanted to keep him for myself, in order that on your behalf he might be my attendant during my imprisonment for the cause of the message of good news. ¹⁴ But I did not want to do anything without your consent, so that your good deed might not be compulsory but voluntarily. ¹⁵ Perhaps for this reason he was separated for a short time in order that for an eon you might receive him back fully ¹⁶ no longer as a slave but beyond a slave, a dear brother. He is especially so to me, but even more to you by natural kinship and kinship in the Lord. ¹⁷ Therefore, since you have me as an associate, accept him as you would me. ¹⁸ If he caused you damage in any way or owes you anything, make me liable for that. ¹⁹ I, Paul, have written in my own handwriting. I pledge repayment. I do not claim to you that you still owe yourself to me. ²⁰ Yes, brother, I am your benefit *i.e., your "Onesimus"* in the Lord. Refresh my inner being in Christ.

Assurance & Need for Lodging

²¹ I have written to you being sure of your compliance. I know that you will do even more than what I ask. ²² One more thing, prepare a guest room for me. I hope that an outcome of your prayers is that I will be made grateful to you.

Closing

²³ Epaphras, my co-captive in Christ Jesus, sends you greetings. ²⁴ Also sending greetings are Mark, Aristarchus, Demas, and Luke, my coworkers. ²⁵ May the favor of the Lord, Jesus Christ, be with your pneuma.

To the Romans

Letter Opening

1:1 Paul, a devotee of Christ Jesus, called to be an envoy because I had been selected for telling God's good news. 1:2 God previously made a declaration through his prophets in the sacred writings 1:3 about God's son, who would be a biological descendant of David. 1:4 However, based on his revivification from the realm of the dead, Jesus Christ, our Lord, was powerfully distinguished as a son of God in a sacred manner. 1:5 It is through him that my companions and I have received a favored status as envoys on behalf of Jesus to bring about a faithful obedience among all the gentile peoples. 1:6 You in Rome are a part of the gentile peoples and we are inviting you on behalf of Jesus Christ.

1:7 I am writing to all who are in Rome—to those whom God loves; to those called to be sacred followers. May you *gentile peoples* experience the benevolence and concord that comes from God, our Father, and from Jesus Christ, who is our Lord.

Occasional Remarks

1:8 First, I give thanks to my God on account of Jesus Christ for all of you because your faithfulness is reported throughout the world *i.e., the empire*. 1:9 For I could present God as my witness—God whom I serve religiously and spiritually by telling the message of God's son—1:10 how I constantly mention you whenever I say my prayers, requesting whether at last I might receive an indication by God's will that it is good for me to travel and come to you. 1:11 For I yearn to see you, so that I might freely share with you a spiritual message that will give you strength. 1:12 What I mean is to be mutually encouraged by you through one another's faithfulness, both yours and mine.

1:13 I want you to know, siblings, that I often intended to come to you, and I have been hindered so far. My purpose has been to have some fruit also among you like I have had among the rest of the provinces. 1:14 I have a sense of obligation to both Hellenes and barbarians, both to the sophisticated and to the uncultured. 1:15 So I have an eagerness to persuade you also who are in Rome. 1:16 For I am not embarrassed by the message, since it has divine potency for restoration to all who are being committed. This happened first to Jews and then to Hellenes. 1:17 For divine justice is being made apparent in it based on the faithfulness of Jesus to instill faithfulness in others, just like it was written, "Now the just will live faithfully" (Hab 2:4 LXX).

Against Pagan Idolatry & Practices

1:18 God's wrath from heaven is being made apparent against all impiety and injustice of humans who hinder the truth unjustly. 1:19 I base this on the fact that the intelligibility of God is apparent to them, since God has made it apparent to them. 1:20 For God's unseen qualities—both God's eternal power and divine character—are perceived from the creation of the cosmos, which can be deduced by the existence of created things resulting in humans being without a defense. 1:21 Nevertheless, being cognizant of God, humans did not honor or show gratitude to God. Rather, their conclusions were baseless, and their senseless mind was dulled. 1:22 Asserting themselves to be wise, they were made fools 1:23 when they altered the magnificence of the incorruptible God into the likeness of the image of corruptible humanity and of birds, of quadrupeds, and of reptiles. 1:24 For this reason God gave them over in their heartfelt desires into impurity to dishonor their bodies in this way: 1:25 they exchanged the truth of God in a deception and they reverenced and served the created thing rather than the creator [May God be blessed into the ages. Amen]. 1:26 For this reason God gave them over into dishonorable passions, for their females exchanged the natural function for what is against nature *by being infertile*; 1:27 and similarly the males, abandoning the natural function of the female *for procreation*, were inflamed in their desire for one another, males with males, subduing the shameful partner, and receiving among themselves the inevitable retribution for their error.

1:28 And just as they did not examine the facts critically and arrive at a proper recognition of God, God gave them over to an uncritical mind, to practice the inappropriate actions, 1:29 being consumed with all manner of injustice, evil, avarice, vice; engulfed in jealousy, butchery, rivalry, treachery, malignity, whispering; 1:30 slanderous, misotheists, insolent, arrogant, boasters, evil schemers, disobedient to parents; 1:31 senseless, faithless, passionless, merciless. 1:32 These people, being aware of God's judgment that those who practice such things deserve death, not only do these things but even applaud such practices.

Censure of the Inconsistent Judge

[P] 2:1 Wherefore, you, friend, are inexcusable, anyone who passes judgment. For when you pass judgment on others, you condemn yourself. For you practice the things you criticize! 2:2 Now you and I acknowledge that God's judgment is equitable against those who practice such things. 2:3 So do you reason, *my friend*, as one who criticizes practicing such things and yet do them, that you will escape God's judgment? 2:4 Or do you disdain the abundance of God's generosity, tolerance, and forbearance, ignorant that the *Christly*-beneficence of God leads you to a change of mind? 2:5 Now, because of your stubbornness and unchanged attitude, you reserve for yourself wrath at the time of wrath and disclosure of God's verdict. 2:6 God "will reward each person according to each person's actions" (Ps 61:13; Prov 24:12 LXX).

2:7 On the one side, to those seeking with endurance of good action a respectable, honorable, and incorruptible character, their reward is unending life. 2:8 On the other side, to those whose lives are based on self-aggrandizement, who are dissuaded by truth, and who are persuaded by injustice, their reward is wrath and fury. 2:9 There will be affliction and distress on every human soul who produces a life of vice—whether the soul of a Jew or a Greek. 2:10 Conversely, there will be respect, honor, and bliss allotted to each one who produces a life of goodness—whether to a Jew or a Greek. ²:¹¹ For God shows no partiality. ²:¹² For whoever breaks a law code without knowledge of the code, they will languish without that knowledge; and whoever breaks a law code in its jurisdiction, they will be condemned by means of the law code. ²:¹³ For it is not the hearers of the law code who are upright before God. Instead, the doers of the law code will be considered upright. ²:¹⁴ For when gentiles, who do not have the Torah, do naturally the precepts of Torah, these people, though not having Torah are a Torah within themselves. ²:¹⁵ They show outwardly the action of Torah inscribed on their minds, their conscious minds making judgments between one or the other rational reflection by either condemning or defending themselves, ²:¹⁶ [on a day when, according to my message, God judges the inner being of humans by means of Christ Jesus].

[P] ²:¹⁷ Now if you label yourself a Judean and take comfort in Torah, boast in your relationship to God, ²:¹⁸ claim to know how God wants you to act, and discern the proper moral choices having been trained out of Torah, ²:¹⁹ and convinced that you yourself are a guide of the blind, a light of those in darkness, ²:²⁰ an educator of the ignorant, a teacher of the young, who possesses the embodiment of the knowledge and truth contained in Torah....
²:²¹ So then, the one who teaches others, do you not teach yourself? The one who proclaims people should not steal, do you steal?
²:²² The one who says not to commit adultery, do you commit adultery? The one who detests idols, do you commit idolatry?
²:²³ Whichever person boasts in Torah, dishonors God by transgression of Torah. ²:²⁴ For "The name of God because of you is blasphemed among the gentile peoples" (Isa 52:5 LXX), just as it is written.
²:²⁵ For circumcision, on the one side, is beneficial, if you practice Torah. On the other side, if you should be a transgressor of Torah, your circumcision has become a foreskin. ²:²⁶ Logically, then, if the fore-skinned man keeps the requirements of Torah, will not his fore-skinned condition be regarded as though he were circumcised? ²:²⁷ And the one who is naturally fore-skinned who keeps Torah will judge you who in spite having the written code and circumcision are a transgressor of Torah. ²:²⁸ For it is not the one who is a Jew by appearance neither is circumcision by appearance in flesh. ²:²⁹ Instead, the Judean is in the inner person, and circumcision is spiritually inscribed on the heart, not literally. This person's approval is from God rather than humans.

Fictive Dialogue on being a Jew

[I] ³:¹ Then what more belongs to a Judean? What is the benefit of circumcision?
[P] ³:² There is much more. Most importantly they were entrusted with the precepts of God.
[I] ³:³ What then? If some were unfaithful, will not their

faithlessness do away with the *covenant* faithfulness of God?

[P] 3:4 No way! Let God be true, though every human is a liar, just as it is written, "So that you might be upright in what you say, and you will triumph when you judge" (Ps 50:6 LXX).

[I] 3:5a But if the failure to act uprightly establishes God's justice, what are we to conclude? Not that God is unjust to inflict wrath.

[A] 3:5b (I'm putting this in a typical rhetorical structure.)

[P] 3:6 No way! If that were the case, then how will God judge the world?

[A] 3:7 (Now if God's truth in me by this fiction abounds into the splendor of God, why am I yet criticized as a gentile sinner? 3:8 And not like we are slandered and as some assert we say, "Let's do what's bad so good results." Their penalty is deserved.)

[I] 3:9a What then *do we conclude is the condition of the Judeans?* Are we superior?

[P] 3:9b No way! For you and I have previously proven that both Judeans and Greeks are all under sin, 3:10 just as it has been written:

"There is not an upright person, not a single one. 3:11 There is not one who comprehends, there is not one who seeks out God. 3:12 All have turned away, together they have become depraved. There is not one who does kindness, not even to one" (Ps 14:1–3).

3:13 "An opened tomb are their throats, by their tongues they deceive, poison of cobras is beneath their lips" (Pss 5:9; 140:3);

3:14 "His mouth is filled of cursing and bitterness" (Ps 10:7).

3:15 "Their feet are quick to spill blood, 3:16 destruction and wretchedness are along their paths, 3:17 and the peaceful path have they not experienced" (Isa 59:7–8).

3:18 "There is no fear of God before their eyes" (Ps 36:1).

3:19 Now we know that whatever the Torah says, it addresses those in the legally-binding covenant, in order that every mouth might be closed and the whole world might be held accountable to God. 3:20 Wherefore, simply by observing Torah, "no person will be considered upright before God," since the only condition brought about by a law code is the awareness of breaking it. 3:21 But now, separate from the covenant of Torah, God's justice has been brought to light. It is supported by the Torah and the Neviim: 3:22 God's justice is by means of the faithfulness of Jesus Christ to all the committed followers. For there is no difference *in God's treatment of Judeans and gentiles.* 3:23 For all act wrong and lack God's splendor, 3:24 though they are considered upright undeservedly by the gracious act through the acquittal brought about by the death of Christ Jesus. 3:25 God planned for Christ Jesus to be an expiatory sacrifice by means of Christ's faithfulness during his savage execution. God did this to prove God's justice because of the passing over of the previously committed sins *of the gentile peoples* 3:26 in God's forbearance, to prove God's justice at the present time, that God is justly upright and considers upright the one who has benefited by the faithfulness of Jesus.

[I] ³:²⁷ᵃ Then what is the basis for boasting *for Judeans*?
[P] ³:²⁷ᵇ It has been shut out.
[I] ³:²⁷ᶜ On the basis of what legal system? Based on our actions?
[P] ³:²⁷ᵈ No, rather based on the concept of faithfulness. ³:²⁸ For we have reasoned that a person is rectified apart from Torah keeping. ³:²⁹ᵃ Or does God only belong to the Judeans? Does God not also belong to the gentiles?
[I] ³:²⁹ᵇ Yes, to the gentiles also.
[P] ³:³⁰ So then, God is One. God will rectify the circumcised based on faithfulness *to the covenant* and the foreskinned by means of the faithfulness *of Jesus*.
[I] ³:³¹ᵃ Then do we invalidate *the covenant based in* Torah by means of the faithfulness *of Jesus through which gentiles are attributed to be upright*?
[P] ³:³¹ᵇ No way! Instead we establish *the validity of* Torah.
[I] ⁴:¹ What then shall we say Abraham, our progenitor, discovered? ⁴:² For if Abraham was regarded as upright based on his actions, he has a basis for boasting.
[P] But not before God. ⁴:³ For what does the writing say? "Abraham was faithful to God and it was **regarded** as uprightness"(Gen 15:6 LXX).

⁴:⁴ Now to the person who performs an action a reward is not **regarded** as a gift but an obligation. ⁴:⁵ Yet to the one not performing a moral action but who puts trust in the one who turns upright the impious, that one's faithfulness is **regarded** as uprightness.

⁴:⁶ In the same way also David refers to the happiness of the person about whom God **regards** uprightness apart from moral actions:
⁴:⁷ "Happy are those whose infractions have been pardoned and whose errors have been put out of sight. ⁴:⁸ Happy is the person against whom the LORD will not **regard** a moral error" (Ps 32:8).
[P] ⁴:⁹ So, then, is this happiness *of David* conferred on the circumcision or also upon the foreskinned? For we say, "Abraham's faithfulness was **regarded** as uprightness."
[I] *Note: Perhaps no response, since the respondent recognizes a trap.*
[P] ⁴:¹⁰ᵃ Then tell me how "he i.e. *Abraham* was **regarded**." Being in a circumcised condition or in a foreskinned condition?
[I] *Note: Again, no response.*
[P] ⁴:¹⁰ᵇ Not in circumcision but in a foreskinned condition. ⁴:¹¹ And he received the covenantal symbol of circumcision as an attestation of his faithful uprightness which he had in his foreskinned condition. This was so that he would be the father of all the foreskinned faithful, who are **regarded** as being upright, ⁴:¹² and the father of the circumcised, who are not only circumcised but also conform to the standard of the faithfulness of Abraham while foreskinned, the father of all of us.

⁴:¹³ For the promise to Abraham or to his progeny that he is to be the beneficiary of the world is not through a legal transaction but through a faithful uprightness. ⁴:¹⁴ For if the *gentile* beneficiaries are awarded based on a legal transaction, faithfulness is ineffectual, and the promise is invalidated. ⁴:¹⁵ For the presence of a law code brings retribution. But

where a law code does not exist, neither can there be a violation. ⁴:¹⁶ For this reason, it is based on faithfulness, in order to be according to beneficence, so that the promise is valid to all the progeny, not only to those who participate in the Torah covenant but also to those whose status is based on the faithfulness of Abraham, who is the father of us all, ⁴:¹⁷ as it is written, "I have established you a father of many nations" (Gen 17:5 LXX), in the presence of whom he trusted God, who enlivens dead corpses and calls the things not existing as existing. ⁴:¹⁸ Contrary to expectation, Abraham hopefully trusted that he would become "a father of many nations" (Gen 17:5 LXX), according to what had been spoken: "So shall be your progeny" (Gen 15:5 LXX). ⁴:¹⁹ And not faltering in his trust, he evaluated his own deadened body, some hundred years old, and the infertility of Sarah's womb. ⁴:²⁰ But he did not disloyally doubt God's promise, but he was strengthened in his trust, praising God ⁴:²¹ and being assured that God was able to do what he had promised. ⁴:²² Wherefore, it was regarded to him for uprightness.

Gentile Inclusion

⁴:²³ Now it was not written for him only, "it was regarded to him," ⁴:²⁴ but also for us *gentiles*, to those who are about to be regarded as upright, to those trusting on God who raised Jesus, our Lord, from among the realm of the dead. ⁴:²⁵ He was surrendered on account of the transgressions of us *i.e., the gentile peoples* and was raised in order for us *i.e., the gentile peoples* to be regarded as upright.

⁵:¹ So then, because we *gentiles* have been regarded as upright based on faithfulness, we *gentiles* have rapprochement with God by participation with our Lord, Jesus Christ. ⁵:² It is through him we *gentiles* have obtained the entrance into this benefit where we hold steady and we base our boasting in the expectation of *receiving* the splendor of God. ⁵:³ And not only this, but we also base our boasting in afflictions, being aware that *coping with* affliction produces endurance, ⁵:⁴ endurance *brings about* tested character, and tested character produces expectation. ⁵:⁵ And expectation does not disappoint, because God's love permeates in us through the divine Pneuma given to us. ⁵:⁶ For while we *gentiles* were helpless, Christ, when the time came, died for the benefit of the impious *gentiles*. ⁵:⁷ For barely will someone die for the benefit of an upright person. For it's true that on behalf of the good person someone does show courage to die. ⁵:⁸ And God shows love to us *gentiles*, because, while we were still *gentile* sinners, Christ died for our benefit. ⁵:⁹ Then, what's even more important, since we have now been regarded as upright in Jesus's violent execution, we shall be rescued by him from wrath. ⁵:¹⁰ For, if, while we belonged to enemy peoples, we have been reconciled to God through the death of God's son, then what's even more important, since we have been reconciled, we shall receive the salutary effects of his life. ⁵:¹¹ And not only that, but we base our boasting in God through our Lord, Jesus Christ, through

whom now we have received reconciliation.

Comparison of Adam & Jesus

5:12 For this reason, just as Hamartia entered into the world-history through one person, and death occurred on account of that error, so death started happening to all people, because all did wrong. 5:13 For Hamartia existed in the world before a law-code was given, but wrong-doing is not charged where there is no law-code. 5:14 Yet death ruled from the time of Adam until Moses, even upon those who did not commit error like the transgression of Adam— who is a type of the one to come. 5:15 So the wrong-doing is not like Adam's, so also is the gift not like the consequence of death. For if many died on account of the transgression of one, much more does the graciousness of God and the beneficent gift abound for the many on account of the one person, Jesus Christ. 5:16 And the gift is not like through the one sinning. For, on the one side, the judgment based on one was unto condemnation, but, on the other side, the gift because of many transgressions results in a vindication. 5:17 For if death ruled through one on account of the transgression of the one, much more the one receiving the abundance of grace and the gift of uprightness shall rule in life through the one, Jesus Christ. 5:18 Therefore, just as through the offense of one person to all people resulted in condemnation, so also through the upright action of one to all people results in life-giving acquittal. 5:19 For just as many were made sinners through the disobedience of one person, so also through the obedience of the one the many are made to be upright. 5:20 And the Torah was introduced, in order that the offense might increase. But where error increased, graciousness exuded, 5:21 in order that just as Hamartia ruled by causing death, so also might graciousness rule because of uprightness resulting in unending life through Jesus Christ, our Lord.

Dialogue with Recalcitrant Gentiles

[G] 6:1 What, then, shall we *gentiles* say? Should we *gentile peoples* persist in our relationship to Hamartia in order that God's graciousness might increase?

[P] 6:2 Not at all. How shall we *gentiles*, who have died to our relationship with Hamartia, still be living in it? 6:3 Or don't you *all* know that, as many of us as have been placed into Christ Jesus, we have been placed into his death? 6:4 Therefore, we have been buried along with him through the placement into his death, in order that as Christ was raised from the realm of the dead through the splendor of the father, so also might we proceed with a fresh life.

6:5 For if we have become implanted people parallel with his death, then also we shall be participants of his revivification. 6:6 We know that the person we used to be was co-executed, in order that the error-ridden body might be extinguished, so that we are no longer mastered by Hamartia. 6:7 For the one *i.e., the criminal* who has been put to death is acquitted from his error. 6:8 So if we have been put to death with Christ, we trust that we shall live together with him. 6:9 We also know that Christ, who was raised from the realm of the dead, no longer experiences death—Death no longer rules over him. 6:10 For when he was put to death, he died to the criminal accusation once for all; Now that he lives, he lives with God. 6:11 So you also need to regard yourselves to be dead in relationship with Hamartia and living with reference to the divine life in Christ Jesus.

6:12 Therefore, stop allowing Hamartia to dominate you, so that you obey its passions. 6:13 No longer offer yourself as tools of wrong-doing but offer yourselves to God as alive from the realm of the dead and yourselves as tools of uprightness in the divine life. 6:14 For Hamartia shall not rule over you. For you are not under the judgment of the law, but under God's gracious acquittal.

[G] 6:15 What, then? Might we continue to commit moral error, because we are not under the judgment of the law, but under God's gracious acquittal?

[P] 6:15b No way! 6:16 Don't you realize that to the one you offer yourselves as voluntary slaves, you are a dutiful slave, whether to commit moral error and receive death or to be obedient and be upright?

6:17 I'm grateful to God that, though you used to be slaves of Hamartia, now you have obeyed from the heart to that form of teaching you have been entrusted with, 6:18 and since you have been freed from the rule of Hamartia, you have become devoted to uprightness.

[A] 6:19a I am saying this in the customary human *rhetorical* form due to your limitation.

[P] 6:19b For in the same way as you offered yourselves as slaves to do unclean acts and to one unlawful act after another, so now offer yourselves as slaves to uprightness resulting in sacredness. 6:20 For when you used to be slaves of Hamartia, you were freed people from being duty-bound to act uprightly.

[P] 6:21a Then what outcome did you use to have?

[G] *Note: Perhaps too ashamed to respond.*

[P] 6:21b About these acts you now experience shame. For the goal of them is to bring about death. 6:22 But now, since you have been manumitted from Hamartia, and have become devoted to God, you have your outcome of sacredness: the goal is unending life. 6:23 For the payback of Hamartia is death, but the graciousness of God is unending life by participation in Christ Jesus our Lord.

No Legal Duty to the "Husband" for Gentiles

7:1 Or don't you *all* know, siblings (for I speak to people who know how legal concepts work) that a law code rules over a person only for as long as the person is alive. 7:2 As an example, a married woman has ties by law to a husband while he lives. If the husband should die, she is released from the law pertaining to her husband. 7:3 Consequently, if she marries another man while her husband is still living, she will be labeled an adulteress. Yet, if her husband should die, she is a freed-woman in relation to the law so that she is not an adulteress if she marries another man. 7:4 Likewise, my siblings, you also have been made dead with regard to being bound by marriage-law by participation with the body of Christ so that you might be "married" to another, to the one raised from the corpses *of the underworld,* for the purpose that we might produce fruits of virtue for God. ⁷:⁵ For when we were *wedded to Hamartia* in our fleshly bodies, the Hamartian passions, based on marriage-law, were titillated in our bodily members to produce the effects of soul-death. ⁷:⁶ But now we have been released from marriage-law by having died to that which we were oppressed, so that we might dedicate ourselves in a fresh relationship rather than an antiquated code.

Soliloquy of the Gentile Soul's Inner Person

⁷:⁷ What, then, shall we say? Equate Torah with Hamartia? No way! Rather it was through Torah that I *i.e., the Inner Person* "knew" Hamartia. For I would not have been aware of my excitement *for marital relations with Hamartia* except Torah said, "You shall not desire *to have marital relations with another*" (Exod 20:17; Deut 5:21 LXX). ⁷:⁸ Yet, Hamartia leaped at the chance because of the commandment and brought to life every desire in me. For where there is no legal code Hamartia is dead. ⁷:⁹ Now at one time, I *i.e., the Inner Person* was living my life without the existence of Torah. When I became aware of the commandment, Hamartia sprung to life. ⁷:¹⁰ But I *i.e., the Inner Person* died. What happened to me was that the commandment that brings life caused me to die. ⁷:¹¹ For Hamartia leaped at the chance because of the commandment and deceived me and through it killed me.

⁷:¹² So then, it is confirmed that the Torah is sacred, and the commandment is sacred, just, and good. ⁷:¹³ You might ask, "Did that which was something good for me cause my death?" I would answer, "No way!" The culprit was Hamartia. Through what was good for me, it produced a soul-death, in order that Hamartia through the commandment might reveal its true nature.

⁷:¹⁴ For we *the soul collectively* know that Torah belongs to the spirited part of me *i.e., the soul,* but I *i.e., the Inner Person* am engulfed in flesh and have been sold as a slave under the authority of Hamartia. ⁷:¹⁵ I *i.e., the Inner Person* am not under control of my actions. I *i.e., the Inner Person* do not practice what I *i.e., the Inner Person* want, but I do what I detest. ⁷:¹⁶ If I do what I do not want, then I confirm that Torah is good. ⁷:¹⁷ I *i.e., the Inner Person* am no longer in control but Hamartia residing in me *i.e., the soul.*

⁷:¹⁸ For I, *the gentile person,* know that goodness does not reside in the choices of my flesh. For the disposition to desire what is morally good is present within me *i.e., the Inner Person,* but effecting good is not completely under my control. ⁷:¹⁹ For I often do not do the good things that I want to do, but I practice the bad things I do not want to do. ⁷:²⁰ If I do that which I do not want, I no longer bring it about, but Hamartia residing in me. ⁷:²¹ I discover a principle that when I want to do good, then *the impulse to do* bad is present within me. ⁷:²² For I delight together with the divine principle of the Inner Person. ⁷:²³ I discern another principle among my bodily members waging war against my mental faculty and making me a captive by the principle of Hamartia which is in my bodily members. ⁷:²⁴ I am a miserable person! Who will rescue me from this death-prone body? ⁷:²⁵ God is to be thanked on account of Jesus Christ, our Lord. To sum up, I serve by

my rational mind by means of God's principles but with my bodily flesh the principles of Hamartia. ⁸⁾¹ There is now no longer any condemnation for those who participate in Christ Jesus. ⁸⁾² For the principle of the life-giving Pneuma in Christ Jesus set you *i.e., my Inner Person* free from the principle of Hamartia and soul-death.

The God-given Moral Capacity for Freedom to Live as God's Offspring

⁸⁾³ For due to the weak-willed flesh *of gentile peoples*, Torah was not able to overcome Hamartia. God, however, by sending his own son in the likeness of the flesh of Hamartia and regarding Hamartia, passed a death sentence against Hamartia by means of God's son's flesh. ⁸⁾⁴ The outcome was that the just requirement of Torah was satisfied in us *gentile peoples* who do not conduct themselves based on the capacity of the flesh but based on the power of Pneuma. ⁸⁾⁵ For those *gentiles*, who conduct themselves based on the capacity of the flesh, discern what has to do with the fleshly appetites and desires. In contrast, those *gentiles*, who conduct themselves based on the power of Pneuma, discern what has to do with the virtues of Pneuma. ⁸⁾⁶ For the discernment of the flesh brings about soul-death, but the discernment of Pneuma brings about vitality and serenity. ⁸⁾⁷ Consequently, the discernment based on fleshly appetites and desires is opposed to God, for it is not conducive to God's Torah, since it is not capable of doing that. ⁸⁾⁸ In fact, those *gentiles* who continue to conduct themselves based on the capacity of the flesh are not able to satisfy *the moral standard of* God. ⁸⁾⁹ But you *gentile followers of Jesus* are not controlled by fleshly desires and appetites but are controlled by the *reasoning* Pneuma, since God's Pneuma resides within you. [If anyone does not have the Spirit of Christ, this person does not belong to Christ.] ⁸⁾¹⁰ If Christ is manifest in your character, then your bodily impulses are dead with regard to Hamartia, but your pneuma is alive with regard to right living. ⁸⁾¹¹ And if the Pneuma of the one who raised Jesus from among the dead ones resides in you, then the one who raised Christ from among the dead ones will immortalize also your mortal bodies by means of God's resident Pneuma in you.

⁸⁾¹² So then, siblings, we are obligated not to our fleshly desires and appetites, to live a life based on those fleshly values. ⁸⁾¹³ For if you live a life based on fleshly desires and appetites, you will experience the death of your soul. ⁸⁾¹⁴ For whoever are guided by God's Pneuma, they are "sons" of God *just like Jesus*. ⁸⁾¹⁵ For you *gentiles* did not receive enslavement to again be fearful, but you received an adoption by which we *Jews and gentiles* cry, "*Abba!*" "*Patēr!*" ⁸⁾¹⁶ The same Pneuma testifies together along with our pneuma that we *gentiles* are offspring of God. ⁸⁾¹⁷ If offspring of God, then God's heirs: God's heirs and co-heirs along with Christ, since we experience life's struggles along with Christ in order that we also might receive divine splendor along with Christ.

⁸⁾¹⁸ For I consider that the currently experienced birth pangs are far surpassed by the future divine splendor to be disclosed to us. ⁸⁾¹⁹ For the anticipation of humanity awaits the disclosure of the "sons" of God. ⁸⁾²⁰ For *gentile* humanity was subjected to

foolish ways of thinking, not wittingly but allowably, with the expectation ⁸:²¹ that humanity would be liberated from the enslavement to mortality unto the liberation of the divine splendor of the "sons" of God. ⁸:²² We recognize that the whole of humanity groans and moans to the present day. ⁸:²³ More specifically, we—those who were among the first to experience Pneuma—groan inwardly awaiting adoption, the release of our mortal body. ⁸:²⁴ For we have been kept by our trust in the future. Future trust of something within view is not trust at all: Who depends on trust for something when it is in view? ⁸:²⁵ If we expect what is not in view, we anticipate patiently.

⁸:²⁶ In the same way *as we gentiles groan for our adoption*, Pneuma assists with our incapacity. For we do not understand how we should pray *regarding the future*, but Pneuma itself makes our petitions for us with unintelligible groaning. ⁸:²⁷ God, the one who discerns how we feel, knows the intent of Pneuma because Pneuma makes petitions in keeping with what God wants for the *qedoshim i.e., the Jewish people*. ⁸:²⁸ We know that everything that happens results for good for those who love God, to those *gentile peoples* being invited *to be part of God's people* according to God's overall plan. ⁸:²⁹ It stands to reason that, those *gentile peoples* whom God knew in antiquity, he also determined in antiquity for them one day to share in the form of the likeness of God's son for the purpose of him being a first-born among many siblings. ⁸:³⁰ It also stands to reason that those *gentile peoples*, whom God made a determination in antiquity, God also invited *to join God's people*. Those invited God also made upright; those made upright God also immortalized.

⁸:³¹ What then shall we say about this? If God is on our side, who can stand against us? ⁸:³² Considering the fact that God did not spare God's own son but delivered him *for execution* for the benefit of all of us, how shall God not also grant everything to us along with him? ⁸:³³ Who will bring an accusation against those whom God has chosen? God makes upright! ⁸:³⁴ Who will bring a judgment? Christ is the one who died—and was raised. He is also at the privileged right-hand of God. He also makes petitions on our behalf. ⁸:³⁵ Who shall remove us from Christ's love? Will difficulty or pressure or attack? Will famine or nakedness? Will peril or sword? ⁸:³⁶ As it says, "For your sake we are threatened with death throughout the day, we are regarded as sheep waiting to be slaughtered" (Ps 43:23 LXX). ⁸:³⁷ On the contrary, we overcome all of these things because of the one who loved us.

⁸:³⁸ For I am convinced that whether we are dead or alive, whether we encounter angels or evil forces, whether we face our present or future fate, whether attacked by agencies of power; ⁸:³⁹ whether we go to the highest height or the deepest depth, whether killed by any wild beast, none of these are able to remove us from the expression of God's love brought to us by means of Christ Jesus, our Lord.

Paul's National Loyalty and Premise of God's Promise

⁹:¹ I solemnly swear by Christ that I am speaking the truth and not lying based on the co-testimony of my own self-awareness and the sacred Pneuma.

⁹:² I feel great sorrow and incessant anguish. ⁹:³ I would vow to curse myself from belonging to Christ if it were beneficial to my physical co-ethnics. ⁹:⁴ I am referring to Israelites to whom belong the adoption, the divine majesty, the covenants, the giving of the law, the sacrificial system, and the promises. ⁹:⁵ To them belong the patriarchs and from them is the Christ by natural descent, the one who has been placed over everything. God is blessed unto the unending ages. Amen.

⁹:⁶ It is not as though God's message *of promise* has fallen down. For not all those who belong to the lineage of *the patriarch* Israel are those *who belong to the nation* Israel. ⁹:⁷ Neither are the descendants of Abraham all his offspring, but "in Isaac shall be designated your descendant" (Gen 21:12 LXX). ⁹:⁸ What I mean is, it is not the offspring by natural descent who are the offspring of God but the offspring of the promise who are regarded as a descendant. ⁹:⁹ For the message of promise is this: "about this time" I will come "and there shall be to Sarah a son" (Gen 18:10, 14).

⁹:¹⁰ Similarly, also is the case of Rebecca, who had intercourse with one man, Isaac, our ancestor. ⁹:¹¹ For before their sons had been born or had done anything good or bad—in order that God's plan based on God's choice might persist, ⁹:¹² not based on deservedness but based on God's call—it was spoken to her "the greater *in age* will serve the lesser *in age*" (Gen 25:23 LXX). ⁹:¹³ As it is written "I have loved Jacob, but I have hated Esau" (Mal 1:2–3 LXX).

Dialogue on the Choices of God

⁹:¹⁴ What, then, shall we say? Is God unfair? Not at all! ⁹:¹⁵ God says to Moses, "I will show mercy to whomever I will have mercy and show compassion to whomever I will have compassion" (Exod 33:19 LXX). ⁹:¹⁶ Consequently, it is not about desiring an outcome or running toward it, but it is based on God's mercy. ⁹:¹⁷ For the writing says to Pharaoh, "For this reason I raised you up so that I might show my power in you and so that my name might be proclaimed in the whole land" (Exod 9:16 LXX). ⁹:¹⁸ Consequently, God shows mercy to whom he chooses, and God causes to be stubborn whom he chooses.

[P] ⁹:¹⁹ᵃ You, *my friend,* will say to me:
[I] ⁹:¹⁹ᵇ "Why does God still assign blame? Who opposes his choice?"
[P] ⁹:²⁰ *My friend,* who are you to talk back to God? "The molded object does not say to the molder, 'Why did you make me this way?'" (Isa 29:16 LXX). ⁹:²¹ Does not the potter have the authority over the clay to make from the same lump an object for special use and one for ordinary use?

⁹:²² So, what if God, willing to exhibit his wrath and to make known his power, bore with much longsuffering objects of wrath set for ruin. ⁹:²³ And what if God is willing to make known the wealth of God's divine majesty upon objects of mercy God had made ready beforehand for divine majesty. ⁹:²⁴ We are those *of the remnant* whom God has called. We have been called not only from among Jews but also from among the gentile peoples. ⁹:²⁵ As God also says in Hosea,

"I will call the people who are not my people 'my people,' and I will call the one not loved 'my beloved'" (Hos 2:23).

"And it shall be in the place where it was said to them, 'You are not my people,' there they shall be called 'sons of the living God'" (Hos 1:10 LXX). Isaiah cries out on behalf of Israel, "If the number of the sons of Israel should be as the sand of the sea, the remnant will be saved. For the LORD will perform a decree exhaustively and expeditiously upon the land" (Isa 10:22–23 LXX).

⁹:²⁹ Just as Isaiah also predicted, "If the LORD Sabaoth had not left to us descendants, we would have become like Sodom, and we would have been made to resemble Gomorrah" (Isa 1:9 LXX).

[I] ⁹:³⁰ᵃ What shall we conclude?

[P] ⁹:³⁰ᵇ The gentile peoples who were not going after uprightness overtook to reach uprightness, an uprightness based on the principle of faithfulness. ⁹:³¹ Israel, though going after the observance of Torah that brings about uprightness, did not reach uprightness through Torah practice.

[I] ⁹:³²ᵃ Why is this?

[P] ⁹:³²ᵇ Because their practice was not based on the principle of faithfulness but as though being upright is based on doing right. They stumbled against a stone that causes people to trip. ⁹:³³ As it is written,
"Look, I am setting in Zion a stone of stumbling and a rock of offense. And the one trusting on him will not be put to shame" (Isa 28:16 LXX; 8:14).

Israel's Role in the Good News to Gentiles

¹⁰:¹ Siblings, my yearning and my prayer to God is for them *the Judean people* and that God will bring about the deliverance *of Israel*. ¹⁰:² For I testify that they have zeal for God but not based on complete knowledge. ¹⁰:³ For they are disregarding God's uprightness *based on faithfulness* and are trying to establish their own. They have not submitted to the uprightness of God. ¹⁰:⁴ For the culmination of Torah is *the coming of Christ to bring uprightness to all who are faithful*. ¹⁰:⁵ For Moses writes about the uprightness based on Torah practice, "The person doing them shall live by them" (Lev 18:5). ¹⁰:⁶ And the uprightness based on faithfulness; Moses says it this way,
"Do not think to yourself" (Deut 9:4),
"Who will ascend into heaven" (Deut 30:12)?
This means to bring down Christ. ¹⁰:⁷ Or,
"Who will descend into the abyss" (Deut 30:13)?
This means to bring up Christ from the realm of the dead. ¹⁰:⁸ But what does Moses say?
"The pronouncement is near you in what you say and what you want" (Deut 30:14).

This means the message about faithfulness *of Christ* which we announce *to the gentiles*: ¹⁰:⁹ If you *a gentile person* profess aloud *with your mouth* that Jesus is Lord and you are really convinced *in your heart* that God raised him from the realm of the dead, you will be saved *from your pagan beliefs and lifestyle*. ¹⁰:¹⁰ For in the heart the person is convinced leading to uprightness, and with the mouth the person makes a profession leading to salvation. ¹⁰:¹¹ For the writing says, "Everyone trusting on him will not be made ashamed" (Isa 28:16 LXX). ¹⁰:¹² For there is no differentiation between a Jew and a Greek, for the same LORD of all bestows riches to all who invoke the LORD. ¹⁰:¹³ For "whoever might invoke the name of the LORD will be saved" (Joel 2:32).

¹⁰:¹⁴ How, then, are they *i.e., the gentile peoples* to make an invocation to the LORD they have not believed? How

should they *i.e., the gentile peoples* believe the LORD about whom they have not heard? How should they *i.e., the gentile peoples* hear *about the LORD* apart from *Jews* proclaiming? ¹⁰:¹⁵ How should they *i.e., the Jews* proclaim except they should be sent? *The Jews have been sent,* just as it is written, "How seasonable are the feet of the one announcing good things" (Isa 52:7). ¹⁰:¹⁶ However, not all *Jews* have been obedient to the announcement. For Isaiah says, "LORD, who has trusted in our hearing" (Isa 53:1 LXX). ¹⁰:¹⁷ Consequently, faithfulness is based on hearing, and hearing is through the pronouncement about Christ.

¹⁰:¹⁸ But I ask, "Have they *i.e., the gentile peoples* heard? Of course!

"Their *i.e. Israel's* voice has gone out into all of the land, and their pronouncement to the edges of civilization" (Ps 18:4 LXX).

¹⁰:¹⁹ But I ask, "Didn't Israel understand? First, Moses says,

"I will make you jealous by not a nation, by a senseless nation will I make you angry" (Deut 32:21).

¹⁰:²⁰ Then, Isaiah is emboldened to say *about the gentiles,*

"I was found by those who did not seek me, I became visible to those who were not inquiring me" (Isa 65:1 LXX).

¹⁰:²¹ Yet, concerning Israel he says,

"All day long I have extended my hands to a disobedient and oppositional people" (Isa 65:2 LXX).

Foot Race Metaphor to Cause Competitive Jealousy of the Jewish People

¹¹:¹ Therefore, I ask, has God disqualified his people? Of course not! For I am also an Israelite from the ancestry of Abraham, of the tribe of Benjamin. ¹¹:² God has not disqualified his people whom he has known previously. Or do you not know what the writing says about Elijah, how he pleads to God against Israel?

¹¹:³ "LORD, they have killed your prophets, they have destroyed your altars; I alone am left, and they are seeking my life" (1 Ki 19:10, 14).

¹¹:⁴ What is the oracular response to him?

"I have kept for myself seven thousand men who have not bent the knee to Baal" (1 Ki 19:18).

¹¹:⁵ Therefore, so also at the present time has God formed a remnant according to a choice based on undeservedness. ¹¹:⁶ If God's choice is through favor, then it is no longer based on actions, otherwise God's favor is no longer favor.

¹¹:⁷ What then? Israel did not obtain *the prize* that is was seeking after. The selected reached. The rest have become calcified, ¹¹:⁸ as it is written,

"God gave them a spirit of insensitivity, eyes not seeing and ears not hearing, until this very day" (Deut 29:4; Isa 29:10).

¹¹:⁹ And David says,

"Let their table become a snare and a trap, and a stumbling block and a retribution to them. ¹¹:¹⁰ Let their eyes be darkened so that they cannot see and bow down their backs continually" (Ps 68:23–24 LXX).

¹¹:¹¹ Therefore, I ask, they have not stumbled so as to have fallen down, have they? Of course not! Rather, through their misstep recovery has come to the gentile peoples to spark their *i.e., Israel* competitive jealousy. ¹¹:¹² If their *i.e., Israel* misstep is a rich prize for *the rest of* humanity and their loss is a rich prize for the gentile peoples, how much more of a rich prize is their completion *of the race*?

¹¹:¹³ I am speaking to you gentiles. Since, then, I am an envoy for the

gentiles, I hold my service with high regard ¹¹:¹⁴ on the condition that I might somehow spark the jealousy of my "flesh *and blood*" and rescue some from among them. ¹¹:¹⁵ For if their loss means the reconciliation of *the rest of* humanity, what will mean their addition other than life from among corpses? ¹¹:¹⁶ If the first portion from the dough is sacred, then the rest of the batch is sacred too. If the root *of a family* is sacred, then the branches *of the family* will be sacred as well.

Dialogue with a Boastful Gentile

[P] ¹¹:¹⁷ If some of the branches *of the family tree of Israel* have been pruned, and you, *my friend*, a wild olive shoot, have been grafted among them and have become a participant of the rich nourishment coming from the root of the olive tree, ¹¹:¹⁸ do not act triumphantly about the *pruned* branches. If you do act triumphantly, remember that you do not support the root, but the root supports you.

¹¹:¹⁹ Then you shall say:

[I] The branches were pruned so that I might be grafted!

[P] ¹¹:²⁰ That's true. They were pruned because of infidelity. You persist by your fidelity. You should not be boastful but fearful. ¹¹:²¹ For if God did not spare the natural branches, neither will God spare you, *my friend,*.

¹¹:²² Notice, then, the benevolence and severity of God. On the one hand, severity toward those who have fallen down. On the other hand, benevolence of God toward you, *my friend,* if you continue in his benevolence. Otherwise, you, *my friend,* will also be pruned. ¹¹:²³ Even those *who have been pruned,* if they do not continue in their infidelity, will be grafted in. For God is able to graft them back in again. ¹¹:²⁴ For if you, *my friend,* had been pruned from what is by nature a wild olive tree and had been grafted contrary to nature into a cultivated olive tree, how much more will these natural branches be grafted back into their own olive tree!

God's Plan for the Ages to be the God of All

¹¹:²⁵ I want you to understand, siblings, this enigma, so that you might not be wise people beyond yourselves. Israel has partially experienced an insensitivity *caused by God* until the fullness of the gentile peoples has entered. ¹¹:²⁶ That is when the entire Israelite nation will be delivered, as it is written, "The deliverer will come out of Zion, he will remove impiety from Jacob. ¹¹:²⁷ This is my covenant with them (Is 59:20–21 LXX), when I take away their sins" (Is 27:9 LXX).

¹¹:²⁸ On the one hand, regarding God's good news *to the gentile peoples,* they *i.e., the Jewish people* are at odds with God for your sake. On the other hand, regarding their selection, they are loved of God for the sake of the ancestors. ¹¹:²⁹ For God does not regret God's calling *of Israel* and God's gifts *i.e., the covenant, the Torah and the sacrifices*. ¹¹:³⁰ For just as you *gentile peoples* had been disobedient at one time but now have received mercy through their disobedience, ¹¹:³¹ so also, they *of the Israelite nation* have been disobedient for your mercy, so they also might receive mercy. ¹¹:³² For God jointly enclosed all *peoples* to disobedience, that he might be merciful to all.

¹¹:³³ Oh, the profundity of the benevolence, sagacity, and intelligence of God! How unfathomable are God's decisions and inscrutable God's choices!

> ¹¹:³⁴ "For who has understood the mind of the LORD, or who has been God's adviser" (Is 40:13 LXX)?
> ¹¹:³⁵ Or,
> "who has given to God, and God must repay" (Job 21:31)?

¹¹:³⁶ Everything is from God, through God, and unto God. To God is splendor unto the ages. Amen.

Personal Transformation and Community Formation

¹²:¹ Therefore, I exhort you, siblings, by the opportunity given to you by God's compassion, to present a living, sacred, and God-pleasing sacrifice of your bodily desires and appetites. It would be a ritual made to enhance your rationality. ¹²:² Stop modeling yourself based on the current social standards but be transformed by a new way of thinking in order that you might examine what actions God wants you to perform that are morally good, right actions, and the best to be done.

¹²:³ What I have to say to you with all the grace I have is that everyone within your group should not make harsh judgments beyond what one ought to think but think sensibly. I say this to each one as God has distributed proportionately the ways to show one's commitment. ¹²:⁴ For in the same way we have many parts in one body and all parts do not have the same action, ¹²:⁵ so we who are made up of many different people are one body in Christ, we are individually parts of one another, ¹²:⁶ and have differing levels of endowments based on the favor granted to us. If God has given to someone the endowment of prophecy, then that person practices prophecy faithfully. ¹²:⁷ But if someone is only a server, that person should also serve faithfully. If God has given to someone the endowment of teaching, then that person practices teaching faithfully. ¹²:⁸ But if someone is only an encourager, that person should also provide encouragement with faithfulness. Those who provide for the needs of others, do it with generosity. Those who manage households, do it with diligence. Those who show mercy with alms, do it with cheerfulness.

¹²:⁹ Love is to be genuine.
Abhor the bad, cling to the good.

¹²:¹⁰ Show affection for one another with sibling friendship.
Guide one another with honor.

¹²:¹¹ Show boldness with diligence.
Be fervent in your pneuma.
Give service to the LORD.

¹²:¹² Rejoice in anticipation.
Endure in troublesome times.
Persist in prayer.

¹²:¹³ Contribute to the needs of the *qedoshim*.
Work hard to show friendship to foreigners.

¹²:¹⁴ Speak well of those who harass you. Do this rather than call down curses against them.

¹²:¹⁵ Be joyful with those who are experiencing joy; weep with those who weep.

¹²:¹⁶ Treat each other in the same way. Don't show better treatment to high-born people. Instead, associate with the lower rank people. Do not

become discerning people regarding them.

¹²:¹⁷ Do not respond to meanness with cruelty. Adapt to what is good for each person.

¹²:¹⁸ If it is possibly under your control, live peacefully with everyone.

¹²:¹⁹ Do not avenge yourselves, dear friends, but give an opportunity for *God's* wrath *through retributive justice*. It is written,

"Retribution is mine; I will avenge" (Deut 32:35),

says the LORD. ¹²:²⁰ Instead,

"If your enemy is hungry, feed him. If he is thirsty, give him a drink. For by doing this you pile fiery coals on his head" (Prov 25:21–22 LXX).

¹²:²¹ Do not be overcome by the hurtful things people do but overcome the hurtful things with good behavior.

Civic Duties

¹³:¹ Let every person submit themselves to governing authorities. For there is no government except that which exists under God. And those that exist have been instituted under God. ¹³:² So then those who oppose government stand against God's institution and they will receive a penalty. ¹³:³ For those who act appropriately have no reason to fear rulers, but those who break the law do. If you want to not be afraid of government, then act appropriately and you will have its approval. ¹³:⁴ For it is God's servant to help you act appropriately. But if you do wrong, you should be frightened. For government does not possess the power of life and death without effect. It is God's servant for adjudicating severe punishment against a wrongdoer. ¹³:⁵ So, it is required that a person is submissive, not only because of the threat of punishment but also to ease one's own mind. ¹³:⁶ For this reason you also pay tributes. For authorities are God's ministers diligently carrying out their duties. ¹³:⁷ Provide to everyone what is your obligation. Provide tribute to the one who is owed tribute. Provide the toll to the one who is owed a toll. Provide respect to the one who is owed respect. Provide honor to the one who is owed honor.

¹³:⁸ Do not be indebted to anyone except to love one another. For the one who loves the other person has fulfilled Torah. ¹³:⁹ For the commandments "You shall not commit adultery, you shall not murder, you shall not steal" (Exod 20:13–15, 17; Deut 5:17–19, 21), and any other commandment, are summed up by this commandment, "You shall love your neighbor as yourself" (Lev 19:18). ¹³:¹⁰ Love does not perform a wrong to a neighbor. Love, then, is the fulfillment of Torah.

[¹³:¹¹ And knowing the season, that an hour is already that you should be stirred from sleep. For our salvation is now closer than when we believed. ¹³:¹² The night is far gone, but the day has come near. Therefore, we must put off the deeds of darkness, and put on the weapons of light. ¹³:¹³ Let us walk decently as during the day, not with orgies and with intoxications, not with strife and jealousy. ¹³:¹⁴ But put on the Lord Jesus Christ and do not make an intention of the flesh for desire.]

Social Duties

¹⁴:¹ Accept *in friendship* those *other gentile followers of Jesus* who are fragile with regard to their level of convincement, but not just so you can have a debate with them. ¹⁴:² One *who is more robust* is convinced that it's okay to

consume anything, but the one who is fragile *with superstition* eats vegetables *and does not consume meat or drink that might have been used sacrificially.* 14:3 The person who eats should not reject the person not eating, and the person not eating should not condemn the person eating, for God has accepted them.

[P] 14:4 "Who do you, *my friend,* who abstains, think you are condemning someone else's servant? It's up to their own master if that servant should stand or fall!" They will stand, for the LORD is able to cause them to stand.

14:5 On the one hand, some people make a judgment that one day is more significant than another day, while other people make a judgment that every day is the same. Let each person be convinced in their own mind. 14:6 For the basis for thinking one day is more significant is to honor the LORD. Those who consume *any food* consume to honor the LORD, by being thankful to God. Similarly, those abstaining *from some foods* do so to honor the LORD by also being thankful to God. 14:7 People do not live to themselves and do not die to themselves. 14:8 For if we should live, we live for the LORD; if we should die, we die for the LORD. Therefore, whether we should live or die, we belong to the LORD. 14:9 For this reason Christ died and lived, that he might reign over the dead and the living.

[P] 14:10 "Why do you, *my friend,* who eats anything, condemn your sibling?

[P] Or you, *my friend,* who abstains, why do you reject your sibling?"

For we shall all be presented before the rostrum of God. 14:11 For it is written, "As I live, says the LORD, every knee shall bow to me and every tongue shall acclaim to God" (Isa 45:23 LXX).

14:12 So then, each one of us will give an account to God.

14:13 Therefore, let us no longer incriminate one another, but discriminate this instead, not to be a cause for a sibling's fall or to be an offense.

[I] 14:14 I know and have been convinced by our Lord, Jesus, that nothing is intrinsically impure.

[P] Except that to the one who determines something to be impure, it is impure to that person. 14:15 For if your sibling is distressed on account of food, you, *my friend,* no longer conduct yourself based on love. Do not bring this one for whom Christ died to *moral* ruin by your food.

14:16 Therefore, do not let your good behavior be a cause for someone's impiety. 14:17 For the realm of God is not food and drink but uprightness and peace and joy in sacred Pneuma. 14:18 For the person who serves Christ in this way is pleasing to God and is considered morally excellent by people.

14:19 So then, work hard at those things that maintain harmony and that bring about the formation of one another.

[P] 14:20 Do not tear down, *my friend,* for the sake of food God's work *in the formation of others.*

[I] Everything is indeed pure.

[P] However, *my friend,* it is wrong by your eating habits to impede another's progress. 14:21 It is not good to consume meat or drink wine or anything else *related to sacrifices to gods* by which your sibling might be impeded. ¹⁴:²² Your commitment is between you and God.

Happy are those who do not condemn themselves by what they approve. ¹⁴:²³ Yet, those who are indiscriminate, if they should eat, they have incriminated themselves, because it was not based on conviction. Whatever is not based on conviction is moral error.

¹⁵:¹ We who are robust are obligated to handle the fragility of those who are not robust and do not satisfy ourselves. ¹⁵:² Let each of us do what is best for the other person for the good of their formation.

¹⁵:³ [For Christ also did not act selfishly, but just as it is written, "The insults of those who insult you have fallen on me" (Ps 68:10 LXX). ¹⁵:⁴ For whatever was written previously, for our teaching was it written, in order that through the endurance and through the encouragement of the writings we might have a basis for expectation in the future. ¹⁵:⁵ May the God who brings about endurance and encouragement grant to us to think alike among one another according to Christ Jesus, ¹⁵:⁶ in order that you might with one accord with one mouth glorify God even the Father of our Lord, Jesus Christ.]

¹⁵:⁷ Wherefore, accept one another *in friendship*, just as Christ accepted you for the splendor of God.

¹⁵:⁸ [For I say Christ became a minister of circumcision for the truth of God in order to confirm the promises of the patriarchs, ¹⁵:⁹ and that the gentiles should glorify God for mercy, just as it is written, "For this reason I shall confess you before the nations and praise your name" (Ps 17:50 LXX). ¹⁵:¹⁰ And again it says, "Rejoice, O nations, with his people" (Deut 32:43 LXX). ¹⁵:¹¹ And again, "Praise, all the nations, the LORD and let all the people praise him" (Ps 116:1 LXX). ¹⁵:¹² And again Isaiah says, "The root of Jesse shall be, and the one who rises to rule over the gentiles, in him the gentiles shall hope" (Isa 11:10 LXX).

¹⁵:¹³ Now the God of hope fill you with all joy and peace in believing, in order that you might abound in hope by the power of the Holy Spirit.]

Proclamation to the Gentiles and Plans for a Visit

¹⁵:¹⁴ I myself am convinced about you, my siblings, that you yourselves are replete with goodness, filled with all understanding, capable of admonishing one another.

¹⁵:¹⁵ I have written more daringly in some sections so as to remind you through the favor given to me by God ¹⁵:¹⁶ in order that I might be the worship attendant of Christ Jesus to the gentiles, mediating God's good news, in order that the offering of the gentile peoples might be acceptable, consecrated by sacred Pneuma. ¹⁵:¹⁷ Therefore, I have a basis for boasting in Christ Jesus regarding the things I have accomplished for God. ¹⁵:¹⁸ For I will not dare to talk about anything other than what Christ has accomplished through me for the obedience of the gentile peoples by what was said and done ¹⁵:¹⁹ in the power of signs and wonders, by the power of Pneuma. So then, from Jerusalem and to the surrounding area as far as Illyricum, I have completely proclaimed the good news about Christ. ¹⁵:²⁰ So I aspire to proclaim the good news where Christ's name is not known, so that I do not build upon another's foundation, ¹⁵:²¹ but as it is written, "To those it was told about him, they shall see; and those who have not heard will understand" (Isa 52:15 LXX).

¹⁵:²² I have been thwarted many times to come to you. ¹⁵:²³ But I now no longer have a place in these regions, and

I have had a desire for many years to come to you ¹⁵:²⁴ whenever I travel into Spain. I plan to pass through *Italy* to see you and to be sent on there by you after I first have finished my stay with you for a while. ¹⁵:²⁵ At present I am going to Jerusalem ministering to the *qedoshim*. ¹⁵:²⁶ For Macedonia and Achaia were pleased to have made some participation toward the poor of the *qedoshim* in Jerusalem. ¹⁵:²⁷ For they were pleased to do this and even obligated to them. For if the gentiles have participated with their spiritual inheritance, they are obligated also to minister to them with their material goods. ¹⁵:²⁸ Therefore, when I have finished this task and have safely deposited this financial harvest, I will make my journey by passing through Rome and then to Spain. ¹⁵:²⁹ I know when I come to you, I will arrive in the fullness of the blessing of Christ.

¹⁵:³⁰ Now I implore you, through our Lord, Jesus Christ, and through the love of the Pneuma to be fervent for me in your prayers to God on my behalf, ¹⁵:³¹ in order that I might be rescued from those who are disobedient in Judea and my service in Jerusalem might be acceptable to the *qedoshim*, ¹⁵:³² so that when I come to you joyfully by God's will, I might be refreshed by you. ¹⁵:³³ The God of peace be with all of you. Amen.

Scribal Addenda with Recommendation Letter

¹⁶:¹ I recommend to you our sister Phoebe, who is a server of the assembly *i.e., synagogue* in Cenchrea, ¹⁶:² in order that you might accept her in the LORD in a way worthy of the *qedoshim* and assist her in any function she might need from you. For she has become a patroness of many people, including me.

¹⁶:³ Pass greetings to Prisca and Aquila, my coworkers in Christ Jesus. ¹⁶:⁴ They risked their own freedom for my life. Not only am I grateful to them but also all the assemblies of the gentiles. ¹⁶:⁵ Also pass greetings to the assembly at their house.

Pass greetings to Epenetus, my dear friend, who was the first to respond to Christ in the province of Asia.

¹⁶:⁶ Pass greetings to Mary, who has labored greatly for you.

¹⁶:⁷ Pass greetings to Andronicus and Junia, my co-ethnics and my co-prisoners. They are significant members among the envoys. They also had been in Christ before me.

¹⁶:⁸ Pass greetings to Ampliatus, my dear friend in the Lord.

¹⁶:⁹ Pass greetings to Urbanus, our co-worker in Christ, and Stachys, my dear friend.

¹⁶:¹⁰ Pass greetings to Apelles, an esteemed person in Christ.

Pass greetings to the members belonging to the household of Aristobulus.

¹⁶:¹¹ Pass greetings to Herodion, my co-ethnic.

Pass greetings to the members who are in the Lord belonging to the household of Narcissus.

¹⁶:¹² Pass greetings to Tryphena and Tryphosa, laborers in the Lord.

Pass greetings to Persia, a dear friend, who has labored greatly in the Lord.

¹⁶:¹³ Pass greetings to Rufus, selected in the Lord, and to his mother and mine too.

To the Romans

¹⁶:¹⁴ Pass greetings to Asyncritus, Phlegon, Hermes, Patrobas, Hermas, and the siblings with them.

¹⁶:¹⁵ Pass greetings to Philologus and Julia, Nereus and his sister, and Olympas, and all the *qedoshim* with them.

¹⁶:¹⁶ Pass greetings to one another with sacred affection.

[¹⁶:¹⁷ I urge you, siblings, to watch out for those who create dissensions and difficulties contrary to the teaching you learned and stay away from them. ¹⁶:¹⁸ For such people do not serve our Lord, Christ, but their own appetites. Through their smooth talk and flattery, they deceive the naïve. ¹⁶:¹⁹ Your obedience has spread to all regions. Therefore, I am delighted about you. I want you to be wise people when it comes to what is good and innocent people when it comes to what is bad. ¹⁶:²⁰ The God of peace will soon crush the adversary under your feet.]

⁽¹⁶:²⁴⁾ The favor of our Lord Jesus be with you.

¹⁶:²¹ Timothy, my coworker, and Lucius, Jason, Sosipater, my co-ethnics, greet you.

¹⁶:²² I, Tertius, the one writing this letter, greet you in the Lord.

¹⁶:²³ Gaius, the host of me and the whole assembly, greets you.

Erastus, the manager of the city, and Quartus, his brother, greet you.

[¹⁶:²⁵ Now to the one able to strengthen you according to my gospel and the proclamation of Jesus Christ, according to the revelation of the mystery having been silent for long ages, ¹⁶:²⁶ but now manifested, and made known through the prophetic writings according to the command of the eternal God for the obedience of faith to all the gentiles, ¹⁶:²⁷ to the only wise God, through Jesus Christ, to whom be splendor for the ages. Amen.]

APPENDIX TWO: CHART OF TERMS

I list here important and often-used terms. Most of these will be translated in a way different than what is typically found in modern English translations. I try to give a brief explanation with a cross reference if I have presented a fuller discussion.

Typical Translation	Greek Terms	My Translation	Explanation
apostle	*apostolos*	envoy	"Apostle" is too specialized and is only a transliteration.
believing, believer(s)	*pisteuōn*	trusting, adherent(s)	Rather than "believers" I use the term "adherents." See faith.
brothers	*adelphoi*	siblings	The term "sibling" is a bit awkward, but I think the plural refers to kinship of males and females.
Christ	*Christos*		It's nearly impossible to know how Paul is using this term. I don't think it is first and foremost an explicit reference to Jesus as the anointed one, the Messiah. It seems to be a name at times. This name might have derived from the same sounding name Chrestus, meaning beneficent one.

Typical Translation	Greek Terms	My Translation	Explanation
church	*ekklēsia*	assembly	"Church" is too specialized. A group of people that meet together is an assembly. There are several places where I want to indicate that Paul may be referring to a household "gathering" of Jews as a synagogue.
dead, the	*nekroi*	dead ones, corpses, realm of the dead	When Paul uses the plural, he is referring to dead people either in Hades or corpses in a cemetery. The expression "from the dead" means "out from among the dead people" or "out from among the corpses." I'm not sure which Paul has in mind. I think Paul believes in a realm of the dead, an underworld (Hades/Sheol) but not in Hell as a fiery, eternal death.
destruction	*apōleia*	moral regress, moral degradation	Paul mainly uses this term in conjunction with "salvation" in the dichotomy of moral progress and moral regress.
faith, belief	*pistis*	faithfulness, allegiance, commitment	I take this term to be about one's commitment to what one is persuaded to be true and right.
Gentiles	*ethnē*	gentiles, gentile peoples	The term refers to non-Jewish people-groups, the other ethnic groups besides Israel. The mistake would be to either make it a term about an individual person apart from their ethnic group's heritage or to seem like it's a term like nation that has a particular political existence and structure.

Chart of Terms

Typical Translation	Greek Terms	My Translation	Explanation
glory	*doxa*	splendor	Paul does use this Greek word based on his reading of the Greek Bible. In other literature *doxa* has to do with fame.
God	*theos*	God, (the one) God	There are places in Paul where he seems to be referring to God specifically as the one God, the God of Israel. Yet, I still think Paul includes concepts of the Hellenistic philosophical view of god or the gods. God exists in a place where God is untroubled by emotions and fate, for example. God shares with humans some level of divinity.
gospel	*euangellion*	good news	"Gospel" is archaic and too specialized. There's no other idiom better than "news" for what Paul is announcing to the gentile nations.
grace	*charis*	divine benevolence	
in Christ	*en Christō*	in the lineage of Christ, participation in Christ	In the same way that a descendant of Abraham is thought to have been "in Abraham" (in his seed), so are those who have a spiritual descent thought to be "in God" or "in Christ." I don't take it to be a mystical union.
Jews	*Ioudaioi*	Judeans, Jews	At times it seems like Paul is referring to citizens of Judea and other times to people who are ethnically and religiously Jewish.

Typical Translation	Greek Terms	My Translation	Explanation
law	*nomos*	Torah	I try to use language that gets away from negative connotations that have come about in Christian tradition and theology. The Greek word has a variety of implications and no one English word captures the subtlety.
Lord	*kyrios*	Lord; LORD	It must have been confusing to refer to Jesus as Lord, in the sense of "master, sovereign," while also referring to YHWH as LORD. As with English translations of the Old Testament, I've chosen to render as LORD any time Paul is not specifically referring to Jesus. The reason for doing this is that I think Paul sometimes is referring to the God of Israel when he uses LORD.
love; beloved; to love	*agapē; agapētos; agapaō*	love; dear friend; to love	I think the words relating to the emotional connection and commitment between people are more synonymous than what has been thought. I think Paul has in mind both the love of family members and the love of friends. I will use "friends" for "beloved" language.
peace	*eirēnē*	concord, serenity	Sometimes Paul is referring to the lack of conflict (national peace is a blessing from God) and other times to a sense of a person being unperturbed. The peace with God through the reconciliation of those at odds with each other that gentiles have received I call "rapprochement."

Chart of Terms

Typical Translation	Greek Terms	My Translation	Explanation
proclamation; to preach	*kērygma; kēryssō*	proclamation; to proclaim	My only point is to avoid overtly Christian language like "preach."
reconciliation; to reconcile	*katallagē; katallassō*	reconciliation; to reconcile	Reconciliation is the condition in which God has forgiven the sins of the gentile peoples and removed the enmity so that God is the God of all peoples.
saints	*hagioi*	*qedoshim*	I've tried to argue and show that Paul uses the term "holy ones" very carefully. I may be wrong, but I think Paul has in mind those of the Jewish nation who are God's holy people. So I'm trying to see if a Hebrew term like *qedoshim* works in contexts. When referring to gentiles, Paul says "called to be *qedoshim*." The calling language, I think, refers to the act of God calling or inviting the gentile peoples to accept the one, true, living God as their God. For more, see page .
salvation, to save	*sōtēria; sōzō*	restoration, deliverance, recovery, moral progress, moral health; to rescue, to be kept	The usual translations of these terms are too loaded with theological meaning and very little other meaning in English. In moral contexts I take them to refer to the therapeutic healing of the soul. In other contexts, the sense is rescue or deliverance from danger.
servant, slave	*doulos*	devotee	"Slave" has too many negative connotations. "Servant" is too mild a term. "Devotee" has religious implications and I think that's the sense Paul uses.

Typical Translation	Greek Terms	My Translation	Explanation
sin, to sin	*hamartia; harmantanō*	error, moral error;	"Sin" is too specialized. The terminology has to do with making a mistake or an error and not specifically a "sin" as in a trespass against God.
spirit	*pneuma*	pneuma	I want to emphasize the technical aspect of the Greek word, so I'm rendering it with the transliteration. See: Spirit, Holy.
Spirit, Holy	*hagion pneuma*	sacred Pneuma	I think the spirit of God in the Bible is a way of referring to God's presence and power in the world of humans. See: spirit.
believe	*pisteuō*	trust	The verb form in Paul mainly has to do with trust and dependence (on God) rather than assenting to the truth of something, as in believing.
uncircumcision	*akrobystia*	fore-skinned	To be "fore-skinned," though a bit awkward, is a more literal and more natural way of understanding the terminology.
we		we (gentiles)	Frequently Paul uses "we" to include him in the experience of the gentile peoples. See discussion on page 4.
you (pl)		you (gentiles there)	For Paul the plural pronoun is a way of addressing the readers and hearers in a certain locale. See: you (sg) and we.

Chart of Terms

Typical Translation	Greek Terms	My Translation	Explanation
you (sg)		you, my friend	In diatribe Paul addresses a singular interlocuter as a teacher to a student. At times, I think Paul let's his gentile audience listen in on him talking to a fellow Jew who is a caricature representing some attitude or action for censure. Other times Paul is addressing a gentile with the same function. See: you (pl) and we.
resurrection	*anastasis*	revivification	The narrative of the myth is that Jesus died, descended to Hades, and after three days was "raised" from the underworld and his life revived or restored. I don't mean to imply some theory that Jesus wasn't dead and was revived from a coma or something like that. My purpose is just to get away from a theologically loaded term. I do think Paul considers what happened to Jesus and what may happen to Jesus-followers (or others who attain the same level of the complete human) is an apotheosis to immortality and divinity.

BIBLIOGRAPHY

Aeschylus. *Oresteia: Agamemnon. Libation-Bearers. Eumenides.* Translated by Alan H. Sommerstein. Loeb Classical Library 146. Cambridge, MA: Harvard University Press, 2009.

Alexander, Loveday. "Paul and the Hellenistic Schools: The Evidence of Galen." In *Paul in His Hellenistic Context*, 60-83. Minneapolis: Fortress Press, 1995.

Annas, Julia. *The Morality of Happiness.* New York: Oxford University Press, 1993.

Aristotle. *Complete Works of Aristotle: The Revised Oxford Translation.* Edited by J. Barnes. Bollingen Series. 2 vols. Princeton, NJ: Princeton University Press, 1983.

Arius Didymus. *Epitome of Stoic Ethics.* Edited by Arthur J. Pomeroy. Atlanta, GA: Society of Biblical Literature, 1999.

Balch, David L. "Rich Pompeiian Houses, Shops for Rent, and the Huge Apartment Building in Herculaneum as Typical Spaces for Pauline House Churches." *Journal for the Study of the New Testament* 27, no. 1 (2004): 27-46.

Balch, David L., Everett Ferguson, and Wayne A. Meeks, eds. *Greeks, Romans, and Christians: Essays in Honor of Abraham J. Malherbe.* Minneapolis: Fortress Press, 1990.

Bartos, Emil. *Deification in Eastern Orthodox Theology.* Eugene, OR: Wipf & Stock, 2006.

Bassler, Jouette M., David M. Hay, and E. Elizabeth Johnson. *Pauline Theology.* Minneapolis: Fortress Press, 1991.

Betz, Hans Dieter. Review of Seneca und die griechisch-römische Tradition der Seelenleitung. Journal of the History of Philosophy 9, no. 1 (January 1971): 86-87.

Bird, Robert. *Paul of Tarsus.* New York: Charles Scribner's Sons, 1916.

Bruce, F. F. *New Testament History.* New York: Doubleday, 1991. London: Nelson, 1969.

Burridge, Richard A. *What Are the Gospels?: A Comparison with Graeco-Roman Biography*. 2nd ed. Grand Rapids: William B. Eerdmans Pub. Co., 2004.

Bøgh, Birgitte. "The Phrygian Background of Kybele." *Numen: International Review for the History of Religions* 54, no. 3 (2007): 304-39.

Cadbury, Henry J. "Erastus of Corinth." *Journal of Biblical Literature* 50, no. 2 (1931): 42-58.

Callahan, Allen Dwight. "Paul's Epistle to Philemon: Toward an Alternative Argumentum." *The Harvard Theological Review* 86, no. 4 (1993): 357-76.

Carson, D. A., Peter Thomas O'Brien, and Mark A. Seifrid. *The Complexities of Second Temple Judaism*. Justification and Variegated Nomism. Vol. 1, Grand Rapids, MI: Baker Academic, 2001.

– – –. *The Paradoxes of Paul*. Justification and Variegated Nomism. Vol. 2, Grand Rapids, MI: Baker Academic, 2004.

Caulley, Thomas Scott. "The Chrestos/Christos Pun (1 Pet 2:3) in P72 and P125." *Novum Testamentum* 53, no. 4 (2011): 376-87.

Celsus. *On Medicine, Volume 3: Books 7-8*. Translated by W. G. Spencer. Loeb Classical Library 336. Cambridge, MA: Harvard University Press, 1938.

Charlesworth, James H., ed. *The Old Testament Pseudepigrapha* Vol. 2. Garden City, NY: Doubleday & Co., Inc., 1983.

– – –, ed. *The Old Testament Pseudepigrapha* Vol. 1. Garden City, NY: Doubleday & Co., Inc., 1983.

Christensen, Michael J., and Wittung Jeffery A. Partakers of the Divine Nature: The History and Development of Deification in the Christian Traditions. Grand Rapids, MI: Baker Academic, 2008.

Cicero. *On Ends*. Translated by H. Rackham. Loeb Classical Library 40. Cambridge, MA: Harvard University Press, 1914.

– – –. *On Old Age. On Friendship. On Divination*. Translated by W. A. Falconer. Loeb Classical Library 154. Cambridge, MA: Harvard University Press, 1923.

– – –. *Tusculan Disputations*. Translated by J. E. King. Loeb Classical Library 141. Cambridge, MA: Harvard University Press, 1927.

Clay, Diskin. "Deep Therapy." *Philosophy and Literature* 20, no. 2 (1996): 501-05.

Cooper, John M., and associate editor D. S. Hutchinson, eds. *Plato: Complete Works*. Indianapolis and Cambridge, MA: Hackett, 1997.

Davies, William D. *Paul and Rabbinic Judaism: Some Rabbinic Elements in Pauline Theology*. New York: Harper & Row, 1967.

Dill, Samuel. *Roman Society from Nero to Marcus Aurelius*. The Meridian Library. New York: Meridian Books, 1956.

Dio Chrysostom. *Discourses 37-60*. Translated by H. Lamar Crosby. Loeb Classical Library 376. Cambridge, MA: Harvard University Press, 1946.

Diogenes Laertius. *Lives of Eminent Philosophers, Volume 2: Books 6-10*. Translated by R. D. Hicks. Loeb Classical Library 185. Cambridge, MA: Harvard University Press, 1925.

Donaldson, Terence L. "Jewish Christianity, Israel's Stumbling and the *Sonderweg* Reading of Paul." *Journal for the Study of the New Testament* 29, no. 1 (2006): 27-54.

Dunn, James D. G. *Jesus, Paul, and the Law: Studies in Mark and Galatians*. Louisville: Westminster/John Knox Press, 1990.

Eastman, Susan. "The Evil Eye and the Curse of the Law: Galatians 3.1 Revisited." *Journal for the Study of the New Testament* 24, no. 83 (2002): 69-87.

Eitrem, Samson, and Leiv Amundsen, eds. *Papyri Osloenses* Vol. 2. Oslo: Dybwad, 1931.

Engberg-Pedersen, Troels, ed. *Paul Beyond the Judaism/Hellenism Divide*. Louisville: Westminster John Knox, 2001.

— — —, ed. *Paul in His Hellenistic Context*. Minneapolis: Fortress Press, 1995.

— — —. "Radical Altruism in Philippians 2:4." In *Early Christianity and Classical Culture*, 197-214. Leiden: E J Brill, 2003.

— — —. The Stoic Theory of Oikeiosis: Moral Development and Social Interaction in Early Stoic Philosophy. Studies in Hellenistic Civilization. Aarhus, Denmark: Aarhus University Press, 1990.

Epictetus. *Discourses, Books 1-2*. Translated by W. A. Oldfather. Loeb Classical Library 131. Cambridge, MA: Harvard University Press, 1925.

— — —. *Discourses, Books 3-4. Fragments. The Encheiridion*. Translated by W. A. Oldfather. Loeb Classical Library 218. Cambridge, MA: Harvard University Press, 1928.

Euripides. *Bacchae. Iphigenia at Aulis. Rhesus.* Translated by David Kovacs. Loeb Classical Library 495. Cambridge, MA: Harvard University Press, 2003.

———. *Children of Heracles. Hippolytus. Andromache. Hecuba.* Translated by David Kovacs. Loeb Classical Library 484. Cambridge, MA: Harvard University Press, 1995.

Finlan, Stephen Kharlamov Vladimir. *Theosis: Deification in Christian Theology.* Eugene, OR: Pickwick Publications, 2006.

Firth, Florence M. The Golden Verses of Pythagoras and Other Pythagorean Fragments. London: Theosophical Pub. House Ltd., 1923.

Fitzgerald, John T. Cracks in an Earthen Vessel: An Examination of the Catalogues of Hardships in the Corinthian Correspondence. Sblds. Atlanta: Scholar's Press, 1988.

———, ed. Friendship, Flattery, and Frankness of Speech: Studies on Friendship in the New Testament World Vol. 82, Supplements to Novum Testamentum. Leiden: E.J. Brill, 1996.

———, ed. *Passions and Moral Progress in Greco-Roman Thought*, Routledge Monographs in Classical Studies. London; New York: Routledge, 2008.

Fitzgerald, John T., Dirk Obbink, and Glenn Holland, eds. *Philodemus and the New Testament World* Vol. 111, Supplements to Novum Testamentum. Leiden; Boston: Brill, 2004.

Fitzgerald, John T., Thomas H. Olbricht, and L. Michael White, eds. *Early Christianity and Classical Culture: Comparative Studies in Honor of Abraham J. Malherbe*, Supplements to Novum Testamentum, vol. 110. Leiden: Brill, 2003.

Fitzgerald, John T., and L. Michael White. *The Tabula of Cebes.* Texts and Translations 24; Graeco-Roman Religion 7. Chico, CA: Scholars Press, 1983.

Fredriksen, Paula. *Paul: The Pagans' Apostle.* New Haven & London: Yale University Press, 2017.

Gager, John G. *Reinventing Paul.* Oxford: New York, 2000.

———. Who Made Early Christianity?: The Jewish Lives of the Apostle Paul. New York: Columbia Press Press, 2015.

Garland, David E. "The Composition and Unity of Philippians: Some Neglected Literary Factors." *Novum Testamentum* 27, no. 2 (1985): 141-73.

Gaston, Lloyd. *Paul and the Torah.* Vancouver: University of British Columbia Press, 1987.

Glad, Clarence E. "Frank Speech, Flattery, and Friendship in Philodemus." In *Friendship, Flattery, and Frankness of Speech,* edited by John T. Fitzgerald, 21-59. Leiden: E J Brill, 1996.

———. *Paul and Philodemus: Adaptability in Epicurean and Early Christian Psychagogy.* Supplements to Novum Testamentum. Vol. 81, Leiden; New York: E. J. Brill, 1995.

Hadot, Ilsetraut. Seneca Und Die Griechisch-Römische Tradition Der Seelenleitung. Berlin: de Gruyter, 1969.

———. "The Spiritual Guide." Translated by Margaret Kirby. In *Classical Mediterranean Spirituality: Egyptian, Greek, Roman,* edited by A. H. Armstrong. World Spirituality, 436-59. New York: Crossroad, 1986.

Hadot, Pierre. *Philosophy as a Way of Life: Spiritual Exercises from Socrates to Foucault.* Translated by Arnold I. Davidson. Edited by Arnold I. Davidson. Malden, MA: Blackwell Publishing, 1995.

———. The Inner Citadel: The Meditations of Marcus Aurelius. Cambridge, MA: Harvard University Press, 2001.

———. *What Is Ancient Philosophy?* Translated by Michael Chase. Cambridge, MA: The Belknap Press of Harvard University Press, 2004.

Hall, Robert G. "Epispasm: Circumcision in Reverse." *Bible Review* August (1992): 52-57.

Hays, Richard B. *The Faith of Jesus Christ: An Investigation of the Narrative Substructure of Galatians 3:1-4:11.* Dissertation Series / Society of Biblical Literature. Chico, CA: Scholars Press, 1983.

Hägg, Tomas. *The Art of Biography in Antiquity.* New York: Cambridge University Press, 2012.

Hengel, Martin. The Atonement: The Origins of the Doctrine in the New Testament. Philadelphia: Fortress Press, 1981.

Herodotus. *The Persian Wars, Volume 3: Books 5-7.* Translated by A. D. Godley. Loeb Classical Library 119. Cambridge, MA: Harvard University Press, 1922.

Hierocles. *Hierocles the Stoic: Elements of Ethics, Fragments, and Excerpts.* Edited by Ilaria Ramelli. Translated by David Konstan. Writings from the Greco-Roman World 28. Atlanta: Society of Biblical Literature, 2009.

Hock, Ronald F. "Paul's Tentmaking and the Problem of His Social Class." *Journal of Biblical Literature* 97, no. 4 (1978): 555-64.

———. "Simon the Shoemaker as an Ideal Cynic." *Greek, Roman and Byzantine Studies* 17 (1976): 41-53.

———. The Social Context of Paul's Ministry: Tentmaking and Apostleship. Philadelphia: Fortress Press, 1980.

Hodges, Frederick M. "The Ideal Prepuce in Ancient Greece and Rome: Male Genital Aesthetics and Their Relation to Lipodermos, Circumcision, Foreskin Restoration, and the *Kynodesme*." *Bulletin of the History of Medicine* 75, no. 3 (2001): 375-405.

Huttner, Ulrich. *Early Christianity in the Lycus Valley*. Leiden; Boston: Brill, 2013.

Huttunen, Niko. *Paul and Epictetus on Law: A Comparison*. The Library of New Testament Studies. London: T & T Clark, 2009.

Inwood, Brad. *Ethics and Human Action in Early Stoicism*. Oxford: Clarendon Press, 1985.

———. "Goal and Target in Stoicism." *The Journal of Philosophy* 83, no. 10 (Oct. 1986): 547-56.

Jaeger, Werner. "The Greek Ideas of Immortality." In *Immortality and Resurrection; Four Essays by Oscar Cullman, Harry A. Wolfson, Werner Jaeger, and Henry J. Cadbury*, edited by Krister Stendahl, 97-114. New York: Macmillan, 1965.

Josephus. *Jewish Antiquities, Volume 5: Books 12-13*. Translated by Ralph Marcus. Loeb Classical Library 365. Cambridge, MA: Harvard University Press, 1943.

———. *The Jewish War, Volume 1: Books 1-2*. Translated by H. St. J. Thackeray. Loeb Classical Library 203. Cambridge, MA: Harvard University Press, 1927.

Justin Martyr. *Dialogue with Trypho*. Translated by Marcus Dods and George Reith. The Ante-Nicene Fathers: Translations of the Writings of the Fathers Down to A.D. 325, 1885-1887.

Klein, Jacob. "The Stoic Argument from Oikeiōsis." In *Oxford Studies in Ancient Philosophy*, edited by Victor Caston, 143-200: Oxford University Press, 2016.

Kloppenborg, John S., and Stephen G. Wilson, eds. *Voluntary Associations in the Graeco-Roman World*. London: Routledge, 2012.

Kraemer, Ross Shepard. When Aseneth Met Joseph: A Late Antique Tale of the Biblical Patriarch and His Egyptian Wife, Reconsidered. New York: Oxford University Press, 1998.

Litwa, M. David. Iesus Deus: The Early Christian Depiction of Jesus as a Mediterranean God. Minneapolis: Fortress Press, 2014.

———. *We Are Being Transformed: Deification in Paul's Soteriology*. Beihefte Zur Zeitschrift Für Die Neutestamentliche Wissenschaft Und Die Kunde Der Älteren Kirche. Berlin; Boston: De Gruyter, 2012.

Long, Anthony A. "Friendship and Friends in the Stoic Theory of the Good Life." In *Thinking About Friendship: Historical and Contemporary Philosophical Perspectives*, edited by Damian Caluori, 218-39. New York: Palgrave Macmillan, 2013.

Lucian. How to Write History. The Dipsads. Saturnalia. Herodotus or Aetion. Zeuxis or Antiochus. A Slip of the Tongue in Greeting. Apology for The "Salaried Posts in Great Houses." Harmonides. A Conversation with Hesiod. The Scythian or the Consul. Hermotimus or Concerning the Sects. To One Who Said "You're a Prometheus in Words." The Ship or the Wishes. Translated by K. Kilburn. Loeb Classical Library 430. Cambridge, MA: Harvard University Press, 1959.

———. Phalaris. Hippias or the Bath. Dionysus. Heracles. Amber or the Swans. The Fly. Nigrinus. Demonax. The Hall. My Native Land. Octogenarians. A True Story. Slander. The Consonants at Law. The Carousal (Symposium) or the Lapiths. Translated by A. M. Harmon 14. Cambridge, Mass.; London, England: Harvard University Press, 2006.

———. The Dead Come to Life or the Fisherman. The Double Indictment or Trials by Jury. On Sacrifices. The Ignorant Book Collector. The Dream or Lucian's Career. The Parasite. The Lover of Lies. The Judgement of the Goddesses. On Salaried Posts in Great Houses. Translated by A. M. Harmon. Loeb Classical Library 130. Cambridge, MA: Harvard University Press, 1921.

Lucretius. *On the Nature of Things*. Translated by W. H. D. Rouse. Revised by Martin F. Smith. Loeb Classical Library 181. Cambridge, MA: Harvard University Press, 1924.

Lutz, Cora E. "Musonius Rufus, 'the Roman Socrates'." In *Yale Classical Studies*, edited by Alfred R. Bellinger, 3-147. New Haven: Yale University Press, 1947.

Malherbe, Abraham J. "Antisthenes and Odysseus, and Paul at War." *Harvard Theological Review* 76 Ap (1983): 143-73.

———. "Gentle as a Nurse: The Cynic Background to 1 Thess 2." *Novum Testamentum* 12, no. 2 (1970): 203-17.

———. "Medical imagery in the Pastoral Epistles." In *Texts and Testaments: Critical Essays on the Bible and Early Church Fathers*, edited by W. Eugene March and Stuart Dickson Currie, 19-35. San Antonio: Trinity University Press, 1980.

———. Paul and the Thessalonians: The Philosophic Tradition of Pastoral Care. Philadelphia: Fortress Press, 1987.

———. "Paul: Hellenistic Philosopher or Christian Pastor?". *Anglican Theological Review* 68, no. 1 (1986): 3-13.

———. *Social Aspects of Early Christianity*. Philadelphia: Fortress Press, 1983.

———. "The Beasts at Ephesus." *Journal of Biblical Literature* 87, no. 1 (1968): 71-80.

Marmorstein, A. The Doctrine of Merits in Old Rabbinical Literature. New York: KTAV, 1968. 1920.

Martin, Dale B. "Paul and the Judaism/Hellenism Dichotomy: Toward a Social History of the Question." Chap. 2 In *Paul Beyond the Judaism/Hellenism Divide*, edited by Troels Engberg-Pedersen, 29-61. Louisville: Westminster John Knox, 2001.

McRay, John. *Paul: His Life and Teaching*. Grand Rapids, MI: Baker Academic, 2003.

Meeks, Wayne A. The First Urban Christians: The Social World of the Apostle Paul. 2nd ed. New Haven: Yale University Press, 2003.

Mohler, S. L. "A Roman Answer to the Salary Question." *The Classical Weekly* 21, no. 14 (1928): 105-07.

Montefiore, C. G. "On Some Misconceptions of Judaism and Christianity by Each Other." *Jewish Quarterly Review* 8 (1896).

Moore, G. F. "Christian Writers on Judaism." *Harvard Theological Review* 14 (1921).

———. Judaism in the First Centuries of the Christian Era, the Age of the Tannaim. 3 vols. Cambridge: Harvard University Press, 1927-30.

Mortensen, Jacob P. B. *Paul among the Gentiles: A "Radical" Reading of Romans*. Neutestamentliche Entwürfe Zur Theologie. Tubingen: Narr Francke Attempto, 2018.

Murphy-O'Connor, Jerome. *Paul: A Critical Life.* Oxford; New York: Oxford University Press, 1997.

Mussner, Franz. *Traktat über die Juden.* München: Kösel, 1979.

Nanos, Mark D., and Magnus Zetterholm, eds. *Paul within Judaism: Restoring the First-Century Context to the Apostle.* Minneapolis: Fortress Press, 2015.

Nock, Arthur Darby. Conversion: The Old and the New in Religion from Alexander the Great to Augustine of Hippo. London: Oxford University Press, 1961.

Novenson, Matthew V. Christ among the Messiahs: Christ Language in Paul and Messiah Language in Ancient Judaism. Oxford: Oxford University Press, 2016.

Nussbaum, Martha. The Therapy of Desire: Theory and Practice in Hellenistic Ethics. Princeton: Princeton University Press, 1994.

———. "Therapeutic Arguments: Epicurus and Aristotle." In *The Norms of Nature: Studies in Hellenistic Ethics*, edited by Malcolm Schofield and Gisela Striker, 31-74. New York: Cambridge University Press, 1986.

O'Neil, Edward N., ed. *Teles (the Cynic Teacher).* Edited by Hans Dieter Betz and Edward N. O'Neil, Texts and Translations, vol. 11. Missoula, MT: Scholars Press, 1977.

Osiek, Carolyn, and David L. Balch. *Families in the New Testament World: Households and House Churches.* Louisville: Westminster John Knox, 1997.

Osiek, Carolyn, Margaret Y. MacDonald, and Janet H. Tulloch, eds. *A Women's Place: House Churches in Earliest Christianity.* Minneapolis: Augsburg Fortress Press, 2005.

Philo. Every Good Man Is Free. On the Contemplative Life. On the Eternity of the World. Against Flaccus. Apology for the Jews. On Providence. Translated by F. H. Colson. Loeb Classical Library 363. Cambridge, MA: Harvard University Press, 1941.

———. *On Abraham. On Joseph. On Moses.* Translated by F. H. Colson. Loeb Classical Library 289. Cambridge, MA: Harvard University Press, 1935.

———. *On the Creation. Allegorical Interpretation of Genesis 2 and 3.* Translated by F. H. Colson and G. H. Whitaker. Loeb Classical Library 226. Cambridge, MA: Harvard University Press, 1929.

———. *On the Decalogue. On the Special Laws, Books 1-3*. Translated by F. H. Colson. Loeb Classical Library 320. Cambridge, MA: Harvard University Press, 1937.

———. *On the Embassy to Gaius. General Indexes*. Translated by F. H. Colson. Loeb Classical Library 379. Cambridge, MA: Harvard University Press, 1962.

Pinheiro, Marília P. Futre, Richard Pervo, and Judith Perkins, eds. *The Ancient Novel and Early Christian and Jewish Narrative: Fictional Intersections*, Ancient Narrative Supplementum. Havertown: Barkhuis, 2013.

Plato. *Timaeus. Critias. Cleitophon. Menexenus. Epistles*. Translated by R. G. Bury. Loeb Classical Library 234. Cambridge, MA: Harvard University Press, 1929.

Pliny the Younger. *Letters, Volume 1: Books 1-7*. Translated by Betty Radice. Loeb Classical Library 55. Cambridge, MA: Harvard University Press, 1969.

Plutarch. *Lives, Volume 1: Theseus and Romulus. Lycurgus and Numa. Solon and Publicola*. Translated by Bernadotte Perrin. Loeb Classical Library 46. Cambridge, MA: Harvard University Press, 1914.

———. Moralia, Volume 1: The Education of Children. How the Young Man Should Study Poetry. On Listening to Lectures. How to Tell a Flatterer from a Friend. How a Man May Become Aware of His Progress in Virtue. Translated by Frank Cole Babbitt. Loeb Classical Library 197. Cambridge, MA: Harvard University Press, 1927.

———. Moralia, Volume 2: How to Profit by One's Enemies. On Having Many Friends. Chance. Virtue and Vice. Letter of Condolence to Apollonius. Advice About Keeping Well. Advice to Bride and Groom. The Dinner of the Seven Wise Men. Superstition. Translated by Frank Cole Babbitt. Loeb Classical Library 222. Cambridge, MA: Harvard University Press, 1928.

———. Moralia, Volume 5: Isis and Osiris. The E at Delphi. The Oracles at Delphi No Longer Given in Verse. The Obsolescence of Oracles. Translated by Frank Cole Babbitt. Loeb Classical Library 306. Cambridge, MA: Harvard University Press, 1936.

———. Moralia, Volume 6: Can Virtue Be Taught? On Moral Virtue. On the Control of Anger. On Tranquility of Mind. On Brotherly Love. On Affection for Offspring. Whether Vice Be Sufficient to Cause Unhappiness. Whether the Affections of the Soul Are Worse Than

Those of the Body. Concerning Talkativeness. On Being a Busybody. Translated by W. C. Helmbold. Loeb Classical Library 337. Cambridge, MA: Harvard University Press, 1939.

Poliakoff, Michael. "Jacob, Job, and Other Wrestlers: Reception of Greek Athletics by Jews and Christians in Antiquity." *Journal of Sport History* 11, no. 2 (1984): 48-65.

Rabbow, Paul. Seelenführung: Methodik Der Exerzitien in Der Antike. München: Kösel-Verlag, 1954.

Rawson, Elizabeth. "Roman Rulers and the Philosophic Advisor." In *Philosophia Togata: Essays on Philosophy and Roman Society*, edited by Miriam T. Griffin and Jonathan Barnes, 233-57. Oxford Clarendon Press: New York, 1989.

Reardon, Bryan P. *Collected Ancient Greek Novels*. Berkeley: University of California Press, 1989.

———. *Form of Greek Romance*. Princeton, NJ: Princeton University Press, 2016.

Reece, Steve. "'Aesop', 'Q' and 'Luke'." *New Testament Studies* 62, no. 03 (2016): 357-77.

———. Paul's Large Letters: Paul's Autographic Subscriptions in the Light of Ancient Epistolary Conventions. London: Bloomsbury T&T Clark, 2017.

Roskam, Geert. On the Path to Virtue: The Stoic Doctrine of Moral Progress and Its Reception in (Middle-) Platonism. Leuven: Leuven University Press, 2005.

Runesson, Anders. "The Question of Terminology: The Architecture of Contemporary Discussions on Paul." In *Paul within Judaism: Restoring the First-Century Context to the Apostle*, edited by Mark D. Nanos and Magnus Zetterholm, 53-78. Minneapolis: Fortress Press, 2015.

Sampley, J. Paul, ed. *Paul in the Greco-Roman World: A Handbook*. Harrisburg, PA: Trinity Press International, 2003.

Sanders, E. P. Paul and Palestinian Judaism: A Comparison of Patterns of Religion. Minneapolis: Fortress Press, 1977.

Schechter, S. *Some Aspects of Rabbinic Theology*. New York: Macmillan, 1923.

Schellenberg, Ryan S. *Rethinking Paul's Rhetorical Education: Comparative Rhetoric and 2 Corinthians 10-13*. Early Christianity and Its Literature. Atlanta: Society of Biblical Literature, 2013.

Schultheiss, D., J. J. Mattelaer, and F. M. Hodges. "Preputial infibulation: From Ancient Medicine to Modern Genital Piercing." *BJU International* 92, no. 7 (2003): 758-63.

Sedley, David. "Philosophical Allegiance in the Greco-Roman World." In *Philosophia Togata: Essays on Philosophy and Roman Society*, edited by Miriam T. Griffin and Jonathan Barnes, 97-119. Oxford; New York: Clarendon Press, 1989.

Seid, Timothy W. "The New and Eternal Covenant." *Quaker Religious Thought* 109 (2007).

Sellars, John. *Hellenistic Philosophy*. Oxford: Oxford University Press, 2018.

———. *Stoicism*. Ancient Philosophies. Vol. 1, Berkeley; Los Angeles: University of California Press, 2006.

———. *The Art of Living: The Stoics on the Nature and Function of Philosophy*. Ashgate New Critical Thinking in Philosophy. Aldershot: Ashgate, 2003.

Seneca. *Epistles, Volume 1: Epistles 1-65*. Translated by Richard M. Gummere. Loeb Classical Library 75. Cambridge, MA: Harvard University Press, 1917.

———. *Epistles, Volume 2: Epistles 66-92*. Translated by Richard M. Gummere. Loeb Classical Library 76. Cambridge, MA: Harvard University Press, 1920.

———. *Epistles, Volume 3: Epistles 93-124*. Translated by Richard M. Gummere. Loeb Classical Library 77. Cambridge, MA: Harvard University Press, 1925.

———. Moral Essays, Volume 2: De Consolatione Ad Marciam. De Vita Beata. De Otio. De Tranquillitate Animi. De Brevitate Vitae. De Consolatione Ad Polybium. De Consolatione Ad Helviam. Translated by John W. Basore. Loeb Classical Library 254. Cambridge, MA: Harvard University Press, 1932.

———. *Tragedies, Volume 1: Hercules. Trojan Women. Phoenician Women. Medea. Phaedra*. Translated by John G. Fitch. Loeb Classical Library 62. Cambridge, MA: Harvard University Press, 2018.

Sorabji, Richard. Emotion and Peace of Mind: From Stoic Agitation to Christian Temptation. Oxford: Oxford University Press, 2002.

Starr, James. "Was Paraenesis for Beginners." In *Early Christian Paraenesis in Context*, edited by James Starr and Troels Engberg-Pedersen, 73-111. Berlin: Walter de Gruyter, 2004.

Stendahl, Krister. *Paul among Jews and Gentiles: And Other Essays*. Philadelphia: Fortress Press, 1996.

Stowers, Stanley K. *A Rereading of Romans: Justice, Jews, and Gentiles*. New Haven: Yale University Press, 1994.

———. "Apostrophe, Prosopopoiia and Paul's Rhetorical Education." In *Early Christianity and Classical Culture*, edited by John T. Fitzgerald, Thomas H. Olbricht and L. Michael White. Supplements to Novum Testamentum, 351-69. Leiden; Boston: Brill, 2003.

———. "Does Pauline Christianity Resemble a Hellenistic Philosophy?". In *Paul Beyond the Judaism/Hellenism Divide*, edited by Troels Engberg-Pedersen, 81-102. Louisville, KY: Westminster John Knox Press, 2001.

———. *Letter Writing in Greco-Roman Antiquity*. Library of Early Christianity. Philadelphia: Westminster Press, 1986.

———. "Paul and Self-Mastery." In *Paul in the Greco-Roman World: A Handbook*, edited by J. Paul Sampley, 524-50. Harrisburg, PA: Trinity Press International, 2003.

———. "Romans 7.7-25 as a Speech-in-Character (Προσωποποιία)." In *Paul in His Hellenistic Context*, edited by Troels Engberg-Pedersen, 180-202. Minneapolis: Fortress Press, 1995.

———. "Social Status, Public Speaking and Private Teaching: The Circumstances of Paul's Preaching Activity." *Novum Testamentum* 26 (1984): 59-82.

———. *The Diatribe and Paul's Letter to the Romans*. Sblds. Chico, CA: Scholar's Press, 1981.

Suetonius. Lives of the Caesars, Volume 2: Claudius. Nero. Galba, Otho, and Vitellius. Vespasian. Titus, Domitian. Lives of Illustrious Men: Grammarians and Rhetoricians. Poets (Terence. Virgil. Horace. Tibullus. Persius. Lucan). Lives of Pliny the Elder and Passienus Crispus. Translated by J. C. Rolfe. Loeb Classical Library 38. Cambridge, MA: Harvard University Press, 1914.

Sweet, Waldo E. *Sport and Recreation in Ancient Greece: A Sourcebook with Translations*. New York: Oxford University Press, 1987.

Tanner, Jeremy. "Portraits, Power, and Patronage in the Late Roman Republic." *Journal of Roman Studies* 90 (2000): 18-50.

Warren, Lunette. "Psychagogy in Plutarch's *Moralia* and *Parallel Lives*: The Image of the Ideal Woman." Ph.D, Stellenbosch University, 2016.

Wasserman, Emma. "The Death of the Soul in Romans 7: Revisiting Paul's Anthropology in Light of Hellenistic Moral Psychology." *Journal of Biblical Literature* 126, no. 4 (Winter 2007): 793-816.

— — —. The Death of the Soul in Romans 7: Sin, Death, and the Law in Light of Hellenistic Moral Psychology. Tübingen: Mohr Siebeck, 2008.

Williams, Sam K. *Jesus' Death as Saving Event: The Background and Origin of a Concept.* Harvard Dissertations in Religion. Missoula, MT: Published by Scholars Press for Harvard Theological Review, 1975.

Wright, N. T. What Saint Paul Really Said: Was Paul of Tarsus the Real Founder of Christianity? Grand Rapids: Wm. B. Eerdmans Publishing Company, 1997.

Zanker, Paul. *The Mask of Socrates: The Image of the Intellectual in Antiquity.* Sather Classical Lectures. Vol. 59, Berkeley, CA: University of California Press, 1995.

Zeller, Dieter. "The Life and Death of the Soul in Philo of Alexandria: The Use and Origin of the Metaphor." *Studia Philonica Annual* 7 (1995): 19-55.

Zetterholm, Magnus. Approaches to Paul: A Student's Guide to Recent Scholarship. Minneapolis: Fortress Press, 2009.